MENTAL STATES

# Mental States

## ORDERING PSYCHIATRIC DISORDER IN FRANCE

Alex V. Barnard

Columbia University Press
*New York*

Columbia University Press
*Publishers Since 1893*
New York Chichester, West Sussex
cup.columbia.edu


Library of Congress Cataloging-in-Publication Data
Names: Barnard, Alex V., 1987– author
Title: Mental states : ordering psychiatric disorder in France / Alex V. Barnard.
Description: New York : Columbia University Press, [2026] |
Includes bibliographical references and index.
Identifiers: LCCN 2026001491 | ISBN 9780231203180 hardback |
ISBN 9780231203197 trade paperback | ISBN 9780231554916 ebook |
ISBN 9780231567367 PDF
Subjects: LCSH: Mentally ill—France—Social conditions |
Mental health policy—France | Mental health services—France |
Psychiatric hospitals—France | Mentally ill—Commitment and detention—France |
Deinstitutionalization—France
Classification: LCC RC450.F7 B27 2026
LC record available at https://lccn.loc.gov/2026001491

Printed and bound by CPI Group (UK) Ltd, Croydon, CR0 4YY

Cover design: Milenda Nan Ok Lee
Cover image: Wirestock Creators / Shutterstock

GPSR Authorized Representative: Easy Access System Europe, Mustamäe tee 50, 10621
Tallinn, Estonia, gpsr.requests@easproject.com

*Les malades mentaux sont des hommes comme les autres,*
*mais ce ne sont pas des malades . . . comme les autres.*

The mentally ill are men like other [men],
but they are not sick people . . . like other [sick people].

—CLAUDE VEIL (1956)

# CONTENTS

# PREFACE

"Did you know that treatment in psychiatric hospitals is different than treatment in other hospitals?" The man pauses. "That there are huge differences in psychiatry between countries?" He glances around the room, looking for a nod, an affirmation. "That the government is really involved in psychiatry and uses it in various ways?"

The man's testimony was easy to ignore. His doctor, after all, had just told the judge that he suffered from paranoid schizophrenia. This was the ostensible reason the man was hostile toward medical staff and refusing treatment. When it was the man's turn on the witness stand, his lawyer pushed him to tell the judge that, yes, he would take his medication and that therefore, yes, he could safely be released from the hospital. Instead, he offered an excursus on cross-national variation in mental health systems, apparently confirming the delusional state that brought him to the hospital in the first place.

To me, though, he seemed entirely correct.

It was the fall of 2016, and I was sitting in the back of a spare courtroom tucked upstairs in a public psychiatric hospital in New York. Perhaps, as a born-and-bred American, nothing happening there should have surprised me: not the primacy of the judge in deciding who stays within a medical facility (and, later in the hearing, what drugs the psychiatrist would be authorized to administer forcibly), nor the ritual of subjecting a psychotic patient to an adversarial cross-examination, nor even that his psychiatrist's master plan was to discharge him in a few days with little more than a prescription and the address of a homeless shelter.

But it all struck me as very bizarre. Just a few weeks earlier, I had been sitting in the back of a different courtroom inside a psychiatric hospital in Paris, France. There, patients had similar symptoms, to which psychiatrists attached the same diagnoses and prescribed identical medications. But judges never demanded that doctors provide a detailed justification for their treatment decisions. They deemed patients far too fragile for hostile questioning. And psychiatrists, far from seeking to discharge patients as soon as they achieved a bare degree of stability, aimed to keep them within the grip of a health-care system that was supposed to provide for them their entire lives.

Thanks to fifteen months spent observing French clinics, social service offices, and courtrooms, interviews with nearly two hundred professionals working within them, and countless hours digging through government reports and ministry archives, I could see the wisdom in this man's madness. His three insights are the backbone of this book. First, even in an era of transnational pharmaceutical companies and the global circulation of psychiatric knowledge, the trajectories of people with the most serious conditions vary enormously across national borders. Second, this difference reflects that psychiatric interventions seek not just to ameliorate symptoms but also to juggle complex and contradictory demands around managing marginalized people, ensuring social order, and promoting autonomy. And finally, the peculiar ways governments use psychiatry to resolve these dilemmas tells us something broader about how modern states transform the populations they care for and control.

Like a long line of inquisitive voyagers, I had gone to France hoping that the solution to the ills of my own country could be found across the Atlantic. A more social democratic system, I dreamed, would keep people with mental illness out of prisons and at *liberté* in the community; it would replace inaccessible services with *égalité* of access; *fraternité* and *solidarité* would overcome stigmatization and exclusion.

I was disappointed. So might be the readers of this book. This book is not a tour of best practices in a system that is reliably better than its American equivalent (although I do think, on the whole, it *is* better). Instead of showing an ideal, it shows difference: the consequential impacts of policy, organizational, and clinical choices made decades ago on the lives of people with serious mental illnesses today. And it is more subtly about how the population created by those choices recursively reinforces these differences, whether through moments of open resistance to psychiatry, like the man's testimony above, or less visible ways of pushing back against the discipline's rules and expectations. This limits the convergence of mental health systems across national boundaries, creating, at the level of both intimate psyches and public policies, very different mental states.

Being a stranger in a foreign land can carry certain advantages. Perhaps an unthreatening haplessness and thick accent helped open doors to facilities often shut to local researchers; an email address linked to a prestigious foreign university probably led to interviews with higher-level officials who ought to have clicked "*supprimer*." Writing about France for a non-French audience means I gloss over some nuances in order to present a digestible overview.[1] This book's three parts, which deal with tensions between expanding care and controlling costs,[2] the contradictions of promoting autonomy in the face of chronicity,[3] and the conflicts between civil rights and social control in involuntary hospitalizations,[4] are each the object of fascinating monographs and dissertations by French researchers. Other exemplary works address transversal issues around how French clinicians classify patients.[5] I draw on them liberally and try to cite them generously. But a French specialist would certainly assess that some detail is lost in translation.

What I hope to offer the (Anglophone) French reader, in contrast, is a fresh perspective that highlights how a national response to serious mental illness that might seem intuitive or natural is in fact quite specific. I have drawn on my own extensive research in the United States to insert a handful of short ethnographic anecdotes that heighten the sharp distinctions between the two approaches. My outsider's assessment helps reveal a surprising coherence in France's system, which is organized around a conception of who "*malades*" are and what they need. This might be invisible to those inside it, for whom institutional fragmentation, contradictory mandates, and interprofessional conflict boil on the surface of this underlying structure. Still, this is an investigation that centers on public psychiatric care for adults in an urban area; the further away we get (such as psychiatric care in the private sector, for children, or in rural zones), the less this book's portrayal of mental health care in France is likely to hold.

I have obviously done quite a bit of translating for this book (checked by a native French speaker when possible), but some things are left in *version originale*. I keep "*secteur*"—the fundamental building block of France's public psychiatric system—as *secteur*, which frees me to use the English "sector" in its more general form ("the health sector"). I have left "*malade*" as just that. The closest English rendering would be "sick person," but there's something meaningful in the fact that *malade* is a noun, whereas English requires it become an adjective. To be a *malade* is not just to carry a medical diagnosis; it is to be a certain type of person—what I call a bureaucratic kind—in the eyes of the state. I actually prefer if the untranslated term gives readers pause because it reminds us that there is nothing inevitable in how we define and label people living with conditions like schizophrenia. The French *"handicap"* can be translated as "handicap," of course, but also its more modern twin, "disability." I use both: I rely on "handicap" to describe specific categories embedded in policy (like "psychic handicap," or *handicap psychique*) but translate it as "disability" when referring to the population in general or the system serving them.

Some terminological choices are more complex than translation. I at times refer to the people at the heart of this book as "the mad." I do this in the spirit of activists and scholars who have worked to reclaim this stigmatizing term (in much the same way as "queer"). They have valorized it as a way of describing psychological experiences, like hearing voices, that appear to be medical problems but don't necessarily have to be treated as such.

Individuals identified with a first and last name have either consented to their name being used or are public figures whose identities cannot be masked. Nearly all the other names used in this book are pseudonyms. When individuals have a formal title ("Judge," "Doctor") I use a (fake) last name; other professionals (like social workers or nurses) are usually referred to by a first name. This is, to be clear, not a sign of a hierarchy of differential respect. It's my best attempt to replicate the dialog I documented as closely as possible.

One of my greatest challenges writing this book has been balancing a critical appraisal of a flawed system with honoring the work of practitioners and patients within it. A wise friend once told me that sociology should be "hard on structures, easy on people." My portrayals of professionals will range from the dedicated and compassionate to apathetic and detached (although I lean toward the former because I saw these characteristics more often). But just as it is a mistake to define an entire person based solely on their illness, it would be an error to extrapolate from my short ethnographic vignettes and categorize individual clinicians as saints or sinners. I ask, in advance, for forgiveness—above all from my research subjects themselves—for the moments where I fail to capture this delicate balance.

MENTAL STATES

# INTRODUCTION

## Precarious Patienthood

Hippocrates saw, from the start, that the struggle over how to treat the mad began with a debate over who the mad actually were. Insanity seemed like proof to the Ancient Greeks that they were puppets in the hands of capricious gods. They missed, the Hippocratics countered, that madness was "nowise more divine nor more sacred than other diseases, but has a natural cause from which it originates, like other affections."[1]

Hippocrates lost the argument for millennia. According to the French social theorist Michel Foucault, up through the Renaissance "the mad were not treated as human beings" but rather as animals.[2] Even physicians believed they were "as mad as wild beasts" and did not "differ much from them."[3] They were left to roam freely in the best of cases, chained and brutalized in the worst.

By the eighteenth century, the mad had recovered a measure of their humanity but lost their specificity. They were lumped indiscriminately with the aged, infirm, and destitute in the English poorhouses or the French *Hôtels-Dieu*.[4] In 1797, the Parisian mad-doctor Phillipe Pinel faced this mass of abandoned and abused humanity and lamented that their condition was "so destitute . . . we found it impossible to classify our patients according to the varieties and degree of their respective maladies."[5] Whether Pinel actually freed the mad from their chains—as legend has it—is a topic of historical debate.[6] What is more clear is that he tried to put an end to their intermingling. He took those he diagnosed as "melancholics" and "maniacs" back with him to his clinic and left the "demented" and "idiots" behind.[7]

The asylums that he and other mad-doctors, soon to be known as psychiatrists, spread through the Western world were billed as symbols of scientific progress and humanism. They were founded on a promise of more accurate classification leading to more effective treatment. In 1838, when a French law mandated the creation of an asylum in each of the country's subnational departments, legislators insisted that "the establishments specifically for madmen should focus exclusively on this type of illness."[8] The state now offered them a bureaucratic, as well as medical, identity as "non-adult assisted persons."[9] This legal designation matched a new therapeutic vision. "Moral treatment," the nineteenth-century innovation that insisted on the curative power of regimented isolation, presumed that mad people "needed to be treated essentially like children."[10] But the childlike madman "remained, in essence, a man," a fragment of reason intact.[11]

This erstwhile triumph became a disaster. If the status of the mad-person as a human being was no longer intellectually in doubt, for a century, their treatment did not reflect that humanity.[12] In 1932, the head of one French asylum complained to the authorities that "every night fifty *malades* are sleeping on straw mats . . . in the corridors . . . even though an asylum is not a pen for sheep nor a campsite . . . [but] a hospital."[13] This problem of hopeless intermixing was not confined to France. A 1966 report by a commission in the US state of California observed that public hospitals had become "a bin marked 'miscellaneous' to receive every personnel problem facing society."[14] Treatments and diagnostic categories come and go, but changes in the social status of the mad come at a glacial pace. Putting them in hospitals had not really made them patients.

In the second half of the twentieth century, a combination of optimism about the efficacy of new pharmaceuticals, a restructuring of welfare states, and humanitarian impulses drove the dramatic downsizing of the asylums (although, in France, not a single public psychiatric hospital actually closed entirely). This process of deinstitutionalization has revamped the perennial project of sorting the mad by dispersing them across many kinds of institutions rather than indiscriminately lumping them in one. As two French psychiatrists wrote in 1975, "psychiatrists must search elsewhere . . . for the solution . . . to the aged and retarded [*sic*] . . . The mission [of public psychiatry] consists . . . in putting the patient in the most logical place, avoiding the lack of differentiation in the traditional asylum."[15]

And so, across the Western world, the elderly went to nursing homes and disabled people to supported living arrangements.[16] At least in theory, people with mental illness—emphasis on the *illness*—would receive medical care on an outpatient basis, integrated into the community. As a pair of prominent French psychiatrists celebrated in 2018, this outcome is the culmination of a decades-long battle to "make mental illness an illness like any other, which can be cured."[17] Just as Pinel had hoped, new diagnoses (now based on genetic biomarkers, neurological pathways, or even gut inflammation) would finally impose scientific order on disordered selves.

Hippocrates would be proud. I am skeptical. In years of ethnographic research in France and the United States, I've seen the chaos firsthand: haggard professionals torn between impossible demands to deliver care and reduce costs, families desperate to get a shred of support from byzantine welfare programs, and patients who will do anything to get away from services they see as serving up little more than coercion and trauma. These depictions lend credence to French scholar Marcel Jaeger's declaration that, in the face of the "perpetual incapacity of the state to define and realize a coherent mental health policy," we should analyze psychiatry "less in terms of how it produces order and more how it never ceases to fail to do so."[18]

For my own country, the United States, this analytical admonition seems apt. The last major federal report on the US mental health system summarized it as "fragmented and in disarray."[19] Sociologist Owen Whooley argues that this depiction is too rosy: the United States doesn't have a mental health "system," it has a "mess."[20] That mess is both cause and consequence of the fact that, despite the pileup of diagnoses heaped on mad individuals, they have no coherent collective identity within the threadbare US welfare state. Being labeled "chronically mentally ill" does not unlock care or support. Rather, the mad might get medication as inmates in a jail, a modicum of income through being designated as disabled by the Social Security Administration, and a slim chance at permanent housing if a municipal government identifies them as "chronically homeless."[21] With a shriveled number of hospitals to treat them and community services subjected to endless waves of austerity, the patienthood of the mad in the United States is partial and precarious.

The rhetoric across the pond is equally dire. A widely publicized 2018 book, *Psychiatry: The State of Crisis*, announced that the French system "is cracking up everywhere."[22] But there's one key difference. In 1958, on the eve of the inauguration of a new system of community care, the French state finally changed "madman" to "*malade*" in the *Code de la santé publique*. This designation became the cornerstone for a system of specialized and segregated solidarity. While in the United States, psychiatrists largely abandoned the mad to serve the worried-well in private practice, in France, public psychiatrists insisted they were their paternalist protectors. As the head of one major union wrote, "the *malade* . . . is an inconvenient being that is expensive . . . His natural defender is the psychiatrist, image and mirror of madness. Their destiny is linked."[23]

Today, this approach to comprehending, classifying, and caring for *malades* is under strain. Politicians, bureaucrats, families, and people with mental illness themselves have called for rationalizing and economizing treatment, promoting autonomy, and better protecting civil rights. Yet these initiatives must contend with the reality of the people that the category *malade* has created: individuals whose care is costly, whose trajectory is one of chronicity and dependency, and whose lengthy hospitalizations are closely bound up with social control. *Malade*, I argue, is an exemplary case of what I call a *bureaucratic kind*, an administrative identity that binds policies, professionals, and populations tightly together. And bureaucracies are not the kind of thing that turns on a dime.

This book is a story of one country's distinctive balance of rights, care, and control—and how it weighs heavily on the medical and social trajectories of the mad. But more broadly, it is an analysis of how state-led attempts to transform the social status of populations are constrained by the very categories that states once imposed.

## SORTING PSYCHOSIS

All of this talk of mental states and bureaucratic kinds might seem a bit abstract to Doctor Laulaire. She was focused on the fact that you could still see the spit from the last time she took a shift at the Infirmary.

Doctor Laulaire, slight with a broad smile, doesn't look like she would work on the hardest edges of French psychiatry. Yet as a medical student, she trained with Daniel Zagury, a forensic psychiatrist. He was legendary for declaring that Salah Abdeslam, the only perpetrator of the November

13, 2015, terrorist attacks at the Bataclan concert hall and cafés in Paris (which killed 130 people) caught alive, was sane enough to be judged for his crimes. As a medical resident, she spent six months at a hypersecure hospital where she recalls treating an "ultra-right-wing" patient who "if he ever leaves, is going to commit a massacre, a real mass murder." Her main gig is in a nearby prison, where she appreciates the "lively" mix of "psychoses, troubles of personality, [and] adolescents who have engaged in violence." On the side, she takes the occasional shift at the Psychiatric Infirmary of the Prefecture of Police (*Infirmerie psychiatrique de la préfecture de police*, hereafter Police Infirmary). The Paris Police Infirmary is where the capital city's law enforcement brings individuals whose disruptive behavior or inexplicable crimes merit a psychiatric evaluation. It was here that a detainee who had pushed someone onto the metro tracks, unhappy with her decision to return him to jail rather than send him to the hospital, spit at her.

It landed on the glass cover of a bookcase holding withered volumes of the *Annales Médico-Psychologiques*, the flagship journal of French psychiatry, dating back to 1843. There would have been eighty-eight volumes when a young Jacques Lacan, the celebrated psychoanalyst, did his residency at the Policy Infirmary.[24] Perhaps Albin Ballestra, who, in 1982, evaded security to offer a rose to President François Mitterrand to celebrate the final match of the French Football League, looked at the 139 volumes in the case while the doctor determined he needed to be sent to a hospital. He would stay there for the next five years. The Police Infirmary has been a way station on some of the most famous trajectories of both patients and professionals in the French mental health system.

Today's case is closer to the Police Infirmary's more banal bread-and-butter. Doctor Laulaire and I are sitting behind a heavy wooden desk when a man is led in by a nurse and security guard. They order him to sit in front of us. He's twenty-one and white. His face, partly hidden by a scraggle of chin-length blond hair, is red, like it's been recently scrubbed after not being washed for some time. He's rubbing his wrists, which show the marks of having been in restraints. The psychiatric resident who did a first evaluation of him last night said he was "extremely oppositional."

There are no pleasantries. "Do you know why you're here?" Doctor Laulaire quizzes.

"I was in jail. I saw a psychiatrist. He said I was not good, that I wasn't 'managing my schizophrenia.' So they sent me here," he replies, flatly.

"But what happened before that? You were arrested at a protest, I see." He had been among the throngs in the streets of Paris remonstrating against a reform to France's labor law.

"Yes. They said I had a weapon—that's false—and that it was an illegal demonstration. There was an officer, he was fixated on me, he stared at me, and he said, 'I'm going to deal with you,' and so I defended myself." Regardless of who started it, the punch he threw at the officer did not go over well. He wound up in jail.

"Is there anything else going on?" Doctor Laulaire asks, her tone softening.

"I lost my son," the man deadpans, "and I have cancer."

Doctor Laulaire ignores these heavy declarations. She flips through his file. "Do you have a family?" she queries.

"Yeah, but I haven't lived with them since I was six. I was placed [in foster care]."

"And where do you live now?"

"Outside. It's been five years. Always outside," he opines.

"And what do you live off of [income]? The intern said that you're not receiving the Allocation for Handicapped Adults [France's minimum income payment (about 800 euros a month) for people with disabilities]."

"I missed my appointment to renew it," he replies.

The man is looking more and more frustrated, but Doctor Laulaire presses on. "When was your last injection [of an anti-psychotic]?" she asks. It's a strategic move. She doesn't actually know if the man is attached to a *secteur*—the organizational unit of France's public psychiatric system—but she's assuming he is, and that his presence at the Police Infirmary is rooted in him not complying with the treatment prescribed for him.

The ruse works. "Who knows [when I last got my injection]? I don't understand why they give it to me!"

"Well, you've had some behaviors that are . . . a bit bizarre."

"I'm bizarre because of the injection, then!" he fires back.

"Sir, what would you think about going back to the hospital?"

"Why?"

"You've been saying some pretty odd things today," she muses.

"The hospital makes everything worse," he protests.

"Frankly, sir, if you don't go to the hospital, you risk going to prison," Doctor Laulaire declares. "You are going to be hospitalized at the demand of a representative of the state. I wish you the best."

The man scowls but doesn't resist. He's been here before. "The psychosis here was not that obvious," Laulaire tells me, "but he's young, and if he escapes treatment now, the psychosis is going to become more entrenched."

The nurse comes back in, and reports, "He's pretty angry. We need to put him in a seclusion room until we can find him a hospital bed."

And why wouldn't he be frustrated? At the Police Infirmary, you see all the failings of the French state up close: social services that can take someone from their parents but can't keep them off the street, disability bureaucrats that cut off someone's only income based on a missed appointment, a police force that routinely uses violence against protesters, and a public psychiatric system that can force a hospitalization but not extend care beyond it. And what Doctor Laulaire does is send suffering citizens back to grind through that same state machinery. She does it based on an extraordinary power delegated to her: to write out a medical certificate authorizing the prefecture to hospitalize someone, in this case, because he was "aggressive toward others," "minimized his illness," and posed a "serious threat to public order."

The Police Infirmary is unique to Paris, a reflection of the Ministry of the Interior's preoccupation with public safety in a country where both state power and sometimes revolutionary discontent are concentrated in the capital. It's easy to see why an institution consecrated to evaluating people brought by the police for involuntary treatment would be a lightning rod for critiques. In 2015, France's General Controller for Places of Deprivation of Liberty (*Contrôleur général des lieux de privation de liberté*) called for closing the Police Infirmary, noting that it had "nothing to do with a hospital appropriate for the mentally ill."[25] In an era where the rights of patients are supposed to be expanding, the Police Infirmary appears to be a gray zone of "non-law" where people are neither patients nor prisoners and thus lack the rights guaranteed to each.[26]

These critiques center on the mixing of roles and responsibilities inside the Police Infirmary: of care and control, detention versus hospitalization, psychosis or criminality. What the professionals at the Police Infirmary would retort is that their job is to disentangle them. "My role at the [Police Infirmary] is simple. I orient people based on whether they're a *malade* or not a *malade*," explains Doctor Laulaire. Later that day, I watch Doctor Laulaire evaluate a woman who slapped someone in a stadium and a man who had shouted homophobic insults on the subway. Both seemed distressed enough that the police brought them to the Police Infirmary. Doctor Laulaire coolly sent them back to the justice system.

Singular as it might seem, the Police Infirmary offers a distilled version of a much broader state function. Before government agencies can treat, educate, discipline, punish, or control, they must *sort*.[27] The history of modern states is a story of steadily more differentiated systems for classifying populations: by their need for welfare and deservingness of it, by race and gender and sexuality, by responsibility and culpability.[28] On the ground, the work of state agents like psychiatrists, social workers, and teachers is at once providing care and clarity: determining who belongs on which bureaucratic pathway.[29] Classifying people sometimes requires overcoming active resistance (coming, occasionally, in the form of a bit of spit). It also means confronting the reality of human complexity, which makes actual people difficult to fit into neatly defined administrative boxes.

Before we delve into the deeper theoretical question—how states sort people who aren't easily sorted—we need to understand the mental health system in which the Police Infirmary is, somewhat controversially, situated. A few aspects of the exchange above are revealing. For one thing, the role of psychiatric hospitals is supposed to be drastically diminished in an era where the lion's share of treatment comes in the form of pills prescribed by an outpatient clinician. Yet Doctor Laulaire deploys hospitalization with the faith that it remains the best way to attach an individual to protective care. Second, while the mixing of policing and psychiatry in the Police Infirmary is fodder for social theorists who view psychiatry as a sinister discipline of social control,[30] Doctor Laulaire is convinced that part of her goal is actually to keep delinquents, deviants, and drug addicts *out*. Third, for her a careful screening at the entrance to the hospital is essential because the finite resources of public psychiatry need to be kept for people who are *malades*. This category sounds like people with psychosis, but it refers to more than just a medical diagnosis. It designates a population in which the state (and not just psychiatrists) has taken a special interest. There's a whole history of institutional change, professional reorganization, and shifting ideologies of treatment that brought the wayward protester described above and the young forensic psychiatrist together.

## DEINSTITUTIONALIZATION AND DIVERGENCE

The best way to throw into sharp relief the particularities of the French mental health system and the dilemmas it creates for professionals like

Doctor Laulaire is through contrast. Comparing France to the United States is, admittedly, a bit arbitrary. But it is also apt. A wealth of sociological and historical studies have revealed the two countries' divergent approaches to the role of the state, the sources of expert authority, and the relationship between doctors and patients.[31] We might imagine these differences would crystallize in distinctive mental health systems.[32] Yet an observer in the mid-twentieth century would be struck by their notable similarities. Both countries were home to some of the largest asylums in the world.[33] Those asylums were in crisis, victims of both overcrowding and underinvestment. The two countries would soon embark on an ambitious experiment in shifting care into the community, that is, deinstitutionalization.

The justifications for the revolution sounded remarkably similar, too. In 1963, President John F. Kennedy told the US Congress that, thanks to new therapeutic breakthroughs, the "traditional methods of treatment which imposed upon the mentally ill a social quarantine, a prolonged or permanent confinement in huge, unhappy mental hospitals" was "obsolete." The "cold mercy of custodial isolation" would now be replaced with "the open warmth of community concern."[34] In France, a 1960 circular by the Ministry of Health was drier but evoked the same recognition: "The majority of [the] mentally ill have medical-social problems that are not fixed by hospitalization, and which hospitalization actually makes more acute."[35] Fortunately, "new therapies and methods . . . permit a significant reduction" in the use of hospitalization.[36] The alternative in both cases looked equivalent: "community mental health centers" in the United States and outpatient "medical-psychological centers" in France.[37]

There was one enormous difference: the role of hospitals. It is the root of profound variation in the organizational structure, treatment approaches, and professional hierarchies of the two systems, and ultimately the very conception of who public mental health is for. Federally funded community mental health centers in the United States would be entirely cut off from the state-run asylums where most psychiatric patients were relegated. Community care would be paid for by Medicaid, a new health insurance program for the poor, and community survival would be enabled by Supplemental Security Income (SSI), a new disability payment. Inpatients were eligible for neither. Faced with an irresistible financial incentive to shift costs onto the federal government through these programs, states slashed the number of people under their direct control.[38] The hospitals that exist today are largely privately run and barely communicate with publicly-financed outpatient providers.[39]

The French took a different path: "sectorization."[40] The 1960 circular envisioned that the country would be divided into geographic territories of around 70,000 people (today there are about 800 such *secteurs* for adults). In each, "a single team . . . would ensure . . . the indispensable continuity between screening, treatment without hospitalization when possible, care with hospitalization, and finally, surveillance and follow-up."[41] Hospital and community care would be linked in a single administrative unit.[42] It is striking that the circular actually insisted that "the number of beds which the country has available for hospitalization is insufficient."[43] France continued to build psychiatric beds well into the 1970s (figure 0.1). Even today, the country has two-and-a-half times more beds per capita than the United States (figure 0.2). Deinstitutionalization shifted the majority of care out of hospitals in both countries. But this "earthquake"[44] was not of a large enough magnitude to shutter a single French hospital entirely.[45]

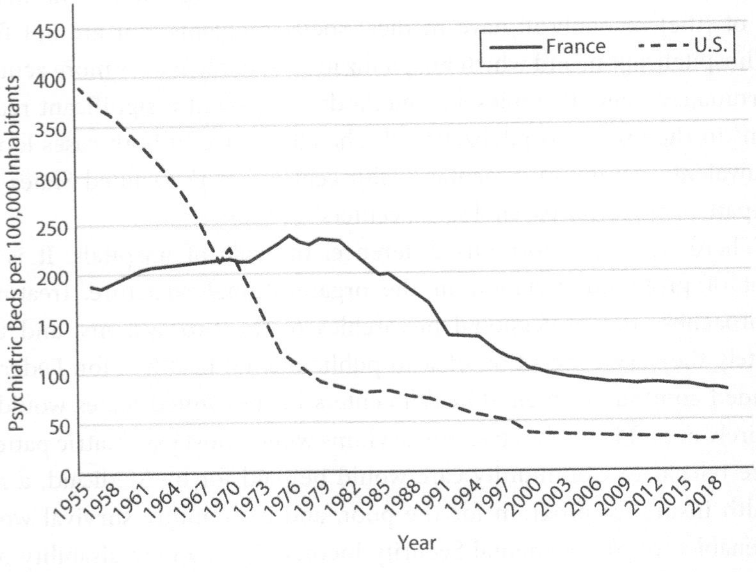


FIGURE 0.1. Trajectories of deinstitutionalization, 1955–2020. *Source*: French Statistical Yearbooks; Mental Health—United States.

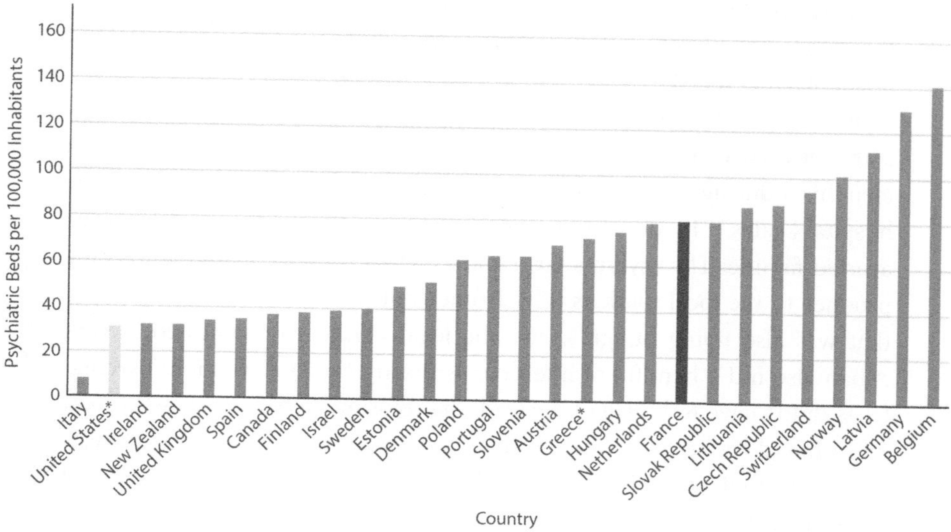


FIGURE 0.2. Number of psychiatric beds per capita, 2020. *Source*: Organisation for Economic Co-operation and Development (OECD).
* Data from 2019.

It is a surprising turnaround. At the point where Kennedy addressed the US Congress, a series of exposés had branded state hospitals as places of abuse and abandonment, making them the "Shame of the States."[46] But France's psychiatric hospitals were more than shameful. They were sites of mass death. During World War II, the occupation squeezed the rations allocated to the interned, which, during the winter of 1942, dropped to 1,000 calories a day.[47] A regional director of health visited the hospital in Clermont-de-l'Oise and described "such a famine that it plunges us into the Middle Ages and seems unbelievable in our era. Rooms full of gaunt *malades*, skin-and-bones and skeleton-like . . . Covered in vermin and scabs . . . for lack of disinfectant and laundry."[48] Some were buried naked in mass graves. The medical dossiers noting the cause of death were sometimes last updated in the 1920s.[49] The "massacre of the mad" led to 45,000 excess deaths out of a prewar asylum population of 110,000. Historians continue to debate whether it reflected a deliberate eugenic policy of the Vichy regime or malignant neglect of a disposable population.[50] The disgrace of some psychiatrists ran deep: "After the Liberation . . . we reflected on the condition of people in concentration camps, and we said, 'in the end, we are the *kapos* [prisoners working for the Nazis], the guardians of the camp,'" one wrote.[51] If ever there were a reason to abolish psychiatric hospitals, this was it.

But the war taught other lessons. At Saint Alban's hospital, in the rural south of France, a young émigré who had fled the persecution of Spanish anarchists during the civil war, François Tosquelles, had thrown open the hospital's gates.[52] By developing links with the surrounding community, he averted famine: The asylum's farm and foraging produced enough to bring produce to the local markets (a welcome contribution to a broader society that was also going hungry), and the local villagers reciprocated.[53] Saint Alban also hid a handful of intellectuals fleeing Nazi persecution. Psychiatrists didn't have to be *kapos*: Instead, the reformist psychiatrists who went on to found the *secteurs* were, in their own eyes, "first and foremost resisters . . . who took refuge behind the walls of the asylums, which became useful protectors."[54]

Under Tosquelles and his protégés, asylums grew into something beyond being safe spaces. Saint Alban's was the incubator for a new therapeutic approach: "institutional psychotherapy." Staff dropped their white coats and hung up the keys to the wards. They invited *malades* to join them in coconstructing the life of the institution. Art therapy groups, theatrical productions, and patient-run clubs flourished. As Jean Oury (who went on to found another hospital based on the same principles, *La Borde*) put it, the idea was that you could "heal the sick by healing the hospital."[55] The transformed asylum would serve the patient population in the same way that a psychoanalyst treated an individual: by shaping their unconscious and challenging their alienation from society.[56]

Institutional psychotherapy altered both the structure of the French public mental health system and the ideology behind it. In the United States, psychoanalytically trained psychiatrists in community mental health centers prioritized treating "pretty co-eds with interesting sex lives."[57] They left the chronically mentally ill patients departing the asylums in the cold, convinced by Sigmund Freud's view that the ravings of the psychotic person were meaningless babble. In France, though, institutional psychotherapy and the work of the famous psychoanalyst Jacques Lacan endowed those words with symbolic meaning.[58] Today, *secteur* patients are rarely placed on the divan for the talking cure. Still, psychoanalysis provides many public psychiatrists a kind of "intelligence of the human psyche" that pulls them to be attentive to a patient's social relationships, not just pathology.[59]

This narrative may suggest a tale of divergence rooted purely in therapeutic approaches and humanitarian impulses. As Isabel Perera convincingly shows, however, the contrast between integrating hospitals with community care (as in France) and separating the two (as in the United States) is also an outcome of professional mobilization and political arbitrage.[60] Even before patients began leaving psychiatric hospitals in large numbers, US psychiatrists abandoned them en masse.[61] When unions representing nurses and staff began fighting against hospital closures in the 1970s, they found few allies among psychiatrists, who had bet that the future was in private practice.[62] Today, psychiatrists play a patently marginal role in running the public mental health system, having withdrawn into churning out medication scripts in fifteen-minute increments.

Once again, France is a study in contrasts. The unions representing public psychiatrists allied with other public workers.[63] They insisted that new personnel for the *secteurs* be in addition to, rather than replacements for, those working in hospitals.[64] The appeal worked in part because the state was acutely concerned about the impact of deinstitutionalization on employment.[65] In 1985, when the state finally inscribed the *secteur* system into law, it guaranteed funding from the most solid of sources—France's national insurance—to that most solid of structures—the hospitals (which would then share the funds with nonhospital services). The system gave psychiatrists a firm base of both medical and administrative power. This more expansive role for psychiatry is matched by their more extensive numbers: there are 50 percent more psychiatrists per capita in France as in the United States. A majority of them work in the public sector (figure 0.3).[66]

This has been a whirlwind tour so let's recap. Both France and the United States deinstitutionalized: The absolute number of people interned as well as the proportion of mental health care delivered in specialized psychiatric hospitals declined dramatically. But hospitals retained a central role in the reformed public system in France. This reflected both ideological factors (a new justification for hospitals tied to institutional psychotherapy) and institutional ones (the strategy of psychiatric professional organizations, in alliance with other public workers, which found a sympathetic ear in the state). This historical trajectory set the stage for a range of distinctive features of the French *secteurs*: the persistence of a psychoanalytic sensibility, a vision of psychiatry as intervening extensively in patients' lives, a hierarchy that continues to give psychiatry a privileged position in organizing the

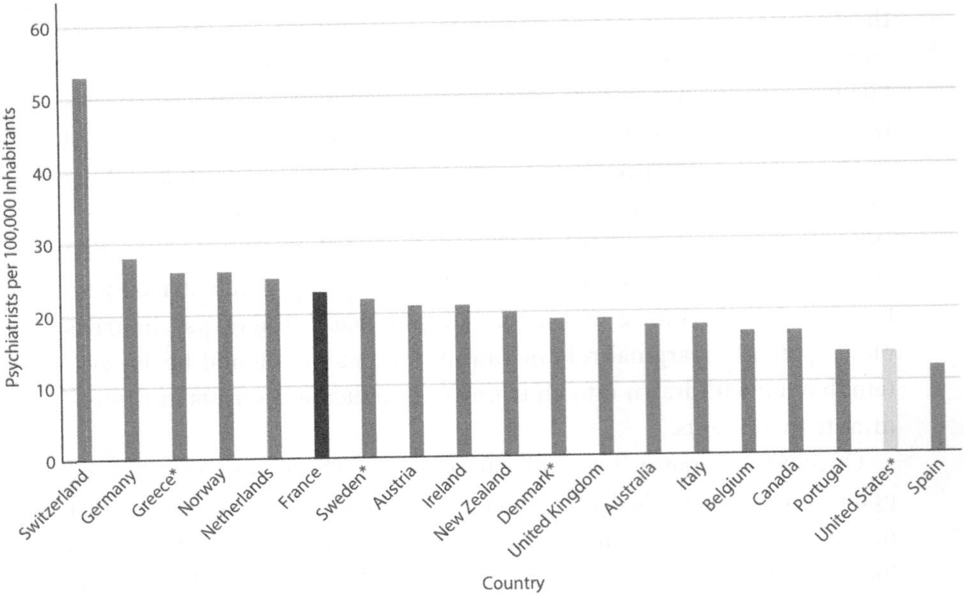


FIGURE 0.3. Number of psychiatrists per capita, 2020. *Source*: Organisation for Economic Co-operation and Development (OECD) Health Stat.
* Data from 2019.

mental health system as well as decision making on the ground, and a close (but sometimes fraught) relationship between the discipline and the state.

This book teases out the implications of one slightly less obvious consequence. As short vignettes scattered through this book will show, in the United States the so-called severely mentally ill largely disappeared. Not only were many former asylum patients abandoned, but they ceased to be a coherent population into which public policy sought to intervene or which psychiatric professionals viewed as their primary responsibility. In contrast, the integration of the old asylums into community care made the *malades* who were once (and, in some cases, still) inside them a ubiquitous reference point in subsequent debates. For this population, care would be permanent, dependency was assumed, and social control was a useful side effect of treatment.

## TRANSMISSION BELTS AND SHOVING MATCHES

In addition to providing a snapshot of the public psychiatric system organized around *malades*, this book also offers a dynamic analysis of how that category shapes and constrains attempts to change it. In this section, I'll consider how states construct people and populations, and in the next, how those populations can in turn remake the state.

Throughout this book, I document conflicts over the right equilibrium of care, rights, and control for the mad. These frequently pit professionals attached to the original principles of the *secteur* (and its *malades*) against state administrators, social movements, and reformist professionals looking to move beyond them. These conflicts are exemplary of what social theorist Pierre Bourdieu called "classification struggles."[67] Battles over, for example, what counts as "good art" or who is a "struggling worker" worthy of government benefits (versus a "welfare cheat") might appear to be about the labels we apply to a social world that already exists out there. According to Bourdieu, however, in truth classification struggles create the very things they purport to describe. The combatants in struggles over what to do with *malades* all claim they have their finger on who *malades* really are; in reality, though, it is through the imposition of a certain balance of rights, care, and control that the population of *malades* comes into being.

If the meaning of "madness" reflects the state of play among warring factions at a given point in time, who is likely to be the dominant player? For Bourdieu, defining *malades* would be foremost the prerogative of the state, for which "one of the most general functions . . . is the production and canonization of social classifications," which it could "impose in a universal fashion, on the scale of a certain territorial foundation."[68] Bourdieu's theory assumes that official categories are internalized by representatives of the state (like public school teachers), who then foist them on citizens, who in turn accept them as the natural division of the social world.[69]

It's a theory that seems particularly adapted to France.[70] After all, in the nineteenth century, the state took a mass of peasants speaking regional dialects and turned them into a unified group of "Frenchmen" through standardized education, legislated cultural traditions and holidays, and integration via military service or state-built transportation networks.[71] (They held on to their 246 different varieties of cheese, which, as President Charles de Gaulle famously quipped, was a sign of a persistent ungovernable streak.) But Bourdieu's approach has extended outside the Hexagon (another name for France) to show how state categories are imposed in all sorts of ways, from defining who counts as (and ultimately executed for being) a pirate to shaping sexual identities.[72] In this book, you'll see clear examples of such state-led reclassification projects, such as a 2005 reform that sought to redefine chronic *malades* as increasingly autonomous people with psychiatric disabilities.

This perspective attributes enormous power to bureaucratic *categories*, which travel a kind of transmission belt from the upper echelons of the state to ground-level professionals and in turn the ways populations come to identify themselves. The problem with this theory is that it is obviously wrong. The notion that official state categories are "spontaneously appl[ied] to all things of the social world" is manifestly out of sync with almost any portrayal of how policy implementation looks in practice.[73] Bourdieu evoked censuses as the ideal site for showing how classifications with no objective truth behind them nonetheless had enormous power when fabricated by the state. Racial categories, for example, become meaningful once people are forced to check a box, and that box checking serves as the basis for allocating benefits and political power.[74] Yet quite a bit of work gets done along the classificatory assembly line. As Mara Loveman shows, in early twentieth-century Puerto Rico, census enumerators bent official criteria for determining who was "white" versus "mulattos." The aggregation of their individual actions whitened the population, even though the US Census Bureau was seeking to show the *non*-whiteness of the colonized.[75] Classification struggles over who belongs in the public mental health system can take the form of overt battles over the allocation of funds, the enumeration of target populations, or criteria for treatment; they can also come in the form of bureaucratic foot-dragging and administrative workarounds.

There's another part of the literature that focuses on bureaucratic *professionals* as the key to understanding how states identify, categorize, and govern their subjects. The real impacts of public policy are not imposed from the top down but are determined from the bottom up as frontline workers juggle competing and contradictory mandates.[76] The categories they use are flexible, emerging ad hoc from professional preferences, local resource constraints, and pressures from management within organizations. Welfare case managers, for example, lean heavily on a binary between "deserving" and "undeserving" poor to determine who can access scarce resources, even though these are not the formal categories inscribed in regulatory rulebooks.[77] Mental health services in the United States, while required by regulation to put a diagnosis on file somewhere, in practice often sort their clientele based on simpler divisions between those who are really sick and those who are simply "bad" or "disruptive."[78] *Malade* looks like it has a similar function: a practical label that allows professionals to separate those who are ill (rather than deviant or delinquent) and thus designate them as meriting psychiatric care.

This perspective suggests that, while the grand logic of social policy might be to discipline, punish, or regulate poor and marginalized populations, the main thing bureaucracies do in practice is to try to get rid of them.[79] Scholars (myself included) have developed a steadily proliferating range of admittedly overlapping appellations for this process: "burden shuffling," "people exchanging," "authority abdicating," or "institutional offloading."[80] Whatever term we use, all of them capture an important piece of the lived experience of those both working in and worked on by the mental health system. Professionals sense that someone is always trying to push problematic clients who ought to be treated elsewhere onto them. Mad people themselves are constantly displaced between a welter of service providers reluctant to serve them.[81] Sociologists have reenvisioned states as fragmented entities with "multiple hands."[82] Rather than constituting a state-constructed transmission belt, those hands are engaged in a perpetual bureaucratic shoving match.

The shoving match perspective, while clearly describing one form that classification struggles can take, has its own limits. Concepts like "burden shuffling" or "institutional offloading" ring true amid the mess of the US mental health nonsystem, where the mad have no consistent or coherent bureaucratic identity. (Note that the concepts cited above were all developed on the basis of research in coastal California.[83]) Yet a framework that highlights chaos is less compelling when we zoom out and compare the trajectories of people with mental illness in different countries. Psychiatrists, social workers, and judges in France aren't exactly consensual cogs in the well-oiled bureaucratic machine Bourdieu envisioned. But they're not always playing the administrative version of hot potato, either. They have a surprisingly coherent sense of the meaning of *malade* and a conception of their roles and responsibilities with respect to it. This formulation of *malade* is sticky, even in the face of state-led projects to reconfigure and reattribute care, rights, and control to it. To understand why, we need to look at the sort of category that *malade* is.

## LOOPS OF A BUREAUCRATIC KIND

*Malade* is not a diagnosis, partly because it captures a range of pathologies from serious depression to paranoid schizophrenia. It is also more than an informal bureaucratic shortcut that frontline workers use to process clients quickly. That's because *malade* isn't really a label for an attribute; it's a description of a type of person. It is a way of designating membership in a bureaucratic *population*, which we need to account for in our transmission-belt theory of bureaucratic *categories* and shoving-match theory of bureaucratic *professionals*.

My starting point is the late, great philosopher Ian Hacking. He elaborated the notion of "human kind" to capture how, when confronted with particular (and peculiar) individuals, scientists and medical professionals aspire to "systematic, general, and accurate knowledge" about them. Elaborating "homosexuals," "alcoholics," or "split personalities" as human kinds is an attempt to create an all-encompassing category which is "sufficiently strong" to provide "laws about people, their actions, or their sentiments."[84] Through the crafting of human kinds, experts develop "principles through which we can interfere, intervene, help, and improve" disordered persons not as individuals but as representatives of a broader population category.[85]

Hacking (and others using the concept) was interested primarily in the relationship between classifications elaborated by scientific experts and their application to their subjects.[86] But he recognized, without theorizing in detail, that some human kinds were also administrative or *bureaucratic kinds* that travel beyond laboratories, professional conferences, and examination rooms into the realm of the state.[87] In an 1838 law, when the French state mandated the creation of asylums for madmen, it conjured up the mad not just as a group of patients but a new bureaucratic kind. Lumping people with disparate experiences of symptoms and suffering into a single group has required the mobilization of a host of techniques of statecraft, from enumerating populations in official statistics to directing them to reside or work together in specific institutions and forcing them to self-identity with a given category in order to access welfare benefits. This book is largely not a work of history that examines the origins of the category *malade*. It does take as its starting point, however, that the category itself has created a population that resembles, in important ways, the way state administrators and public psychiatrists originally imagined it: chronically ill, dependent on open-ended and costly care, and necessitating control from a stern but benevolent psychiatric corps.

The power of Hacking's framework stems from the way it puts theory into motion. When I said in the previous section that theories of the power of state-led projects to reclassify populations (such as those of Pierre Bourdieu) overstate their case, it's in part because they have under-considered the way that populations created in the past weigh on projects to create the populations of the future. As Hacking elaborates, "new sorting and theorizing induce changes in self-conception and in behaviour of the people classified."[88] But precisely because these changes are unpredictable, they force modifications in the way bureaucratic kinds are identified and treated. Instead of a horizontal shoving match or a vertical transmission belt, we get a spiral: "kinds are modified, revised classifications are formed, and the classified change again, loop upon loop."[89] Public policies and professional practices are constantly playing catch up with classifications that have slipped out of their hands.

Consider the case of autism.[90] In the 1980s, a revision to diagnostic categories shifted autism from being a rare condition marked by extreme withdrawal and self-harm into a continuum of behavioral and communication differences that emerge early in life. For parents, this new classification had a certain appeal: It suggested that, far from needing to be indefinitely confined to institutions, their children could receive new therapies that would adapt them to a more normal life. Because these nonpsychiatric interventions successfully altered autistic people's behavior, it seemed to confirm the change in classification: Autism was not in fact a mental illness or a fixed disability but a mutable developmental syndrome. As the spectrum broadened, however, it included an increasing number of high-functioning individuals. This had the unintended effect of facilitating the mobilization of autistic people themselves. They in turn pushed for autism to be reclassified as a form of neurodiversity to be celebrated and protected, not treated. Any future attempt to reconceptualize autism, even with the weighty backing of the state and the expertise professionals can marshal behind their diagnoses, will have to contend with the many autistic people now assembled around a classification that once applied to almost no one.

The neurodiversity movement's "rebel[lion] against the knowers, the classifiers, the science that classifies them," as Hacking put it, is paradigmatic of the potential for the groups created by classifications to become active participants in classification struggles around them. This poses all sorts of challenges for public policy.[91] By collecting mad people together and placing them in institutions riven with degradation and abuse, states certainly laid the groundwork for mobilization by "survivors" or "ex-patients."[92] By switching "mad" from an epithet to a proud identity, for example, such movements constitute a barrier to treating madness as something to be involuntarily cured (and thus mad people as a population to be, in effect, eliminated). An analogous but less adversarial version of this looping effect comes from contemporary recovery movements. Here, even people who have been willingly labeled with psychiatric categories nonetheless demand a new approach that goes beyond locking people into a diagnostic category for life and offering only medication as a response, towards one that emphasizes the potential for thriving in spite of ongoing illness and the need for nonmedical interventions—like social support from "peers" with lived experience—to achieve it.[93] To remind us of Hacking's insight, the point is these movements are only possible because people were lumped together as mentally ill in the first place.

It would be difficult to make the case that antipsychiatry or (ex-)patients' movements have been a significant factor in public policies intended to transform the French psychiatric system.[94] It is true that, in the 1960s and 1970s, critiques of mainstream psychiatry from thinkers like Michel Foucault or Félix Guattari were hyperpublicized in French media and intellectual circles.[95] For a moment, some psychiatrists even feared such "psychiatricidal" challenges: In 1977, the Union of Hospital Psychiatrists cautioned its members to be "extremely vigilant" in imposing involuntary hospitalizations to avoid "play[ing] the game of anti-psychiatrists."[96] But currents like institutional psychotherapy managed to take critiques of old-school asylum psychiatry seriously while repurposing them toward reforming, rather than abolishing, psychiatric institutions (where, even in celebrated places like St. Alban's, interventions like electroshocks remained in use).[97] As the head of that psychiatric union concluded in his memoir, "anti-psychiatry in France was a bubble of soap" that had popped by the 1980s.[98]

In Hacking's world, though, a population does not have to mobilize intentionally to transform the classifications applied to them. In their quotidian interactions with professionals and public policies, *malades* constitute, as French sociologist Bruno Latour famously put it, a "reality that resists."[99] Resistance can take the simple form of an aggregate response that differs from that which state administrators expect. It can range from not showing up to consultations in the *secteurs* to applying for the wrong benefits at a welfare office. The result is to stymie attempts to categorize them in new ways, place them in different sets of institutions, or alter how they participate in treatment. This book thus nuances transmission belt theories by showing how new ways of classifying and governing populations are constrained by how states have classified and governed populations in the past. As you will see in part III, for example, reforms that attempted to turn the mad into rights-bearing citizens with a prerogative to refuse psychiatric treatment struggled when faced with a population who, through their treatment as *malades*, had begrudgingly come to see psychiatric control as a form of necessary care on which they were dependent.

Paying attention to the way populations interact with state classifications also provides analytical leverage for seeing an underlying structure to the pell-mell of bureaucratic shoving matches. The medical, social, and judicial professionals I investigate in this book may very well imagine that they are intervening using different official categories (assessing medical need for patients, functional limitations for people applying for disability benefits, or the validity of consent for a hospitalized person seen in a hearing, for example) and prioritizing different identities (that of a patient, a disabled person, or a legal subject, respectively). But in France, people with mental illness typically enter the circuits of state care and control through the health system, which constructs them as *malades*. Institutions downstream must contend with the common set of characteristics, problems, and needs that being a *malade* entails. The looping process thus also links together horizontally distinctive state agencies, who grapple with the consequences of the way that other professionals—whether they are collaborators, rivals, or seemingly disconnected actors operating in an entirely different institutional domain—have administered the same bureaucratic kind.

In her work comparing economists in France, the United States, and Britain, Marion Fourcade argues that differences in how the discipline intervenes in society stem from the ways states "structure the individuals who carry them out."[100] I am taking her observation that "different societies create different types of individuals"[101] one step further: It's not just the professionals, but the *malades* in that system themselves, who are structured in a nationally specific way. That population then offers its own unintended contribution to France's distinctive mental state—a set of government institutions with fundamentally distinctive conceptions of who the mad are and, in turn, what should be done to and for them. The result is, despite the widespread narrative of ungovernable chaos and policy failure with which I started this book, a discernible order to the disorder.

This book unfurls this argument about the dynamic interplay between state policy, professional practices, and the populations they produce in three parts. In each, I examine a policy reform intended to alter the balance between rights, care, and control in the trajectories of *malades* before showing how the bureaucratic kind of *malades* shaped what reform meant on the ground.

Part I examines the health system itself. A global movement has called on psychiatry to move from addressing "mental illnesses" among a narrow group to the "mental health" of society as a whole.[102] This expansion is only possible if psychiatric care is made more economical through rationalizing tools like best practice protocols, cost-benefit analyses, and guidelines for stepping stabilized patients out of the public mental health system. In chapter 1, I show how French public psychiatrists have resisted calls to offer medical treatment to a widening range of social and psychological problems, and have fought back against public health programs intended to allow them to do so. They have done so in the name of concentrating resources on the people they, exercising their own professional judgment, deem as *malades*. I will examine the limits of this approach in chapter 2, where we'll watch professionals in an outpatient clinic try to hold the lines separating *malades* from a broader mass of psychological suffering and social deviance that threatens to overwhelm them. The result is care that, while congruent with the original spirit of the *secteur* system, is costly and largely assumes that *malades* are the chronic, permanent wards of the public psychiatry system.

Part II switches from analyzing the classification of *malades* in the health system to their transformation in broader social policy. The *secteur*'s vision of lifetime protection by a paternalist psychiatric system is out of sync with a growing mandate, sweeping welfare states across the Western world, to replace passivity with the active pursuit of autonomy.[103] Chapter 3 charts a 2005 reform that sought to transfer partial responsibility for *malades* to France's disability system, which offers a range of benefits—from help adapting workplaces to access to independent housing—intended to enable independence. But as I show through ethnographic observations in a French Disability Office detailed in chapter 4, the characteristics of the dependent *malades* being produced by the *secteurs*, and the expectations of the self-advocating disabled people they were supposed to become, often clashed. Part II thus shows how different bureaucratic kinds applied to the same people can collide to disrupt the state transmission belt in unexpected ways.

The starting point for part III is the proliferation of rights, promulgated by institutions like the United Nations and the World Health Organization (WHO), in alliance with disability movements, to protect the mad from the practice that most sets them apart from other sick people: involuntary treatment.[104] This vision faces strong headwinds, though, as states fixate on instrumentalizing psychiatry to manage populations they perceive as disorderly, risky, or dangerous.[105] Chapter 5 examines virulent debates about forced treatment, which in 2011 culminated in the introduction of systematic judicial reviews of all involuntary hospitalizations. This seemed destined to provoke a clash between white coats and black robes. Chapter 6 delves into those hearings on the ground. In the face of patients resisting care, courts encouraged them to recognize their suffering and consent to care from public psychiatry. They redefined "rights" in terms of procedural regularity and access to medical care—largely leaving *malades'* right to refuse treatment to the side. Judges, a profession seemingly well positioned to mount a frontal challenge to psychiatrists, ceded their own jurisdiction, based on shared assumptions of who *malades* are and what they needed. The loop between new policies, professional practices, and bureaucratic kinds produced surprising convergence on a new balance of care, control, and rights, in place of an anticipated shoving match.

There are more than theoretical stakes here. Psychiatry is a global discipline. Pharmaceutical companies have international reach. The categories in the *Diagnostic and Statistical Manual* spill across borders.[106] Yet what struck me as an outsider in France was the extent to which the trajectories of people with mental illness continue to diverge dramatically despite a growing consensus about the importance of community care, the value of autonomy, and the necessity of civil rights. The differences stem less from disagreements about what people with mental illness *have* but who they *are*: Are they socially and economically dysfunctional or disabled by a medical condition? Deviants to be punished or ill but dangerous people to be treated forcibly? As I will show, the bureaucratic kind of *malade* is both armor and a straightjacket. It protects French patients from some of the worst dysfunctions of the US mental health system while profoundly limiting the possibilities for mad citizens.

The field research for this book was conducted a decade ago. The book's conclusion brings us to the present. French public psychiatry is in deep crisis, offering care that—across a range of comparative metrics—is ineffective, overly institutional, and heavily reliant on coercion. Yet the original intuitions of the *secteur* system provide a strong base: a guarantee of access to specialty care across the French territory, a commitment to addressing both social and medical needs, and public policy that recognizes the specificities of psychiatric care (such as the need to oversee and regulate the use of involuntary treatment). The system's failures stem in large part from the same gaps in sociological theory I identify: our failure to take seriously the way the people the state is supposed to serve engage (or not) with the categories and programs imposed on them.

# PART I

## Between Sickness and Health

Who should be served by the mental health system? Answers range from four-tenths of 1 percent to 100 percent of the population. Four-tenths of 1 percent because that's the estimated population prevalence of schizophrenia, which is nearly ubiquitous across human societies and increasingly understood as requiring some kind of medical treatment.[1] When governments set up asylum systems in the nineteenth century, their focus on confining mad men and women meant that they leaned toward that four-tenths figure. When the size of public hospitals crested in 1954, about .39 percent of the US population was interned.[2] France hit .24 percent in 1976.[3]

One hundred percent because, when governments started tearing down the walls of asylums, they also put cracks in the barriers that separated the mentally ill from everyone else. As the prominent psychiatrist William Menninger told the US Congress in a 1956 hearing, "When we take . . . common, everyday emotional disturbances . . . into account, the toll of mental ill health must be reckoned as one in one, for there isn't a person who does not experience frequently a mental or emotional disturbance severe enough to disrupt his functioning as a well-adjusted, happy, and efficiently performing individual."[4] In France, psychoanalysis, which became culturally ascendant in the 1960s, suggested that everyone struggled with a degree of neurosis, providing a justification for an expansive remit for psychiatric interventions.[5]

There is no easy way to adjudicate where the real need for mental health care falls between .4 percent and 100 percent. Clinicians cannot refer to brain scans or blood tests to determine if someone is truly mentally ill.[6] Perhaps everyone could benefit from psychotherapy or mood-enhancing drugs from time to time. In France, however, public psychiatrists long insisted that their efforts should be concentrated on mental *illnesses*—a bureaucratic kind, *malades*, with conditions like schizophrenia, bipolar disorder, or major depression—while issues of mental *health*, like stress or anxiety, should go to private psychiatrists or primary care physicians.[7]

This neat division between public care for the sick and private interventions for the worried but healthy is under strain. In developed countries, a turn toward neoliberalism in the 1980s has meant both cutbacks to social services and an ideological shift that attributes individuals' failure to succeed in an increasingly ruthless labor market to psychological dysfunction, not economic exclusion.[8] As theorist Alain Ehrenberg describes, the result of these twin transformations is a "protean ensemble of suffering which is erupting everywhere" and seeks to "find a response in mental health."[9] It threatens to overwhelm public mental health services with people now too precarious to pay for private care and, in so doing, dissolve the specificity of *malade* as a distinctive bureaucratic kind. This process of what social scientists refer to as "medicalization," which redefines ever-more psychological states and behaviors as requiring clinical intervention, is the first key force discussed in part I of this book.[10]

Yet for public mental health systems, heightening solicitations to provide care sit uncomfortably with another set of forces, also rooted in the brutalities of contemporary capitalism. These are incessant demands to limit the drain that the mad place on government coffers. The porous boundaries of what constitutes mental illness is a challenge for administrators and regulators, who struggle to economize services that are open-ended, variable in their efficacy, and sometimes combine care with social control.[11] In France, mental health care went from consuming 9 percent of (steadily rising) health spending in 1998 to 15 percent by 2020.[12] As elsewhere, policymakers and the Ministry of Health have demanded that the system embrace techniques of "rationalization" alongside medicalization.[13] Rationalization implies an imperative to "efficiency . . . the attainment of the same outcome at a lower cost and with fewer resources" by focusing on "increase[s] in productivity, minimization of financial costs, optimization of resources, and 'outcome targets.'"[14] The treatment of amorphous suffering in the human spirit must thus justify itself in the technical language of soulless accounting.[15]

Part I examines how medicalization and rationalization intersect at the edges of the public mental health system. It charts the clash between two competing versions of who should get into care and who should be left out. As I will show, since the 1960s, a dominant wing of the French psychiatric profession has insisted that these lines should be drawn through a logic of what I call "bounding": sharp divisions (decided upon by professionals themselves) between *malades* who receive intensive, open-ended care and everyone else, who receive time-limited treatment, or none at all, in the public system.[16] Although rationing care in this way can seem harsh, bounding also appears to many professionals to be the only way to deal with the reality of a population of *malades* that *sectorization* has made their responsibility. Their care is costly and thus, by necessity, narrowly concentrated.

But there is another logic that, rather than resisting rationalization and medicalization, embraces them. I call it "scaling": an attempt to calibrate care carefully to meet the momentary needs of each individual, depending on their placement on a smooth continuum that stretches from health to illness. While scaling has its proponents in the French Ministry of Health, advocacy organizations, and an important wing of psychiatry itself (among more internationally oriented, university psychiatrists), it's by looking to the United States that we can see what scaling looks like on the ground when taken to its logical conclusion. A brief visit to California will help us to see the stakes of the debate: where reforms might lead, and what proponents of bounding—with their commitment to treating *malades*—fear.

## SCALING FOR BEHAVIORAL HEALTH IN CALIFORNIA

In one Northern California clinic where I spent a year and a half observing weekly triage meetings for new clients, scaling looked like an all-out response to a woman whose mental illness consisted of an (apparently incorrect) belief that her son has croup (a barking cough caused by an infected throat).

Avril, a psychologist who manages the mobile crisis team that responds to emergency calls in the community, is presenting the case. When we meet, she tells me that she calls her clients "consumers" because "it reminds us that we're here to serve them." Thus, her presentation of this forty-one-year-old white woman begins unsurprisingly with what the consumer wants: "She says she's looking for 'holistic care for mind and body.' She recognizes us as a 'powerful force' that she wants as a 'friend and not a foe.' "

I look down at the intake sheet, which states she is in "constant, high-profile crisis in the community." At the top, under diagnosis—a box that sometimes has five or six *Diagnostic and Statistical Manual* categories written in it—I read just one: "somatic symptom disorder."

"Wait, what is somatic symptom disorder?" one team member interjects.

"Well, she presents with some qualities of a personality disorder, but the symptoms are not clustered in a way that would support a full diagnosis," Avril explains. So they have used the woman's conviction that her son has chronic croup as the basis for a diagnosis in order to meet California's strict medical necessity criteria.

Still, it's not somatic symptom disorder that the team is treating. Michael, the clinic's director, is already in the loop. The woman was living in a "rat-infested, moldy camper" by the waterfront, which the city towed. He elaborates, "When they took away her camper, she went to a city council meeting and talked so long that they had to go into recess. We're getting pressure to do a full-court press here."

That mobilization has been underway for a while. The clinic has specialized teams that conduct homeless outreach, visit potential clients in the hospital, and respond to crisis calls. It is a powerful engine for medicalizing a host of social and psychological problems. The homeless outreach team has now visited the forty-one-year-old woman seventy times. Avril explains, "She has rejected several offers of housing based on this croup thing . . . Her medical beliefs have been a barrier to getting services, including shelter." On this basis, Avril is recommending that the woman go onto a Full-Service Partnership (FSP), the clinic's most intensive level of care. These teams of social workers chase clients to deliver antipsychotic injections in McDonald's bathrooms or to distribute socks and safe-injection kits under freeway underpasses.

This level of care is expensive—over $20,000 a year—and there are only sixty spots for the clinic's catchment area of over 100,000 people. The criteria are strict and formalized in an elaborate decision tree that the clinic's team consults religiously. Clients have to have multiple enumerated risk factors, like comorbid substance use and homelessness. The woman is unsheltered and has been seen multiple times using methamphetamine in public, so she meets that bar. But someone also needs to have a certain number of emergency room (ER) visits, contacts with crisis teams, or days spent in jail.

Brian, the head of the team, is skeptical: "This is someone who made it forty-one years without being in the system . . . I get that she's having a lot of contact with [the homeless outreach team], but we're generating those ourselves. It's not a classic presentation." That last line is important. Brian has been with the FSP since it was created in 2004. For him, cases like these are emblematic of an ongoing shift in who is prioritized for public mental health care in California: "I've been doing this for eighteen years, and now we have 80 percent of people for whom the main issue is substance abuse. We have fewer and fewer people with classic severe mental illness. Instead, we're moving towards people . . . who might have bipolar, but it would be manageable if they weren't on meth."

Despite Brian's skepticism, the clinic's psychiatrist, Doctor Stevens, presses the case: "Let's try it, we can document our efforts, reevaluate in a few months, and if we need to, make the case for withdrawing care."

"Fine," Brian concedes. "Where do we find her?"

"She's usually at [intersection] with a cardboard sign," Avril replies. And so the woman's mental health treatment for—was it somatic symptom disorder? Homelessness? Disrupting a city council meeting?—began.

Three unstated assumptions of scaling structured the team's decision to assign this woman to the highest level of mental health care—even though, as Brian remarked, at other places and times she might be deemed not mentally ill at all. The first was a particular vision of what was actually being evaluated and treated. The team put the accent on the woman's drug use, homelessness, and disruptive crises. This reflects a nationwide transition from treating symptoms to addressing behaviors, evident in the steady rechristening of many "mental health" departments as "behavioral health" departments.[17] I asked Carla, a social worker turned clinic director in San Francisco who started in community mental health in the

1970s, if this shift meant downplaying the inner life of the person. She replied:

> No shit. If you're still into psychoanalysis, you're in the wrong field. Go into private practice . . . I'm a dyed-in-the-wool social worker. But just sitting and doing interpsychic exploration is not what the taxpayer pays us to do. We have so many trauma clients, but [in treating them] . . . you encapsulate, you don't uncover . . . you don't delve into the past. You stay in the here and now. What do you need to do right now to contain your emotions and behaviors?

Within this logic, "mentally ill" and "addict," "deviant," or "criminal" are not really separate bureaucratic kinds but bundles of behaviors, risk factors, and costs to the state that make them frequently overlapping. The pathological (or not) origins of problematic activities (like smoking meth in public) become less relevant.

A second piece of the team's approach is to imagine behaviors as existing on a scale. Clinicians worked to place their clients on a smooth continuum from unproblematic and invisible to disturbing and disruptive.[18] As one US psychiatrist explained it to me, "The issue of severity, I like to say, is more a 'state' than a 'trait' . . . Folks can be in deep trouble for a while, and then they may not be at the same level, and that is going to vary over time." Precisely because this woman might move down this continuum of severity, Doctor Stevens could imagine she would ultimately step out of the public mental health system to a lower level of care or none at all—a stark contrast to French clinicians' conviction that their *malades* needed care for life.[19]

In the team's eyes, one of the upsides of focusing on criteria like going to the emergency room and/or being homeless is that they can be counted, quantified, and measured in a far more objective and reliable way than subjective distress.[20] Scaling has thus facilitated the transformation of the crucial decision of who gets care in the public sector from one based on inscrutable professional judgments to one formalized as carefully elaborated criteria and flowcharts (see figure I.1 in part I for an example from one California county). These tools are useful because they help clinicians meet the rationalizing goal of delivering just the right amount of treatment at the right moment. As Martha Long, the longtime director of

Behavioral Health Diagnosis 1) ______ 2) ______ 3) ______

**Is provisional diagnosis/diagnosis an included diagnosis for MHP services** ☐ Yes ☐ No ☐ Unsure

Documents Included: ☐ **Required Release of Info completed** ☐ MD notes ☐ H&P ☐ Assessment ☐ Other: ______

Primary Care Provider ______ Phone: (____) ______

| List A (check all that currently apply) | List B (Check all that currently apply) | List C |
|---|---|---|
| ☐ Persistent mental health symptoms & impairments after psychiatric consult and 2 or more medication trials in past 6 months<br>☐ Co-morbid mental health and serious health conditions (specify below)<br>☐ Behavior problems (aggressive/assaultive/self-destructive/extreme isolation) (specify below)<br>☐ 3+ ED visits or 911 calls in past year<br>☐ Significant current life stressors [e.g. homelessness, domestic violence, recent loss] (specify below)<br>☐ Hx of trauma/PTSD that is impacting current functioning**<br>☐ Non-minor dependent<br>☐ May not progress developmentally as individually appropriate without mental health intervention (ages 18 to 21only) | ☐ 2+ in-patient psychiatric hospitalizations within past 18 months<br>☐ Functionally significant paranoia, delusions, hallucinations**<br>☐ Current & on-going suicidal/significant self-injurious/homicidal preoccupation or behavior in past year (specify below)<br>☐ Transitional Age Youth with acute psychotic episode<br>☐ Eating disorder with related medical complications<br>☐ Personality disorder with significant functional impairment**<br>☐ Significant functional impairment (not listed above) due to a mental health condition** | ☐ Drug or alcohol addiction and failed SBI (screening & brief intervention at primary care) |

| | Referral Algorithm | |
|---|---|---|
| 1 | Remains in **PCP care** with Beacon consult or therapy only | ☐1-2 in List A and none in List B |
| 2 | Refer to **Beacon Health Strategies**(eFax (866) 422-3413) | ☐3 in list A (2 if ages 18-21)and none in list B OR<br>☐Diagnosis excluded from county MHP |
| 3 | Refer to **County Mental Health Plan** for assessment (Fax – 510-346-1083) | ☐ 4 or more in list A (3 or more if ages 18-21) OR<br>☐1 or more in list B |
| 4 | Refer to County Alcohol & Drug Program (1-800-491-9099) | ☐1 from list C |

FIGURE 1.1. Evaluation criteria and assignment algorithm in a California county. *Source*: Alameda County Behavioral Health Department.

the famed mental health program in Long Beach, California, explained: "It's categorizing that you have to be very careful about . . . You want to provide the amount of support someone needs and not one iota more."[21]

Scaling in this way is indeed a logical response to the challenges these clinicians face. As a result of public awareness campaigns, school psychological screenings, and early intervention programs, public clinicians are deluged with demands for care. Politicians also push for medicalization: They want clinicians (not police) to respond to 911 calls and for outreach teams to make the rounds of homeless encampments. Yet mental health in California has also been subjected to nauseating seesaws in its funding.[22] As recently as the 2008 Great Recession, brutal budget cuts expelled one-third of clients from public mental health caseloads.[23] In the face of these competing demands, rigorous rationalization—focusing on the most disruptive of behaviors, carefully dosing out treatment, and pushing clients out as soon as possible—was not just a rational response; it seemed like there was no alternative.

## BOUNDING FOR THE REAL *MALADES* IN FRANCE

When I arrived in France in 2015, I heard about plenty of initiatives that sounded like scaling (minus references to "consumers" or "behavioral health," both of which my informants found farcically American—that is, superficial). Recent mental health plans, for example, have put the accent on public health tools like destigmatization, mental health first aid delivered by laypeople, and prevention education, which would expand psychological interventions to a broader swathe of the French population.[24] Administrators in the Ministry of Health, themselves under pressure from their colleagues (or in effect overseers) in the Ministry of Finance, have demanded that *secteurs* titrate treatment more rationally and adopt protocols to rigorously evaluate who really needs care in the public system and to send elsewhere those who don't.

On the ground, however, professionals remain committed to another approach, which I call "bounding." Bounding focused not on classifying symptoms or behaviors but on *people*. I asked Doctor Poulain, a psychiatrist working in a psychiatric *secteur* in Reims, how she decided who had a real mental illness that merited public mental health care. Her answer was striking:

> What do you mean a "real illness"? . . . In psychiatry, you don't care for illnesses, you care for ill persons . . . When you care for an illness, you don't care for people, you care for organs. And what organ are you going to target in psychiatry? You're really in the shit! . . . To imagine that illness is only in the brain . . . is just completely false . . . You can't care for someone in a serious way in psychiatry without being in relation with someone. You can't care without the person.

Determining who belonged in the *secteur* was not a matter of placing individuals on a continuum. Instead, it meant sorting them into three separate kinds: real *malades*, people with mere psychic troubles, and others' whose problems with addiction or criminal behavior were not psychiatric. Clinicians insisted that the best way to do so was not through elaborate protocols but by professional judgment.[25] As I discovered, bounding shapes not only who gets served in *secteurs* but how: If scaling tends toward the

TABLE I.1
Bounding and scaling

| | Bounding | Scaling |
|---|---|---|
| **Position in classification struggles** | Resisting medicalization and rationalization on assumption that care is costly and should be concentrated. | Embracing medicalization and rationalization to produce care that is calibrated to individuals and far-reaching in the population. |
| **Approach to allocating care** | Focus on evaluating *people* and placing them into typological kinds (e.g., real *malades*, people with psychic troubles). | Focus on evaluating *behaviors* and placing them on a continuum of disruptiveness (e.g. number of emergency room visits). |
| **Process of classification** | Hierarchical (dominated by psychiatrists) and subjective; reliant on professional judgment and skeptical of outside pressures. | Ostensibly objective; based on quantitative counts; open to input from nonmedical entities (e.g., municipal government). |

individualization of treatment, bounding favors the homogenization (or, perhaps, equality) of interventions for people within a given bureaucratic kind (table I.1).

In chapter 1, I will describe how, in public policy debates, a powerful segment of public psychiatrists resisted medicalization and rationalization, which they saw as diluting the resources devoted to real *malades*. The problem, as I will explore in chapter 2, is that *secteurs* are legally expected, as public services, to serve everyone. The result was something that looks not like the careful and efficient calibration of allocating care via rationalization and more like simple rationing. In a context where they were supposed to say yes to everyone who asked for their services, professionals found informal ways to say no and to concentrate their limited resources on real *malades*.

As a way of managing the dilemmas between costs and care, scaling looks good to consultants in the French Ministry, and bounding has plenty of appeal to street-level professionals. But neither can ultimately resolve the thorny question of how to manage demands for care and limit costs. A system in the United States that assumes everyone can achieve a modicum of behavioral control and move to a lower level of care has to face the reality of people with serious mental illnesses who don't. As I will show in this book, clinicians in France, convinced that they can deliver permanent care to a small group of *malades* while minimizing the amount delivered to everyone else, cannot actually deliver enough treatment to meet the demands of either.

*Chapter One*

# THE BOUNDARIES OF "SANTÉ-MENTALISME"

Every time I have spoken to an Anglophone psychiatrist who knows something about the French mental health system, they know something about *Secteur* 59G21. *Secteurs* are the building blocks of French public psychiatry: each *secteur*, which is responsible for all the people living in a catchment area of around 70,000 people, includes beds in a hospital, an outpatient clinic, day hospitals, and apartments for patients. *Secteurs* are staffed by a team of nurses, social workers, and psychologists—and managed by psychiatrists. *Secteur* 59G21 covers a low-income suburb of Lille, a struggling postindustrial city in the north of France. For decades, its charismatic head, Doctor Jean-Luc Roelandt, worked to puncture the segregated world of French psychiatry and—as he put it in a 2001 national report on going "From Psychiatry Towards Mental Health"—to "integrate psychiatric care . . . into the much vaster field of health."[1] Roelandt drew eclectically on models like the open and unlocked hospital wards of Trieste Italy, the patient-run Clubhouses of Quebec, support programs led by trained "peers" with lived experience of mental illness of the United Kingdom, and the Assertive Community Treatment model of intensive community treatment piloted in Wisconsin. He in turn convinced the World Health Organization (WHO) to situate a Collaborative Center for Research and Training in Mental Health in Lille, although the center notes that, for many French mental health professionals, it's best to "keep quiet about the international sources of principles and recommendations."[2]

Roelandt's *secteur*, which is laser-focused on keeping the *secteur*'s patients in the community and out of the hospital, is not just seductive for international audiences. It is catnip for the French Ministry of Health. In May 2016, I tag along during a two-day visit his team organizes for a few high-level administrators. We start at the *secteur*'s main office, where Baptiste, a psychologist, kicks off the tour. "We operate under principles of health democracy," he explains. "That means, first, that our care is integrated with the needs of the community, and second, that our users are participating in our system of care." The representative from the Ministry of Health, however, quickly pulls us from first principles to brass tacks: "How are you deciding who to serve here?" Baptiste pivots to something I rarely heard referenced in French *secteurs*: epidemiology. "When we do a survey, 30 percent of people [living in the *secteur*'s catchment area] have some issue with 'mental health.' Maybe half actually say, 'I want to do something about this.' But that's still huge! And in this area, there are only three private psychiatrists." Here we have already arrived at the central tension of part I in this book: a clinician facing enormous need, squaring off with a government official worried about paying for a potentially limitless system of care.

How do they manage? "We're mobilizing elected leaders, social services, and generalist doctors to organize the first level of care," Baptiste explains. Once someone calls the *secteur*, though, they're screened using a formalized questionnaire and given a meeting with a nurse within forty-eight hours. Baptiste takes us into a room that looks like a command center to show what comes next. There's an enormous board with names written on cards under categories: "Medical-Psychological Service of Proximity," "Intensive Care Integrated in the City," "Therapeutic Family Placement." Every morning, the team discusses high-risk patients, bumps them up or down a level of care, and then hits the road. Nurses spend 75 percent of their time visiting patients at home, Baptiste tells us proudly. I've figured out why no one seems concerned that the main office of *Secteur* 59G21 is poorly signed and hard to reach on mass transit: because the "users" (I almost never hear "patients" during my visit) don't actually come here.

We head out to visit some of the *secteur*'s satellite offices in community centers, the therapeutic apartments it manages in public housing complexes, and its employment programs for users looking to return to work after recovering from their illness. On our way, I comment to Baptiste that the model feels familiar to me from shadowing mobile clinical teams in California. "That's the point," Baptiste tells me. "We're really operating on an Anglo-Saxon model." That model is scaling: rationalizing care by ramping it up and dialing it down based on where an individual is, in this moment, on a continuum of need.

Over lunch, I hear why that Anglo-Saxon model appeals so much to the Ministry of Health official. She asks about the personnel costs of such frequent contacts with users in crisis. A young psychiatrist explains, "Our goal is not to give people permanent care, like many *secteurs*. We're trying to activate someone's personal networks. Once someone is stabilized, a generalist doctor can start doing their prescriptions."

A nurse proudly cuts in, "Our model is one that challenges the traditional idea, which is '*malade* now, *malade* forever.' Our goal is to delegate. Pass the baton."

I see the biggest cost savings at the end of the day.[3] We drive to the gigantic university hospital, where a single unit—ten beds—is run by *Secteur* 59G21 (many *secteurs* have fifty or sixty beds). We wander onto the unit through sliding glass doors. There are no cards to swipe or keys to turn because this is an unlocked ward. It's also half empty. Two users stand up from a table where they've been painting with watercolors. One exclaims, "Oh, it's another visit!"

The other, a young woman who identifies herself as a designated spokesperson, explains: "Our courtyard is much smaller than at the old asylum"—the specialized psychiatric hospital at Armentières a few miles away, which dates to the seventeenth century—"but here we have our own rooms, and so much more privacy."

The official asks Baptiste about the average length of stay. "Eight days," he responds, "though we're trying to get it lower." The official looks surprised: The average length of a psychiatric hospitalization in France in 2016 was about thirty days.[4] Baptiste presses, "We basically realized that at 1,000 euros per day for a hospitalization, you could just give it to someone on the street and their mental health would get a lot better." Roelandt's *secteur* hasn't been handing out cash, but the statement evinces a core trade-off: To provide intensive services in the community, you have to get personnel and funds out of the hospital. Roelandt is explicit that this breaks with the fusion of hospital and community in the *secteur*: As he wrote, his "citizen psychiatry . . . supersedes the strategy of French sectorization" because it "promotes the closure" of places of "exclusion" like psychiatric hospitals.[5]

The international world of psychiatry knows about Lille as the apex of French psychiatry. But when I ask French psychiatrists who are part of the old guard—the ones who rediscovered Sigmund Freud, manned the barricades during the student and worker revolts in 1968, and accompanied the cautious downsizing of asylums in the 1970s—they send me to Reims. It's another peripheral city in the northeast of France. The *secteur* there has been led for a couple of decades by Patrick Chemla. As one psychiatrist told me, rather than hosting ministerial delegations, "Chemla is the head doctor who resists the normative, financial accounting machine" the Ministry of Health has unleashed. Chemla's *secteur* is rooted in the principles of institutional psychotherapy, even in an era of increasing austerity. Its website declares its commitment to "welcoming a person in psychic suffering through multiple responses based in the city . . . In each of these places, the emphasis is put on listening and the collective dimension. Therapeutic clubs, linking patients and clinicians, are a place for constructing the daily life of these places of care."[6]

The *secteur*'s main outpatient clinic is located two blocks from the cathedral in Reims; it couldn't be more central. This is an asset because, unlike in Lille, here the patients are supposed to come in and participate in the quotidian activities of the *secteur*.[7] The nurse who welcomes me takes me into an enormous activity room decorated with art from patients and a posted list of "Principles of Democratic Psychiatry" from the radical Italian psychiatrist Franco Basaglia. Today, the mood is somber. She recounts, "We had a patient who had been coming here every day for twenty years. He was really at the heart of our music club. This week, he passed away." People here generally don't transition to lower levels of care. They die, to be remembered above all by the *secteur* professionals who were serving them for life.

My host for the visit is Doctor Poulain, who tells me she couldn't complete her residency in general medicine and thus switched to being a psychiatrist—an option that reflects how marginalized French psychiatry once was. Speaking of the old asylum where she trained, she comments, "It's paradoxical because it was a place of imprisonment and relegation, and yet it was in a psychiatric hospital that I really learned medicine." She leads me upstairs past a pottery workshop. A woman streams out the door and starts tugging at Doctor Poulain's sleeve; a battery of words spilling out.

Poulain gently detaches the woman's hand and tells her she'll be back in an hour. "You look like you haven't spent too much time around people in the midst of psychosis," she comments to me, noting that I am not nearly as nonplussed as she is.

Unlike with the psychologist in Lille, my first attempt to get her to explain who gets served in the *secteur* doesn't get an elaborate response: "It's a public service and it's free," she tells me, shrugging. When I press her, she admits that broader social changes have made that principle harder to act on: "There's a displacement of social misery toward psychiatry. . . . This makes into our responsibility the suffering that is a consequence of the way society crushes the individual . . . [through] the cruelty of work . . . and foreigners who are displaced by misery and conflict." She confesses that they send some of those patients to the private system: "We're obligated because our resources are limited. We take the people who are very sick or don't have resources."

But then she told me about a case that seemed to fit neither bill: "I saw a young man today who had very poignant troubles. He had sex for the first time, and afterward, he was completely wiped out, he went to see an endocrinologist . . . he even stopped his studies . . . So there's a block that we needed to remove." She tells me she treated him with a quick dose of psychoanalysis. I tried to understand by what criteria this individual met the *secteur*'s standard for care, but I hit a wall when Doctor Poulain tells me, "It's really variable from one practitioner to another, depending on their availability . . . and how we're going to listen to the patient." The issue, she suggested, was not identifying where someone fell on a measure of symptoms but rather professional reflection about the patient's situation in its entirety: "You need to give time to the person in front of you, get down to the nitty-gritty. When someone comes to see you, you don't know what they have. . . . You need to discuss, ask a colleague. . . . It's in psychiatry that I learned that." The scaling that I saw in Lille is a logic of ranks and quantitative metrics; what I saw in Reims was more a mix of expert judgment and artisanal *je ne sais quoi*.

I carry my unanswered questions to my interview with Doctor Chemla, on whose desk a picture of Freud sits prominently. He, too, doesn't have much to say about how the *secteur* makes decisions about who to serve: "We work with institutional, therapeutic, and psychoanalytic criteria.

We can translate that into managerial terms for the director of the hospital, but they know they [the managerial terms] are meaningless. No problem." He thunders, "The problem is coming from the ministry, which is beginning to threaten us with a new schema of organization!" He's talking about a new reform, passed in February 2016, that would submit psychiatry to some of the same pressures as the rest of the medical system to adopt quantitative evaluations and to increase productivity in care. "Psychiatrists ought to be in a position of resistance and combativity . . . against a delirious economism of ultraliberalism . . . [but] we have a desire to self-destruct," he declares. He evokes the famous death instinct of Freud: "Thanatos is winning."

The *secteurs* in Lille and Reims and their heads—Roelandt and Chemla, respectively—are both inheritors of the same tradition: public psychiatry at the service of the French populace. They face the same competing pulls from a society demanding more care and a national health insurance system hesitant to cut a blank check to deliver it. Lille represents one rationalized model founded on an implicit logic of scaling: epidemiological analysis of population needs, close collaboration with nonpsychiatric institutions to reduce the number of people who require specialized care, and treatment modulated based on someone's momentary placement on a continuum of distress.

This chapter, however, is about how psychiatrists like Doctors Poulain and Chemla have struggled to defend an alternative model for resolving dilemmas between care and costs: bounding. Reims is an archetypal example of the bounding model. As this chapter shows, many public psychiatrists have resisted society's and key state actors' demand that they address a broader range of suffering, insisting that they must concentrate resources on a single bureaucratic kind of suffering: *malades*. Bounding has proven difficult to dislodge because of the way that the conception of *malades* as the primary responsibility of the *secteurs* is inscribed in the structure of the system itself. The result is psychiatric *secteurs* that have an open door at the center of town but do little to recruit patients actively through awareness campaigns, screening, or networking with other service providers. This first chapter describes the origins of the conundrum that clinicians on the ground constantly navigate: an inexorable rise in demand for services, a dwindling budget—and, without Lille's scaling model, no tools to reconcile the gap.

## FEAR OF REACTIVITY

Scholars have frequently described psychiatry as an "imperialist" discipline that seizes on any opportunity to colonize new psychic terrain.[8] The famed 1960 circular inaugurating the *secteur* policy, written by close allies of public psychiatrists in the Ministry of Health, seemed to endorse such expansionist aims. It opened by declaring that "the importance of mental illnesses among the social plagues"—think tuberculosis, alcoholism, or child maltreatment—"is every day more preoccupying."[9] In analogizing mental illness to a social contagion, the ministry implied that the clientele of the *secteurs* was nothing less than the French population as a whole. Within a given geographic area, the *secteur* was charged with "assur[ing] for all the *malades*, men and women, indispensable continuity between detection, treatment without hospitalization when possible, care with hospitalization, and finally, surveillance and post-cure."[10] There were to be no exceptions. As ministers have reminded psychiatrists periodically since: "The psychiatric *secteur* is, above all, the obligation for a public service to welcome and care for every patient who resides within a given geographic area addressing themselves to it."[11]

Yet even as they embraced a shift toward community care, many public psychiatrists sought to limit their own reach and responsibilities. The modifier—"all" or "every"—has never been the issue. Instead, it's the noun: Who counts as a *malade*? In 1966, the luminaries of French psychiatry gathered for a conference debating who exactly the nascent *secteurs* were supposed to serve. Henry Ey, the General Secretary of *L'évolution psychiatrique*, which organized the conference, offered an ambitious opening allocution: "I would like to call attention . . . to the immensity and urgency of the task which is waiting for us . . . as formidable as that of national education."[12] How immense and formidable? His elaboration was surprising: "It is not excessive to say that 1 to 2 percent of the French population will ask for psychiatric care in a given year."[13]

From the beginning, French psychiatrists were setting boundaries. Lucien Bonnafé, who helped shepherd the *malades* of Saint Alban's Hospital (as well as a number of Jews hiding among them) through the occupation during World War II, weighed in at the conference: "I am a psychiatrist. Sometimes I treat easy cases that are quickly cured, but above all I treat severe disadaptations that are persistent . . . The psychiatric system of which we are speaking . . . should be made to confront the most important of needs. And among them, even the smallest objective analysis puts at the foreground . . . schizophrenia, the chronic illness *par excellence*."[14] Georges Daumezon, another lion among the postwar psychiatric reformers, elaborated that "the *secteur*, as I wanted it, was something that could take on, not the 'mental health' of a zone (this seems like a sociological perspective that is foreign to me) but the *malades* of a zone."[15]

In effect, when public psychiatrists envisioned a system serving all *malades*, it was not one whose doors were open to everyone (even if, like in Reims, the clinic was located in the center of town). Rather, they wanted a system that would not slam the door shut for the "*malades* who are undesirable, perturbing, uncontrollable, discouraging," as one partisan of sectorization put it.[16] And the way to "block the permanent rejection of the *malade* by different institutions," attendees at the 1966 conference argued, was to put all the institutions serving them in the "hands of the same team."[17] This principle was foundational to the distinguishing feature of the *secteurs* vis-à-vis community mental health centers in the United States. As one French *secteur* psychiatrist observed: "In the United States, the system is very siloed, with community teams that have no relationship with the teams in the psychiatric hospital. The divorce is at a maximum . . . The *secteur*, it is the joining of the community and the psychiatric hospital."[18] By adopting this institutional structure, the state de facto endorsed the idea that *secteurs* would mobilize these multiple institutions in the service of a single group: chronically ill, usually impoverished, once-institutionalized people with psychosis.

What's surprising about this to an outsider with a sociological perspective is how fearful psychiatrists were of interventions that risked bringing too many people under the mental health system's remit. General Secretary Ey concluded his 1966 discourse, "Psychiatry should not 'inflate' at the demand of a number of '*malades*' who are not actually [*malades*], or due to the abusive image of a society that wants to make psychiatry in charge of the happiness of everyone."[19] When US psychiatrists were promoting the results of community surveys to highlight the huge scope of mental health problems, French psychiatrists were arguing such surveys were meaningless because "if one accepts uncritically the reported morbidity rate," it is virtually impossible to "imagine the immense psychiatric resources that have to be developed" to respond.[20] It's rather remarkable that even as they built a system designed to serve "all the *malades*," neither public psychiatrists nor the central state ever ran epidemiological studies to determine how many there were. *Malade* was left an undifferentiated category without a race or class in both official policy and practice. One major effect of sectorization was to eliminate the division of men and women, agitated and calm, acute and chronic patients into different wards in the old asylum and mix them together in integrated hospital units.[21]

Social scientists vaunt their discovery of reactivity, or the way that metrics actually create the realities they purport to measure.[22] Psychiatrists' epistemic lens of bounding has arguably allowed them to see this sociological insight for a while. Time spent going into schools to conduct screenings for emotional disturbances or running destigmatization campaigns to encourage people to ask their doctor if they are suffering from an anxiety disorder will create mental health problems that would not have existed otherwise. And that undermines care for a small group of *malades* who aren't hard to find because they went straight from the asylums into the *secteurs*. From this vantage point, an ebullient activist and a coolly rational consultant, described in the next section, could seem like an existential threat.

## THE ACTIVIST AND THE CONSULTANT

The intensifying efforts of politicians and activists to burst the traditional boundaries of public psychiatry and address a wider spectrum of need became evident to me, somewhat paradoxically, inside a bubble. In May 2016, I visited the *Cap sur la santé mentale*—a giant plastic dome erected on the grand plaza of *La Défense* in Paris. As Ségolène Neuville, the ministry's secretary charged with disabilities, declared at the opening ceremonies: "We share a determination to change the way our society views mental health"—namely, by making it an issue of concern and topic of discussion for the entire public, and not just a small group of mental health professionals.[23] This admittedly made holding a public awareness event in a bubble an odd choice. The attendees were a predictable who's who of advocacy groups, joined only by the occasional confused tourist.

At the first panel (also broadcast over the radio), a psychiatrist from a nearby university recited a familiar set of figures: "This is a massive problem. Statistics show 1 to 2 percent of the population has psychosis, five to ten depression in a given year, and 20 percent over their lifetime. For anxiety, I can't even cite statistics. It's everyone." Aude Caria, who ran a group called Psycom in Paris (which works closely with Doctor Roelandt in Lille), followed up: "We know that this is a problem that concerns everyone, but there is not enough information . . . We are trying to get people to know that every one of us can do something for our mental health. It's not just something that concerns psychiatrists." The next speaker, Tim Greacen, brought to his intervention not just a strong Australian accent but an Anglo-Saxon flair: "The big revolution that has happened in other countries is the realization that mental health is something that is fantastic. It's a positive value, something that we all can have, and imagine and construct together. Knowledge of health needs to belong to everyone, not just health professionals."

Earlier in my research, I had spoken to Greacen at Maison Blanche, a major Parisian hospital. He had moved to France with the intent of introducing concepts like "empowerment" from the HIV/AIDS movement and later pivoted to promoting user participation in the mental health system. He didn't hold back about his adopted home country: France "operates on the model of the savior, the health professional, who comes to the poor person who is suffering." What he envisioned was something more proactive. "They should be doing health promotion in schools, teaching people about mental health and drugs and alcohol. Right now, there's very little health promotion, all the spending is on 'care' and not prevention. France doesn't really have a Ministry of Health. It has a Ministry of Illness," he inveighed.[24] I countered that at least psychiatric treatment is universally accessible and free in France. "Sure, there are no barriers to access," he replied, "except that people don't dare to say they have a mental health problem because the stigmatization is enormous here." He wasn't exaggerating. In one study of twenty-seven countries, people with schizophrenia in France were the third most likely to report having experienced discrimination.[25]

His lament spoke to a broader push. Top officials in the Ministry of Health have been aggressively advocating for scaling up attention to mental health for decades. In 2001, when the minister introduced a new mental health plan, he explained that "by not limiting itself to psychiatry and its major clinical presentations (schizophrenia, psychoses, etc.), this plan includes the care of mental troubles or behaviors and psycho-social problems. It's not only the crazy person that [the plan] deals with, but everyone affected by psychic suffering."[26] Subsequent national plans in 2005, 2012, and 2018 promoted campaigns to reduce stigma around seeking psychological help, screen children for autism, and train laypeople to provide psychological first aid to people in distress. Whether these programs helped address unmet need (as activists like Graecen insist) or actually created that need through a medicalization of nonpsychiatric problems (as some skeptical public psychiatrists argue), they reflected a state-led attempt to inject a logic of scaling into French policy.

For Greacen, the right way to respond to social demands for medicalizing suffering is to empower people to manage it themselves. Lise, a consultant with the National Agency for Supporting the Performance of Health Establishments, was focused on helping *secteurs* do their part as well. The key was rationalizing the care they delivered along the lines of what I saw in Lille. Lise trained as a clinical psychologist but was quickly disillusioned. French psychologists are subservient to psychiatrists and not even reimbursed by the French national insurance program.[27] So she left. Lise spent ten years working for Britain's National Health Service, famous for its ruthless cost-benefit evaluations and carefully tiered levels of care. She returned to serve as a consultant just as the Performance Agency was, in 2012, opening its first mission in mental health. "Our goal is to support performance," she explained, "which means a better service for the patient, clinicians who are happier with their work—and, naturally, economic efficiency."

One thing the agency was looking at when we met in 2015 was how to reduce wait times for a first consultation in the medical-psychological centers (*Centres médico-psychologiques*, hereafter "Clinics"), the outpatient clinics at the center of the *secteurs*. Lise told me, "If a Clinic tries to take charge of everything, any which way, it's going to be overwhelmed." But for her, the issue "is not having too many people [asking for care]. It's a question of organization." Much like in the United Kingdom, she said, "What we need is something graduated; you have a specialized team trained in initial evaluations. And then you decide whether a person should see a psychologist, a specialized nurse, a psychiatrist—or someone outside [the *secteur*]." She envisioned a scale of professionals who the health system would assign based on where a patient was, at a given moment, on a continuum between health and illness. Like in Britain, a patient might first be sent to take a short course online about managing symptoms of anxiety before being given a script for medication by a primary care doctor.

Alongside better titrating the intensity of care, Lise wanted public psychiatrists to learn how to end it. She noted, "In France, we have a sentimental attachment to keeping a patient's file open for life, we never close it." Yet as a report she coauthored concluded, psychiatry could only address expanding demand by moving from a "management of stocks"—that is, treating a fixed group of *malades*—to a "management of flows" of people moving in and out of care.[28] Figuring out when to close a file, of course, would require a clearer sense of what public psychiatrists were supposed to be doing. But, she noted, "We basically have no indicators [for evaluation] in mental health . . . But we're developing them. Things like the number of people hospitalized unnecessarily, or who don't come to their first appointment at a Clinic." Moving the needle, she insisted over and over again, "is really not an issue of having more resources, it's the way in which they're divided."

Greacen and Lise drew on two different vocabularies: the first, personal empowerment and community responsibility, and the second, professional specialization and rationalized cost-benefit calculations. Yet their work emerged from the same roots. France could reconcile demands for more care with cost controls through individualized interventions adapted to a broad continuum of need. Inside this bubble, a logic of scaling appeared perfectly rational. When it collided with a logic of bounding outside, the result was acrimonious.

## DEMEDICALIZING DEPRESSION

Béranger, a psychologist in charge of mental health programs at the National Institute for Prevention and Education for Health, saw psychiatrists' fear of reactivity firsthand. He bemoaned to me (echoing Graecen), "Prevention is relatively undeveloped in France . . . We have a very medical orientation. We take charge of patients once they develop a pathology, but everything else is private life." Béranger arrived in 2007 when the ministry was actively seeking to use public health interventions to improve psychological well-being across the population. As Isabelle Prade, the official charged with psychiatry, told me, "For me—and this is the position of the minister as well—mental illness is within mental health. The only difference is the intensity [of both symptoms and treatment for them]." Yet Béranger quickly learned how incompatible this vision was with the principles of bounding, and the extent of resistance to medicalizing suffering at the mental health continuum's less-severe end.

In 2005, the National Plan for Psychiatry and Mental Health allocated 7 million euros to the Prevention Institute for a public awareness campaign, "Depression: Know more to escape it." It observed that "no national information campaign has been carried out in the field of mental health" of the kind visible in the United States or the United Kingdom.[29] The justification for such a campaign seemed sound: "Depression is under-diagnosed and under-treated . . . In France, only 47 percent of diagnosed [depressed people] receive treatment by medication . . . Only 5 percent receive correct medical interventions."[30] As Béranger elaborated, "Behind the campaign, we have epidemiological figures that show that 8 percent [of French adults] have had an identifiable episode of depression in the last twelve months, nearly 20 percent over their lifetime." The idea, he explained, was pretty simple: "We wanted to say, 'Depression is an illness, it can happen to anyone, and there are treatments and professionals to help you face it.' "

Calling depression an "illness," Béranger noted, was "an attempt at destigmatization . . . because we know at the level of the population, there's an attitude of, 'These are people who could make a bit more of an effort [to be better].' " Nonetheless, the campaign trespassed an important distinction. Since 1980, the *Diagnostic and Statistical Manual* (*DSM*)—the bible of US psychiatry—no longer considers the origin of someone's symptoms as a factor in diagnosis.[31] But, as Béranger recounted, "The way depression is characterized by the *DSM* is not something that conforms to the culture of French psychopathology." In the psychoanalytically infused French tradition, the distinction between endogenous depression with no external cause and an exogenous depression in response to outside circumstances is crucial. It separates a real illness from a temporary and normal response to adverse conditions.

The campaign ultimately consisted of an innocuous website and a pamphlet. It nonetheless became a fracas. There was an enormous uprising among psychoanalytically trained psychiatrists who claimed, in Béranger's words, that the campaign was "medicalizing . . . reactions to catastrophic social circumstances that largely explain their troubles." Professionals were also unhappy because the campaign included a list of questions for people to ask themselves about their symptoms "before consulting a doctor."[32] This, they alleged, was encouraging people to self-diagnose. Diagnosis was medical professionals' private turf. The outcry reached the Minister of Education, who apparently asked the Minister of Health to withdraw the campaign.

The conflict intersected with a wider moral panic about the expansion of psychiatric treatment across the French population. Aude Caria from Psycom, an organization involved in the campaign, recounted that part of the frontal attack against the Institute for Prevention came from psychiatrists who "reproached them for playing into the hands of pharmaceutical companies and doing a campaign to get people to take antidepressants." In the eyes of many French professionals and policymakers I spoke with, such a campaign was overkill. France's problem was an *over*use of psychopharmaceuticals. During my fieldwork, dozens of them offered some variant of the figure that France was the largest consumer of antidepressants in Europe. (This stat comes from a study carried out in six European countries in 2000, which found that 19.2 percent of French people had consumed a psychotropic medication in the last twelve months; Spain was second at 15.5 percent, and Germans were lagging at 5.9 percent.[33])

There are a few caveats here. First, Europe has more than six countries. Second, the large figure for psychotropic medication is driven in part by benzodiazepines (like Valium) prescribed to elderly people to help them sleep.[34] If we look only at consumption of classic antidepressants like Prozac, as of 2022, France was below the European average and had rates half those of Anglo-Saxon countries.[35] France is actually the rare country where the consumption of psychotropics has gone down in recent decades.[36] Still, the stat touched a cultural nerve. As one psychiatrist interviewed by *Le Monde* put it, the statistic exposed the harmful confluence of pharma's "industrial logic of selling more without ceasing," doctors with "nothing [else] to propose [to] their patients who come to express a social malaise," and a population that "wants an immediate erasure of their suffering, without effort."[37]

That is, the backlash to the public awareness campaign around depression in 2007 stemmed both from the fear from psychiatrists that "poor mental health" and "mental illness" were becoming interchangeable and from a broader cultural anxiety about the medicalization (or perhaps the Americanization) of suffering.[38] This resistance helped maintain a narrow, bounded role for public psychiatry. One ministry official deadpanned, "Since that campaign around depression, we have deprioritized mental health, because it went so badly."[39] While Béranger quickly clarified in our conversation that the Prevention Institute was still working on issues like alcohol use, suicide, and parenting, it was clear they danced around the term "mental illness" as classically understood.

No one in these debates questioned the legitimacy of psychiatry as the right response to mental illness per se. Rather, the concern was that public health campaigns, and the new demand for care they might incite, would pull resources from treating the *malades* for whom psychiatry was indisputably needed. The head of a Parisian psychiatric hospital explained why she rarely collaborated on public awareness events: "There's a destigmatization, the *psy* is a lot less scary. And at the same time . . . French society is complaining. We see a growth of people who come to the *secteur* for malaise, burnouts. There's a kind of swell arriving and we say to ourselves, 'What is our mission?' Because if we accept this surge . . . we're going to be less present for our schizophrenic patients . . . I read recently that we have the responsibility for caring for 'mental health.' That's beyond psychiatry, it's well-being . . . it's so huge that it's scary."[40]

Toward the end of our conversation, I asked Béranger what his institute could do for *malades* whose medicalization no one contested. He replied, "In France, psychosis is not really an issue of public health because we know it's going to wind up being cared for whether or not we do any campaigns about it. If you're schizophrenic . . . you're eventually going to get diagnosed, and there's a whole system of psychiatry that's ready for you." This was not a conclusion reached through hard epidemiological data. It was a logical deduction from the universal access promised by the *secteur* system—access that a surge of people who were not really *malades* could threaten. " 'Mental health' is making a mess in psychiatry," Béranger concluded. "What even is mental health?" he wondered. And so, better to put one's time and limited resources elsewhere.

## CITIES OF SUFFERING

At the same time as public health campaigns were pushing psychiatry to widen its reach to include people suffering from depression, other initiatives encouraged it to broaden its horizons to see economic precarity, delinquency, and addiction as part of its mission as well. In the 1990s, the French population faced the harsh forces of globalization and deindustrialization alongside cuts to the social services supposed to mitigate their effects. Mid-decade, a report from a ministerial commission observed how cash-strapped work, welfare, and education programs were, "running up against a problem which is poorly-defined, but heavy, disturbing, and new—that of suffering, the poor well-being of a significant number of people."[41] In the face of rising rates of drug use, school dropouts, and disruptive public behavior, it was, the report argued, "urgent to enlarge the practical ambitions of public psychiatric *secteurs*" and expand their collaboration with other social service providers.[42] In the United States, such challenges were met with a new focus on behavioral health, which recognized that addressing homelessness and avoiding overdoses were equal to treating symptoms among the core responsibilities of psychiatry. At the risk of being repetitive, though, in France, public psychiatric unions made it clear that that the discipline would be dragged into this new role reluctantly at best. In a document released at the same time, the unions insisted on the priority of "assur[ing] psychiatric care to the most chronic, fragile, and disadvantaged *malades*," which was being threatened by demands for "psychiatric treatment for social problems."[43]

As was often the case, there was a disconnect between competing visions and practical realities. The lines between medical and social interventions were blurred as soon as psychiatric patients began leaving asylums to return to the communities. *Secteur* personnel needed to find public housing or a minimum income for released patients. The keys (literally, in the case of housing) to these social services are held by municipal governments. Those governments face their own demands. As Laurent El-Ghozi, a city council member from a working-class suburb of Paris ("it has been run by communists since 1935"), explained to me, "Since 2000, when we do 'participatory diagnoses' [of need for new social programs] . . . mental health is almost always among the top three priorities." A half-dozen municipal officials that I interviewed confirmed that demands that public psychiatry scale up to address a continuum of suffering were not just coming from the Ministry of Health. They were emerging in community meetings, electoral campaigns, and quotidian encounters between citizens and municipal welfare workers.

The lever for getting municipalities to address the social needs of mentally ill *secteur* patients and pushing *secteur* psychiatrists to address the medical needs of the general population of municipalities has been more recently the local councils of mental health (*conseils locaux de santé mentale*, or councils). Councils have been receiving increasing state funding since 2010; there are now 260 across France.[44] I was lucky enough to follow the attempt to create a new council in one arrondissement of Paris over several months in 2016. At a first meeting, Armand, a psychologist funded by the city to help the effort, gives a quick overview for attendees: "Councils are a place for concertation and coordination between health professionals, psychiatrists, social services, service users, and any other local concerned parties."

The mayor's adjunct for health then steps in: "As you know, the municipality has been trying to increase its role in addressing the health needs of precarious populations or irregular migrants. In meetings on health, mental health kept coming up. We have high rates of addiction and multiple hospitals in the district with which we need to be collaborating."

Armand ticks off some of the actions the council might focus on: public awareness campaigns during the yearly Week of Information on Mental Health, creating a committee for the management of complex situations, initiatives on preventing Islamic radicalization, and addressing issues around housing. The last topic prompts nods from the dozen municipal social workers and *secteur* professionals seated around the table. "On one hand," he explains, "there's an issue of stigmatization: Some public housing doesn't want to take people because of their illness. On the other hand, you can have troubles with neighbors which can be a barrier for people remaining in their housing at all."

A nurse from the *secteur* chimes in to affirm: "Housing is a big challenge for us. It's so key for maintaining care."

For elected officials I spoke to, councils were a worthwhile investment of time because they might enlist psychiatry to respond to complaints about neighbors yelling at all hours of the night, the fire hazards created by hoarders, or adolescents smoking pot in apartment block stairwells. A citizen psychiatry, of the kind envisioned in Lille, would be an active collaborator in providing targeted, short-term interventions, in line with a logic of scaling. When viewing these problems through the optic of bounding, though, French professionals are skeptical.

A few weeks later, I observe a follow-up meeting, which begins with a presentation from a representative of Habitat Paris, the main public housing authority. "We have nineteen thousand units in the district," she reports, "and have been dealing with a rash of arsons. We have a lot of people who have done damage and . . . Well, not to stigmatize, but they have '[psychiatric] troubles.'" She recounts a specific case: "We had someone who was supposed to be followed in the *secteur*, but he wasn't adhering to his treatment. One day, he turned on the gas in the apartment and left, naked. He made his way to the Clinic, where they hospitalized him." He returned to his apartment upon discharge. When he threatened the doorman of the building, the doorman called the police, who visited the apartment and hospitalized the man again. The representative pulled up some photos on her PowerPoint: "This is really extensive damage to the unit. He removed all the wallpaper and the electrical sockets."

The psychiatrist at the head of the local *secteur* nods, "Yes. We determined he wasn't ready to be housed independently. So he's still staying in an apartment we run directly." This was a clear pattern: When *malades* struggled in the wider community, the tendency was to bring them home—that is, to the *secteur*.

Armand, however, believed that a council could do better. A few weeks later, he convenes a working group to manage "complex situations" in housing. He opens by passing out photocopies of a form that building landlords could send to the Clinic to flag a problematic situation.

From the start, the head of the *secteur*, arms folded, is skeptical: "You need to have a meeting first, to triage these, before this even gets to us . . . The information is very subjective, and I don't know why we would intervene."

A representative of the landlord's association jumps in, sounding frustrated, "But this is the problem! Now, we call the Clinic and they ask 'Well, is this psychiatric or not?' How am I supposed to know?"

Armand tries to bring the spiraling conversation back to the form: "So, we have a question here, 'The person's troubles seem to be of what nature?'"

A social worker from the *secteur* intervenes: "Only a doctor can determine this."

At this point, Armand seems a little beleaguered, "Well, we can just have them put the facts: threatened the neighbors, threw things out the window."

"Those are just behavioral troubles . . . if you're seeing someone in danger, you should just call the fire department," a nurse says. By the end of the meeting, they settle on a drastically reduced form. The *secteur* makes no commitment to act on it.

National surveys show the *secteur* professionals are key participants in nearly all councils.[45] Yet Armand suggests that, even when they show up, a reticence to expand the *secteur*'s mission is common: "Everywhere I go to start a new council, the psychiatrists are not at all thrilled. They tell me, 'We know how this is going to go. We'll see the elected officials, they're going to say they have a list of people in public housing that they don't know what to do with and they want us to intervene . . . they're going to give me new clients, and I already have enough.'" Armand himself seems to buy into this framing, however: "We have one psychiatrist who comes [to the council] and explains, 'Not everything is mental health. There are people who are annoying, but it's just because they have a bad character' . . . We shouldn't medicalize everything, we should not turn everything into psychiatry."

*Secteur* psychiatrists welcomed the aid of municipal governments in finding housing. They regularly knocked on the doors of people who were flagged by social workers as psychotic. They even relied on local police to help them hospitalize *secteur* patients who stopped coming to their appointments. Working with people who were impoverished and suffering was at the core of their definition of public service. It's just that they were doing all these things for their patients—the ones that they deemed *malades*.[46]

## RESISTING RATIONALIZATION, IGNORING INCENTIVES

We have now seen how a segment of public psychiatrists resisted pressures for medicalization, whether via public health campaigns to destigmatize depression or municipal initiatives to intervene in public housing. We will now consider the fraught collision between a logic of bounding and the economic rigors of rationalization.[47] Recall what the latter meant to our ministry consultant, Lise: a gradation of care between professionals, cost-benefit analyses to optimize psychiatric interventions, and an end to open-ended treatment in favor of stepping stabilized patients to lower levels of care.

The traditional financing of *secteurs* was not conducive to any of that. It's almost perfectly designed to support practices that, from within a logic of scaling, look totally irrational—but that, in contrast, facilitate bounding. Starting in 1985, each *secteur* received a global budget: a fixed amount that they could then divide between inpatient care and community-based services, like clinics, day hospitals, or *secteur*-monitored therapeutic apartments.

This allowed *secteur* teams ideally to shift smoothly between classically medical interventions, like writing prescriptions, to activities that would be hard to count and reimburse, like liaising with families. A global budget, needless to say, gives psychiatrists significant discretion over both who to serve and how to do it. It allowed for enormous heterogeneity among them, as the contrast between Lille and Reims makes clear. *Secteurs* vary by a factor of thirty in the number of hospital beds and twenty in the number of patients on their active file.[48]

The French public psychiatric system has never faced the violent gyrations in funding experienced by its US counterpart. Nonetheless, the state has waged a long-running battle to contain health spending—which, clinicians recognized, was actually about more than just saving money.[49] As one bemoaned, "It's through financial constraint that the public authorities intend to reorganize psychiatry"—to create a rationalized, medicalized discipline. One of the most contentious examples was when, in the 1990s and early 2000s, the Ministry of Health pushed to replace the global budget with a radically different form of financing called "payment by the activity" (*tarification à l'activité* [T2A]).[50] Adapted from Medicare in the United States and adopted elsewhere in French hospitals in 2003, payment by the activity is based on the estimated average cost of treating an episode of a given pathology. It incentivizes shorter hospitalizations and increased volume.[51]

The payment scheme had the support of many psychiatrists based in universities, who saw it as a way to get other psychiatrists to adopt more effective treatments.[52] One leader in a reform-minded union told me, "Under the global budget, if you have 1,000 outpatients and you give them 20,000 consultations or 1,000 consultations, it's the same funding!" He slapped the table, "The future of citizen psychiatry will depend on the possibility of valorizing, financially, ambulatory care as an alternative to hospitalization. I'm convinced!" The reform would funnel resources toward *secteurs* (like Jean-Luc Roelandt's in Lille) that responded to greater demand by delivering more and cheaper treatment, which invariably meant care outside hospitals.

When details of the proposed funding scheme were unveiled in the early 2000s, though, they proved wildly unpopular. The union head above reported that, when the professional organizations of French psychiatry got together in 2003, 80 percent of attendees voted against adopting T2A.

Because T2A would require much more careful documentation of diagnoses and treatments, psychiatrists (correctly) saw it as a tool for administrative intrusion into decisions that, in a system organized around classification via bounding, were made based on professional discretion. By encouraging hospitals to compete against one another to attract more lucrative patients, T2A seemed to be a Trojan horse for the marketization of the public hospital system. Some psychiatrists decided to make the logistics of implementing T2A harder by declaring a "strike against statistics" in 2004,[53] coding most cases as "F99: psychic troubles without other indicators" in medical records. This rendered the already complex technical challenge of identifying typologies of patients and determining the average costs of their care almost insurmountable. In 2006, a national report on T2A for the health system writ large stated that "the T2A in psychiatry poses methodological problems that are not resolved"[54] and left it at that.

By the time I made the rounds of the Ministry of Health during fieldwork in 2016, reform looked more like tinkering on the margins. For example, one state official described an initiative embedded in the contracts that any health establishment (like a hospital) has to renegotiate every five years to maintain its authorization. She was currently working on a stipulation to improve access to outpatient clinics: "In the contracts, we are trying to make Clinics open at least twice a week until 8 p.m. . . . [or] offer more consultations to people without an appointment. We want their delays to be shorter, and for them to visit patients at home. Very concrete." Given budgetary cuts, she admitted, there "weren't a lot of carrots," but they could offer small financial incentives for changing practices.

The newly installed head of one *secteur* described how it looked from her perspective: "We can see that the question of budgets is going to be more and more on the front burner. They're now requesting that we commit to providing a certain number of 'acts'"—that is, consultations—in the *secteur*'s contract, "even though we have several personnel [who left and] who haven't been replaced. And it's not going to stop there." This psychiatrist correctly saw that these expectations promoted both rationalization and medicalization, pushing her to scale up interventions to address a broader patient pool. She was skeptical it would work:

> When I arrived [in the *secteur*], we were obligated not to fill one post for a nurse, but the contract said that for each 500 additional acts in

> the clinic, we would get 900 euros. The maximum we could "win" through this was 8,000 euros, which we could use for training, cultural activities, whatever we want . . . I think we can agree that proposing a few hundred euros in exchange for reducing the number of nurses, working with one less person [is not compelling] . . . I told the financial director [at the Regional Health Authority], "I'm not in the habit of thinking like this . . ." I'm not against [the goal] in principle. I think as a public service, we have to do our best work, we shouldn't go home too early, we have to be accountable for what we do . . . But contracts, and especially [financial] incentives, I don't like that . . . We are supposed to be focused on the most complicated cases.

Focusing on the most complicated cases meant a flexibility in what care to deliver and how much. To her, that could never be captured in a contract.

My interviews were filled with stories of small acts of resistance to the creeping forces of managerialism in public psychiatry. There were clinicians who refused to put diagnoses in the electronic medical record to stymie the consultants hired by the ministry to evaluate the costs and benefits of care.[55] Others filled them in but kept a parallel paper record, where they could continue to use psychoanalytic categories like "transference" and "neuroses." Then there were nurses who refused to accelerate the so-called acts at the Clinic because that would inevitably mean shortening the time they spent listening to the person in distress in front of them. There was a trade-off, however: A lack of data made it difficult to allocate resources more equitably or standardize an inconsistent range of treatments available depending on which *secteur* a patient wound up in.

Perhaps most important was that this resistance didn't work. Psychiatric professional organizations may have successfully preserved the autonomy offered by a global budget, but they couldn't preserve that budget itself.[56] A lump sum payment is easy to cap. By the time of my field research, the budget for each *secteur* was growing more slowly than inflation. Psychiatry was losing ground relative to other disciplines in medicine, which had embraced rationalizing reforms to their finances.[57] "It's been a losing strategy, clearly," sighed one hospital director, "psychiatry is the fifth wheel of the carriage—it's absolutely not a priority, no one in the ministry is willing to die for it." There were other, more expensive and prestigious disciplines to reform. Public psychiatry could slowly die on its own.

## CONCLUSION: DILEMMAS OF DIVISION

For whom is public psychiatry responsible? This chapter analyzes struggles over the response to this question in France as an example of a general dilemma facing mental health systems: how to reconcile simultaneous demands from society and the state to medicalize an expanding range of psychological conditions and behaviors, in a moment where health systems face growing pressure for rationalization and cost controls? I've argued that we can understand these conflicts as rooted in the clash between distinctive logics of what public psychiatry is actually treating (people versus behaviors, for example), how to evaluate these conditions, and which professionals using what tools should do so. They speak to broader patterns in the different ways states can demarcate bureaucratic kinds.

I've identified two logics that present their own solutions to the dilemmas of medicalization and rationalization. What I call scaling has come to dominate behavioral health care in the United States. Various pieces of it have been promoted in France by standard bearers, including activists like Tim Greacen or reformist psychiatrists like Jean-Luc Roelandt. Scaling imagines mental health as a continuum. Public health interventions (like early screening or destigmatization campaigns) keep people with mild distress on the lower end of that spectrum. Carefully calibrated, time-limited medical interventions push people who are on the higher end of the continuum back down to lower levels of severity. In contrast, bounding draws a sharp line between a small, defined group of real *malades* and a qualitatively different mass of people with psychological or behavioral problems. It jealously guards the judgment of professionals in drawing those distinctions, against the formalized symptom scales and cost-benefit analyses that facilitate scaling.

Scaling may be the logic favored by policymakers, but bounding is embedded in the structure of the *secteur* itself. From the start, *secteurs* needed to find a way to allocate resources that would meet their primary mission of caring for the *malades* long confined to psychiatric hospitals who, in contrast to the United States, were rolled into France's community care system. Perhaps because of its deep institutional grounding, bounding also appeared, as Pierre Bourdieu put it, in the "categories of thought" that most of the actors with a hand in that system "spontaneously appl[ied] to it."[58] In other words, even those who sought to reform the *secteur* system saw some sense in the division between treating genuine *malades* and addressing a wider range of mental health problems on which the *secteur* was founded. I spoke with Denys Robiliard, a socialist member of the National Assembly. As of 2015, he was the parliamentary point person for the ministry. When I asked him about initiatives to expand the reach of psychiatry, he told me, "We have to put priorities, and it's absolutely unimaginable that we don't treat psychotics . . . We should reaffirm that . . . And if we give into the '*santé-mentalisme*' "—a wordplay that suggests "mental health" is a kind of "sentimentalism"—"we're going to end up with no time for them."

The final conclusion of the 1966 conference, cited at the beginning of this chapter, declared that "the *secteur* will have demonstrated its effectiveness when there are no longer, in the back of the asylums, schizophrenics who are practically abandoned."[59] Even as they saw sectorization's flaws, characters like Béranger (running public health campaigns at the Prevention Institute) or Armand (shuttling between different local councils of mental health in different arrondissements) believed *secteurs* had largely met this mandate. There was something in the community for anyone who was really *malade*. Adopting scaling might put this achievement into question—and accede implicitly to the specters of neoliberalism and Americanization.

Classificatory logics like bounding or scaling provide a coherent way of understanding the world. But they don't necessarily solve all the problems the world throws at them. Austerity was inescapable. When nurses retired, their positions were going unfilled. Beds were being eliminated. For all public psychiatrists' fear that interventions like screening or awareness campaigns would generate mental health problems that wouldn't otherwise exist, the French population was asking more and more of the *secteurs* even without such public health interventions. The public system went from serving around 2 percent of the population in the mid-1990s to 3.7 percent of adults by 2019 (figure 1.1).[60] If public psychiatry wasn't willing to adopt scaling in response, what did the alternative look like on the ground?

Doctor Antipa, a Greek émigré who was head of a Parisian *secteur* for a long time and now ran a center providing psychoanalysis for the poor, was one of those who believed the *secteurs* could reserve the majority of their resources for real *malades* while sprinkling around enough care for anyone else who showed up, in a manner consistent with the spirit of public service. But when I asked him how he adapted to budget cuts

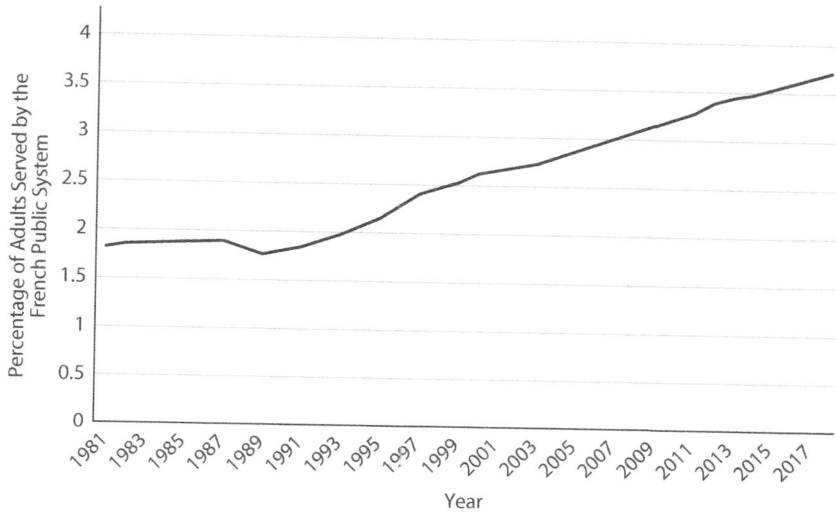


FIGURE 1.1. Proportion of adults served by public *secteurs* in France. *Sources*: Zambrowski, *Moderniser et diversifier les modes de prise en charge de la psychiatrie française*; Joly, *Prevention et soins des maladies mentales*; and Lopez and Turan-Pelletier. *Organisation et fonctionnement du dispositif de soins psychiatriques, 60 ans après la Circulaire du 15 Mars 1960*.

and increased demand, he replied, "I didn't succeed in doing much. We've arrived at the point where there is such a crowd coming that we are obligated to change one of the core elements of [the *secteur*'s] identity, which is that it welcomes the whole world. And it's not easy to decide which 'world' we're going to welcome."

"So you're obligated to do some kind of triage?" I asked.

"In practice, yes," he replied, "But if you consider different criteria that would permit you to not welcome everyone, they all pose problems. It's not evident. We've realized we can't take everyone, but then you go into the discussion, 'now what?' It's not obvious."

Psychiatrists rarely articulated clearly how they dealt with these challenges. But, as we'll see in chapter 2, they put bounding into practice every day. The result looked less like rationalization—with its promise of giving everyone just the right amount of care at the right time, and not one iota more—and more like rationing: a triage that withholds scarce medical resources for some in order to save them for others deemed more urgent and more deserving.[61]

*Chapter Two*

# RATIONING FOR REAL *MALADES*

The clinicians at the *secteur* where I conducted my fieldwork determine the boundary between sickness and health on Friday mornings. It's 9 A.M. on one particular morning, but the waiting room at the medical-psychological center (*Centre medico-psychologique*, or "Clinic") is already filling up. A middle-aged white woman is standing at the glass separating patients from secretaries; she's rocking back and forth on her feet and demanding a prescription renewal for antianxiety medication. Another woman, wearing a hijab, hustles past me to the door; she's trying to block her face with a piece of paper. An older man, sharply dressed in slacks and a button-up shirt, sits next to me and apologizes profusely for reasons I don't understand. I can overhear another secretary answering a steady stream of calls. She is making an appointment for one person to come in for an intake, reminding them to bring proof of their address to show they live in this *secteur*'s catchment area.[1] She chastises another patient for missing their appointment, notifies them that their doctor is not in today, and gives the address of an emergency room. One of the Clinic's psychologists opens the door separating the waiting room from the rooms where clinicians meet with patients. She waves me in and offers a *café allongé* in a plastic cup. After I cross the threshold, they never leave me with the patients again.

A few minutes later, Nurse Pauline, the head nurse of the Clinic, walks out to the tiny courtyard, where a few nurses are grabbing a quick cigarette.

"They're done," she announces. The *secteur*'s doctors have finished their weekly meeting. Most are now heading back to their posts in the nearby hospital, local emergency room (ER), and *secteur*'s day program. The nurses, two social workers, a psychologist, and a secretary hustle into the back conference room. Doctor Delignon, the head psychiatrist of the *secteur*, is still there with Doctor Kuorio, fresh from medical school. They're busy discussing what to do with a longtime patient's dog while his owner is stuck in the hospital. The secretary passes out a paper summarizing the Clinic's activities for the previous week. Friday triage meetings have a long agenda, and there are patient consultations starting at 10 a.m.

The agenda begins with a section addressing "miscellaneous questions." A father came to the Clinic to discuss his daughter, who is being treated by a private psychiatrist for an eating disorder. They can't pay anymore. He's wondering if, at seventeen, she needs to go to the separate public system for children and adolescents. "Take her," Nurse Pauline declares, "It makes no sense to send her elsewhere when they're going to transfer her to us in a few months."

An older male nurse presents the next case: "This monsieur is no longer being treated by us, but he called asking for a renewal of his valium prescription. He doesn't want to stop by the Clinic for it but is asking to have it sent.'"

Doctor Delignon is adamant, "This man is an addict. We don't have patients who don't come to the Clinic. Tell him to come in."

Next up are the emergencies and hospitalizations. Twenty-one patients have contacted the Clinic in crisis this week; two were hospitalized on the spot (one involuntarily) and another two sent to the ER for further evaluation. The *secteur* also conducted three home visits. In one, they went in force: one doctor, four nurses, and a specialized police unit. They rehospitalized a patient who had not shown up for his antipsychotic injection.

The focus of the meeting, though, is the new patients. This week, twenty-six people were given an initial appointment for a consultation with a nurse; sixteen actually came. When I interviewed a group of four nurses, I mentioned the elaborate guidelines and evaluation scales used in California to make the high-stakes decisions of who gets care in the public system and who has to keep looking. Patrice, a thirty-year veteran, told me: "Well, we have scales and tables like that in our heads, unconsciously." Sandrine, just a few years out of school, followed up: "We all have a different style, but there's a common thread. You need a minimum of information about the history of the person, their family, what they do in life, why they came here, if they're coming on their own or someone sent them. If it's troubles with sleep, with food. We're looking for symptoms that we can bring into our meeting [on Fridays]."

The results of these interviews are typed into a two-hundred-word summary, copied into the weekly report, and reviewed on Fridays. Today, we're running the gamut. There's a police officer complaining of sadness and fatigue; Delignon notes that she sounds "pretty depressed" and speculates that "there might be something more going on." Doctor Beaufils, a young psychiatrist uniformed in a sweater and five-o'clock shadow, counters that it looks "pretty typical." They'll see her in two weeks, but they will try to convince her to go see a private psychiatrist afterwards. A sixty-year-old man was sent by a judge with an obligation for him to receive treatment after being arrested for public urination. "Put him with a male psychiatrist," Delignon declares, "And warn him he may go pee pee in his office." They'll sign his paper for the judge and encourage him not to come back. Another new arrival was violently assaulted at the restaurant where he worked; he's been unemployed and having nightmares since. "He's someone we should see soon," Doctor Kuorio announces, "We really need to get a better sense of the situation." She directs a social worker to contact the municipality to check on whether he has any income coming through government benefits.

Toward the end of the list, we get to the *secteur*'s core clientele. The patient is a nineteen-year-old woman coming for an intake at the Clinic after leaving the hospital. She was there involuntarily, at the request of her mother, for seventy-one days after having a psychotic break, dropping out of school, and causing disruption inside a store. Patrice reports: "In the interview, she responded with yes or no without giving details. She said she did not want to talk about her hospitalization but wouldn't say why." Doctor Delignon adds some particulars: "We talked about her this morning. She's completely resistant to treatment and does not realize she has a disease. She is extremely fragile." At the clinic, she's going to see the same doctor she had on the inpatient unit, a continuity in line with the original vision of sectorization. The only problem is that her doctor can't see her for thirty-one days. There are plenty of *malades* who are also waiting. The meeting closes with a review of *secteur* patients seen by psychiatrists in local ERs (six, with one hospitalized for depression and another for borderline personality disorder) and psychiatric evaluations requested for somatic patients (twenty-nine) by doctors in nonpsychiatric hospitals.

Doctor Delignon was very clear about the dilemmas these meetings posed. In one breath, she proudly told me how the *secteur* model meant that "we never have to stop following someone. We can say, 'Treatment for life,' which means care but also accompaniment toward rehabilitation, recovery. . . . We have a global budget and so we can do what we want . . . and the patient pays absolutely nothing!" But in the next instant, she noted, "The budget is not exactly enormous, and if we see one patient or forty, it's the same [budget]." The predicament was stark: "The risk we have with the clinic is that we've been asked to serve everyone, but it's not possible. So we have to do the triage ourselves, and the heart of our vocation, it's mental illness."

In this second chapter of part I, I use observations at the clinic to determine what exactly the heart of the vocation of a public psychiatrist is. Doctors and nurses draw sharp boundaries around the bureaucratic kind of real *malades*. They classify the rest in two more amorphous groups: people with psychic troubles and individuals whose problems are not psy (and thus outside the appropriate ambit of psychiatric intervention). This logic parallels that evoked by public psychiatrists and their allies in policy debates. On the ground, however, we see how bounding is under constant strain from the complex reality of human beings who inevitably trespass simple categories. In the end, these practical challenges have only reinforced professionals' insistence on the sharp division between mental illness and mental health long institutionalized in the French system.

## THE SPIRIT OF THE *SECTEUR*

There are around eight hundred *secteurs* for adults in France, which meant eight hundred different mixes of treatment sites—acute-care hospitals, day programs, therapeutic apartments, family placements—and eight hundred distinct cocktails of therapeutic interventions—from psychoanalytic talk therapy to electroshock—available.[2] It's impossible to say that the *secteur* I studied, serving a neither particularly rich nor particularly poor arrondissement of Paris, is representative. But at least it adheres to the model of sectorization as originally conceived: a diverse range of services inside and outside the specialized psychiatric hospital to which it is attached. As Doctor Delignon told me: "It's very enriching for the patient to have different practices. In our *secteur*, they're not stuck [with one kind of treatment]. My training is mostly psychoanalytic, but I also studied at a university hospital [where biological approaches are privileged]". Still, she was clear about her primary role: "Our number one mission is to be a doctor and to prescribe [medication] so a patient can function outside [the hospital]. . . . After that, we can do something else if we want."

For all their variability, almost every *secteur* has a medical-psychological center. These all-purpose outpatient clinics are "symbols of the move from asylums to the community," a veritable "archetype of the values of access and continuity of care which constitute the *secteur*."[3] Doctor Delignon is particularly proud to have "one of the most accessible clinics in France." And this is a fair point: this clinic is open beyond normal working hours and on the weekends. When I spoke to the nurses, Manu enthusiastically emphasized that "we're one of the secteurs [in Paris] that has lots of services on the exterior [of the hospital]." Patrice jumped in, "Yes, we're really open to the city." Rather than hospitalizing patients, for example, this clinic can bring them in on a daily basis to get their medication, giving nurses a chance to check in.

Yet the *secteur* wasn't exactly advertising its services. The clinic was on the bottom floor of a nondescript building with no sign facing the street. From Doctor Delignon's perspective, there just wasn't much need for publicity, given the forces bringing more patients to the clinic's unmarked door: "There's more destigmatization. We've gone to meet with all our partners—social services, the fire department—in our district. There's also an ongoing precarization of society, which means people can't pay for a private doctor." As a result, the clinic, which was staffed by two doctors, ten nurses, six psychologists, two social workers, and four secretaries (plus doctors who spent the majority of their time in the hospital but rotated through) was facing a patient population of nearly three thousand. New arrivals frequently waited one month for a first consultation with a psychiatrist.

Before delving into the *secteur*'s triage in more detail, I want to make three observations based on this chapter's opening vignette. First, everyone from this *secteur*'s team whom I interviewed shared the ideal of the *secteur* as a public service open to everyone. When I asked Doctor Beaufils what worked well in France, he quickly replied, "It's the access to care. . . . We're never going to refuse a patient because she doesn't have money, doesn't have papers, doesn't have insurance. . . . There's no monetary pressure on the access to care. . . . I'm very happy to work in France because of that." He added a quick caveat: "But the *secteur* is really made for heavy psychotics. . . . If they're coming to us, it's because they're very sick." The meeting above belies this point. Neither the idea that the *secteur* is just for people with schizophrenia nor the notion that the *secteur* treats everyone is quite true. Some people are pushed to go into the private sector. Others are given a single appointment so they can attest to a judge that they're getting care, even if they aren't. *Secteurs* might rush treatment in emergencies and give appointments with huge delays at other times. These decisions are not capricious but stem from an unarticulated logic that ethnographic observation helps reveal.

The second observation is that, in a world of bounding, these decisions emanate from professionals acutely attuned to their restricted resources but exercising significant discretion in how to allocate them. Neither the process for evaluating new patients nor the criteria for making decisions is defined from above. I spoke to an official in the French High Authority of Health, which elaborates best practices in medicine. When I pressed her on who regulated access to *secteurs*, she fumbled: "Well, first off, I would say, 'No one'. . . . We [the High Authority] deal with clinical practices, but the administrative decision of classifying and orienting people is not part of our job. . . . There is a principle of medical judgment that still prevails." She suggested I check with a few other agencies about whether they were providing any guidance: the Regional Health Authority (the referent for mental health there said, "It's not regulated, and it's better that way"), the Ministry of Health ("That's not at all regulated"), and the National Association for Performance in Health ("We haven't made any recommendations on that").

A third observation is what is strikingly absent from orientation discussions in the clinic: diagnosis. According to French theorist Robert Castel, diagnosis "determine[s] the institutional fate" of the mad person. This assumption seems shared by the participants in high-level debates in France over each new translation of the *Diagnostic and Statistical Manual (DSM)*, with its steady proliferation of checklist-style disease categories that threaten a more humanist, psychoanalytically inspired approach.[4] In most cases, though, clinicians on the ground have greeted new revisions to psychiatry's ostensible bible with a shrug.[5]

That's partly because, in practice, diagnosis was not determinative. According to Doctor Beaufils: "I think it's impossible to standardize [psychiatry] like another medical specialty. Of course, not all heart attacks are the same. It depends on the person. But frankly . . . we have as many illnesses as we have *malades*." To him, a diagnostic category in itself was far too crude to decide whether a patient was really of the bureaucratic kind "*malade*." Regulators have gradually arm-twisted psychiatrists into at least putting a diagnosis into the electronic medical record, and *secteur* team meetings could involve elaborate discussions of the content of patients' psychosis or structure of their personality. But diagnostic categories do not play a particularly consequential role at the time of initial admission. As Nurse Guilhem told me, "It's not the diagnosis that directs us; it's the current situation of the person. . . . It's case by case, it's individual, it's qualitative. Even if on paper they have the same criteria [diagnosis], we can't make a decision based on just filling in a box, we're nothing like the Americans here."

I agree with these assessments, to a point. The *secteur* team did reason largely in terms of situations and people rather than pathologies and symptoms. But Friday meetings took the particular inputs of individual patients and grouped them into three rough categories, to which we now turn.[6]

## ALL IN FOR THE REAL *MALADES*

The exemplar of the *secteur* patient is someone with psychosis, which was usually both cause and consequence of poverty. The following write-up from a nurse captured the archetype:

> Man, seventy-two years old. Sent to us by [inpatient unit]. Patient is afflicted by a chronic psychosis, single without children, lives alone. Hospitalized at the demand of the prefecture[7] for delirious decompensation (persecution with a sexual theme) and hallucinations (with syndrome of mental automatism). . . . While delirious, he left his domicile to hide in a hotel to escape voices. Broke into a neighbor's room and the employees called the police. The [audio-visual hallucinations] have disappeared under Risperdal, but he remains attached to his delirium. . . . He says that he is recovering his autonomy and his

> faculties little by little. Partial critique of his troubles, good contact, correct clothing, coherent statements, and adapted response.

The case provoked no debate and no enthusiasm. In a sense, that's the way it's supposed to be. One doctor explained to me, "There are patients who are a bit of hot potatoes. . . . [People] that no one wants to occupy themselves with, but the advantage of the *secteur* is that there's no patient that no one occupies themselves with." After the nurse finished, Doctor Delignon instructed the secretary to give the patient a rapid meeting with Doctor Beaufils. She dispatched the social workers to confirm the stability of his housing. The nurses would make sure he came in regularly to receive an antipsychotic injection. Although professionals like Nurse Guilhem had told me they evaluated the current situation of the person in its entirety, the entire situation of some people was already encapsulated by the very contours of the bureaucratic category of *malade* into which they were placed. The social situation of a *malade* was that of a patient of the state; their social relationships were, ideally, with the *secteur* and, less ideally, with the police or ER.

Forty years after France began deinstitutionalization in earnest, the fastest way into the *secteur*'s active file was still through a hospitalization. If someone was concerning enough that one of their colleagues saw fit to hospitalize them, this was a strong sign they belonged at the clinic (and not, say, with a private psychiatrist) on discharge. On the flip side, hospitalization was often the go-to response at signs of psychosis. Nurse Patrice led one conversation for a thirty-four-year-old woman:

> She was sent to us by [private psychiatrist] who follows her for addiction to alcohol and medication. She's eight months pregnant with a girl. She reported both sexual and psychological mistreatment during childhood at the hands of her father, although her mother denied it ever happened. Her father died recently and the mourning has been complicated. Now, she's declaring she has images of violence toward her daughter. She even stopped eating for fifteen days to kill her and currently only eats yogurt. At the same time, she says she wanted the pregnancy. Right now, she sleeps little and displayed a cold affect. She has a sentiment of depersonalization. She says she's okay for a [psychiatric] consultation right now. I'm requesting a rapid appointment.

After the presentation, there is a long silence, followed by a sigh from another nurse.

Then Nurse Pauline jumps in: "She needed to be seen by Doctor Delignon *before* today."

Doctor Kuorio nods emphatically: "We should plan a hospitalization. We're talking about infanticide here."

Pauline concurs: "Yes. This is an emergency. I'll call inpatient and check on a bed." When the secretary announces Doctor Delignon has an opening next week, Pauline replies, "Not good enough. Clear someone off her schedule."

At this point, the conversation moves into frustration about the patient not making it to the *secteur* sooner. Gaia, a psychologist, laments, "Why are we only seeing this person now if she started talking about killing the baby months ago? What was [private psychiatrist] thinking?"

"Something like this needs to be brought up first in the meeting," Pauline reiterates.

Nurse Patrice defends her own assessment: "If you look at what I wrote, it's less clear about the urgency. There's nothing about suicide, no history of attempts"

Doctor Kuorio isn't convinced: "No way. She's having deliria about killing her child."

Nurse Pauline closes, "This could take two or three months to stabilize. If she gives birth in the hospital, that's just how it is."

The next week, Nurse Pauline demands an update. Patrice reports that the woman was seen by Doctor Delignon, who proposed she come for a hospitalization the next day; however, the patient didn't show up. The clinic team then went to her house to hospitalize her involuntarily. A few weeks later, Doctor Delignon announces, to palpable pride on the team, that the woman had given birth and mother and daughter were doing well. She goes on, "She's a very interesting patient, very complex delusions, but finally asking for help. Our biggest concern at this point is the husband, who also seems sick."

So far it might sound like *secteur* professionals make decisions based on a diagnosis of psychosis, even if they used much rougher categories than those you'd find in the *DSM*. But in my data, it was actually uncertainty about patients' medical and economic situations, as well as concerns about the impacts of illness on patients' families and social linkages, that clinicians evoked to justify a more assertive response (table 2.1). Consider a sixty-year-old man, who was seen by Nurse Sandrine: "This is someone being sent to us by his generalist doctor. He was hospitalized two years ago as a danger to himself, in the context of massive suicidal ideation. He's had multiple passages through the ER for alcohol overuse. In our interview, he came off as sad but not suicidal. He says he sleeps all day and has no desire to work. He is originally from a poor family in Denmark but claims he was once a highly successful architect. He has two kids but one has cut off all contact, and the other is angry about his alcohol use. He is married to an Italian but won't discuss it. He expresses regret about leaving Denmark and, despite being here for two decades, still hasn't mastered French."

Doctor Delignon offers her assessment: "This is being passed off to us because he has just overwhelmed every other place that has tried to treat him. His depression is too much for an addiction doctor. He's in the process of completely disinserting himself from society, and we need to be here for him. Who is it going to be, given all of that?" The secretary proposes an appointment with one of the *secteur*'s doctors in four weeks. "Fine, but let's bring him in for another meeting with a nurse right away," Delignon states. "I want to know if he's coming to us because he is being kicked out by his wife. This looks like someone that the whole world is trying to get rid of. He's too heavy. Definitely not an easy person." Although

TABLE 2.1
Reasoning evoked in clinic decision making*

| **Justification for an accelerated appointment or higher level of care** | | **Justification for a delayed appointment or lower level of care** | |
|---|---|---|---|
| "Isolated," "fragile," "vulnerable" | 27% | No demand for treatment | 19% |
| Risk to family | 18% | Psychological/reactional | 18% |
| Lack of resources | 13% | Not severe | 16% |
| Uncertainty about situation | 13% | Not psychiatric | 13% |
| Severe | 11% | Secteur inappropriate | 8% |
| Prior secteur treatment | 5% | Can pay private doctor | 8% |
| Risk to self | 5% | Not urgent | 8% |
| | | Administrative† | 4% |

* This table codes instances where a reason for a decision was explicitly articulated. In some cases, no reason was given and decisions were made without discussion.

† For example, not having an address in the *secteur*.

past suicidal ideation was a cue to take the case seriously, Doctor Delignon was as concerned about the patient's social inscriptions as his mental state. In my analysis of over two hundred intake decisions, "isolation" came up more even frequently than "severity" as justification for bumping someone up the queue to meet with the *secteur* team. While *secteur* professionals described themselves as focused above all on people with psychosis, the meaning of *malade* has evolved to encompass a wider range of situations for which no solution outside the *secteur* is forthcoming.

In his ethnography of a French general hospital, Pierre-André Juven shows how the financial incentives tied to payment by the activity have led clinicians to focus on those whose cost of treatment was standard for their diagnostic group. In contrast, professionals push away complex patients who were "problematic as a result of the cost of their care."[8] Operating with a global budget and a strong shared ethos of their core clientele, however, the *secteur* did the opposite. In a crisis, it would throw the kitchen sink at a destabilized patient—from involuntary hospitalization to therapeutic apartments, to intensive support from nurses.[9] Once things went back to baseline, however, most real *malades* wound up with similar care: a monthly consultation with a psychiatrist, visit with a nurse for medication, and occasional follow-up from a social worker to ensure they were receiving benefits.

Bounding lends itself to practices of what sociologist Evitar Zerubavel calls "lumping" and "splitting." This approach tends to "play down" differences within a category and "exaggerate" differences between them.[10] This relatively homogenous care for *malades* was arguably the most equitable approach to a large caseload of serious patients for whom there was no obvious alternative to the *secteur*. But ensuring it required splitting *malades* from the broader wave of suffering coming to the clinic door.

## TRIAGING PSYCHIC TROUBLES

The central place such malades occupied in my interviews with professionals at the clinic belies the fact that they are a small proportion of cases brought up in Friday meetings. Nurses characterized only about 20 percent of new patients as having psychotic symptoms (which is not far from available statistics about the people served by *secteurs*).[11] Far more common were people presented as suffering from anxiety or depression, or a mix of the two (anxio-depression syndrome). They were trailed by insomnia, eating disorders, suicidality, and trauma.[12] When nurses wrote up these cases, they indicated that these people came not for care but rather for support, aid, advice, or just to talk. The following summary prepared by Sandrine was representative:

> Woman, forty-four. Referral: herself. She demands support. Says that her partner has quit her home, leaving her with four children. Now housed by a pair of friends. The children are struggling to understand what happened, and she is having difficulty in dealing with their reaction. Unemployed for fourteen years. No prior treatment. Anxiety, trouble sleeping, crying, no dark ideas. States that she "wants help passing this difficult moment."

Cases like these were emblematic of inexorable demands for medicalization, what French scholars have characterized as an "overflowing of social [problems]"[13] and never-ending "enlargement of demands tied to psychic suffering."[14] *Secteur* professionals were unequivocal that these cases were not the core of their vocation. "I don't even know what mental health is," Doctor Kuorio told me, "I am concerned with mental illness." Yet here these patients were, demanding care from a public service formally unable to say no yet focused on the psychotic patients to whom it would have to say yes over many years.

Because the response to *malades* often seemed obvious, the conflicts and tensions during Friday meetings centered on what to do with these cases. At times, this was articulated as frustration with the social service agencies sending people the *secteur*'s way. In one instance, Nurse Florence presents an aging man with chronic health issues who she had visited at home at the request of a municipal social worker. She makes the case for the *secteur*'s social workers to get involved: "He stopped receiving his pension because he didn't fill out his paperwork. The apartment was filthy, the bed had no sheets. Supposedly he's living on two hundred euros a month and has worsening diabetes. He reported to me some suicidal ideation."

"Of course he does!" Nurse Pauline cuts in. "Look at the situation, he's living on two hundred euros and he's going to be on dialysis."

Doctor Kuorio adds, "We need to get in touch with the municipality. Everyone has their task and they need to be doing theirs."

Nurse Pauline hammers the point, "How is there no one else that can help this person get their paperwork in?"

"Sure, he has medical issues, but this is a social problem," Doctor Kuorio closes.[15]

The *secteur* was founded to serve one main category of person: *malades*. That focus could be maintained because other public services would exist for people in other bureaucratic categories, like the nonworking poor. But amid neoliberal retrenchment, the *secteur* often felt alone in its standing commitment as a public service to saying no as little as possible. For all the exasperation, Doctor Kuorio ultimately added the man to her crammed schedule.

Cases like these were not just less severe than real *malades*. They were of a qualitatively distinct type. Surveys find that 60 percent of French people using mental health services (both public and private) characterize themselves as having a "psychic trouble."[16] They define this largely in the same way as professionals do: a condition originating in environmental factors, which demarcates it from an inner pathology. "Troubles," one article in a French journal of psychiatry explained, are a "translation of the English 'disorder,' and corresponds to the endless expansion . . . of social and individual suffering, in the extensive field of 'mental health.'"[17] One public psychiatrist evinced her skepticism toward these situations: "There are people who need to talk. . . . In the countryside, you have the priest or the baker. But in Paris, there's a line to buy a baguette, so you won't have time to talk. . . . So that becomes the problem of psychiatry. . . . But for me just needing psychological support, that's different from an illness."

Whatever they said, the professionals I observed at the clinic were in a bind. They lacked any rationalized system for assigning distinctive levels of care. They had a team of psychologists, who in some systems (like that in the United Kingdom) would be the frontline response to less-severe troubles. However, the French psychologists I interviewed insisted on the necessity of focusing their psychotherapy on the same *malades* being treated by the psychiatrists. So how did professionals address these demands for care?

One simple heuristic was to deprioritize troubles that had an identifiable cause in favor of those whose origins were uncertain (and therefore potentially pathological).[18] The team discusses a seventeen-year-old girl who had been pushed to go to the clinic by her mother and a psychologist at school. Nurse Manu opens: "This is a patient with previous treatment from age seven to eleven for trichotillomania [pulling out her hair] but hasn't had any problems since. This summer she suffered a sexual assault—she fell asleep at a party and, when waking up, her friend admitted, 'I abused you.' Now she is having flashbacks and a sentiment of disgust. Since then, she's had difficulty falling asleep and finding it impossible to get up. She uses alcohol on weekends. She admits to smoking marijuana frequently but says she's not the one who buys it."

Doctor Delignon announces, "Well, she should see someone . . ." and throws out the name of a doctor who was not present. The secretary reports that there is no open slot for a month-and-a-half. Delignon declares that acceptable: "That's okay. This isn't urgent."

In contrast, situations where the origins of illness were unclear were more likely to spark a vigorous reaction. Patrice presents a thirty-five-year-old woman coming at the recommendation of her primary care doctor for anxiety and depressive symptoms: "She's originally from Bolivia, very religious. There's some trauma in her biography, including sexual assault. Her father was killed violently in Colombia. She's working as a cleaning lady. Basically afraid of everything, afraid of strangers, afraid of foreigners. She has anxious ruminations and perturbed sleep. She is increasingly isolating herself in her housing. There's clearly a lot of sadness, but no dark ideas or suicidal ideation. She also claims she's lost thirty kilos on a diet." Doctor Delignon asks if her primary language is Spanish; Patrice replies, "Her French is, we might say, approximate."

Guilhem, the secteur's head nurse, observes, "This is a heavy history." Patrice nods, "I proposed that she come back to meet with me, just for support." Nurse Pauline approves, "Yes, good. What's aggravating the situation now?" "I tried to find out, but I couldn't get more details," Nurse Patrice admits.

Doctor Delignon turns to the secretary: "Well, get her in quickly to [Doctor]; she speaks Spanish. Let's have her start psychotherapy too. We've got to explore, explore, explore, and see if there's something more behind this symptomology."

The reasoning behind the *secteur* team's decisions, primarily handed down by psychiatric fiat, was rarely articulated. But here, two people having both experienced sexual violence provoked very different levels of engagement. The second patient's more inexplicable decline justified intensive investigation compared to first patient, whose severity seemed bounded by its clear—if awful—cause.[19] As I found in my coding, characterizations of patients as having troubles that were deemed "psychological" or "reactional" to external circumstances were one of the most common arguments for delaying or limiting care (table 2.1).[20]

These kinds of mental shortcuts were useful for reconciling increased demand with a commitment to guarding resources for real *malades*. There were moments, though, where the team knew it was offering little to soothe very real suffering. This was evident in one presentation from Nurse Sandrine: "This is a young woman, seventeen—she turns eighteen next month—coming to the clinic on the advice of a friend. She has been cutting her arms with scissors, which stems from frequent conflicts with her family. She asked that we do not send letters to the house about appointments because she does not want her parents to find out. She's been humiliated and persecuted by her ex-boyfriend. Claims she's only barely sleeping or eating. She's fearful of death, dark ideas and suicidal ideation without an immediate plan."

"She should definitely be seen," states Doctor Delignon, confirming the obvious.

The secretary looks around, and finally finds a window for a doctor in forty days. There's a pause. "Maybe one of us [a nurse] could see her first?" Nurse Manu offers.

"Yes. We have no choice," Delignon laments.

"She can come back to the clinic if there's an emergency," Nurse Pauline notes, trailing off.

Not every depression that was a reaction to external events was mild. As I could see in weekly reports, more and more patients with serious suicide attempts were leaving the hospital with appointments at the clinic a month in the future. Protecting the logic of bounding, which both constituted the *secteur*'s core population and privileged professional discretion in identifying it, meant failing to scale up care to protect the health of clearly vulnerable individuals.

## REFERRALS TO NOWHERE

One of the few clear modes of reducing the resources going to people with psychic troubles was to refer them to private psychiatrists. By my count, the *secteur* did this for 12 percent of people who came in for a first evaluation.

While some older public psychiatrists moonlighted as psychoanalysts in private office, the symbolic distance between the public and private branches of the profession is enormous. One university psychiatrist working in the hospital to which my *secteur* was attached declared to me: "There aren't enough schizophrenics, real *deprimés* [depressed people] for all the psychiatrists to have work, so what do they do? They go to Boulevard Saint-Germain and take a client that isn't really sick, but the grand bourgeois [who is] a little stressed, or women who are bored or have complicated children. These psychiatrists are trained at the expense of society, and we pay them to care for people who have a little blues of the soul."[21]

When I asked Doctor Kuorio who should be referred to private psychiatrists, she emphasized the difference between someone who needed the team-based approach and extra-medical resources the *secteur* could offer versus "someone who has personality problems or is sad just for a short-term reason [or] anyone who just needs a consultation but doesn't need all our support. They just need someone to follow them, consult with them, listen to them, maybe eventually prescribe medication. Private doctors can do that. But they don't need a day hospital, they don't need a nurse, they don't need to come to the clinic every week for medication. They don't need to be hospitalized. They don't need the *secteur*. They just need 'someone.'"

In practice, though, the clinic operated based on an even simpler shortcut. In one instance, the nurse prefaced a reading of the intake summary to Doctor Halaby, the head psychiatrist of the clinic. "Should I start with his salary," Nurse Manu smiles.

"Sure," Doctor Halaby replies.

Manu says, "He makes three thousand euros [a month] and works at [a major insurance company]."

"Do we even have to discuss this?" Halaby muses.

"Just to add a bit more detail," Nurse Manu continues, "he appears to have an anxio-depression. He lost his mother in June and is having troubles with his two sisters subsequently. He describes troubles with stress, difficulty sleeping, and a deterioration of his marital relationship."

At this point, Nurse Pauline and Doctor Halaby are already talking on the side about a recently hospitalized *malade*. This new patient's income, in this case, was overriding. When Manu comments, "His discourse did have some 'mystical elements' [potentially a sign of bipolar mania] . . ." Doctor Halaby looks up, cuts the conversation, and declares, "Private."

Rationing through referrals assumed a coupling of high income and low severity. Psychiatrists often acted as if that association existed even when it plainly didn't, as in the case of one forty-five-year-old woman who came to the *secteur* after a stint in a private hospital. Nurse Sandrine leads: "She's leaving a hospitalization at [Private Hospital] where she was voluntarily hospitalized [for fifty-eight days] for depressive symptoms with suicidal ideation—she had images of jumping out a window—in the context of professional difficulties. . . . She's had problems of adaptation since emigrating to France. She is socially isolated and quitting work. The suicidal ideation is still present, although rarer, and she claims no intention of carrying it out. No real previous treatment: she had a consultation at [hospital to which the *secteur* was attached] a few years ago, but they decided no further treatment was necessary."

The *secteur* had already (apparently incorrectly) deemed the woman as not needing its services, and the woman was now being sent to them by the private sector on the basis of being too severe. Nonetheless, Doctor Delignon responds with a single word: "Private." The reasoning was obvious: those who could go elsewhere should. If she could pay for private inpatient, she could pay for private outpatient, too.

While only a few of the *secteur*'s patients lived in extreme poverty—as was the norm for public mental health services in the United States—many were on the edge. I counted the number of times nurses referred to patients' employment: one-quarter were unemployed, one-quarter were students, and most of the rest worked in low-level service jobs. Clemence, one of the social workers in the *secteur*, told me: "We are seeing more psycho-social troubles than psychiatric ones. Sure, we have the cases that are a bit brutal: the guy who's eighteen, smokes a bunch of pot, completely falls apart and thinks he's a bird, and that happens whether you're rich or poor, black or white, ugly or beautiful. But we have more people for whom it's like, 'Okay, yeah, with that life, who wouldn't go crazy?'"

"And is that a problem for psychiatry to deal with?" I wondered.

"Maybe it's not psychiatry, but it develops over time, and it needs treatment," Clemence replied.

"But treatment in the *secteur*?" I pressed.

"I mean, there's nothing else. It's still suffering," Clemence said.

When doctors attempted to shunt this misery into the private system, they often received pushback from the nurses. They—like the social workers—were often the upwardly mobile children of working-class families, and more aware of social situations that were far from the lived experience of psychiatrists, who typically came from more privileged backgrounds. Some nurses also had experience with the fact that France's universal, free health-care system could be anything but for people unable to advance the fees for a private consultation (before later reimbursement by the national insurance system) or who lacked the private supplemental insurance that comes from white-collar employment.[22]

Nurse Manu leads one discussion: "Madame is forty-five years old. She came to us after being referred by the ER for anxio-depression. She lives in an eighteen-square-meter apartment. Never married, no children, and her father recently died of Alzheimer's. She worked as a secretary but stopped in 2013 during a traumatizing relationship with a boyfriend. She told me she is 'disgusted with herself.' She's had four months of suicidal ideation, without a plan, saying 'I want to leave, but I don't want to go.' Her generalist gave her multiple antidepressants, but they've had no effect. She was somewhat flirty. I'm suggesting Doctor Halaby."

"Where does she work?" asks Doctor Halaby, who seemed to have missed part of the presentation.

"She was a secretary," Manu reiterates.

"Great. She can go to a private doctor," Halaby replies.

Manu protests: "She can't pay eighty euros, even if she's reimbursed [by insurance]."

Doctor Delignon comments, "[Private psychiatrist] loves flirty patients!"

"She can't pay!" Manu repeats, incredulous.

Manu later told me, exasperated, "There are times when we really don't agree with the private sector orientations. We're the ones who have to tell them [the patients], and they don't understand." One patient was she was sent to a different private psychiatrist for three weeks in a row, and each time recontacted the nurses to report the psychiatrist was not taking new patients. These were, in the words of Elizabeth Chiarello, "road[s] to nowhere," who used the phrase to describe referrals to absent addiction services in the United States.[23]

The failure here is not all on the shoulders of the *secteur* professionals. The slow transformation of public asylums into the combined in- and outpatient *secteur* system starting mid-century was shadowed by a veritable explosion of private psychiatrists. Now, though, 50 percent of private psychiatrists are over the age of sixty.[24] Like private doctors in France more generally, they have lobbied successfully to be allowed to set up their practices wherever they'd like, creating vast "medical deserts" in some departments of France where there are almost no private psychiatrists. A public psychiatric system that was supposed to be one among multiple tools for responding to the needs of the population felt to professionals like the only one.

Referring patients to private care that didn't exist exacted a psychic toll on clinicians. An experienced nurse in another clinic confessed, "Normally, the *secteur* is a public service . . . Except that, effectively, there are criteria. . . . We send people to the private system, it's not very 'public service,' but that's how it is." Rationing in order to focus professionals' activity almost entirely on *malades* reinforced the *secteur* as a place for chronic patients who never seemed to get better. They were cared for by professionals constantly confronted with moral dilemmas for their proud identities as public servants.[25]

## DRUNKS, DELINQUENTS, AND DENIERS

In the United States, the embrace of behavioral health has shifted the center of gravity of public psychiatric interventions toward managing deviant, delinquent, and disruptive comportment. Yet when in chapter 1 I discussed local councils of mental health and public health campaigns in France, I showed how public psychiatrists at times actively fought against programs that would flag these kinds of situations as needing care. Their efforts weren't enough. Third parties still sent the *secteur* a steady stream of alerts by phone or email. Doctor Halaby told me with a sigh: "We are obligated to deal with alerts from everywhere. Families, neighbors, social workers are identifying people who they don't know but who are making noise, who have behavioral troubles, who are dirty. Every week, every day, we receive messages that 'Monsieur X is not doing well. What are you going to do?'. . . . We really need to investigate and analyze the situation that has been flagged for us, to see if there really are psychiatric symptoms, before we invite the entourage [to the clinic for a meeting]. We have enormous work to do, and I'm tired." Part of that work, I will show, is identifying who fit into a loose category of "not psy" and sending them back to the addiction services or judicial institutions that were supposed to be administering them.

During the Clinic's biweekly nurses' meeting, the team discusses the case of a thirty-year-old woman who appeared to be descending into paranoia. As Nurse Sandrine notes, "We were contacted by this woman's parents, who are concerned about their grandchild. The relationship between the grandparents and their daughter have been tense for some time."

Nurse Pauline, the head nurse, refocuses the conversation: "But what do we have at the clinical level here?"

Nurse Manu is also in on the case: "We know she took her daughter out of school after the [terrorist] attacks [of November 2015 in Paris], claiming that it wasn't safe."

"Lots of people did that," Pauline dismisses.

"Well, she had a crisis ten years ago, but she wasn't hospitalized," Sandrine comments. "There's a family history of suicide. Overall, the grandparents are definitely not clear here about what's happening."

Doctor Kuorio intervenes: "This situation worries me. This is a woman who think she's being persecuted. She has isolated her daughter and forbidden her to have contact with her friends. We should plan a home visit."

Nurse Pauline continues her skepticism: "Imagine we go with the police, beat this woman's door down, and she's delirious. We do an [involuntary hospitalization]. What happens to the girl?"

"We should do something," Manu pleads. "She [the mother] is basically holding her daughter hostage in the house."

"Let's be very prudent here. The grandparents should get documentation from the school that the granddaughter has been taken out of school inappropriately. The grandparents are mostly talking about social and family problems. That's not psychiatry. We should send a message to the daughter telling her to come in, and see what happens," Pauline proposes.

"So we don't push too hard on this?" Kuorio confirms.

"We keep an eye on it," Pauline replies.

Although decision making in the clinic tended to be hierarchical, in this case, Nurse Pauline's role in shuffling the overbooked schedules of the nurses, several of whom could be tied up for hours by a visit to the (potential) patient's home, was crucial. But when I asked how often someone actually responded to these invitations—essentially, emails or phone calls saying, "This person has expressed concern for you, would you like to come in for a meeting?"—Doctor Halaby admitted it was "a very small proportion, not a lot."

In taking a passive approach to bringing people into care, teams manifested that long-standing fear of reactivity that satisfied ethical and organizational imperatives at once. As one report put it, many teams "will not privilege an action which forces the door of those who don't ask [for care] next to the quantity of people demanding care who are waiting for a response."[26]

The clinic used the benchmark of a clearly formulated demand for care as a broader screening tool (table 2.1). It allowed the *secteur* to avoid responsibility for patients it didn't want by sifting out those patients that didn't want the *secteur*. This was the case of a twenty-year-old woman who had been seen in the *secteur* a few years prior, before disappearing. Now she was being sent back by an ER after being evaluated for anorexia. Nurse Patrice reports: "She's currently obsessed with counting calories, BMI [body mass index]14.2.[27] But in our interview, she stated that she 'doesn't want treatment because I will lose control' and does not want to be 'only doing well because I'm taking medication.' This is someone who was sent to a day program after a previous hospitalization three years ago, and she didn't stick with it. Then we sent her to a private psychiatrist and she never followed through."

Doctor Delignon replies, "This is going to be totally unmanageable."

Nurse Pauline concurs, "Right. Lost her friends, no work plans, parents paying for her schooling . . . She doesn't want anything."

"Totally ambivalent," Delignon adds.

Nurse Patrice observes, "She is motivated for help with her eating, but nothing else."

"I guess we have to take her because she was sent by the ER," Doctor Delignon admits. "But she's never really going to be cared for here." The discussion ended with her being given an appointment fifty-one days in the future, to which the team assumed she would not come. The fact that her main problem was presented as behaviors around food suggested that her problems were more on the order of personality than mental illness, pushing it beyond the clinic's usual purview.[28]

There was one profession that might seem to have the authority to override the *secteur*'s resistance to addressing problematic behaviors: judges. France has seen a dramatic rise in legal obligations for care, under which individuals are allowed to leave prison or avoid punishment on the condition that they receive psychiatric treatment.[29] A judge explained to me,

"If we see someone who presents a certain number of mental difficulties that at some point contributed to some criminal action . . . we're not going to let that person go back into society without putting in place something. We want to avoid politicians accusing us of being irresponsible . . . We're going to do everything that guarantees the security of our citizens."

This aspiration ran into a wall on Friday mornings at the clinic. Manu helped quickly dispatch one case: "Twenty-two-year-old male. He's coming in the context of an obligation for care after driving a car under the influence of drugs and alcohol."

"So why didn't this go to an addiction doctor?" Doctor Delignon asks, sounding annoyed.

"To be clear, he has no demand here. He's coming because he has to," Manu replies.

"It doesn't sound like this is even pathological," Doctor Delignon insists.

Nurse Pauline concludes, "Give him to an intern"—a medical trainee rotating through the *secteur* as part of their training—"have her sign the paper, and don't give him a second appointment."

When I followed up with the nurses, they were unapologetic. As Manu told me, "It's true that when we see 'obligation for care,' we are going to say right away that it's a person who doesn't want care, the appointment is going to last five minutes and they just want a paper to show the judge."[30]

Recall that *malade*, as it was defined in the 1960s (or perhaps left largely undefined), did not have an age, race, or gender. But, of course, the patients at the clinic *did* have a gender: nearly 60 percent of new arrivals were women.[31] They were not evenly distributed across the typologies the *secteur* used to allocate care. The overwhelmingly female team at the clinic was attuned to the harms, harassment, and trauma women faced in French society, and recognized that the psychic troubles created by these factors merited some kind of care. Men were overrepresented among the *grand malades* who needed to be contained via involuntary hospitalization or intensive surveillance. While some scholars have argued that men's addiction or disruptive behaviors grow out of the same soil of suffering as women's withdrawal or self-harm, the former were far more likely to be deemed "non-psy."[32]

In one meeting, Nurse Agathe read a letter from an addiction doctor about a forty-nine-year-old man recently hospitalized for alcoholism: "The doctor is saying that he diagnosed him with bipolar disorder, which was previously masked by his alcoholism. He is 'fragile' and 'has not fully accepted his treatment.' The letter states, 'Given the complexity of this case, follow-up at the clinic is indispensable. Ideally, this would include multiple treatments per week.' "

Nurse Pauline scoffs, "No."

Nurse Agathe insists: "Doctor Delignon had said she might be willing to take him."

"I'm going to write her and say if this person is already regularly going to appointments in addiction medicine, he should get all his treatment there," Pauline replies.

"Can they do psych meds?" Nurse Patrice wonders.

"I don't know, but they can do blood draws. We can't," Nurse Pauline counters.

"In any case, I don't even think he wants to be treated at the clinic," Agathe admits.

Here, the team spurned the framing that drug use and mental illness were comorbid in favor of an assumption that it was one or the other. One psychiatrist noted the distinctive French approach in this regard: "There are people who are more addicts than *malades*. I know that's a less clear distinction in the United States, but here, a pure addict is going to addiction medicine, not psychiatry. There are psychotics who consume [drugs], but people who arrive at addiction through life events, personality problems . . . They're going elsewhere."

The doctor's comment that "there are psychotics who consume drugs" is revealing. An astute reader may have noticed that the rules for deciding who gets served in the Clinic don't apply to everyone. A *malade* could be drunk, delinquent, and in denial and still be admitted for treatment without a second thought. *Secteur* professionals assumed that they would occasionally have to go to their houses with police in tow to hospitalize them involuntarily. But for those of a different bureaucratic kind—people with psychic troubles, or those with troubles that were not *psy*—the criteria for treatment at the clinic grew stricter.

## THE REVOLVING DOOR

We've talked about how people enter care at the clinic, but how about exiting it? The 2008 national guide for best practices for clinics observed that "the shrewd reader will have noticed that if the question of how to enter into the clinic has been discussed . . . the end of treatment has not even been cited."[33] For some interviewees, the decision of when to stop serving people in the *secteur* simply did not exist. Clemence, the *secteur*'s social worker, reiterated, "There's a culture of public services which are free and that are permanent. That's our strong point." By now you've seen the trade-off: Permanent care for some, paid for with a fixed budget, means rationed care for others and a minimal interest in recruiting new patients.

In truth, the discourse of care for life ignored perhaps the greatest contradiction in the functioning of the clinic: many *malades* were not remaining in active care. Around 10 percent of patients presented during Friday meetings were signaled as "resumption of following," which meant that their dossiers had never been closed, but they had been gone for long enough that they needed to be reassigned. Nurse Manu read aloud one such case:

> Male, forty-one. Was followed by the clinic from 2010 to 2015. First hospitalization was for catatonia [a sometimes-fatal manifestation of schizophrenia]. Stopped care in agreement with Doctor Clech. In interview: difficult contact, distrusting, coherent discourse, no thought troubles, loss of life force [*élan vital*], medium mood, no suicidal ideas, anxiety tied to fear of a relapse as in 2010. Okay to restart treatment.

No one I spoke to in the *secteur* believed that *malades* could be cured. Instead, agreements to halt treatment reflected an implicit acceptance that the *secteur* did not have the resources to maintain its grip on resistant patients who were not in crisis.

Having *malades* dropping in and out of care was tolerable, if not ideal, in the cases of people suffering quietly from chronic symptoms, but this was more starkly concerning for patients with histories of violent behavior. One Friday meeting was dominated by the presentation by a psychiatrist from another *secteur*, Doctor Chancel, whose patient was moving to the arrondissement I studied: "This is a fifty-seven-year-old patient with a history of hospitalizations and defenestration [jumping from windows]. He first appeared in the ER in 2006, declaring that voices in his head were telling him to destroy his computer. He was pushed into care by his partner, who's really the one driving this. But he stopped medication and therapy. In 2007, he returned to the hospital through [involuntary hospitalization at the demand of the prefecture] because he was caught being disruptive at the Arc de Triomphe. We placed him on ten milligrams of Risperdal. If you look at his records, we do see that he gets better with treatment, with reduced delirium, but absolutely never really gains insight [into his illness or need for care]."

Nurse Pauline asks, "How long did you hold him [in the hospital]?"

"Two months. Not that long," Doctor Chancel replies.

"Then what?"

Doctor Chancel continues, "That's the mysterious part. [pause] And then in 2013, he jumped out a window."

"Wait, what happened from 2008 to 2013?" Doctor Delignon cuts in.

"We completely lost sight of him," says Doctor Chancel. "After he jumped, he was in intensive care, but they didn't call us in for a psychiatric evaluation. When he was in rehabilitation, a psychologist evaluated him and wrote that there was no sign of delirium. Then this year, his companion reported to us that he was again leaning out of windows, so we hospitalized him. He got out a few months ago."

When Doctor Delignon hears that the patient has two children at home, she declares: "We need to do a visit to his domicile and know what the situation is. We can propose a meeting, but we also need to go *chez lui*. This worries me."

Doctor Chancel comments, "We think that he is stable now."

Delignon insists, "I don't want him to throw the little one out the window! A little child, a man like this, that raises some red flags."

Doctor Chancel then summarizes the man's current care: "He's currently on a program of care [a protocol that requires a patient to accept outpatient care or be rehospitalized]. We think that's the only reason we see him."

"Then we need to maintain him on that program," Delignon confirms.

"We are currently seeing him twice a month," says Chancel

Delignon replies, to my surprise, that "That's not possible for us. We'll put him on a monthly injection and ask him to come in for it."

When the other *secteur* psychiatrist left, Doctor Kuorio comments, "I can't believe it, a psychotic like this, left alone for years."

Nurse Pauline adds, "And why did no one go see him when he was hospitalized [from injuries from his suicide attempt]?"

Yet for all their critiques of the other *secteur*, Doctor Delignon was proposing less intensive care that he was already receiving. We can see here the flattening implied by bounding: the *secteur* generally couldn't offer more than one appointment per month to its stabilized patients with schizophrenia, and this man would be no different—despite the risks.[34]

The extent to which the *secteur* was overwhelmed sometimes came through even more clearly. Nurse Agathe leads off one Friday meeting's discussion of "miscellaneous questions" by recounting a recent encounter with a long-term male patient who had immigrated from Dubai: "The patient came to the clinic asking to see a doctor immediately because he didn't feel well. The secretaries asked him to wait, and he started making threats and knocking on the glass. There was a rapid intervention from the team [of nurses] to calm him down."

Doctor Delignon is directive: "For now, we're going to require he not come to the clinic. If there's an emergency, he needs to go to the ER. We've planned a hospitalization for Monday. We'll see if he comes. He's been taking crack, but claims he's trying to stop."

"What do we do if he does come?" Agathe enquires, looking worried.

"You'll have to call the police," Delignon affirms.

Nurse Agathe frowns. As one of the nurses told me in the interview, "Normally, the clinic is supposed to be a protected place [for patients], a place where the police can't come."

Guilhem, head nurse of the secteur, turns to Doctor Delignon: "What about after his hospitalization?"

Delignon replies, "We'll see. I'd like him to be followed here, but we need to make sure he comes for his appointments, not just showing up whenever and making a fuss."

Nurse Sandrine points out the danger on weekends, when there are only two nurses at the clinic: "Even if he's in treatment, he's still going to be taking drugs."

"After the hospitalization, you should continue to have him come to the hospital for his consultations [rather than coming to the clinic]," Nurse Pauline suggests.

"I don't know. We are already completely overwhelmed there," Delignon remarks. The nurses look unsatisfied, and Doctor Delignon comes to the patient's defense: "Apparently, he's been on the street for two months. That's definitely destabilized him. He's a complicated patient."

"We have no shortage of complicated patients here," Pauline remarks, defending the nurses' position. "But only some of them make threats."

The patient did not show up for his Monday hospitalization. The nurses discussed the case at their Tuesday meeting. Agathe asked, “So what do we do if he shows up for his injection?”

Doctor Halaby suggests, “If it’s something simple like that, maybe just let him in.”

“He should be hospitalized. Involuntarily,” Agathe retorts.

“Does this man even need care?” Pauline wonders.

“He’s an addict, but he has psychotic symptoms,” Halaby notes.

“Okay, how do you want me to organize treatment for him?” Pauline asks. “He seems more like a psychopath than a psychotic.”

“So here’s the plan,” Doctor Halaby offers in a conciliatory tone. “If he shows up, either give him an injection, call the police, or take him to the ER. We’ll adapt to his ‘demand.’ ”

The social worker was looking through his dossier and comments, “It looks like he doesn’t even have [immigration] papers. He might not be in France long.”

When I spoke to actors around Paris, many of them cited the clinic I studied as very “containing” (“*contenant*”) because it was open seven days a week and could ask patients to come in every day to take medication. Yet there were clearly patients, like the one just described, who seemed to surpass the *secteur*’s capacity to contain them.

The situation, everyone agreed, was getting worse. Outside hospitals, the tool for attaching patients to care is not mechanical restraints or locked gates but human relationships. That requires humans. As Doctor Halaby explained, “The *secteurs* are facing increasing administrative pressures. Problems with managing beds. The doctors are working here for shorter and shorter periods. . . . For the team, it’s difficult to see your colleagues leaving. For the patients, it risks a rupture in care. I think it’s a bit of suffering for everyone.” Yet she, too, was departing for private practice: “It’s been nine years that I’ve been here, and honestly, it’s harder and harder. . . . All the administrative responsibilities on top of the clinical ones, it’s exhausting and not at all gratifying.”

It wasn’t just *malades* who were dropping out of the clinic.

## CONCLUSION: DOUBLING DOWN ON REAL MALADES

I opened part I by asking, “Who should be served by the mental health system?” I noted that, in the last century, answers have ranged from

0.4 percent to everyone. In October 2024, the prime minister of France settled on a figure: At a press conference, he declared, "One French person in five is touched by a question of mental health . . . and to them, we are going to bring some help."[35] In a dramatic development for a field that my interviewees bewailed as being treated often as the poor stepchild in health policy, he announced that mental health would be the Grand National Cause of 2025. This came with a national destigmatization campaign, new services to screen adolescents, and strengthening care for mental health by generalist practitioners. (He lost his job two months later, but his replacement kept the National Cause designation.)

The response of mental health professionals themselves, though, was ambivalent. A communiqué from major unions representing psychiatrists, nurses, and psychologists, plus the directors of psychiatric establishments and the national patients' association, expressed their concern that "the dimension of psychiatric care not be forgotten within the context of this grand national priority."[36] This aspiration to "bring some help" to one in five French people, cautioned one hospital director, was a "vacuum cleaner . . . [sucking] more money for the lightest patients."[37] Some skepticism was certainly warranted: The declaration came from the mouth of a conservative politician preparing a budget that would restrict funding for health care. But the apprehension that mental health would leave out psychiatry (and its *malades*) also reflected a deep cultural and institutional division that was reinforced by practices of bounding on the ground.

Before considering that division in more detail, imagine how such an announcement might fit into a system of scaling. This approach, which rests on the construction of mental health as a continuum, assumes that by identifying problems early (facilitated by reducing stigmatization), some people (like adolescents) could manage their own psychological troubles and avoid developing mental illness at all. If screening programs did discover more people who needed treatment, that's all the more reason to define levels of care clearly, strengthening the role of generalist doctors or psychologists in taking on mild or moderate conditions. That leaves public psychiatry with the resources to offer intensive interventions to the most severe cases—and then step them down.

Professionals no doubt resisted this vision in part because it implies restricting the autonomous professional judgments that the French public system privileges. But it also reflected that scaling, in their eyes, was ill-adapted to the reality—as they experienced daily on the ground—of the population they saw as their duty to protect. As one veteran psychiatrist told me:

> You need to understand—the *secteur* is made to take care of all the pathologies of a given territory, and that means the heaviest pathologies. These are maladies that are durable, chronic. I see a lot of patients I've known for thirty-five years. The care is repeated and repetitive because the treatments aren't that effective. These are people who are not capable of . . . going anywhere else, and so we're obligated to keep them, rehospitalize them from time to time.

Scaling looks great in a consultant's PowerPoint, but that's why it was worth taking a detour to discuss what I saw in California in practice: undertreating people whose behavior is not disruptive enough to place them at the high end of protocols of prioritization but who are too sick to thrive with what's offered to those on the lower end of the continuum. For French professionals, *malades* ultimately showed up whether or not anyone ran a public awareness campaign and, once they were there, never successfully graduated to the less intensive levels of care that the prime minister was seeking to boost.

Yet bounding had its own internal contradictions because populations couldn't actually be sorted in the way that logic presumed. In the face of the public's demands for a psychiatric response to psychological troubles, neither the *secteur*'s attempts to push them away or to resolve them with minimalist interventions seemed to work. Bounding perhaps made sense when it was embedded in a robust welfare state for every different bureaucratic kind, where *malades* could go to public psychiatry and the poor, the addicted, or those involved in the criminal justice system could go elsewhere. But today every other wing of the French state seems as overrun as the clinic. Despite best efforts at rationing, the standard package of monthly psychiatry appointments, occasional support from nurses, and injectable antipsychotics was not enough to prevent a portion of the *secteur*'s *malades* from drifting in and out of care. Sometimes this had grave consequences: Recall the patient who, after several years off the *secteur*'s radar screen, jumped out a window.

If anything, these ground-level challenges have reinforced the line between mental health and illness. Years after my fieldwork ended in 2016, the coronavirus pandemic brought a new "wave of need" crashing down on public psychiatry.[38] More recent statistics about access to psychiatric care are dire. New patients wait an average of three months for a first appointment.[39] In response, public psychiatry has actually been putting an increasing proportion of its resources into hospitals, which remained the most indispensable service for *malades*.[40] If rationing at the doors of the clinic failed, it could be more brutally effective at the gates of the hospital. One nurse told the French publication *Libération* that he was "practicing wartime medicine, triaging the *malades*. The serious ones, we will take on, the others we put to the side."[41] Rather than becoming far-reaching, care was becoming more concentrated. And instead of being rationalized, it only became more costly. No one thought this was an optimal situation, but the alternative is not obvious. As long as budgets are limited, serious illnesses are incurable, and society demands more care for a proliferating spectrum of psychological states and social situations, the allocation of care will be unsatisfying.

One of the key arguments of this book is that the classifications imposed on a population by one of the state's many hands will stick even when that population gets handed off. As you have seen, the *secteurs* defined *malades* as a group perpetually dependent on them, even as *secteurs* struggled to keep them stabilized in the community. France's disability system imagined, however, that they could be a different kind of person: increasingly autonomous people with psychic handicaps. But this project had to contend with the fact that they were not fabricating a population from a blank slate; they were reclassifying people who had already been categorized and treated as *malades*.

# PART II

## From Chronicity to Autonomy

What future can the mental health system offer its patients? You wouldn't know it from today's morose depictions, but the old asylums were astoundingly effective at curing illnesses and restoring independence. An 1801 report to the French Ministry of the Interior on the new asylums promised that "these establishments . . . [can] give back to society nearly two-thirds of those who until now were condemned to perpetual seclusion by a lack of care."[1] Across the Atlantic, mad-doctors were making even more extravagant claims. Worcester State Hospital in Massachusetts, one of the country's first public asylums, delivered to the state legislature in 1833 the suspiciously precise statistic that 82.25 percent of recent admissions had been cured.[2]

Later experience proved that these figures were optimistic. By the 1950s, over one-third of the population of French psychiatric hospitals had been institutionalized five years or more.[3] Hospitals not only failed to cure chronic mental illnesses; they also fabricated "withdrawal [and] detachment" on a "massive scale."[4] Ken Kesey, in his 1962 novel *One Flew Over the Cuckoo's Nest*, described the population of the state hospitals, which were then interning a half-million Americans: "Across the room from the Acutes are the Chronics. Not in the hospital, these, to get fixed, but just to keep them from walking around the streets. Chronics are in for good, the staff concedes."

Yet by the time Kesey was writing, a revolution was afoot. In 1952, Parisian pedestrians started noticing dramatic changes at Sainte Anne's, the local asylum: "The windows facing the street were opened in the spring and summer, and the clamor of patients would normally be audible along the Rue d'Alésia . . . After June 1952, the local merchants began pulling aside Jean Thuillier [a psychiatrist] . . . and asking him with wonder: 'Doctor, what are you doing with the patients up there? We don't hear them anymore.'"[5] The answer was that Doctor Thuillier and his colleagues were treating the Chronics with Chlorpromazine, the first antipsychotic medication.

Medications did more than transform the interior of hospitals. In his 1963 message to the US Congress, President John Kennedy reported that, while the average stay for schizophrenia in state hospitals was eleven years, modern psychiatry had demonstrated that "two out of three" could be "treated and released within six months." Patients were moving on to a life of "wholesome and constructive social adjustment."[6] The promise of community care was that the chronicity of mental illness—instead of the sufferers of it—could be banished.

Just a few years after Kennedy's speech, however, medication's triumph over chronicity (like the triumph of asylums a century earlier) was in doubt. In 1966, Pierre Deniker, a coinventor of chlorpromazine, told the World Congress of Psychiatry, "Chemotherapies have been around long enough now for us to know their action in cases treated since their inception. . . . Many patients, who had first been stabilized at an excellent level . . . so that their social functioning was almost normal, then had progressive attacks after five or ten years which defeated every therapeutic attempt." Psychiatrists had been right, he reiterated, in identifying that extended stays in the hospital had been a chief "factor in chronicity." But he and his compatriots needed to "acknowledge that illness is also such a factor."[7] Drugs could blunt delusions and paranoia, but they were less effective in addressing the negative symptoms of schizophrenia: apathy, withdrawal, and passivity.

In short, policymakers and professionals across the Western world were unprepared for the fact that deinstitutionalization would create a population of people who, despite living in the community, were nonetheless deeply impaired.[8] They required more than just medication and therapy;

they needed the whole host of things the asylums had been providing: food, clothing, shelter, and a modicum of social interaction. The mad were now destined not just to be patients but also beneficiaries and clients of a host of social programs. And as innumerable studies of welfare programs have shown, to be a supplicant of the state was to receive a "daily lesson in . . . subordination."[9] If less degrading than the experience of internment in an asylum, it looked little like the independence and inclusion that deinstitutionalization had originally promised.

In recent decades, though, what we expected from welfare recipients—be they clients, beneficiaries, or indeed mental health patients—has changed. Government programs, like cash welfare, once provided security and protection while imposing passivity. They are now supposed to promote active self-reliance instead.[10] "Autonomy" is not just an opportunity, writes sociologist Alain Ehrenberg, but a "collective expectation of each person . . . an imperative" to which even the most marginalized should aspire.[11] This new vision is not just a top-down exhortation. Movements of people with disabilities have been at the forefront of demanding that the state switch from providing minimalist survival for the incapable to active support for developing capabilities.[12]

Part II is about this collision: the aspiration of autonomy, constantly threatened by the sticky reality of chronicity.[13] In takes us from the focus in part I on how states identify and demarcate populations to how they transform them. Insofar as bureaucratic kinds are, as Ian Hacking puts it, "sufficiently strong" to provide "laws about people, their actions, or their sentiments,"[14] they also carry with them expectations about the predictable and consistent ways people in a given category are supposed to relate to the state. The people in welfare-to-work schemes, drug rehab facilities, or prisoner reentry programs are expected to have, or at least develop, a particular way of articulating their needs, responding to authority, and using government services.

What happens, however, when different state agencies expect the same people to belong to distinct bureaucratic kinds? Part II traces a project to empower people with mental illness by recognizing them as part of two populations at once: *malades* receiving treatment for a chronic illness from psychiatry, and people with a psychic handicap moving toward a future of growing autonomy within a revamped disability system. To understand how peculiarly French this mélange is, let's check on how life in the community has transformed the lives of people who once belonged to bureaucratic kind of "asylum patient" in the United States.

## ABANDONMENT INTO AUTONOMY IN THE UNITED STATES

As I found in ride-alongs with a team of community paramedics attached to the fire department of one coastal California city, the United States has an effective strategy for overcoming chronicity in order to promote independence. It involves ignoring the former and defining down the latter. The most seriously mentally ill are abandoned into autonomy.

The team I shadowed was focused on a few dozen individuals on whom just about every other social service agency had given up. We chatted with one woman sprawled on a mattress in an alleyway who, after years of contact, still refused to give any name beyond Dragonfly Galaxy; passersby kept calling 911 on her behalf when they saw the gaping, untreated sores on her arms and legs. We spent a few minutes trying to convince a chronic alcoholic with a traumatic brain injury to return to his homeless shelter. He refused, but he'd reappear after he passed out and hit his head on the pavement, was picked up by an ambulance and taken to an ER, and discharged. It wasn't all defeat. We visited one of the team's success stories: a man with schizophrenia who, after years on the street, had won the golden ticket and been placed in a subsidized single-room-occupancy hotel. The smell of rotten food strewn across the floor was nauseating, but we passed a few pleasant minutes teaching him to play the brand-new saxophone on which he had, for whatever reason, spent his entire disability check.

Where was the local mental health department in caring for these individuals, I wonder. "We call them every day," Derrick, my guide, tells me, "just to wear them down." Outpatient teams and inpatient psychiatrists find all sorts of reasons not to take the team's clients: They don't show for appointments; they won't take their medications; they don't appear in jails or ERs enough to meet the prioritization criteria imposed by a logic of scaling. The silently suffering thus have the freedom that comes from being largely left alone.

Every once in a while, the system leaps into action. We're driving back to the station when a call comes in reporting a man with a grave disability—an inability to provide for essential food, clothing, or shelter that has brought him to the doorway of death. That qualifies him for an involuntary psychiatric evaluation in an ER. Derrick turns on the sirens (mostly for my amusement, I think) and we speed across the city to a decrepit supported housing complex. We walk up a creaking staircase covered with torn carpet. The hallway is filled with worried-looking residents, two case managers responsible for providing a threadbare safety net for them, and a pair of police officers. They announce, "Great, you're here, we're gone" and sashay in the opposite direction when we walk past.

Three firefighters in full flame-protection gear break down a door at the end of the hallway. Inside, a gaunt man with a yellowing beard is splayed out on a tangled mass of sheets. The linens are soaked in urine. The tiny room—maybe twelve-by-twelve feet—is filled with buzz saws and a haphazard wooden structure reaching the ceiling, purpose unknown. "You're coming with us," Derrick tells him firmly.

The man declares, "Everything here is being recorded by the FBI [US Federal Bureau of Investigation]" and responds that he is, not, in fact, coming with us.

Derrick clarifies, "You're coming with us whether you want to or not."

He snaps on a pair of latex gloves, grabs the man firmly, and leads him downstairs. He's strapped to a gurney and lifted into the back of an ambulance. "This is a kidnapping!" the man protests. He is off to the county hospital.

I visit the city a few months later and ask Derrick if he remembers what happened to the man. He struggles to recall the case. Overwhelming suffering and neglect tend to blot out individuality. Eventually, the name comes to him. He looks the man up in the city's system. "He stayed two days [in the hospital], and they dumped him," he reports. The fire hazard he created in his tiny room and the stench of death emanating from it was enough to scale up interventions to the level of hospitalization. Care dropped back to zero when he failed to show for his follow-up appointment. The paramedic team ran into him recently. He had been evicted and claimed he hadn't eaten in a week.

"Not a happy ending?" I posit.

"No, not a happy ending," he tells me.

It's a common denouement to the sorry saga of the one-time asylum population writ large. In the 1970s and 1980s, the question of what the Chronics were up to in the community was of significant sociological interest.[15] Psychiatrists developed classifications and treatment approaches for putative human kinds like "young adult chronics" and "dilapidated dhronics."[16] There were, it should be noted, lots of welfare programs serving these groups. A 1977 report from the Federal Comptroller General found 135 such sources of support, concluding "almost every type of service needed by mentally disabled persons in communities can be financed wholly or partly with Federal funds."[17] But this population never cohered into a specific bureaucratic kind. As a follow-up report in 1980 concluded, "persons disabled by chronic mental illness" had been "inadvertently victimized by a lack of consistent national policies . . . [for] planning, coordination, implementation, funding, monitoring, and evaluation of a coherent system of care."[18] The authors elaborated, at last, a "National Plan for the Chronically Mentally Ill."

The plan was never implemented. Perhaps it was because a network of private boarding and nursing homes proliferated to keep the chronically ill population both out of sight and off public mental health departments' caseloads.[19] Maybe it was a distinctively-American unwillingness to accept that some people are not on a trajectory toward productivity and self-improvement.[20] In any case, discussions of chronic mental illness faded from popular discourse even as the people themselves dropped out of discussions of the public mental health system. Today, more attention is paid to the chronically homeless—a population into which many former asylum patients have landed—than the chronically mentally ill (figure II.1).

Decades later, the public mental health system embraced the idea that it should promote empowerment, replacing the "lack of control, sense of helplessness, and dependency" that many treatment users felt with an "assumption of responsibility" for "liv[ing] with the consequences of their choices."[21] Honestly, though, "recovery" asks that mental health professionals catch up with what people with severe mental illness have already been doing since the 1960s: scraping together resources and surviving on their own. For many, the public mental health system is a marginal presence. They might get housing on the basis of being chronically

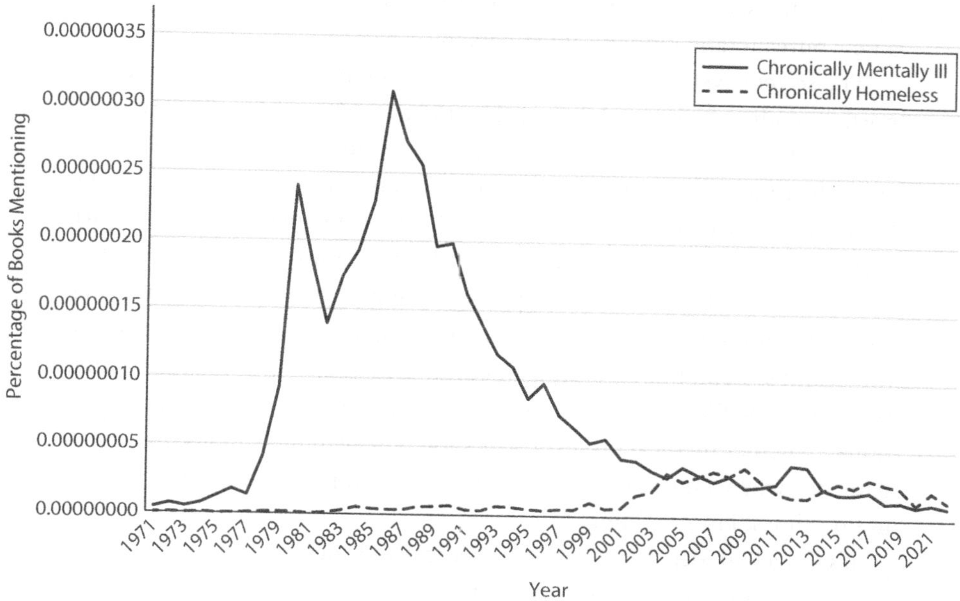


FIGURE II.1. English-language references to "chronically mentally ill" versus "chronically homeless." *Source*: Google N-gram.

homeless, a paltry social security check thanks to a designation of disability, or court-mandated substance use services subsequent to an arrest for a minor misdemeanor. But in the United States, "chronically mentally ill" is not really a bureaucratic kind strong enough to tie this population durably to a set of state agencies expected to meet the full range of their needs.

## THE CONSTRAINTS OF CHRONICITY IN FRANCE

This excursion into how the United States has balanced autonomy and chronicity accentuates how, a few decades after deinstitutionalization began in earnest, France confronted a near-opposite dilemma. The people being labeled and admitted to psychiatric services, as you saw in part I of this book, have long been assigned to the bureaucratic kind of *malade*. This label carries a promise of lifelong care but also a heavy expectation of chronicity and a limited horizon of autonomy. The struggle charted in part II is the search for a way to escape these constraints through assigning a new bureaucratic kind: disabled person.

The *secteur* system promised not just treatment but a host of other supports extending far beyond the usual boundaries of medicine. (The running joke was that nurses in the *secteurs* are "professionals trained in assembling IKEA furniture."[22]) Doctor Mailhol, a psychiatrist nearing retirement after being involved in decades of policy debates, explained to me the spirit that animated reformers in the 1960s and 1970s: "Our vision of the *secteur* was a bit totalizing. We did everything. The goal was to handle housing, social integration, rehabilitation, constructing a family, all of that, but in the health system, not separating 'medical' and 'social' like in a lot of other countries." He liked telling the story of a conference where a speaker questioned whether medical professionals should be helping patients manage in daily life, when a nurse interjected, "But sir, when I go with a schizophrenic to buy shoes, I'm providing 'care.'"

It's not a bad idea: If people have medical and social needs, why not provide both under one institutional roof? But while the United States failed to offer comprehensive care for chronicity, the French system was unprepared for people who demanded anything beyond it. Providing aid with footwear probably helped people walk around the community with a greater degree of autonomy, but it was coupled with ongoing dependency on an all-encompassing health system.

As we will see in chapter 3, in recent decades, a range of stakeholders have mobilized for an alternative. Madame Coulon, the vice president of France's National Union of Families and Friends of People with Mental Illness/Psychic Handicaps (*Union nationale de familles et amis de personnes malades et/ou handicapées psychiques* [UNAFAM]), expressed her frustration to me with the system she was thrust into when her son was first hospitalized: "We talk about 'deinstitutionalization,' but in reality, the mentally ill were still stuck in the psychiatric institution, even when they lived elsewhere. They depended on psychiatry. They remained in the health system. Psychiatrists have a hard time talking about 'people;' they can only speak of '*malades*,' 'their patients.'" She and parents like her waged an improbable struggle to have their children rebaptized "people with psychic handicaps." This cumbersome administrative designation would nonetheless open up a whole new set of services designed for a very different bureaucratic kind from *malade*.

A 2005 reform made this a possibility. Its passage was, to Coulon, a "revolution": "This law made the mentally ill, for the first time, citizens with the rights of other citizens." She went on, "For these citizens, everything around housing oneself, feeding oneself, having pastimes, accessing nature, social integration, work—they are going to be accompanied by professionals who are not from the health system: not psychiatrists, not nurses, but social workers and educators." Perhaps most important, these new professionals would be operating with the state-imposed mandate that "disabled persons can only exercise fully their citizenship . . . under conditions of the maximum restoration of autonomy."[23] *Malades* would escape the constraints of chronic illness by becoming both sick *and* disabled.

Chapter 4 will reveal, however, how difficult it can be to put human beings into two different bureaucratic kinds at once.[24] I conducted months of observation in a Departmental Home for Disabled People (*Maison departementale des personnes handicapées*, or Disability Office), the administrative entity responsible for allocating the disability benefits that were supposed to make their recipients autonomous. For evaluators on the ground, the people with mental illness sent to them didn't have the characteristics of the applicants they were used to. For people living with blindness, paralysis, or Down syndrome, disability is relatively fixed.[25] Symptoms of mental illness are variable. The goal of the Disability Office is to figure out what a person can't do and propose compensation for it (a human aide to help someone shower, for example). People with mental illnesses can do just about everything—get up, get dressed, eat breakfast—but sometimes they don't. The new system expected that people with disabilities would elaborate what they need via a so-called life project. But *malades* often didn't want any help. Or perhaps having been through a *secteur* system that rendered them pliant, many were hardly ready to be transformed into disabled citizens who were active and self-advocating.

The attempt to create a dual identity actually revealed that, as one national official charged with this transformation told me, "We are a country of 'little boxes.' . . . You're black or white, schizophrenic or normal, [mentally disabled] or intelligent. You can't be multiple things. You can't be *malade* and disabled at the same time." But, as Hacking tells us, categories for humans are not static. Instead, "people classified in a certain way tend to conform to or grow into the ways they are described; but they also evolve in their own ways, so that the classifications and descriptions have to be constantly revised."[26] Faced with the difficulty of transforming people with mental illness into people with disabilities, bureaucrats and service providers fell back on reemphazing the status of such people as *malades*. But through this process, the meaning of *malade* stretched to allow for chronicity and a measure of autonomy at the same time. The preexisting characteristics of the population of *malades* were not just a barrier to realizing the intentions of policymakers; they changed the French health and welfare systems in unintended ways.

*Chapter Three*

# A HANDICAPPED REVOLUTION

"I'll tell you, it's the doctors in this *secteur* who have a psychic handicap," declared Sarah, one of the full-time social workers stationed upstairs at the outpatient clinic I studied.

The process of turning a *malade* into a person with a psychic handicap starts at 10:00 a.m., right after the weekly triage meeting. The Clinic's two full-time social workers are joined by some of their seven colleagues who work throughout the *secteur* (in its inpatient units or day hospital, for example). Sometimes, it takes a team effort to decrypt the handwriting in the spiral notebook where psychiatrists write their requests for benefit applications. At moments, doctors suggest that the person apply for mutually exclusive aid, as was the case when the psychiatrist wrote "professional retraining/protected workshop"—the former a disability benefit focused on returning disabled people to the ordinary milieu of work, the latter sheltered employment for those who cannot return. Another commonly appearing directive was "RSA/invalidity pension/AAH," which were acronyms referring to minimum income supports for three very different populations: the precarious and poor, incapacitated workers, and disabled persons. They might have just written, "Figure something out," which was what led Sarah to quip that the real disability was on the psychiatrists' side.

These meetings revealed that, for all the *secteurs'* historical aspiration to care for the holistic needs of *malades*, the doctors at the top of the hierarchy were too overwhelmed to know much about the daily lives of their patients. That responsibility fell to the social workers. They dominate the mental health system in the United States, but in France they have a lower status and no clinical training.[1] Social workers have a strong ethos, though: as Clemence (Sarah's full-time collaborator) told me, "That's the difference between us and the doctors. They'll say 'I encountered this *malade*' . . . [but] while a medical diagnosis is interesting, we're focused on the person above all."

Thinking of a person as more than just a *malade* is the first step in making a successful application to the Disability Office. As Sarah explained, "You have to put the limitations in everyday activities up front. So the doctor will put 'a-pragmatism' [a symptom of lack of motivation] and I'll write that the person is 'isolated,' that they miss a lot of meetings, that they can't manage to work." In one instance, Doctor Beaufils sent an email flagged "URGENT" about an elderly, longtime patient with paranoid schizophrenia. She lived in public housing but had hoarded enough detritus to turn it into an apartment-fire-in-waiting. She was refusing all treatment, but the doctor thought getting a personal assistant paid for by the disability system could help her clean up and ward off an eviction.[2] But while his email talked about her "bizarre contact," "disorganized thinking," and "low morale," Sarah fired off an e-mail in response lecturing, "I need some real information about her autonomy. That's what the Disability Office is looking for." The social workers were the passageway between the health system and the disability system, each of which faced the same people but looked for very different things.

Patients created their own barriers to transforming mental illness into impairments that would be legible to the Disability Office. Under the new disability system inaugurated by the 2005 reform, disabled people were supposed to take the lead in their own applications. An official in the national agency for disability told me proudly: "We used to have very passive evaluations [before the creation of the Disability Office in 2005], the person was not a participant. The doctors said what the situation was and decided what was necessary. Now, we have evaluations which are participatory. The users themselves are going to tell us what their 'life project' is and we will respond as a function of that."

This seemed like empty pablum to Clemence. She quipped, "I pretty much only do disability demands for people who don't think they're disabled. They'll come see me and say, 'I'm great, ready to live alone, I don't need anything, thank you very much.'" *Secteur* patients rarely seemed to seize on the opportunities for autonomy offered by the disability system. "It's completely paralyzing for me to ask them what their 'life project' is," she reported. "Often it's, 'survive with 800 euros a month [the amount of the Allocation for Handicapped Adults]' and so we just leave that blank. What's the point in writing 'be in care and eat' as a 'project?'"

Now we're getting to the core of the issue: The health and disability systems operate under fundamentally distinctive logics, which reflect the once-quite-separate bureaucratic kinds they administer. The disability system serves a specific population that meets a defined set of criteria. It usually requires that people want whatever benefits it is offering. The *secteurs* are supposed to serve anyone and, at least for a subset of *malades*, will twist an arm to get them to accept those services. Doctor Clech, who managed the hospital ward in the *secteur* reserved for the toughest patients, told me:

> To do an application to the Disability Office, the person needs to be in agreement. To be in agreement, he needs to be aware of his handicap. And in fact, that's variable. There are some who are aware right away that they're not going to get there [live without disability benefits], and others not at all. I have a patient who is twenty-five. It's his second hospitalization in two years. He's had electroshocks, really heavy treatment. But he refuses the Disability Office. He has said to me several times, 'If I accept that, that means I'm sick, that means I'm crazy, there's nothing left for me but to die.' So what do you want me to do? For us, there are criteria. For him, there aren't.

Doctor Clech could override patient (non)consent if she wanted to hospitalize someone and bind them further to the kind of *malade*. But she did need consent to send them elsewhere.

As such, in some cases, the transformation of *malades* into disabled people, which might have begun downstairs in the weekly Clinic triage meeting when a case was dispatched to the social workers, ended an hour later when the social workers came together. In one instance, the team opened the notebook to see a demand for "Disability Office/Allocation for Handicapped Adults." Clemence went downstairs to the Clinic to retrieve the medical dossier. As she read off different features of the case, Sarah mocked the absurdity of the assumption that the person would collaborate in a demand to the Disability Office: "Hospitalized after robbing and stabbing someone."

"Hah," Sarah guffawed.

"Request for a visa rejected," Clemence added.

"Hah, hah."

"Chronic drug use."

"Hah, hah, hah."

"Has a project to do a professional training to become a baker, but does not read or write."

"Hahahahahahahaha." The laughter was fake, the incredulity real.

Clemence closed: "We're going to fail at the Disability Office."

She began drafting an email to Doctor Kuorio, and Sarah interjected, "Don't be so nice. There's absolutely nothing we can do here—he's not stabilized, there's no papers, there's no project. What do they want?" Even if he had papers, few disability associations would take a chronic drug user with a history of violence to help him realize his (in this case, quite clear) life project of becoming a baker.

This chapter traces the political debates and historical evolutions in French social policy that created the bureaucratic chasm the social workers were trying to bridge. At its heart is a struggle led by the National Union of Families and Friends of People with Mental Illness to gain state recognition of "psychic handicap" as a passageway between the medical and disability systems. The promise was that someone would receive treatment from the health system and a range of benefits from France's disability system at the same time. Materially, those benefits might include a monthly income, employment supports, or access to a residential institution. Symbolically, they were much more: belonging to an entirely new bureaucratic kind. According to the 2016 National Strategy for Psychic Handicap, this shift of money, policy, and personnel from the health to disability services would "go beyond stabilization of troubles . . . to the promotion of capacities . . . and access to a chosen social and working life."[3]

It was a noble project, and one behind which nearly all of the major actors in the French public psychiatric system ultimately lined up. But the alchemy it envisioned was always riven with tensions between the desire to assimilate people with mental illness into the world of disability and the reality that psychic handicaps seemed distinctive enough to demand a specialized response. In chapter 4, we will see how the challenges that Sarah, Clemence, and the other social workers faced in transforming chronic *malades* into autonomous psychically handicapped persons played out in the place they were applying to: the Disability Office.

## THE BIG SORT OF 1975

Categories like "mentally ill" or "handicapped" were so full of meaning that, by the time I conducted my fieldwork in 2016, relabeling *malades* as "disabled" was a revolution. Yet these divisions made little sense before the 1970s. Asylums were, in the words of sociologist Gil Eyal, a kind of "blender"[4] that scrambled together various kinds of dependencies and deficiencies that could be traced to minds, brains, souls, or social situations. A historical detour into how psychiatrists, the state, and parents tried to sort out these populations will help us understand why bringing them back together—that is, rechristening *malades* as also disabled—later proved so difficult

In 1961, people characterized as "senile," "mentally retarded," or having organic brain disorders made up 40 percent of the asylum population.[5] They were the most abandoned patients in an already abandoned asylum system. Doctor Mailhol, who as of 2015 was on the verge of retirement and will play a key role in the pages to come, recounted a story that still makes my heart sink reading the transcript: "My first job was in an absolutely intolerable hospital . . . for children as young as four. Some people had been there thirty years. It took me months to discover that my ward had a patient who was autistic, blind, and deaf . . . because in the back of the ward, there was another room that I didn't even know was there, where the nurses locked him in to get rid of him for the day, so the doctors could just leave and go fishing or something." One historian found a medical dossier for a man, born in Cambodia, who had been placed in the hospital for "vagrancy" before World War II. As of 1967, his physician described him as an "asylum robot": an "old young man who was forgotten in the asylum because no one knew what to do with him."[6]

At the dawn of sectorization, though, French psychiatrists were trying to firmly establish themselves as doctors for patients, not wardens of robots. Psychoanalysis furnished a new understanding of severe mental illnesses as dynamic psychological processes and not immutable biological facts.[7]

The effects of neuroleptics provided the evidence this might actually be true. In 1955, Henry Ey, a prominent leader in the sectorization movement, declared, "It isn't true that schizophrenia is installed fatally in the individual. [It is neither] a genetic law of destiny, nor an inextricable virus, nor an irreversible illness; it is a 'form of reaction' in each individual that puts into play all the forces and weaknesses of his psychic existence . . . and it can happen that the process stops, the *malade* triumphs, and we can speak of 'remission.'"[8] Here's the important point: French psychiatrists were not denying that mental illnesses were chronic conditions, as some of the greatest optimists in the United States envisioned. They were rather embracing the idea of "cures that came when they were no longer expected," such that "one should never give up on chronic patients."[9] Yet making this vision true in practice meant not just redoubling their efforts to heal the healable. It also required getting rid of the incurable. The problem was that, at the time, there was no alternative, state-recognized bureaucratic kind into which the unwanted and untreated asylum nonpatients with intellectual or developmental disabilities could go.

Fortunately for psychiatrists, the parents of these incurables were taking matters into their own hands, sharply aware of their children's poor treatment in the health system. They joined together to create associations that built and managed residential schools and protected workshops.[10] According to a government report, the "opening of these new establishments . . . extracted a whole category of people from psychiatric hospitals."[11] There was another, parallel world growing that consisted of rehabilitation centers focused on retraining and reintegrating people with physical limitations, like those made "invalid" by accidents at work or "mutilated" by war, into employment.[12]

In the 1960s, the French state pivoted from building a welfare state for families headed by healthy male breadwinners to building "catch-up regime[s] . . . designed to cover up the holes in the social system"[13] for those outside that norm. According to administrative lore, this project of filling these gaps with new bureaucratic kinds was playing out in cabinet meetings during the 1970s:

> At the council of ministers, every time they talked about national defense, the renovation of the docks, or commerce with China, she [the Secretary for Social Action Marie-Madeleine Dienesch] asked,

> "And the handicapped?" One day President [Georges] Pompidou snapped and said, "My friend, make me a law, but a law that solves all these problems, really all of them. I don't want to hear about the handicapped anymore."[14]

The story is perhaps apocryphal but not outlandish. It illustrates the state's enormous power, as Pierre Bourdieu described it, of "production and canonization of social classifications."[15] And so in 1975, the Law in Favor of Handicapped Persons created, as the minister put it, "a true social statute for the handicapped."[16] This new human category resulted from the (not at all intuitive) grouping of "maladjusted" children, "mutilated" warriors, and "invalid" workers. They could now benefit from a monthly Allocation for Handicapped Adults, aid in finding employment, and a now unified system of protected workshops and residential institutions.

French psychiatrists' opposition to provisions in the law of 1975 was ferocious. The virulent debate was over articles of the law that would create a new set of establishments for "handicapped adults who cannot acquire a minimum of autonomy," which would include the "mentally ill whose condition no longer requires their maintenance in a psychiatric hospital."[17] For the head of the Union of Hospital Psychiatrists, though, such establishments would be sites of "apartheid," a "new ghetto."[18] Just as psychiatrists were trying to integrate their patients into society, the law was creating a new form of institutional "segregation."[19]

There's a heavy dose of corporatism in all of this. At the time, Doctor Mailhol was actively involved in (and later president of) the Foundation for Aid in Mental Health–Croix Marine, which helped push sectorization forward by setting up apartments, employment centers, and day hospitals throughout France. He noted, "We had, you might say, a captive population, with the idea that the *secteur* was going to take care of everything—prevention, care, and accompaniment. But all that was happening in the health system, and everything needed to remain there." There was a more ideological component as well that reflected both idealism and a hierarchy of worth: "If psychiatrists were hostile to 'handicap,' it's in part because it called to mind, at least unconsciously . . . the 'idiot.' Because [Jean-Étienne-Dominique] Esquirol [a prominent early nineteenth century psychiatrist] said: 'It's a fixed state, definitive, there's nothing to do' . . . The 'handicapped' is a person who doesn't need care but just needs some help and a bed. And the idea that we're not going to treat these people [as mentally ill] any more, you take away the medical dimension, it's intolerable." Again, even if mental illness was not curable, it was nonetheless treatable, in a way that disability, in psychiatrists' minds, was not.

Psychiatrists' argument that the categories "handicap" and "mental illness" should be kept administratively separate won out. The Office for Mental Health in the ministry declared that putting mentally ill people in establishments for disabled people was "very dangerous" because "the sick person is an evolving subject" who needed more than a "depot where they have no medical guarantee."[20] The report concluded instead that "the mentally ill should remain the charge of the *secteurs*, who are the only ones capable of assuring them the necessary continuity of care and . . . permit[ting] them to acquire a certain autonomy." These ministerial directives revealed the logic through which the French state was thinking about vulnerable populations. In a law that was designed to cover the holes in the welfare system by giving a social status to disabled persons, there was no need to provide for people with mental illness. They both had a bureaucratic status—mentally ill—and were already covered—by the *secteurs* and their psychiatric hospitals. By the end of the decade, " 'handicap' and 'mental illness' " had become, according to sociologist Nicolas Henckes, "mutually exclusive terms."[21]

Many of my interviewees from UNAFAM lamented decades later that their children were excluded from the 1975 law. This isn't quite right. The law gave no definition of "handicap" and left it up to departmental commissions to determine who got benefits.[22] When I asked Doctor Mailhol what happened next, he smiled. As he explained, psychiatrists worked their way into the commissions and ensured that their patients benefited from the new Allocation for Handicapped Adults.[23] And that? "It changed everything. The *secteurs* could set up associations which would rent apartments outside the hospital to *malades* who now had some money. So you had people living in collective apartments, accompanied by nurses, and that was what permitted them to return to society." He concluded, "By 1980, that's when the psychiatric hospitals really emptied out."[24] The average length of stay in psychiatric hospitals was sliced in half, from 234.5 days in 1970 to 114.5 in 1980.[25] Psychiatrists critiqued the law of 1975 by insisting that mental illnesses were dynamic and susceptible to change, and merited ongoing interventions. Ironically, though, that law helped make this claim true, both by transferring people with disabilities away from psychiatry and helping *malades* get out of hospitals and into the community.

## LIBERATING THE LEFT BEHIND

The thing about this story of the mass departure of *malades* from psychiatric hospitals, though, is that it ignores the *malades* who were left behind. This population, which found a place neither in the new disability system nor the supposedly integrating services of the *secteur*, ultimately destabilized the neat divisions that the 1975 law created.

*La Clinique de la Borde* is, on first impression, a bit of a *bordel* [mess]. As soon as we park outside the hospital, an older man in the throes of delirium is grabbing at the door and then—as soon as he steps outside—the leg of *La Borde*'s head psychiatrist, Philippe Bichon. Left on my own, I walk toward the central building of the hospital: an old château, nestled in the forests and farmland of *Loir-et-Cher*, an hour and a half by train from Paris. A group of five people sit at a picnic table outside drinking tea and talking raucously, wildly gesticulating to drive home their points. After introducing myself, I immediately wonder who is a professional and who is a patient.

I get my answer when one middle-aged man—wearing no uniform and no lanyard—starts ranting about the High Authority of Health's accreditation process: "There's a loss of singularity. At the beginning, here, the staff were neither 'medical' nor 'social' . . . now we're obligated to choose."

"What is your training in, then?" I ask.

"Philosophy."

*Le Borde* has, indeed, long served as a "legendary pilgrimage site within the French intellectual world,"[26] which is an impressive accomplishment for a hospital widely understood to be a resting place for the most chronic of people with chronic psychosis.

According to its founding mythos, in 1953, psychiatrist Jean Oury abandoned the decrepit asylum of which he had been made head doctor (at the age of twenty-nine), bringing with him thirty-three patients and a few nurses.[27] After two weeks of sleeping "here and there," they occupied an old château that had been ruined in the war. There, Oury embraced a philosophy of care that drew from "psychoanalysis, phenomenology, surrealism, and Trotskyist-anarchist politics."[28] The approach at *La Borde* eventually coalesced around the notion of institutional psychotherapy and the promise that the hospital itself could be a tool of disalienation.

Doctor Mailhol, who was among those who tried to carry this therapeutic approach from hospitals like *La Borde* and sprinkle it throughout the *secteurs*, told me, "We were trying to put the patients in the position of participating, of having responsibility, of having the possibility of choosing, of being actors and not simply submissive to care. So we created therapeutic clubs, structures for activities, for theater." I go to the meeting of *La Borde*'s club, held in a wood-paneled room with a big fireplace that reminds me of a hunting lodge. The pensioners—*La Borde* does not call them patients—have a lively debate about the menu for the upcoming Bastille Day celebration. After the two nurses overseeing the meeting remove a man in a wheelchair who abruptly starts screaming, the pensioners launch into a prolonged discussion of how best to organize the sale of cigarettes. Although each day the pensioners create a handwritten schedule adorned with unique drawings and describing a range of musical, educational, and artistic activities, the buying, selling, and smoking of cigarettes is invariably the main event.

Afterward, a woman, who both looks and talks as if she is a scion of the Parisian bourgeoisie, declares that she will be my "*poisson-pilote*" ("pilot fish"). This apparently means that she is giving me a tour. I ask for the origins of the label, and she cautions me, "There are lots of things like that here. It takes four years to really get to know *La Borde*. That's what Jean Oury"—who died in 2014—"always said."

She adds, "So I stayed four and a half years before I left the first time." But, she smiles and says, "I came back." Her repeated, open-ended hospitalization is, needless to say, the stuff of nightmares for economists in the Ministry of Health.

Indeed, everyone I talk to at *La Borde* has been there for years. The pensioners often seem as committed to the place as the psychiatrists. She introduces me to one of *La Borde*'s success stories: a man who was discharged to a nearby apartment after over a decade at the hospital but who still comes back every day "because he likes it so much here." He launches into a breathless twenty-minute monologue about Donald Trump (who, as of the summer 2016, was himself in the throes of a delusion that he might actually become president of the United States) and particle physics. *La Borde*, to put it lightly, cuts a strong contrast to the ever-shortening stays in public hospitals in France. It does so by design. In 1998, Oury declared "the fashion of short [hospital] stays is criminal. Schizophrenia is a chronic illness. Life—it's chronic. It's not because you make someone leave [the hospital] that they're cured."[29]

That last point offers a fair condensation of why people in the Ministry of Health despise *La Borde* and the approach to chronic *malades* it embodies. In 1991, the national insurance system threatened to cut the hospital's funding given its inability to "account for the additional costs incurred by the practice of institutional psychotherapy."[30] *Le Borde* survived, but a structure that for some is a totem of the highest ideals of French psychiatry is, for others, a symbol of what's wrong with the discipline. Institutional psychotherapy, one ministry official told me, is little more than "psychoanalysis plus walls" that is a "machine for chronicity." Doctor Bichon tells me that he's just waiting for the High Authority of Health to yank the clinic's authorization, whether over its dilapidated state of its buildings (a patient had recently been killed in a fire) or the ad hoc distribution of medicines. They are "paper-vores," he declares, "They just want to eat paper! So everything we do has to have a paper attached."

Doctor Bichon sees the decades-long stays common at *Le Borde* as reflective of a prolonged therapeutic battle against chronicity; for the ministry, it represents a surrender to dependency. "Hospital patient" is, after all, possibly the most expensive human kind that exists. Doctors are among the priciest government workers you can assign to just about any task. The vision that patients would recover their subjectivity through collectively haggling over cigarettes in a hospital or that *secteur* psychiatrists would visit their patients at home and nurses would stay behind to aid them to assemble furniture was bound to collide with budgetary reality eventually.

By the 1990s, the ministry was intensely focused on why patients were lingering in hospitals for years at a time. Some psychiatrists insisted that the truly "inadequate" hospitalizations were a function of the fact that they were still stuck with people who "did not really belong in psychiatry," such as those suffering from mental retardation or senility.[31] But when the ministry commissioned a study, 60 percent of people who had been hospitalized for more than nine months were diagnosed with schizophrenia—the realest of real maladies.[32] I talked to the consultant who led the study, who told me: "It [their ongoing hospitalization] was a product of the health system! That is, for those who were most trapped in their schizophrenia, we weren't offering them any possibilities, any life experiences that would allow them to develop social competencies and to live in an ordinarily milieu. It was the form of our medical response that was making them deficient." There's also a linkage with the limitations created by a logic of bounding identified in chapter 2: Even when they wanted, *secteurs* struggled to focus enough intensive care on a subset of chronic *malades* to keep them in the community.

For the ministry, the solution was clear. In the 1990s, the state closed 33,000 hospital beds in psychiatry and opened 30,000 in establishments for the disabled (figure 3.1).[33] The assumption that opening the latter institutions is the way to close the former responsibly is clear in the archives. A 2008 memo identified 26 percent of hospital beds—some 11,000 in total—as used "inadequately," at a cost of 750 million euros per year.[34] It argued

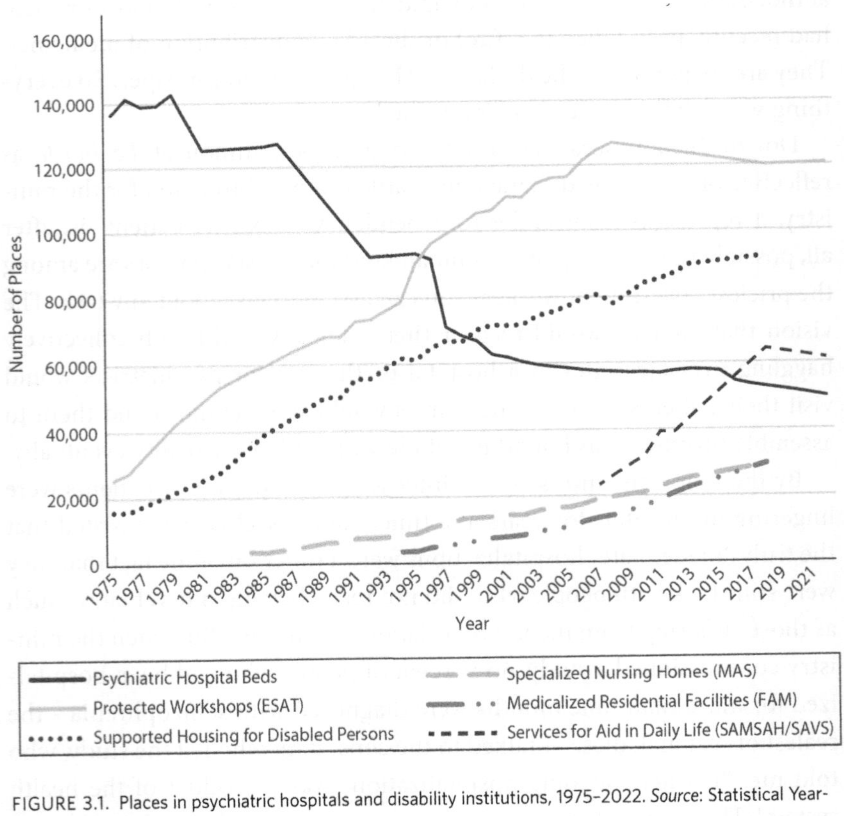


FIGURE 3.1. Places in psychiatric hospitals and disability institutions, 1975–2022. *Source*: Statistical Yearbooks of France.

that nearly 50 percent of those lingering in hospitals could live in the community with the help of disability services focused on providing aid in daily life, 35 percent in supported housing with occasional medical support, and 15 percent in a nursing home. Psychiatry must take a back seat; beyond medical treatment, these supports would be provided by the disability system, saving 350 million euros. The age of institutional psychotherapy, in which being confined to a hospital could be an improbable spark for psychic liberation, was over.

## THE HOPEFULNESS OF HANDICAP

While state administrators were expanding institutions in the disability system, parents like Madame Le Gal were crafting a novel bureaucratic kind to fill them. As she recounted to me, when her son came home from his first hospitalization for schizophrenia at age twenty-one, she didn't find the rich tissue of medical and social services the sectorization system promised. "It seemed like there was nothing between the hospital and the family, except the occasional consultation at the Clinic." There were protected workshops and supported housing in the disability system that could have helped her son, "but they were all designed for people with mental handicaps." That's a confusing term, but, after 1975, it enveloped people with developmental and intellectual disabilities while excluding those with mental illnesses.

In 1998, Madame Le Gal banded together with other parents to create *Espoir*-54, an association whose name is an amalgam of the word for "hope" and the number designating her department, Meurthe-et-Moselle. They started with a program that would organize social activities and help people with severe mental illness run errands in the community. A few years later, they added meetings to coach people to look for work. But the situation was frustrating: "The people with physical handicaps, the blind, they had money to buy buildings, and we were in an unused school, paid for with a yard sale."

Fast-forward to 2015, and the future for *Espoir*-54 was looking, well, hopeful. Madame Le Gal is now the president of the General Association for Aide and Accompaniment of the Psychically Handicapped (*Association générale d'aide et d'accompagnement pour handicapés psychiques*). The federation groups together over four hundred associations, many started by parents. They manage a host of interventions within the disability system, albeit only those serving people with psychic handicaps like her son. They are even swallowing up the Foundation for Aid in Mental Health–Croix Marine, the organization founded in 1952 by psychiatrists to provide social services within the medical system. "They came to us," she says. "They were out of money." More than that, she argues, "Their model was outdated." Psychiatrists, she said, never could get beyond their paternalist and protective attitude toward chronic *malades* to see the potential for the autonomy of the psychically handicapped. "For us, we walk alongside the person, encounter them in their humanity, find a path together. We ask, 'What do you want to do? What is your desire?'" she told me.

Her vision aligned with that of Ministry officials I interviewed. A referent for psychiatry in the ministry told me with borderline contempt, "With sectorization, the psychiatrists said: 'We can do everything, should do everything, can do everything; we can handle dysfunctions between mothers and children, psychiatry for elderly people . . . we know how to find housing, work.' Except that today, the *secteur* doesn't know how to do everything, it no longer has the means to do everything, and so it needs to work with others." Madame Le Gal evinced a similar view, twisting Doctor Mailhol's favorite example: "It's time for psychiatry to pass the baton. Is it really the role of the psychiatrist to go with someone to buy shoes? They say, 'That's our role,' but some are finally realizing that we know how to do that better than they do."

There was a big problem, as parents like Madame Le Gal recounted. The state was pushing people out of hospitals and narrowing the activities of the *secteurs*. But because the 1975 law had not fully incorporated people with mental illness, there were few new places being built specifically for people with "psychic handicap"—a term that emerged out of nowhere into public discourse in the 1990s, pushed by UNAFAM (figure 3.2). But just saying the term "psychic handicap" did not change that to be mentally ill was still administratively separate from being disabled. In 2001, UNAFAM sought to change that: It released a white paper that made a "plea to make exist a category of persons that did not exist" because, without it, "we had no public policies for it, because it was not identified." The goal was thus to ensure that "authorities for welfare will share available resources and official recognition to ensure that the rights of these persons"—those with a "psychic handicap"—were better respected.[35]

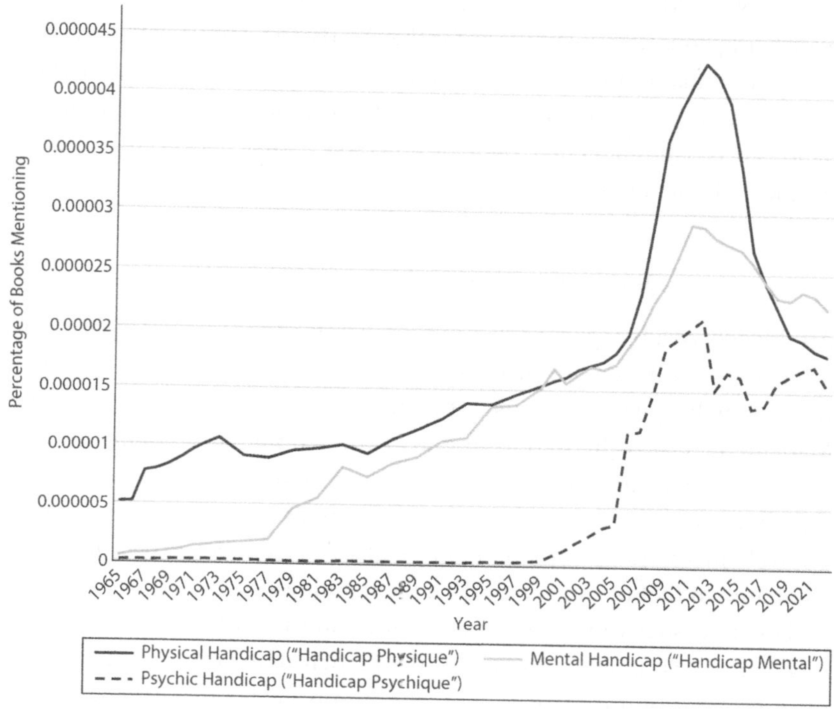


FIGURE 3.2. French-language references to different forms of handicap from 1965 to 2021. *Source*: Google N-gram.

The National Federation of (ex)-Patients in Psychiatry (*Fédération Nationale des Associations d'(ex) Patients en Psychiatrie*) joined the effort, alongside a range of psychiatric professional organizations. Doctor Mailhol from the Croix Marine told me, "It was clear to everyone that the future was in the disability system, and so we joined with UNAFAM." He admitted that, "Up until a few years before, we heard at our conferences, 'We're not going to dump our patients on the disability system!' But you don't hear that anymore. . . . We realize now that being recognized as handicapped doesn't take something away from the *malade*, it brings them something . . . It doesn't block us from providing care." Whether public psychiatrists had a real change of heart or were acceding to a changed reality, they were largely on board.[36]

In response to the white paper, the government commissioned a report on "people handicapped as a result of psychic troubles." The report repeated what UNAFAM had claimed: While some people with mental disorders were being housed in institutions for the elderly and people with autism or cranial trauma, "until now these programs have not, or very little, benefited people handicapped by mental illness." It concluded, "The recognition of handicap is a fundamental right of a person"[37] that had been denied to people with mental disorders.

## DISABILITY RIGHTS AND REVOLUTIONS

All this talk of a recognition of handicap being a fundamental right seems a bit excessive if we are just talking about funding for nursing homes rather than hospitals. But I suggest we take UNAFAM literally: Parents like Madame Le Gal really were trying to create a whole new population that fused two bureaucratic kinds, that of "*malade*" and "disabled." It was crucial that disability offered what Neil Gong refers to as a new "social prognosis," a novel "predict[ion]" of "the kind of life a person can expect to live"[38] compared to that of someone with a mental illness.

This new social prognosis rested on a radical shift in the meaning of "disability" writ large. In the 1990s, the French state faced a steady pileup of resolutions and directives from the European Union and the United Nations demanding, as the 1996 European Social Charter put it, that signatories "guarantee to disabled persons . . . the effective exercise of rights to autonomy, social integration, and participation in the life of the community."[39] When it came to these new mandates, France was, as an article in *Le Monde* put it, "Not the most advanced."[40] In 2000, the National Commission on the Rights of Man delivered a withering assessment that disability in France was a "major cause of exclusion" because of "discrimination in employment, education, access to transports, and even respect of human dignity."[41] Only 2 percent of disabled adolescents, they reported, were integrated into mainstream schools. And all that was before 2003, when over ten thousand vulnerable French people died in a summer heatwave. Many of these aged or disabled people were in institutions that failed to protect them. There were echoes of the Massacre of the Mad of World War II: a national catastrophe that shook an outdated system of social welfare to its core.

It was a propitious time for reform of the disability system because President Jacques Chirac had a special interest in it. He was prime minister in 1975 when the first major law on disability was passed. He was thus not kidding when he declared, in a 2002 speech at a national conference organized by associations for disabled people, "For a long time, the combat that has brought you here has also been mine."[42] He declared that disability would be one of three grand national causes for his term, which would involve the "mobilization of everyone" to support a "project of integration and personal success." Subsequently, he proposed a law that would provide a host of new benefits to help "compensate" individuals for their disabilities. The Secretary for Disabled People explained the new logic vis-à-vis the 1975 law: "Before, we privileged protection and care in specialized structures. . . . Now, we are insisting on individual life projects and the promotion of accompanied autonomy."[43]

This new discourse centered on rights, autonomy, and integration came from more than just government officials repackaging a new international narrative. They also faced significant lobbying. The 1975 law conferred care for people with disabilities onto private associations; this meant that, by the turn of the century, there were huge and well-financed organizations ready to demand change.[44] In 2002, the organization representing parents of children with developmental disabilities dropped off a petition with 200,000 signatures demanding an "emergency plan for disabled people" at the Elysée Palace.[45] The Association of Paralyzed People of France was even more militant. In 2003, *Le Figaro* reported that the association, "strong with its 34,000 members, 30,000 volunteers, and hundreds of thousands of donors, decided to grab peoples' attention . . . by organizing sensational actions in eighty-four French cities." They "covered up cars parked in spots reserved for disabled people"—I am told this is a distinctively French form of protest that involves enveloping a car in a tarp and adding an angry note—and "blockades of buses by human chains." The group "denounced the 'injustice of not being able to circulate freely.' "[46] Even for a government used to handling a restive population, these actions hit home. Rewrites of Chirac's original bill strengthened requirements for accessibility and integration.

If the lead-up to what would ultimately become the Law for the Equality of Chances, Participation, and Citizenship of Disabled Persons of 2005 was contentious, one aspect of it was not. In his 2002 speech, Chirac mentioned almost in a sidenote, "It is evident that too many people—those with multiple handicaps, cranial trauma, and psychic handicaps—are today without a solution."[47] Some interviewees believed Chirac had a soft spot for mental illness because his daughter suffered from anorexia and had been hospitalized in psychiatry. In any case, for UNAFAM, this small reference had enormous implications. Their press release after the speech declared that they had "fought for years for the recognition of psychic handicap. We welcome this presidential declaration with great satisfaction."[48] In truth, UNAFAM kept a low profile in the whole debate.[49] But it had hitched its wagon to a conception of disability that had radically changed.

By vote of the National Assembly, the population that UNAFAM had fought to "make exist" came into official being on February 11, 2005. The law came with hundreds of millions of euros in financing (paid for savings from the elimination of a national holiday, the Monday of Pentecost), new benefits, and an entirely novel administrative apparatus for determining eligibility for disability benefits, the Departmental Home for People with Disabilities. Unlike its 1975 precursor, the law also gave a definition for disability:

> It constitutes a disability . . . any limitation of activity or restriction of participation in life in society . . . experienced by a person as a result of a substantial, durable, or definitive alteration of one or multiple physical, sensorial, mental, cognitive, or psychic functions, from a poly-handicap, or an invalidating health problem.[50]

Parents, psychiatrists, and policymakers all understood that, from this point on, both responses to the chronic condition of people with severe mental disorders and the promotion of their autonomy would be tied to their reclassification as having an "alteration of . . . psychic functions."

Don't lose sight of the stakes here. Gaining access to the disability system meant getting a share of services for housing, employment, and aid in daily life that were rapidly expanding, just as psychiatric hospitals were shrinking. In recognition of how much was riding on this new classification, in 2005, UNAFAM changed its name: the National Union of Friends and Families of the Mentally Ill became the National Union of Friends and Families of Psychically Ill/Handicapped Persons.

## SPECIALLY HANDICAPPED

Madame Coulon once worked as a teacher, but when her son fell sick with schizophrenia, extracting what he needed from his *secteur* became her consuming occupation. Once she realized that psychiatrists could give him medication but not accompany him through the challenges of living with a chronic illness, her occupation became changing the whole system. I already quoted Coulon at the start of part II, but because she repeated the same phrases to describe the law of 2005, I will repeat them here as well: "Entering the field of disability was a long combat, but it was a revolution. Even some psychiatrists understand that it was an enormous turning point." But no one knows better than Coulon that, when your revolution consists of a single modifier in a sentence defining disability, it leaves a lot of work undone. She ticked off her responsibilities: head of the commission that runs her department's Disability Office, representative for families in working groups on psychic handicap at the National Fund for Solidarity for Autonomy, and vice president for UNAFAM in charge of lobbying the government around implementation of the law of 2005. A revolutionary, indeed.

Advocates often talked about people with psychic handicap as a population that existed out there, even if the state had failed to recognize them. From a sociological perspective, though, people like Coulon were contributing to a process by which a new classification and the bureaucratic kind it applied to would, in the words of Ian Hacking, "emerge hand in hand."[51] The process was fraught with contradictions, however. The way reformers fleshed out what they meant by "psychic handicap" would ultimately pose challenges for the bureaucrats who were supposed to make the dual identity of *malade*/disabled real.

We can see this by walking through the three features of psychic handicap identified in the 2001 white paper published by UNAFAM and its allies: first, "intellectual capacities that can remain intact;" second, a "variability of manifestations . . . that demand constant adjustments" in responses to them; and third, a "continuing importance of medical care."[52] You should note an irony here: Activists were defining "psychic handicap" via the same arguments psychiatrists once used to argue that mental illnesses were *not* disabilities.

Let's start with the first criterion. "Psychic handicap" was, from the start, defined against something else: "mental handicaps," the term that post-1975 had come to describe people with developmental or intellectual disabilities like Down syndrome. UNAFAM's president at the time supposedly sat down with the head of UNAPEI, the association for mental handicaps, and settled on the terminology. As he recounted, "We're talking about people with mental illness, but 'mental handicap' was already taken, so we had to find another word, to distinguish our population. Why 'psychic'? 'Mental' is from Latin—spirit, soul, everything in the head, that's not physical. So we just took the word 'spirit' with a Greek root, 'psychic.' We're lucky that in French there are two words for the same object with different roots."[53]

Defining the category of "psychic handicap" in opposition to "mental handicap" had major implications for the institutions that would care for them, accompany them, and promote their autonomy. Recall that a core concern of groups like UNAFAM was that, even as spots opened up in the disability system in the 1990s, they weren't dedicated to people with psychic handicaps (because those people didn't exist administratively). After 2005, there was a quick way to rectify this. With increasing prenatal testing, over two-thirds of children with Down syndrome in France are aborted. This left associations for the developmentally disabled with more and more open spaces in supported housing, protected workshops, or services that organize daily activities. To the government officials I talked to, there was a great opportunity to fill underused spots with underserved people. A person from the municipal government in Paris working on the disability dossier told me, "We have a system that is so specialized and rigid. But you can be multiple things at once! You can be a blind person with mental troubles, an aging person with a handicap who gets Alzheimer's. I'd like to see the field of mental handicap open up a bit to psychic handicap. Do we really need to be so compartmentalized?"

For interlocutors like Mesdames Coulon and Le Gal, the answer was a resounding yes. On this point, Madame Coulon gave me a keen lecture on the functioning of the French state: "The difference is crucial, because everything in France depends on plans which target specific populations. So we have to put the specificity up front; otherwise, we wind up in the blind spot of public policies." In my interview with Madame Le Gal, I noted that many people with conditions like schizophrenia lived with impaired cognition, and the aid they might receive in managing daily life might look similar to those for people with intellectual disabilities.[54] She bristled:

> [Psychic handicap] is an evolving handicap, [intellectual] deficiency much less. There are professionals who don't understand this, and create life projects [for people with psychic handicaps] that are just "the person will go to the movies, we will bring them." That's mental handicap: "we try to do things with people. No worries, but it's not going to change." Psychic handicap is totally different. All the other forms we know—mental, sensory, physical—are stable or degenerative . . . Psychic handicap, it's tied to an illness . . . which fluctuates . . . it can get better!

Her distinction brings us to the second feature activists identified, which was the "need for constant adjustments." The French state largely concurs that developmental disabilities are "stable, durable, and irreversible."[55] This coincides with a bureaucratic process of identifying disabilities that privileges limitations that are stable and objectively identifiable via an IQ scale or a hearing test. My observations in the Disability Office will show, in contrast, that the precise thing that made psychic handicaps hopeful—their capacity to fluctuate—meant that existing models for identifying them didn't really apply.

The final part of the definition UNAFAM gave for this population was that "medical care remains important." This seems obvious, but it stood out in a disability system that was in some sense "created against the hospital, against the health system," as the interministerial delegate for disability put it in an interview with me. The disability rights activists behind the 2005 law were drawing on a discourse that redefined "disability" not as a medical flaw of a person but a problem of a maladapted environment. They wanted compensation, not cures.

There's an interesting road not taken here: that followed by the parents of autistic children. French child psychiatrists long presented autism as a rare form of infantile psychosis needing psychoanalytically inspired interventions. Parents of autistic children began agitating in the 1990s for a "right to an educational, not psychoanalytic response."[56] In 1996, the government accepted the discourse that France was behind in adopting cutting-edge behavioral autism therapies and defined "autism" as a "handicap" and, by fiat, *not* an illness.[57] Some psychiatrists I spoke to were genuinely concerned that the movement would at some point reach "their" *malades*, for whom responsibility would pass entirely to the disability system.[58]

Madame Coulon insisted that psychiatrists really did not need to be so worried: "The associations for the families of people with autism are very combative and reject, violently, the involvement of their loved ones with psychiatry. So they talk about 'cognitive handicap.' They don't want to talk about 'psychic' because it's tied to 'psychiatry,' which they obstinately refuse. We don't refuse psychiatry, we know our loved ones need psychiatric care of quality and continuity, long-term. We're not hostile. It's the big difference." Part of the reason why the 2005 law aroused so little resistance from psychiatrists was precisely the fact that recognizing psychic handicap did not constitute a direct confrontation with medical power.[59] But compensation for handicap and treatment for chronicity, you'll see in the next chapter, were not always easy to put into place at the same time.

There's one other specificity of psychic handicap that will come up in chapter 4. The 2002 government report that followed UNAFAM's call to recognize psychic handicap observed that these individuals would have an "incapacity to decide and to act" tied to a limited self-awareness of their condition, often meaning that "the person cannot themselves defend their rights."[60] In discussions of the 2005 law in the National Assembly, one deputy raised a concern: "The law is not taking account of the difficulties specific to mentally ill persons with respect to their incapacity. . . . as a result of their illness . . . to formulate a life project."[61] That nothing was incorporated into the law about this partly reflects UNAFAM's weak lobbying power. But it also highlights that incorporating this specificity of psychic handicap was fundamentally incompatible with the vision of the new bureaucratic kind of disabled person. In a system founded on cooperation and aiming toward autonomy, forcing people to accept services is antithetical.[62]

The point here, again, is duality. In the older system, *malade* and handicap were mutually exclusive. But under the new regime, people with conditions like schizophrenia were to be both mentally ill and psychically handicapped, receiving care for their symptoms and compensation for their challenges in daily life. On a deeper level, this meant that they would be served by a medical system traditionally centered on managing chronicity (sometimes involuntarily) and a disability system focused on enhancing autonomy. In a practical sense, each system would have to address its side of the *malade*/disabled bureaucratic divide, without negating the other.

## CONCLUSION: SEEING DOUBLE LIKE A STATE

The very particular story of psychic handicap speaks to a much more general challenge in contemporary social policy.[63] The modern state has "many hands"[64] that intervene in proliferating moments across our lives. Poor and marginalized people in particular must engage with a multiplicity of state agencies to meet their needs. They might face intrusions from child welfare workers, parole officers, or eligibility investigators all at once.[65] But nearly all of us cumulate multiple officially recognized identities. We are taxpayers, licensed drivers, Social Security recipients, and green-card holders, not to mention bearers of all the variables—race, gender, ethnicity—registered by the US census.

A less-remarked trend is that many classificatory designations that were once irreconcilable are now overlapping. In the United States, it used to be that you could not be identified as "gay" by the state and be of the bureaucratic kind "soldier." Now you can be both. People once called "mentally retarded" and placed in specialized institutions can now receive support on the basis of "disability" *and* access mainstream educational services as "students."[66] The story of *malade* and disabled represents a similar case of duality replacing mutual exclusion.

In many cases, this cumulation and combination of categories is not problematic. Sometimes a particular designation by the state carries with it very limited expectations of the person so labeled. Qualifying for Social Security, for example, requires little more than an administrative check that a person is relatively old and has paid into the system. The focus of part II, however, is on categories that are not just administrative labels but bureaucratic kinds. They entail not just the presence of a simple set of attributes (like age or income) but the expectation of a certain, consistent way of engaging with the state. Traditionally in France, to be *malade* is to passively accept the aid of a medical system in a never-ending battle against chronicity; after 2005, to be disabled is to advocate for self-inclusion in programs designed to enhance autonomy. These categories then shape professional interventions to alter them reciprocally.

Of course, "seeing like a state" entails what political scientist James Scott calls a "heroic simplification" of complex people into reductive typologies.[67] But while scholars have mostly considered the push and pull between people and categories—the way people do or don't conform to how states see them—we have more rarely considered what happens when multiple agencies are seeing the same people in a different way. What happens when the state sees double? Pierre Bourdieu suggested that the state's capacity to rework individual classifications into a coherent system that serves its own ends is substantial. The state is able to ensure both logical conformity, or "the same categories of thought, of perception . . . of reality," and moral conformity, "agreement on a certain number of values."[68]

This chapter has shown that the idea that the same *malades* can be mentally ill and psychically handicapped has achieved a kind of moral conformity thanks to an ascendant vision of the citizen as an increasingly independent actor. As Nicolas Marquis observed, in France, "beyond the conflicts of theories, of positions . . . [autonomy] seems to get everyone to agree. No one is against promoting the autonomy of the patients, and certainly not the patients themselves, at least in theory."[69] In sharp contrast to their resistance to the inclusion of "their" *malades* in the 1975 law consolidating France's disability system, public psychiatrists largely acquiesced to the integration of psychic handicap in the 2005 reform. The president of France himself concurred with parents that recognition of disability was an essential right, one on which their future independence and self-direction hinged.

But what about logical conformity? Sociologists Guillermina Altomonte and Adrianna Bagnall argue that autonomy is not something that can be granted by fiat, but has to "get done" in practice.[70] In this case, it requires that the state both see double and act double on the same population, to treat and to accompany, without one undoing the other. Yet the very people advocating for lumping people with mental illness into the broader category of disability also insisted on all sorts of qualifiers that would split them from it. Unlike autistic people, they needed an ongoing relationship with psychiatry. Unlike those in wheelchairs, their limitations would fluctuate over time (much like, in fact, a chronic illness). Unlike people with Down syndrome, their intellects would be preserved (enough, in fact, that they might not want to be lumped in with people with Down syndrome at all). Advocates wanted the state to see double but also to see differently.

In French government documents, there are all sorts of new consultant-speak and bureaucrat-ese floating around to explain the collaboration that implementing these dual human categories would entail. In this new system of "articulation," professionals would move beyond the "silos" of "the hospital, the social, and the [disability system]"[71] in order to favor the "fluidity of the trajectory of life in search of coordination, continuity, and coherence between different domains of accompaniment."[72] As we will see in chapter 4, however, the transition between categories was anything but smooth.

*Chapter Four*

# DESIGNATING DISABILITY, ENABLING INDEPENDENCE

In a bottom-floor conference room of a government building in Paris, the Commission for Rights and Autonomy of Disabled Persons is holding the French state's feet to the fire. These commissions have the ultimate responsibility in each French department for granting a host of benefits for people with disabilities, ranging from a minimum monthly income to support in looking for employment, to authorization to enter a residential institution. Membership in the commission is evenly divided between government officials, unions and service providers, and associations representing disabled people. You don't have to stay for much of one of the weekly meetings to see who's in charge. "We're the ones dominating the [commission]," Madame Coulon, from the association for the parents of people with mental illness (UNAFAM), tells me.

This week, the commission is discussing a forty-four-year-old man from Cameroon who had previously received the Allocation for Handicapped Adults (*Allocation aux adultes handicapés*, hereafter "Allocation") because of an injury to his leg as a child. The commission had summoned a member of the professional evaluation team of the Departmental Home for Disabled Persons (*Maison Départementale des personnes handicapées*, or "Disability Office"), which occupies the rest of the building and makes recommendations to the commission. They want the evaluator to explain why she did not renew his allocation, thus throwing him into a labor market that was, as of 2016, not exactly flourishing. The evaluator defends her assessment by explaining what she saw when she summoned him for an interview: "When he arrived, he was walking without a cane. He told me he took public transport to get here."

Her presentation is cut short by the representative of the association for the blind: "You can't say he's not disabled because he took public transport. He probably made herculean efforts to get here—because you insisted he come."

A woman representing deaf people starts signing furiously. Her translator declares, "You haven't said anything about his situation improving. How are you taking his rights away like this?"

The director of an association managing professional retraining for people with disabilities adds, "This [discussion] is pure theory. We need to see him."

At the next week's meeting, the man is invited to plead his case. He limps in and sits down at the head of the tables around which the members of the commission are arrayed. The head of the commission, an elected official from a poor district of Paris, asks him to explain his situation. He recounts that he initially came from Senegal to get an operation on his leg, and stayed when he found work as a window washer. "My boss made some adaptations for me, at first, but then he fired me," he confesses, looking downcast.

The head of the commission sounds sympathetic: "You want to work, don't you?" He replies yes. The man opens a manila envelope and pulls out some X-rays.

Another association representative declares from her wheelchair, "We don't need to see that. We know the challenges disabled workers face."

When he leaves, the representative of an organization of parents of disabled students announces, "We need to help him find work where he can sit. He says his employer was making accommodations, but I bet his coworkers mistreated him because of his impairment."

The representative of the association for the deaf jumps back in, "Let's give him a retraining."

A representative from the central state—there to guard the government's purse strings—replies half-heartedly, "He can't even read or write."

The representative from UNAFAM shoots back, "Then his project of professional reintegration is going to take time. We should give him the

Allocation to help him through the process." The commission overrules the recommendation of the Disability Office evaluator. They award the Allocation for five years, alongside a costly professional retraining to help the man prepare for the (seated) employment of his choice.

That representative from UNAFAM who demanded the reinstatement of the Allocation is Monsieur Vautrin. When I interviewed him in early 2016, he was waiting for his forty-five-year-old son with schizophrenia to leave the hospital, where he has been for the last eight months. "He's going to go home and be all alone," he stated, mournfully. "The Clinic is sick of him, they'll give him medication, but we're going to need to find him something else to accompany him, give him a social life, help him around the house." That "something else" is likely to pass through the commission. As he explained to me, "Mental illness, that has existed for two thousand years. But now we have the recognition of this particularity, 'psychic handicap.' It allows us to put them in a box, next to the others." Those others are long-recognized physical, sensory, or mental [intellectual or developmental] disabilities. He was well-positioned to sit on the commission and represent people with psychic handicaps, he elaborated, because after a long career as an engineer for public works projects, "I know how to be a needle to prick them [the state] in the buttocks." In short, he's on the commission to make sure that people like his son get access to disability benefits—just like the others.

The 2005 Law for the Equality of Chances, Participation, and Citizenship of Disabled Persons created the Departmental Homes for Disabled Persons and the commissions that oversee them to "put into action, from a single place, the trajectory of a disabled person toward the compensation of his loss of autonomy."[1] During the lead-up to the legislation, associations for people with disabilities demanded that the old, impersonal bureaucracy of disability determinations be razed and replaced with one that, one government official explained, offered a "warm welcome, ready to listen." And indeed, downstairs, in the meeting room of the commission, this new mandate seemed to be prevailing. Associations representing disabled people forced government officials to listen patiently to tales of how denials of benefits harmed disabled peoples' ability to survive, work, and achieve their dreams.

There was just one problem. At the departmental commission meetings, parents from UNAFAM were there in force; their children were not.

I never once see someone with schizophrenia come in to argue their case. Many are still receiving benefits; in general, only appeals against Disability Office determinations go to the commission. But in a deeper sense, if the new bureaucratic kind administered by the disability system was people who would drive and defend their own applications, it seems ill-adapted to *malades*, for whom a refusal to recognize or accept what they needed was assumed. This is one reason that, on the top floor, among Disability Office administrators, there was a bit more skepticism.

It's probably a good sign that Arthur is the bureaucrat in charge. A recent graduate of France's ultra-prestigious *École Nationale d'Administration*, he is one of what Pierre Bourdieu calls the "state nobility." These elites, the theorist writes, are bearers of "state magic": They can create a "conformity between words and things, between discourse and reality"[2]—between, you might say, the aspirations of the 2005 law to create a new kind of disabled person and the benefits and services that conjure them into being. Arthur himself is unsure of his mystical powers. For one thing, the year we speak, in 2015, the Disability Office in Paris is processing applications from 40,000 people requesting 100,000 benefits.[3] "It's a massive activity that doesn't make it easy to be precise," he tells me. But that's exactly the vision: to give support that is calibrated to a person's needs and life project. Some of his lieutenants are even less sanguine: "We are trying to make lace through an industrial process." (This is my best literal translation from the French). "We have made a gas factory," another tells me. (I look it up when I get home: It means "convoluted").[4]

Arthur ticks off some of the reasons why psychic handicap is a psychic headache.[5] First, he notes, "There's the frontier with medical care. Compensation is not the same thing as care," but in his view, people with psychic handicaps don't seem to do well if they're not already stabilized effectively by the *secteurs* (which, as we saw in part I, is not a given). Then, he adds, "There's the variability of the troubles" created by mental illness. This is a problem because "almost all our benefits were conceptualized for physical or sensorial disabilities," for which his team could objectively identify the limitations people faced and grant a fixed level of assistance. Finally, and most problematically, "in our approach, the person is supposed to define their life project, and we're supposed to take that into account." But, as any psychiatrist will tell you, one potential symptom of schizophrenia is denying that you have schizophrenia.[6] These contradictions capture why the conditions the Disability Office was supposed to classify as "psychic handicaps" frequently appeared more "psychic" and less "handicap."

I will focus on two sets of benefits: first, those geared toward the positive autonomy and self-reliance offered by paid employment, and second, those that get people out of the autonomy-destroying situation of extended hospitalization. As a team of French researchers wrote (channeling Simone de Beauvoir), "One is not born psychically handicapped, but one becomes one . . . [through] recognition by institutions,"[7] and Disability Office determinations were essential for making exist the population that activists had envisioned. In the daily work of evaluators, psychic handicap came to seem like a bureaucratically split personality, an illogical and contradictory amalgam that carried mutually exclusive expectations for the people to whom the label was applied. Yet these barriers to the state project of reclassifying *malades* as "disabled" did not simply block reform. The way that *malades* defied the neat categories of the health and disability systems ultimately contributed to a hybridization of these separate arms of the French welfare state.

## DIAGNOSING DESERVINGNESS

Anne sits between the enthusiasm for addressing psychic handicap downstairs at the commission and the frustration of the administrators upstairs. This is literally true. She runs the Pluri-Professional Team for Professional Insertion. They meet twice a week on the third floor of the five-story Disability Office to discuss cases where a person has requested one of a basket of benefits that help a disabled person find and keep employment—and, if they can't, give them the Allocation. She's also in between insofar as Arthur, on the top floor, is her boss and Monsieur Vautrin, UNAFAM's representative on the commission downstairs, is her dad. "We're a family business" she laughs. She combines the activist commitment you might expect from someone whose brother has been hospitalized dozens of times with a dedication to the Disability Office's bureaucratic mission: "We're not the police and we're not here to moralize. We're here to open up rights and respond to a disability."

While much of this chapter will focus on frictions and tensions, a lot of what Anne's team did was rote. This was particularly the case when the team confronted demands for the Allocation sent to them by the *secteurs*.

In theory, one big change after 2005 compared to the disability system that had been legislated into existence in 1975, when people with mental illness began receiving the Allocation in large numbers, is that this determination is no longer supposed to be based purely on a diagnosis. As a state official told the evaluation team during a training at the Disability Office I attended, "We [evaluators] are supposed to position ourselves not on the diagnosis, or even the severity of the diagnosis, but the repercussions in the life of the person, the limitations of activity and participation of that person." Moving beyond diagnosis was also about promoting autonomy: supporting people in their individuality rather than as part of a broad, leveling category (say, "*malade*"). Madame Coutel, involved both in her department's commission and state working groups, reminded me, "If you put ten people with schizophrenia around a table, you're going to have ten different situations, ten difficulties, ten capacities. These illnesses have a different impact from one person to another in terms of cognitive ability, social ability. A diagnosis alone doesn't permit us to evaluate someone's need."

In practice, though, a medical certificate from a *secteur* psychiatrist confirming a serious illness provided a tempting shortcut. This was the case for a thirty-eight-year-old woman who migrated to France as a teenager. Anne read her life project: "I would like to have stable employment, to marry, and to have children."

"She's running out of time for the children," Laura, a Disability Office psychologist, remarks.

That wasn't her only problem. The doctor reads from her medical certificate: "She was hospitalized in 2011 for schizo-affective disorder. She's now stabilized on an injectable antipsychotic."

"That's good!" Anne remarks.

"Yes, but she has a chronic delirium. She hasn't worked in years."

"She's had little short-term contracts here and there," Marie, a psychologist from Pôle Emploi, the public employment agency, clarifies. "But she always gets fired for persistent absenteeism. When we last saw her, she wanted to work at a day care which seemed . . . not adapted."

"Now she's saying she is hoping to start a business selling specialized 'hair products,'" the generalist notes, her emphasis on "specialized hair products" making a veiled illusion to the woman's African origins.

The rest of her medical certificate is sparse. In nearly all the questions, beyond the one describing her diagnosis, her psychiatrist had written "nothing of note." But the basics of her diagnosis and treatment were enough.

"Let's give her the Allocation for five years," Anne declares. "This is not something that's going to improve." She turns to me and laughs, "It's better for her . . . Maybe not for the state!"

This rapid decision to grant an Allocation was in keeping with what the social workers in the *secteur* perceived happening: as Clemence, at the Clinic, told me, "We have very few refusals, because we don't demand the Allocation for nothing. Our schizophrenics, I think they all have it [the Allocation]." The case above speaks to the power of the construction of *malades* as needing permanent and protective solidarity, even in the branches of the state removed from places where that construction originated.

It also reveals that *malade* is a moral category as well as a medical one. In the United States, people with mental illness receiving Social Security benefits have been the subject of endless attempts to purge them from the rolls as malingering and undeserving.[8] Yet when I raised this concern with my interviewees, they were quick to push back on the idea that an Allocation was a barrier to employment. Marie, the psychologist from the employment agency, told me, "Someone who has no resources, who's sleeping in the street, who doesn't know where they're going to eat—they're not going to have an easy insertion into the labor market. The Allocation provides security in someone's trajectory [toward employment]. Maybe for other disabilities, it can be a barrier, but not for people with psychic handicaps." In the case above, schizophrenia and the heavy medication and hospitalization that came with it seemed to create a presumptive deservingness. In this case, it trumped all the potential judgments—say, of being a nonwhite immigrant surviving on benefits—that might have come into the discussion.

*Malade* was a bureaucratic kind strong enough to outweigh race and gender, which are otherwise more socially salient identities, in a way that other sources of disability did not. Consider the case of a fifty-three-year-old woman born in Egypt. She had previously received the Allocation during a diagnosis of breast cancer, from which she had fortunately recovered. She was asking for renewal based on serious arthritis. "She's also obese and has chronic knee pain," the generalist comments. "She's not going to work, this woman"—and she never had. Anne's team felt that, by the letter of the law, she qualified for the Allocation but decided to bring the case to the commission on the ground floor.[9]

The generalist's presentation to the commission starts with an impassive overview of her medical situation and difficulties in everyday life, but then she breaks character: "The regulatory texts are clear: the issue is whether she has a disability that presents a substantial barrier to employment. But even though she has a high school diploma, she's never worked. She has made children. That was her personal choice." She makes a point of noting that her husband, also an Egyptian migrant, is unemployed and that, after decades in France, they still speak Arabic at home.

The head of the commission, a municipal official, is a bit more cautious: "We need to be consistent. The issue here is what her impairments are and the barriers to employment they create."

"The barrier is that she's never tried to work!" explains the representative from an association for people with physical handicaps.

"How many children has she had?" asks another representative, which provokes some hushed muttering around the table.

Anne jumps in to defend their assessment: "In our criteria, we don't take into consideration someone's past employment history."

"We need some more objective elements to clarify this situation," the head of the commission concludes. They direct the team to bring the woman in for a face-to-face evaluation. Anne tells me she didn't speak enough French to litigate her case. They ultimately reject her request.

Decisions about the Allocation could break the other way, even for individuals with parallel social identities and medical conditions. One could imagine that a fifty-one-year-old woman, born in Guinea, might have a lot to talk about to the woman just described: the challenges of being a racial minority in France, raising a large family on a shoestring, or the lingering impacts of breast cancer in remission and chronic pain. In addition to a medical certificate citing these issues, this woman also had a document from a *secteur* Clinic noting that she suffered from a "reactional anxiety-depression" with a "light" medication treatment that had "no impact on her autonomy." It "posed no indication for a Disability Office application."

When she came to the commission to appeal the denial of her Allocation, she simply repeated, "My work is just too hard."

"That doesn't really tell us anything," a doctor noted, in interrogatory mode.

She simply repeated it: "It's too hard."

The commission wanted to know all about it. They asked her to walk them through her struggles to find work as a cleaner without papers (she only regularized her immigration status in 2013). It was a sad story: midnight metro trips across the city to keep short-term contracts and employers not willing to adapt her job to her disability.

When she left, the generalist declared, "I think given what we've seen, we should reverse our decision [to refuse the Allocation]." The commission concurred.

Anne whispered this to me: "We see this all the time—'the cleaning woman who did too much cleaning.' Her body is all used up."

There are two overarching points to make here. The first is that, for all the bewailing of the Disability Office as a "gas factory," its industrial process was making one form of lace quite reliably. Evaluators on what Josh Seim characterizes as a "welfare assembly line"[10] smoothly translated medical certificates from *secteur* psychiatrists into a basic income for *malades*. This didn't transform them into a new bureaucratic kind of "autonomous disabled person." Then again, people in all bureaucratic kinds need to eat, and for that, eight hundred euros a month is helpful. The second is that evaluators looked at *malades* with a singular optic. *Malades* avoided some of the racialized and gender judgments of worth applied to other applicants—a sign of the Bourdieusian "moral conformity" behind the idea that being classified as having a psychic handicap was a right too long denied to them. The category, however, posed a series of more practical contradictions. Let's look at them.

## OBJECTIFYING THE INVISIBLE, SUBJECTIFYING THE SKEPTICAL

Laura, a psychologist working with Anne on the team for professional insertion, faced a big problem in conjuring up a transformation of *malades* into people with a psychic handicap: They tended not to show up for the occasion.

It is a nearly universal fact of targeted welfare programs—the ones that require figuring out if a person belongs in this or that bureaucratic kind—that "in order to exercise their social rights citizens must disclose their private problems to officials."[11] This is doubly so in the reformed disability system in France, which requires that the state see both someone's objective limitations in daily life and their subjective desire for how to overcome them. When the paperwork doesn't provide these details, Laura steps in. She serves as an investigator of peoples' needs and advocate for meeting them: "I get people to tell me things they'd never tell their psychiatrist," she tells me proudly.

My first day sitting in, however, I can't assess whether this is really the case. Three people with appointments, three no-shows. "What kind of disability do you think they have?" I ask.

"Oh, psychic handicap, of course," she replies.

The next time I join her, we have a bit more luck. The first interviewee is a "young schizophrenic": twenty-three and just out of a three-week, involuntary hospitalization. According to his dossier, he's there because he (or perhaps his psychiatrist) is asking for professional training adapted to his illness and an Allocation to tide him over until he finds work. When he comes in, I see the tells of heavy medication: shuffling gait, drooping eyes, sagging shoulders (the demoralizing effects of being locked in a hospital for weeks could also be contributing). Laura opens with a question that—given the Disability Office's focus on life projects—seems like a bad sign: "Do you know why you are here today?"

"Not really," he replies gruffly.

"You're here so I can learn a little bit about the difficulties you feel, the things that bother you, the things that are blocking your return to social and professional activities."

"I feel isolated," he offers, without elaborating.

"Okay. Let's talk about that. What do you do beyond going to the Clinic?"

"I lift weights. But I stopped." The man offers no further explanation.

"How about any friends?" Laura asks, hopefully.

"No one."

Laura starts running through the standard list of activities the office uses to gauge autonomy: getting out of bed, getting dressed, managing public transport. Every response: "*Ça va*" ("It's okay"). Laura pivots to asking about his medical situation: "Why were you hospitalized?"

"Because the doctor misunderstood me," the man says mysteriously.

"Were you hearing things, seeing things?"

"No, he [the psychiatrist] just didn't like my behavior."

Laura leaves it there, and brings the conversation back to the present: "Are you feeling anxious?"

"Maybe."

"How about depressed?"

"A little."

"What about tired?" Laura presses.

"Possibly."

Laura betrays no exasperation but puts it bluntly: "It actually seems like you don't have a lot of complaints right now, so I am trying to figure out whether it makes more sense for you to go to a retraining to put you in the 'ordinary' milieu of work or if you should go to a protected workshop [sheltered employment for people with disabilities]."

"Oh, I'm already working twenty hours a week. I clean up at the Eiffel Tower," he clarifies.

"Wait, so are you looking to change to a protected workshop?" He clearly has no idea what it is, and she explains.

"Why not?" he replies. "I'd like a place that doesn't go too fast, with people like me."

"Okay, but you're going to need to ask your psychiatrist to send a new application specifying that," Laura cautions. "What's going to happen now is my team is going to evaluate your request [for a training and disability income], but because you're already working, we'll probably say no. You can always ask again if things change."

He leaves, and I ask Laura how she thinks it went. "Well, he's in denial. He hasn't accepted that he has an illness that is chronic, that will be there his whole life." She later shows me her write-up: "It is difficult for monsieur to evoke his difficulties. He has no complaints." She concludes paradoxically that he should be recognized as having a disability in the most severe category (because of his schizophrenia) but that the office should reject his (really his psychiatrist's) request for a retraining. Is that what he actually needed? In the end, it wasn't clear at all; maybe he needed to be in a protected workshop with people like him or a service for aid in daily life to get him out of the house. But to put those into a life project, he would need to know that they existed first.

These kinds of situations create frustration all around. At the Clinic, Doctor Kuorio told me, "It's a bit of a problem that I apply for my patients, they go to the Disability Office, and they do super well, they don't seem sick, and so afterward I have to call them [the Disability Office] and renegotiate, explain everything."

An ill-timed or poorly worded request could be as complex as an absent one. I sat in on one meeting of Anne's team where they considered a forty-four-year-old North African man. The generalist summarized the certificate written by a *secteur* psychiatrist: "Okay, this one is not going to be too complicated. He's a paranoid schizophrenic, psychotic, and not stabilized. He has apragmatism [a lack of initiative], disassociation, and incoherent ideas."

Laura observes, "Looking at the list of his medications, he's got to be a zombie."

"Right," Anne concurs, "His doctor is saying he has a hard time bathing, and he needs help in daily life." Based on his certificate, the individual appears to be a good candidate for one of the signature measures of the 2005 law, the Benefit for the Compensation of Handicap. It offers up to 12,000 euros a month to pay for help cooking or bathing, allowing individuals to live independently in the community. But this wasn't part of the individual's life project, as Laura notes: "Unfortunately, he crossed out the box asking if he wants the benefit. He wrote, instead, that he wants professional retraining."

The generalist is adamant: "No way. The certificate says he's in complete denial of his pathology. How can he be asking to work?"

"All we can do is say he still needs medical care, give him the [Allocation] for five years, reject everything else, and that's it," Anne concludes. The individual's independent decision *not* to request the benefit disqualified him from receiving something that could very well have helped him be more independent. One psychiatrist who had been trying to get more of his patients disability benefits opined on the situation: "When your disability is relational . . . and to access the system you have to know how to manage your relationship with others, it's like if you said to someone who doesn't have legs, 'To go to the Disability Office, you need to do a 110-meter hurdle course.' For [psychic handicaps], they've never thought about how to put in an access ramp."

There was another issue. Many Disability Office evaluators shared they saw themselves as having a calling of offering solidarity to disabled people. The central state is pretty insistent that they do so carefully and following precise rules. The Disability Offices, I have noted, are not supposed to diagnose illnesses or even pronounce which particular disability a person has. As one trainer told new evaluators in a session I attended, "What you are studying is not a handicap but its consequences for daily life." Evaluators fill out a forty-page form that asks about everything from the number of stairs in someone's dwelling to their ability to maintain sexual relationships, and the state is pushing to standardize these evaluations. One project declared a goal of ensuring the "the objectification . . . [of] the needs of the person . . . and responses to them."[12] Evaluators like Anne and Laura are living in a bureaucratic world that was far from an earlier era of what French sociologists called the "politics of the administrative window," in which petty potentates allocated benefits following their own whims and prejudices.[13]

But objectifying an invisible disability that touches a person's subjectivity was complicated.[14] In the example above, the psychiatrist had marked on the medical certificate that the person needed help bathing, getting dressed, and preparing food. Often, though, the team would open a medical certificate describing a person as having chronic schizophrenia, multiple hospitalizations, heavy treatment—and complete autonomy in daily life. The problem stemmed from a fundamental difficulty of trying to fit psychic handicaps into an evaluation system designed for physical or sensorial disabilities. Madame Coulon from UNAFAM noted: "The problem is that people [with psychiatric handicap] can physically get up, dress themselves, prepare food—but their illness means that sometimes they don't do it! And no one knows how to evaluate it." Indeed, as she pointed out, precisely because families—or, sometimes nurses from the *secteurs*—might be visiting every day to tell *malades* to brush their teeth and go shopping, it wasn't always clear what the disability system was supposed to be compensating for. Compared to applicants with other kinds of disabilities, the Disability Office rarely refused benefits for people because they were "too disabled" or "not disabled enough" for a given benefit; they concluded instead that they simply had "insufficient information" to decide (table 4.1).

TABLE 4.1
Reasons for rejection from at least one disability benefit

| | **Mental Disorder ($n$ = 59)** | **Other ($n$ = 147)** |
|---|---|---|
| Still in treatment | 39.0% (23) | 4.1% (6) |
| Insufficient evidence | 23.7% (14) | 19.0% (28) |
| Not in treatment | 13.6% (8) | 4.8% (7) |
| Administrative ineligibility (working, migration status) | 6.7% (4) | 22.4% (33) |
| Impairment insufficiently severe | 5.1% (3) | 35.4% (52) |
| Benefits as demotivating | 3.4% (2) | 4.8% (7) |
| Impairment too severe | 1.7% (1) | 6.8% (10) |

In the absence of objective elements about the person's autonomy in daily life, Anne's team leaned on medical criteria that, according to the 2005 law, were supposed to be independent from a determination of disability. Anne noted that this was particularly the case with depression, which in her view (much like those of a *secteur* psychiatrist) could mean anything from a serious illness to an understandable but transitory reaction to a difficult social situation.[15] She explained the contradiction: "If someone isn't getting care, too bad for them, but that doesn't mean we're not going to recognize a disability." She admitted, however, "To see if someone has an identifiable psychiatric pathology, we're still obligated to try to grab onto something: Have they received a treatment, consultations, a hospitalization?"

This logic was visible in the case of a fifty-four-year-old who worked as a painter until 2002, when he was physically attacked at work. The team had sent him for multiple professional retrainings, but his failures meant he was now applying for the Allocation. Marie, from the public employment agency, describes their interview: "This is a case of really serious depression. He presents well, he's friendly, but he's never going to get a job."

"From what you're saying, though, I'm not hearing anything that makes it sound like he gets the Allocation," Anne replies, noting that the certificate did not come from a psychiatrist.

"This is a severe depression. It's long running, it's not a psychosis, but it can be just as invalidating. He has no resources, this monsieur!" the psychologist protests.

"Then he should be in care," the generalist replies. "If someone has a certificate from a primary care physician that says 'severe depression' but there's no treatment, we should be pretty skeptical." The team denied the application.

In the process of making lace in an industrial process, evaluators sought objective, replicable methods to delineate disability. Yet this ultimately undermined their own independence. The medical certificates and treatment decisions of *secteur* psychiatrists—or their decision to provide neither—were only supposed to be one element of Disability Office evaluations. But without active self-advocacy from people with mental illness to provide needed information about their daily lives, they became determinative. In practice, if *secteur* (or, worse, private psychiatrists) were prescribing only a light antidepressant, they were also inadvertently prescribing a rejection for disability benefits.

## PROFESSIONAL PROJECTS AND WORKING DELUSIONS

Employment has a special and long-standing place in France's response to both disability and mental illness. In 1958, a government circular celebrated that "work has always been honored in psychiatric hospitals" on the theory that "whatever the perfection of biological treatments that can be dispensed, they are insufficient if *malades* remain unoccupied."[16] The topic remained important enough that the 2016 theme for France's "Week of Information on Mental Health" was "Mental Health and Work." Meanwhile, returning people to work has long been at the core of France's disability system. In 1957, France's Law on the Reclassification of Disabled Workers effectively made disabled *workers* exist before disabled *persons* (the latter taking until 1975).[17]

Nearly everyone I spoke to insisted that people with real psychic handicaps wanted to work, not live on benefits. The head of one specialized job search program expounded, "We can be working on a 'professional project' to help a person work at McDonald's, and people are so proud of their ability to be half-slaves . . . There's such pride in taking charge of one's life, being capable of something, of having a bank card. That really keeps people going." It is little surprise then that activists were eager for the people with psychic handicaps conjured up by the 2005 law to begin taking advantage of the disability system's measures for promoting employment. These were wide-ranging. The Disability Office can give people a protected legal status that allows employers to count them toward their quota of 6 percent of employees having a disability. It also orients applicants toward a special unit in the public employment agency and can pay for professional retraining. These programs are aimed to get people into the "ordinary milieu" of work. Those who meet criteria of a "reduced capacity" to work or needing "multiple social, medical, psychological, and educational supports"[18] could go to protected workshops (discussed in the next section).

Yet this commitment to getting people with a psychic handicap to work ran into difficulties when the expectation of a stable disability clashed with fluctuating symptoms. Laura invited me to attend an interview with a thirty-six-year-old woman. Her medical certificate from a *secteur* psychiatrist is grim: She has "serious personality troubles" that rendered her unable to manage the basics of daily life. When she comes in, I'm struck by how pale she is; as the certificate said, she rarely leaves the house.

"I'm not sure why I'm here," the woman admits.

"We brought you in because you asked for both the Allocation and professional retraining, and we wanted a bit more detail," Laura explains. She reviews her family history and then asks, "What can you tell me about schooling?" The woman gives a loud sigh. "Catastrophic?" Laura wonders.

The woman is already fighting back tears: "Yes . . . I didn't think I would cry, but I was in high school for six years, struggling, but because I wasn't creating problems, no one thought to contact my mother." The woman recounted her scattershot work history: a short stint in a day care that "went very badly;" training as a teacher's aide for which she "just couldn't do my homework;" a live-in nanny for a family that were such "lunatics" she "had to leave in the middle of the night." By 2013, she was unemployed and deeply depressed, stuck in a one-hundred-square-foot apartment with her boyfriend. The municipality cut off her paltry welfare payment because she failed to report his (miniscule) income from working in fast food. As Laura wrote in her notes, "Eviction is not far off."

Then the interview took a more positive turn. Laura queries, "How are you managing in daily life? Can you take care of everything on your own?"

"Not really," the woman confesses. "For a long time, I was only going out because the Clinic made me come. I've been on a merry-go-round of antidepressants. The social worker there prepared a dossier for the Disability Office, but I just . . . couldn't file it. But then I saw a brochure for a SAMSAH [*Service d'accompagnement médico-social pour adultes handicapés*, a team to help people with disabilities take care of shopping, file administrative papers, and socialize] at the Clinic, and I reached out. They force me to get out, just to meet for a coffee right by my building. They helped me apply here. I need to work. But the problem is, I can put on a face to get a job, but I can never keep it. I have tons of experience, but no diploma because every time I have to turn something in . . . I'm totally capable, but I just can't do it."

Laura takes a comforting tone: "Well, to start, we're going to see about getting you some income."

"I don't want the Allocation. It's work that interests me," the woman interjects.

Laura responds by listing some of the potential work programs the office can qualify her for. When she mentions a training specially adapted for people with disabilities, the woman lights up: "That's what I'm missing.

I couldn't sleep last night, I was so nervous, I almost didn't come. But that's what I want to do."

Laura cautions: "Okay, but we're going to have to do it carefully. [The state] only wants to pay for retraining you once, and it's expensive, so you're going to have to know what you want to do first. So we may send you to a specialized preorientation to work on your project before training." The woman has come to seem more and more energetic throughout the interview. She expresses her gratitude and leaves.

Afterward, I ask Laura what she thought. She replies, "When you see someone like that, and you know how much effort it was for them to get out of the house and come here, you have to act fast and take advantage of the moment." In her write up for the professional insertion team, she notes: "Madame is a very fragile woman in a critical social situation. She has grave personality troubles, marked by extreme anxiety, lack of initiative, and relational difficulties. . . . Nonetheless, it is essential to accompany her from here forward in a new project of reinsertion. We should seize on her current momentum in life and sudden increase in energy. She has capacities and is excited by the idea of a retraining. We should proceed step by step so that she feels secure. Nonetheless, in light of the elements observed in the interview, an Allocation would be justified in the meantime."

I query Laura about this last point: "Are you optimistic she'll get work?"

I am gutted by the reply: "No, she'll cry in her interview with the counselor [at the employment agency] and they'll write, 'Not ready, still needs medical care.'" The woman's limitations were hard to pin down—she wasn't blind or in a wheelchair—and yet these limitations were potentially overpowering.

One reason to be skeptical of her chances was the convolutions of France's disability system and the vagaries of mental illnesses. The former is organized as a long series of steps: A person with a psychic handicap applies to the Disability Office, which sends them for an evaluation by one of its external partners, then directs them to a specialized preorientation, at the end of which they will go to a center for professional retraining, where they validate a "project of professional insertion" and have a short "placement in situation" followed by an internship. After graduation, they make their way to a specialized wing of Pôle Emploi, the public employment agency.[19] Whether this was a particularly effective strategy for any person with disabilities is debatable, but in any case, the system had the "strict precondition" that someone would be "stabilized . . . at the medical level"[20] before the first step. Or, put another way, it assumed that a disability was not fluctuating, which was precisely one of the three features of "psychic handicap" as originally defined. As one psychiatrist who specialized in work evaluations admitted, "The notion of 'handicap' in psychiatry is not that interesting if it just means that it's stable and fixed, and if 'stabilization' means not being in an acute situation, then we can say it's a chronic illness . . . but that doesn't stop the fact that there's a great deal of fragility and an equilibrium that is by nature unstable."

Fluctuating preferences could be as problematic as fluctuating symptoms. A forty-two-year-old man with an undergraduate degree in applied math, whose schizophrenia had been stabilized for over a year, seems like a decent candidate. While the applicants at the Disability Office were disproportionately marginalized and racialized (including, unsurprisingly, those with psychic handicaps), the rich kid who suffers a psychotic break at the end of university was an archetype that occupied a significant place in the minds, if not the actual caseloads, of the team. In this particular case, though, Marie from Pôle Emploi gives a negative report: "His problem is that he can't decide his professional project. In 2011, he was working on a training to become an electrician, but he declared that it was 'too manual.' I don't know what do with him even though he has a degree!"

Anne wonders, "Okay, concretely, do you think he's going to find work in the ordinary milieu, or should he go to the protected sector?"

"Hah," the psychologist replies, "He didn't check that [protected workshop] on the application, and it's not worth talking to him about it."

The generalist doctor cuts in, "His psychiatrist is writing that he'd like to be a conflict mediator or monitor in a school. How is this even possible?"

Marie nods: "Back in 2011, we did the whole evaluation, but he was aggressive and demanding. He refused everything!"

Anne tries to salvage the conversation: "He could go to the preorientation, work on his project."

Marie is pessimistic: "He's not going to succeed. He won't finish anything, he'll come back to us, and we're going to have to start everything again." The team rejectes his request for retraining.

The overwhelmed specialists from Pôle Emploi, fighting an uphill battle against a febrile job market, often seemed unsympathetic to people with mental illness. But when I interviewed the representative, her frustration made a bit more sense. "Often, with psychic handicap, it's people with behavioral issues and they're immediately in conflict with everyone." She went on, "But we can't just go to employers and say, 'Please take this person because their psychiatrist thinks that will do them some good.' We have a network of businesses that are sensitive to handicap, and we don't want to lose them."

The damned-if-you-do-damned-if-you-don't justification for denials was to say that someone with a psychic handicap was either "still in treatment" or "not in treatment." I almost never saw these arguments made for other disabilities (table 4.1). A fifty-three-year-old woman who was currently receiving the Allocation applied for a retraining, after years of attempts to return her to her previous profession as a pharmacist had been unsuccessful. Marie observes: "I saw her at the agency a few weeks ago and she was clearly delirious, so that raised the question, is this someone who can work? When you see her, there's definitely a problem."

The generalist looks up: "The medical certificate says 'chronic psychosis' but not much else. She goes to the Clinic once a month and needs to work to 'occupy herself.' But the certificate is a year-and-a-half old, a lot can happen in that time in psy."

Marie adds, "We need to know what that psychiatrist is even talking about. The person I saw is not someone I can send to one of our partners [a center for professional retraining]."

Anne closes: "This one is easy. We tell her she's still in care. Write that she's not conscious of her situation and that's incompatible with retraining." After watching people with mental illnesses cycle in and out of work programs, evaluators wound up sending people back home—to the *secteurs*.

France ranks highly in international measures of efforts to get people with mental illness back to work.[21] And I saw lots of effort: many evaluations, many discussions, many programs and benefits. The end result was often to transform peoples' fervent desire for a paycheck into acceptance that it was incompatible with being a *malade*. As one psychologist explained to me, "People are coming forty-eight hours after they've been discharged [from the hospital] . . . [and] saying, 'I want to work.' That word has so much meaning. We are there to detect if they're just saying, 'I need to exist socially' or 'I need to get out of the house.'" Her ultimate goal, she said, often was "helping people realize that there are things that are just no longer possible. We operate based on the principle of reality. . . . We don't want to mobilize people toward something that they should be grieving." People in a fluctuating state and in denial were not really disabled but just sick. Protection from illness via psychiatric care trumped the pursuit of autonomy in the disability system.

## PROTECTED FROM EMPLOYMENT

For some people, the Disability Office was the last stop on their path to the administrative identity of "disabled": The evaluators determined that they could not work and so they started receiving an Allocation, or they established that they had a reduced mobility and gave a special parking permit. For others, however, it was just one step. The Disability Office could also provide a referral to France's vast network of private institutions serving people with disabilities—which themselves had a say in who they serve.[22] One such orientation could be to the protected sector of work, which is organized around Establishments of Service and Aide Through Work (*Établissement et service d'aide par le travail*, hereafter "protected workshops"). The sheltered employment they provide, which often segregates disabled people and entails subminimum wages, is easy to deride. In the United States in 2016, Barack Obama's administration was seeking to eliminated protect workshops wholesale just as I was doing my research.[23] But being in a protected workshop, many interviewees argued, offers more fulfillment than being stuck at home. In the world of protected workshops, we see how the features attributed to the bureaucratic kind of "psychic handicap"—variable limitations tied to motivation and interpersonal relations, a sharp (and morally loaded) distinction from intellectual disabilities, and a need for ongoing medical care—conspired to reinforce the medicalized identity of *malade* to which the disability system was supposed to be an alternative.

People with mental illnesses long had a foothold in a protected milieu, even if it was not built for them. A 1978 circular allowed protected workshops to take patients from psychiatric hospitals on the condition that "the reception of the mentally ill remains limited in order to . . . not distract from the role of [protected workshops], which remains above all the reception and employment of handicapped persons."[24] Those "handicapped persons," at the time, were people with developmental disabilities like Down syndrome. Some enterprising psychiatrists actually created their own protected workshops, conceptualizing work as therapy. An old-guard *secteur* psychiatrist told me, "Often, the project of readaptation of a patient can go through a period of protected work. . . . It gives people a little distance from the identity of 'mentally ill'. . . . Sometimes it works, sometimes it doesn't." The quote highlights that, while both the disability and *secteur* systems value work, this shared valorization rests on divergent understandings. "Work" in the disability system has always been about getting paid for being productive.[25] But psychiatrists were mostly trying to get their *malades* to engage in meaningful activities, any meaningful activity, as an extension of treatment.

I could see in my observations at the Clinic how protected workshops could figure into the kitchen-sink approach that the *secteur* took toward real *malades*. For a twenty-one-year-old man born in Thailand and who came to France as an adoptee at age seven, Patrice reports: "He's consulting after a hospitalization for psychotic troubles, with persistent audiovisual hallucinations and troubles with language and comprehension . . . He currently lives with his father, goes to sleep at 5:00 a.m., and spends his time playing PlayStation."

Doctor Delignon is worried about a young man stuck at home: "Let's get him into the day hospital and prepare him for a protected workshop. He should be doing regular activities. Is he at least getting the Allocation?"

"No, nothing," Patrice clarifies.

"Okay, let's get Sarah [the social worker] to check in at the Disability Office. We need to take charge of this person's autonomy," she closes.[26]

When I visited one long-standing protected workshop in Paris (organized by former *secteur* psychiatrists), I understood why Delignon thought even a patient with chronic hallucinations could have his autonomy managed in its direction. I visit the workshop floor and can't for the life of me figure out what the work being done actually is. The director tells me proudly, "We don't have any screening out of workers. If you can say, 'I want to work,' you can do it. Here we give everyone the same salary, not tied to their productivity. The work is less profitable, but who cares?"

But the state does care. As of my fieldwork in 2015, protected workshops employed 116,000 workers and constituted nearly one-third of its spending on disability.[27] The state covers the difference between the value of whatever goods and services a protected workshop produces and what the protected workshop pays its workers (usually a little over the value of the Allocation and around the minimum wage). The state would like for that price tag to go down.[28]

To do so, the state is turning to people like Pierre. He's gray haired and stocky, fitting my mental image of the shop-floor supervisor he, in fact, is. I interview him in his office, where a glass window overlooks a vast, neatly ordered space. There's one group sorting through piles of documents and another sitting at a bank of computers typing away. He tells me, "Here we're not a charity created by parents, and we're not run like the *club de pétanque* [a leisurely ball game] next door. We were created by an association of large businesses, and that's where I worked most of my career." He went on, "Over the years, I had the experience of integrating people with mental health problems into some of the places where I worked and eventually decided to change careers and come here." He adds "I've been touched in my family by mental illness, so it was important for me." I am not surprised.

He recounts two changes in the world of protected workshops, both of which appear favorable to people with psychic handicaps. The first is that the traditional populations served by protected workshops are disappearing. Literally: "Protected workshops were really created for intellectual deficiencies, problems like Down syndrome. . . . Now, with prenatal testing, there's a lot fewer being born." There was a more unambiguously-positive side of it: "Lots of people with intellectual disabilities, they are receiving a totally different accompaniment in childhood and now they're searching for a totally normal life"—and working in more ordinary contexts. After 2005, the state thus envisioned filling existing protected workshops with an expanding population of people with psychic handicaps.[29]

This change in population seemed, on the surface, to go hand in hand with the push to make protected workshops economically self-sustaining. Recall that the advocates who introduced the concept of psychic handicap insisted relentlessly on the preserved intellectual faculties of their population vis-à-vis those with mental handicaps. As Madame Le Gal told me, "To go into a protected workshop [designed for people with mental handicaps] and propose to someone who is intelligent [a person with a psychic handicap] to do some repetitive activity, to just make cardboard boxes, or put a cap on top of a bottle for six hours a day, talk to them like they're children, it's mistreatment. . . . We have people who did a doctorate in philosophy!" Pierre was less polemical and more practical: "Lots of simple tasks are being done in other countries at lower cost, so we've had to adapt and increase our skill level." This meant subcontracting to provide data entry, website updates, and processing of administrative documents such as payroll. His workers were increasingly going off-site: "We're deinstitutionalizing too . . . We want people to be as autonomous as possible." Net effect: "We're the most profitable protected workshop in Paris."

In visits and interviews at four different protected workshops, I still saw the perpetual difficulty of pushing people with psychic handicaps into institutions that were not constructed for them. Pierre evoked a familiar challenge: "The issue is that you have people whose problems are extremely variable. Today, I have a meeting at [hospital] about someone who has been with us nine years, who has worked directly at two large enterprises, a great office worker. But he's just coming out of a four-month hospitalization, and we have absolutely no idea if he can come back and, if so, how we'll support him. You have to reinvent everything every time." A psychologist who worked with an agency that helped people authorized to go to protected workshops find one, in accordance with their personal project (yes, even here there's a series of steps before actual employment), put it this way: "We have people who one day are capable of taking tons of initiative, tons of responsibilities, technical stuff . . . and another day they can't tie their shoes. That's the difficulty, it's not that they can't do it, but they just don't!" This creates all sorts of problems. People with "preserved intelligence" and with behavioral problems might be more productive, but they also need more surveillance. France's inflexible labor code makes it difficult for protected workshops to give part-time work. But full-time work, protected workshop operators were convinced, leads to breakdowns and unpredictable work stoppages when people fall (mentally) ill.

Pierre had settled on a revealing formula for making his protected workshop work for a population of people with psychic handicaps: defining them as something else. As he told me, "It's extremely simple: The difference between our protected workshop and one for people with intellectual disabilities is that our population is just *malades*. We don't talk about handicap here, just illness." If your template for disability is someone with Down syndrome—stable, amiable, and compliant, at least according to the archetype—and your institution is built around that, those smart, well-qualified people with schizophrenia aren't disabled, regardless of what the Disability Office says.

This had some concrete impacts. Pierre had two hundred people sent to him per year by the Disability Office for on average of nine open spots (the whole protected workshop had about eighty workers), so he could be choosy: "We have a rule that anyone here has to be followed by a *secteur* psychiatrist, not just so that they're under treatment but also that we know who to call if there's a problem and we can send them back to their Clinic if needed." While the idea of the 2005 reform was to create a new human kind partly detached from the medical system, in practice, "the person with a psychic handicap [is] also a patient,"[30] as one government report mentioned in passing.

At the Disability Office, I could see how the project to transform people with mental illness into workers with a psychic handicap broke down in much the same way with respect to protected workshops as with programs to get people into the regular labor market. The professional insertion team opened up a dossier from a thirty-three-year-old man, born in France, who wrote: "Project of work: florist; project of life: pride; project of personal life: connection."

Laura laughs, "I'm guessing this one is psy."

No doubt. His medical certificate from a *secteur* psychiatrist says that he has schizophrenia, suicide attempts at age fifteen and twenty-five, and multiple hospitalizations. An older medical certificate counseled against him working, and so the team had rejected a previous demand for professional retraining. Now, however, there's an update: "Fluctuating delirium but autonomous in daily life."

The generalist comments, "I guess this is better for the protected milieu?"

Anne replies, "Maybe. Let's bring him in for another evaluation. In the meantime, let's extend the Allocation by two years. The certificate is a few months old and he's probably already in rupture with treatment anyway."

The doctor nods her agreement, "Makes sense. It's not fair to throw him into the world of work if he's not ready."

In some ways, the doctor was just conceding to the harsh reality of France's labor market, in which the unemployment rate for people with disabilities is twice as high as the general rate.[31] But she was also recognizing a broader cultural division. France's generous sick leave system is based on, as one psychiatrist put it, "a strong cleavage between 'I am sick' and 'I'm going to work' that exists in the heads of everyone."[32] Once someone was perceived more as a *malade* than a disabled person, then they fell on the not-working part of the binary. As such, for *malades* with a persistent, if fluctuating, chronic illness, the disability system rarely said never. They endlessly declared, "Not yet."

## DEINSTITUTIONALIZATION, REINSTITUTIONALIZATION

Despite the lofty language of "integration" and "citizenship" in the 2005 law, the idea of finding an often permanent place in an institution still looms large in France. Recall that both parents and the central state turned to psychic handicap as a tool for dislodging a population of people with chronic illness stuck in psychiatric hospitals, which had created a vicious cycle whereby the absence of autonomy increased institutional dependency. The alternative "place" for some was in a residence of medicalized accommodation (*foyer d'accueil médicalisé* [FAM]) or home of specialized accommodation (*maison d'accueil spécialisée* [MAS]). These are effectively nursing homes, the latter with more intensive medical support than the former.

I heard again and again, from parents to psychiatrists, to ministry officials, that the heart of the problem was not that hospitals wanted to keep people for a long time—far from it—but that there were not enough places in these alternative institutions. Madame Le Gal, from the federation that wanted to provide those places, emphasized this point: "In France, there are between thirteen thousand and eighteen thousand people hospitalized full-time because they cannot find a place in the disability system. That's expensive! There's nothing left for them to do. There is no particular treatment for them, except what they're already taking. They're bored to death."

In the 1970s and 1980s, psychiatrists (with perhaps a lack of reflexivity about the psychiatric hospitals they were running) called these institutions "ghettoes" that constituted "apartheid" and "segregation." I decided to see for myself if this was true. I visited a FAM in a nondescript suburb of Paris (so nondescript that I missed it on my first two passes on a bus). The head of the eighty-bed establishment is a former psychiatric nurse, but he has stories that reinforce why loosening psychiatry's grip seemed, to many, so important:

> There are people who were at the hospital ten, twelve, twenty years. When we opened, we took someone who hadn't talked for a decade. In our establishment, we say hello to people when we see them. Even

> if they don't respond, we try to create a connection. This monsieur had a visit from his father every week, regularly. The father would talk to him alone and his son didn't respond. When the father would leave, he would say, "Goodbye my son, until next week." . . . He did the same at the FAM as at the hospital. But one day, the father heard his son respond, "Goodbye, papa." The father exclaimed, "He talked to me, he talked to me!" And the son told us, "No one used to listen to me. Here you do."

There was no question that this is a less restrictive place to live than any public hospital I visited. Residents have their own room with a private bathroom. There's a common room replete with flat-screen TVs, a Ping-Pong table, and a few arcade games, not to mention a theater, a room for aquatherapy, and a relaxation space with soft toys and music. All of this comes comparatively cheap. The director tells me, "The disability system costs two or three times less than the health system. Let's not kid ourselves. A hospital is 900 euros a day, I'm at 265."

At this point, even old-guard psychiatrists like Doctor Mailhol are behind the idea of stabilized chronic patients leaving hospitals for a FAM or MAS. Getting approval from the Disability Office really wasn't a barrier, either. I asked the director, Arthur, if I could observe the unit where they evaluated requests to go to residential institutions. He told me it wouldn't be very interesting, because they approved almost all of them. The problem, Arthur explained, was what came next. He explained, in characteristic frustration with the "gas factory" of which he is a foreman, "We are never sure if there's an institution that actually wants to take someone. . . . As you know, when we decide someone needs to go there, it means staying home [or a hospital] is not really appropriate. . . . So it's a bit annoying to orient them to establishments that are saturated, and we just say, 'Call them' and there are no places." His lieutenant in the unit for residential institutions told me that the city had 377 people, of whom 150 had a psychic handicap, who had been approved for an institution but hadn't found a place.

This transfer is so complicated because of underlying differences in the logic of France's health and disability systems. As we saw in part I, as public services, French *secteurs* have to serve anyone who asks for their aid, in addition to a segment of people who do not. The disability system, on the other hand, relies overwhelmingly on nonprofits.[33] They have a private prerogative to refuse individual applicants sent to them by the Disability Office. And many were built for people with cognitive or physical disabilities. Noted a ministry official, "Disability establishments are being confronted with a public that is new for them because people with psychic handicaps were not a disability public but a health public. If they have a list of people [applicants], we know they're going to look for someone who is not coming from psychiatry." Reorienting facilities to accept people with psychic handicaps meant, in practice, making them more like hospitals: training staff on managing behavioral crises, installing new infrastructures for dispensing medication, and retrofitting buildings (for example, by creating windows that are blocked from opening) to prevent suicide.

This slow conversion was unsurprisingly quite frustrating for the social workers in the *secteur* tasked with finding a place for a person occupying a scarce hospital bed. According to Sarah, the disability system was simply not realistic about the population they were dealing with. "We had one patient with a three-year hospitalization. He would collect cigarette butts and eat them and drink hand lotion. We found a place for him [in a FAM], but they sent him back to us saying, 'He wasn't willing to participate in group activities, he just wanted to eat cigarette butts.'" Now he was monopolizing a bed indefinitely—and contributing to the ministry's statistics about inadequate hospitalizations. Sarah sighed, "I spend a lot of time selling our patients, and they [institutions] say, 'We don't want people with behavioral troubles' and I'm like, 'That's the definition of our population.'" In one 2023 survey, over half of *secteurs* reported an average wait of over a year for getting a patient into a disability institution.[34]

Finger-pointing went both ways. Some people in the disability world felt that the health system was fabricating people ill-prepared for even the most halting steps toward independence. The head of the unit at the Disability Office for placing people in institutions told me:

> Look, in psychiatry, at the hospital, you're in your room, you wake up at a precise hour, you take your treatment, you have breakfast, and then you wait. Maybe once or twice a week you have an activity. . . . But the rest of the time, absolutely nothing happens. . . . So you're not at all ready to restart a social life, even in an establishment. . . . In the hospital, everything is organized for you . . . When you arrive in a FAM or MAS, you need to get yourself up, live collectively, activities in the

> morning and afternoon, and if you're not prepared, it's exhausting. So that creates behavioral troubles, frustration, anger, incomprehension, and so you go back to the hospital.[35]

*Malades* might not fit in the bureaucratic kind of "disabled person" if they show too much deviation from the population institutions imagine themselves serving: limited in autonomy, yes, but working toward having more, conscious of their limitations and compliant with institutional rules.

This lack of a fit between bureaucratic kinds and particular institutions structured political debates and reconfigured policy responses. I caught up with Madame Coulon, the tireless revolutionary from UNAFAM, toward the end of my fieldwork. As we sat down for coffee, she pulled out a copy of the country's third autism plan, which was backed by a new infusion of 205 million euros. "We've been much less demanding" than the other associations, she regretted, adding, "In the next presidential election, we're going to ask every presidential candidate what they're going to do about psychic handicaps, and insist on a plan with concrete actions and real funding." That might actually transform "person with psychic handicap" from a label into a real population.

But when I raised the issue of a lack of places with officials in the ministry and staff working on disability in the National Assembly, they all kept changing the subject back to autism. The prioritization of autism over psychic handicap (meaning, primarily, people with schizophrenia) was, as Madame Coulon suggested, partly reflective of successful lobbying that has convinced policymakers of a grievous "French delay" in responding to autism, of which "exile" to structures in Belgium is a scandalous symptom.[36] But there's a deeper reason why people with psychic handicaps waiting for a bed in a FAM or MAS could never provoke the same panic. In 2013, in response to legal pressures, the government commissioned a report on people who were "without a solution": They had been approved for an establishment by the Disability Office, but they had not found one. The report denounced that, for many people with developmental disabilities or autism, the result was a "brutal use of hospitalization . . . which doesn't resolve anything and results, finally, in the failure of staying a long time in a psychiatric hospital."[37]

As Madame Coulon was quick to point out, there were also many people with schizophrenia who fit this profile. She told me, "The authors of the report did not think that people with a psychic handicap were really among those who had 'zero solution.'" People with autism in a psychiatric hospital could be seen as "no solution" because associational lobbying, state policy, and public discourse had all defined autism as a nonpsychiatric kind. A psychiatric hospitalization was thus, by definition, inappropriate. A long hospitalization for people with schizophrenia was not ideal, but it wasn't categorically unacceptable. When I interviewed an official who had been in charge of implementing the report, she told me, "I know [Madame Coulon] is always insisting on [addressing] long-term psychiatric hospitalizations [for people with schizophrenia], but we've never really gotten into it. . . . We're looking for solutions for people who have none, but those people in the psychiatric hospitals, *ça va*, they have a roof and they have care."

The status quo this discourse meant accepting was disturbing. Forty years after inappropriate long-term hospitalizations became a preoccupation for policymakers, and nearly twenty after the 2005 law was intended to banish them as an autonomy-killing response to chronicity, the number of people condemned to this situation has barely budged. In 2018, seventeen thousand patients were still blocked, at a cost of 2 billion euros per year (nearly one-quarter of public psychiatry's budget).[38] A dual identity of *malade* and disabled person might be the best way to meet their needs, but in the interim, they were confined to being *malades*.

## CONCLUSION: FINDING AND LOSING AUTONOMY IN ILLNESS

Chapter 3 charted the legislative consecration of a dream: that people long confined to the world of psychiatry could find a place (literally and figuratively) in the disability system. This project achieved a degree of what Bourdieu calls "moral conformity": a consensus among activists, policymakers, and professionals that doing so could promote autonomy and help salvage an overwhelmed health system. Through acts and omissions, however, people with mental illnesses broke the logical conformity on which the system depended, rupturing the correspondence between the attributes of the bureaucratic kind "disabled" and the characteristics of the *malades* assigned to the category. As Ian Hacking reminds us, however, these mismatches are never the end of the story: Instead, "[kinds] are modified, revised classifications are formed, and the classified change again, loop upon loop."[39] These loops transformed not just the meaning of *malade* but the very structure and divisions of the state supposed to serve them.

It is worth qualifying this chapter's pessimistic tone. National statistics show that people with "psychic deficiencies" now occupy 23 percent of places (such as in protected workshops or nursing homes) in the disability system.[40] This is an enormous shift in the institutional trajectories of people with mental illness. Given the architecture of the 2005 law, it is a surprise, however, that not all of them were passing through the Disability Office. I interviewed the director of an innovative Service for Medical-Social Accompaniment of Disabled Persons in Paris (SAMSAH). He himself was a psychiatrist, but his team included neuropsychologists, peers (people with lived experience of mental illness), and employment specialists. "Our role is preventative," he explained, "We're trying to intervene as early as possible to keep young people in society." The problem was that SAMSAHs were "made for people who are disabled," whereas "we work to avoid becoming disabled." However, he had signed an agreement with the Disability Office to allow him to admit people to his SAMSAH, file an application after the fact, and get approval without meeting the level of impairment required for recognizing a psychic handicap. His program was proposing to provide medical and social interventions with a single, multidisciplinary team. It sounded a bit like the original vision of sectorization.

This idea of psychic handicap as something to be prevented was gaining purchase within the ministry for the same reason that people a decade before were arguing for recognizing psychic handicap: As one official told me, "Our idea is to avoid chronicity and handicap . . . That's what maximizes autonomy, to prevent a handicap."[41] The 2016 National Strategy for Disability made a notable shift to discussing programs for people "at risk for psychic handicap."[42] The strongest argument for deemphasizing psychic handicap as a classification was that many people who ostensibly had all the features of a psychic handicap were voting against it.[43] When I spoke to staff in public housing complexes; counselors in the public employment agency; and, of course, *secteur* professionals, they all offered the same lament. Many people obviously needed the support that the disability system could provide, but they refused the self-recognition that writing a life project required.[44]

I asked the person in charge of psychic handicap in the ministry what they were doing about the problem of nondemand, and her solution was, in some ways, to put herself out of a job: "There's this rejection of the label 'disabled person' by *malades*. It's very strong. Yet to benefit from our policies of accompaniment in housing, employment, you have to have this label. We're in the process of reflecting on this." New programs like Housing First (which puts mentally ill people directly into independent housing) and Place and Train (which installs people immediately in the job market and provides supports on-site) broke with the step-by-step logic of the disability system. They relied on a hybrid model, mixing both professionals and funding from the health and disability systems. The *secteur* I observed in chapter 2 was working to set up its own SAMSAH to provide disability-system-style accompaniment. These reconfigurations were stretching the meaning of *malade* to allow for a greater margin of autonomy than the paternalist protectors behind the *secteurs* originally envisioned.

In response to the frustration of getting chronic patients out of hospitals into disability institutions, some hospitals have settled on another strategy, one which provides a good segue to the end of this chapter. In unveiling regulations for the FAM and MAS after the 1975 law, the central state prohibited hospitals from running their own, insisting that "the creation of disability entities can obviously not be carried out within psychiatric institutions, symbol of internment and madness."[45] In 1996, the state lifted this prohibition. Since then, hospitals have been chasing and recapturing the funds supposedly being transferred to the disability system. I spoke to one hospital director who described a project to transform one hundred hospital beds on the outskirts of Paris into a MAS based on the fact that the hospital beds were "not adapted and actually generating chronicity." I asked her if this was really in the spirit of the 2005 law, and she told me, "The policy in favor of the disability system I find completely legitimate, but given my place as a director of a health establishment, my objective is not going to be to aid in the transformation of health financial resources into disability ones."[46] The stark contrast between *malade* and "disabled person" was founded on a strict separation of institutions, professionals, and culture between the two systems. The endless loops were breaking down these boundaries.

In 2017, I interviewed a *secteur* psychiatrist at a hospital outside Paris. Afterward, he drove me to lunch, which meant wending our way through quite literal ruins of abandoned hospital wards that once housed thousands of patients. He pointed wistfully to where they used to bring in horses and donkeys for the patients to pet. We passed the grounds of the old farm where patients produced the vegetables that got them through the Massacre of the Mad in World War II. And then, suddenly, incongruously, there was an old building with what looked like a new coat of paint. Jaunty colored letters above the entrance announced: "*Maison d'accueil specialisé.*" An old hospital ward with, ostensibly, a new mission. I wondered if the residents thought of themselves as having a psychic handicap—or just as *malades.* I don't want to exaggerate the continuity here. As the director of the FAM reminded me, having a key to your own room is not a trivial thing, and hospital patients don't get one. Still, it's hard to imagine this as the revolution that Mesdames Le Gal or Coulon imagined.

The right equilibrium between treating chronic illnesses and promoting individual autonomy is not obvious. The United States has recently swung away from its more laissez-faire approach of abandoning its most chronically mentally ill citizens into a marginalized, impoverished independence. States like California have adopted laws that expand the ability to force people deemed unable to meet their need for food, clothing, shelter, and medical treatment into institutions that can provide them.[47] There's an understandable appeal to the French approach, which has sought to avoid the most desperate forms of neglect by wrapping individuals within the protective bureaucratic kind of *malade.* But as we will see in part III, its hardest edge came when individuals rejected that label and were forced back into it nonetheless.

# PART III

## Balancing Rights, Control, and Care

The thorny contradictions between civil rights, social control, and medical care raised by involuntary psychiatric treatment were supposed to be resolved by now.

For centuries, only control mattered.[1] The pretense that constraint in the asylum was a form of medical care, to be imposed by a doctor, is of recent origin. In Anglo-Saxon countries, the decision of commitment was long taken by a jury of one's peers; in prerevolutionary France, the prerogative to sign the notorious *lettres de cachet* rested with the monarchy.[2] When reforms, like the notorious 1838 Law of Madmen, required a medical certificate for admission, it added at a façade of treatment to the equation.[3] According to Robert Castel, social control would henceforth be justified by a physician's "largely fictitious" psychiatric diagnosis, which provided a "prognosis of dangerousness" that would "condition completely" the "social destiny" of a *malade*.[4]

It wasn't until the mid-1950s when the conceit that hospital psychiatry was a form of medicine—and that, like most branches of medicine, it could treat people consenting to its ministrations—came to seem like a real possibility. In 1962, a report in New York in the United States declared, "The bars are disappearing—from most of the windows. The wards are quiet—save for an occasional moaning or outburst of shouts. The harsh words—asylum, lunatic, straitjacket—are dying out, as new ways of thinking replace the old. In mental hospitals in New York State, as elsewhere throughout the world, the last ten years have been years of revolution, the revolution against violence."[5] In France, the same date that the state promulgated the famous *Circulaire* of March 15, 1960, intended to get patients out of hospitals into the community, it instructed those hospitals to "open up to a maximum . . . and progressively reduce locked units."[6]

This was an era of a psychiatry so confident in what it was offering that it could trust the mad to accept it. Amid the civil rights fervor of the 1960s and 1970s, psychiatrists faced a proliferation of measures to limit involuntary commitments. The American Psychiatric Association concurred: "[M]ost persons who need hospitalization for mental illness can and should be informally and voluntarily admitted to hospitals in the same manner that hospitalization is afforded by any other illness."[7] For their part, French psychiatrists believed that discussions of civil rights and judicial oversight were irrelevant: As the Union of Hospital Psychiatrists argued, "the best guarantee of liberty that can be assured for our patients is the quality of care offered to them."[8]

Psychiatrists' claim that good care alone could ensure both rights and control was self-serving. But it wasn't entirely wrong. In the mid-twentieth century in the United States, almost everyone in asylums was there involuntarily; by 1980, it was only one-quarter of them.[9] In France, too, as community-based services were expanding, "*malades* . . . who protest or refuse care became the exception."[10] A 1986 report observed that hospitalizations demanded by the state seemed to be "decreasing ceaselessly" such that only an "irreducible remainder" of 3.3 percent of patients in psychiatric hospitals were there via this mechanism.[11]

This paradise of care, largely unencumbered by judicial intrusion over rights and without the most hard-edged forms of control, would not last. For one thing, the "societies of control" that arose in late capitalist countries ceased to be content with simply locking up individual madmen and women. They wanted them surveilled and disciplined as part of a new, more comprehensive system for managing at-risk populations.[12] Paradoxically, at the same time, while the rights of the mentally disabled have been among "the very last human right[s] to be recognized,"[13] recognized they increasingly are. International treaties and conventions, as well as World Health Organization directives, have all called for an end to involuntary hospitalizations entirely.[14]

How, then, do mental health professionals manage an intensifying clash between mandates to protect civil rights, societal demands for social control, and a desire to impose treatment on people who refuse it? To theorize the equilibrium point of these struggles, I turn to sociologist Erving Goffman who—unlike analysts who take psychiatrists' claims of their own potency at face value—entered the asylum from the ground floor.[15] For Goffman, the end point of internment was not a patient who was an entirely-passive plaything of medical authority but merely one who was "serviceable." That meant the patient's behavior was just deferential enough to "be fed into the administrative machinery . . . to be worked on smoothly by routine operations"[16] in a context where too few staff were chasing too many internees. Patients could carve out a modicum of space for themselves, albeit only by being serviceable in the moments when the hospital needed them to be in order to "reduce the administration's management problem."[17] That meant performing "quiet, obedient behavior" in the pill line, for example, or offering a "contrite admission of illness" in interviews with psychiatrists."[18]

What makes a patient serviceable to public psychiatry today has changed. The endless internments of yesteryear are incompatible with a modern mental health system that is supposed to be delivering active and cost-effective treatment to an expanding number of people. The quiet obedience of psychiatric patients is, at least in theory, giving way to the active pursuit of autonomy. In part III of this book, you will see how judges and psychiatrists operating in this new reality try to cobble together serviceable patients: people who are receiving just enough care to keep them under a fragment of control and exercising just enough rights to make their sojourn in a hospital legally legitimate—but not so many rights as to actually get them out of those hospitals.

Serviceability is not about a totalizing system for managing societal risks or the ascendance of civil rights. It calls our attention instead to the minimum kind of cooperation that institutions need to keep functioning and that professionals require to keep their work flowing. And because these quotidian requirements are contextual, they vary from place to place. Thus, in this part of the book, we will take a detour to a courtroom tucked in the back of a psychiatric hospital in New York City. It will help show how different an equilibrium between rights, care, and control can be when the organizational pressures on psychiatric hospitals and the ethos of legal professionals supposed to keep them in line vary.

## COMPLIANT CALCULATORS IN NEW YORK

If there is one right that is sacrosanct in New York, it is the right to haggle. In the winter of 2016, I observed nearly two hundred hearings in the municipal courts that ruled on whether to continue involuntary hospitalization for people who objected to them.[19] One case is for a middle-aged man diagnosed with schizophrenia. He had been hospitalized dozens of times and promptly disappeared after each one. When it comes time to cross-examine the inpatient psychiatrist, the man's attorney proffers a novel strategy to keep his client compliant: "Would you be willing to lower the dose of his [antipsychotic] injection from 400 to 300 milligrams?"

The psychiatrist replies, skeptically, "It's possible, but it's not certain it would be therapeutic."

"So you'd do it then?" the attorney seizes.

"His current dosage is what would keep him in the community and out of fights but . . . I'll give it a shot," the psychiatrist concedes.

When the man himself takes the stand, the attorney encourages him to pledge to adhere to the deal. His client is uncertain: "The meds make me sick, and I don't have the condition [schizophrenia] that it's prescribed for."

"Would you feel better if you had a lower dose?" the attorney presses.

"I mean, the lower the better, I guess."

"So if the doctor prescribed it, you'd take it?"

"I don't want it but, if they insist, I'll take it . . . in oral form," he yields.

The judge sits back, looking satisfied. He orders the psychiatrist to release the patient on assisted outpatient treatment. This program obligates him to accept treatment outside the hospital and encourages him to stay in his homeless shelter so clinicians can find him.

This scene was a bizarre culmination of a long process of expanding civil rights and the role of the judiciary in enforcing them. By the mid-1950s, New York had 85,000 state hospital beds (enough that, if they were in one place, they would be the ninth-largest city in the state). In the early 1960s, a commission organized by the New York State Bar Association visited Bellevue Hospital in Manhattan to see how people got into those beds. The answer was disturbing:

> In the corridor outside, the patients who have requested a hearing, dressed in pajamas and hospital bathrobes, wait in a straggly gray line to present their protests against being "sent away." A psychiatrist reads to the judge the physician's report setting out the initial observations and recommendations on the need for care. Most patients, when called into the courtroom, talk up in their "defense;" their stories are sometimes rambling and incoherent, sometimes only a pitiful plea to go home. There is no regular representation of the patient's rights . . . The hearings may not meet minimum constitutional requirements.[20]

In the early 1960s, civil rights were in the air, and patients whose due process protections did "not meet minimum constitutional requirements" were not serviceable. In 1964, New York reformed its mental health laws, putting an end to indefinite commitments and creating a specialized corps of lawyers, the Mental Hygiene Legal Service (MHLS) to counsel patients on their rights and advocate for their discharge.[21]

This entry of lawyers into the asylum marked a stark contrast with France, where both legal professionals and legal discourses of rights were largely absent in this period. Whether it really made a difference is less clear. Early studies of New York's specialized MHLS lawyers found they were reluctant to challenge the medical diagnoses underpinning commitment, instead focusing on negotiating with psychiatrists and setting up aftercare.[22] Why would they be more adversarial? This was the era (on both sides of the Atlantic) of great optimism about a psychiatry that was successfully eliciting consent from more and more patients and moving them increasingly swiftly back to the community. Even the 1962 Bar Association investigation, which had decried farcical commitment hearings, was sanguine about the institutions where they were held: "Every person with a serious mental illness needs some care and in many cases must go to a hospital . . . Rapid noncompulsory admission . . . is good for most patients."[23]

This legal-medical bonhomie was not to last. An era where involuntary commitments largely gave way to voluntary treatment started to go into reverse in the 1980s. As promised community services failed to materialize and as cuts during Ronald Reagan's presidency created a flood of homelessness, hospitals like Bellevue were overwhelmed with patients willing to feign symptoms to get upstairs for want of a bed or hot meal.[24] There were not many beds left. Not only had state hospitals been dramatically downsized, but the remaining beds were filled up with unhoused people that the mayor ordered swept up from Grand Central Station or the Port Authority Bus Terminal.[25]

In a context where the system was manifestly unable to provide care for the most severely ill, it's unsurprising that the MHLS lawyers representing patients moved away from advocating that their clients get psychiatric treatment toward fighting against any psychiatric control.[26] There was a profound cynicism underlying this advocacy. As one young lawyer told me, "Psychiatrists cannot get people to buy into this idea that they have mental illness. They can just give them two weeks of synthetic sanity, which doesn't change anything." His skepticism about psychiatry's ability to change his clients' subjectivity was mirrored by his doubt that it could change their social situation. When I asked him how he felt about advocating for homeless patients to be released from the hospital, he replied, "You can't factor in that someone is going to go on the street if you let them out. I mean, after two more weeks, they're going to do the same thing [go to the street]." If they could leave, they needed to leave: "This [the hospital] isn't the Hilton, you don't have a right to be here." This skepticism will cut a sharp contrast with this lawyer's French counterparts. The latter perceived a psychiatric system that, while struggling, could still use involuntary hospitalization as a temporary measure that might attach patients to the *secteur* for the long term.

No one believed that individuals like the New York City man negotiating his medication dosage was on track to become an independent, self-governing citizen. But even the most irrational patients could become serviceable as compliant calculators: people with enough rationality to assess that a few days of medication adherence in the hospital would hasten their discharge and thus allow them to choose to stop complying again once they were outside.

Such was the case for an elderly man whose unwillingness to communicate with the treatment team meant that they had not refined his diagnosis beyond "psychosis, not otherwise specified." The psychiatrist was asking for court authorization to deliver medication involuntarily.

The MHLS attorney opens his cross examination of the psychiatrist by noting, "There's no guarantee he'll get better with meds, isn't that true?"

"Well, it's . . ." the psychiatrist stumbles.

"Of course not!" the judge declares. She turns to the patient: "Listen, do you want to go home?"

"Yes, but those things [medication] are poison!" he protests.

"If you want to go home, you have to take meds," the judge insists. She turns back to the psychiatrist: "How long until his mood stabilizer reaches a therapeutic level?"

"Usually about a week, but we like to keep them to observe . . ."

"Okay, I'm ordering the medication, but you only get to keep him for one week if he takes them."

No one would call this outcome ideal, but it was serviceable: The patient's discharge after a week would meet the minimum requirements of an under-resourced system. The man had an opportunity to exercise a modicum of choice, demonstrate some capacity for self-control, and accept the limited care that the system could actually provide. Then he could leave and open up a bed for the next in line.

## SUFFERING CITIZENS IN FRANCE

France has been grasping at a very different equilibrium for a very long time. "If you look at the debates that they had around the law of 1838 [the Law of Madmen]—we're talking almost two hundred years ago—the question of the relationship between public security, the organization of public life, and health . . . it was all articulated from the very beginning," explained Michel, the director of a psychiatric hospital in Paris. That famed law, mandating a psychiatric hospital in every department, made psychiatry into a "grand public service, which required a national and obligatory organization." This, Michel approvingly noted, prefigured the comprehensive, territorial approach of sectorization.

But the law also reflected a fundamental ambiguity about the status of asylum patients and the purposes of involuntary treatment.[27] One report published in the run-up to passage of the law observed that the legislature faced a "difficult determination [about whether] . . . establishments for the insane should be considered more as hospitals or as detention centers. On one hand, they exist to intern individuals who can harm society; on the other, they are intended to cure individuals who are sick."[28] In the end, asylums would do both. One pathway into the hospital was a voluntary placement (a misleading term) by which a person could be interned based on the demand of a third party (usually kin) and a medical certificate attesting to the "need to have the person undergo treatment in an institution for the insane."[29] A second route, placement by office, allowed the prefecture to request hospitalization for people whose mental disturbance "might compromise public order or the safety of persons." This was an odd mechanism: The 1962 investigation by the New York State Bar cited earlier reviewed commitment statutes around the world and concluded that this second pathway was "unusual" and "should be avoided because it is a police measure."[30] Without a doubt, this role in imposing involuntary hospitalization on people deemed disorderly made psychiatry into a "political discipline . . . over which the state has a lot to say,"[31] as Michel put it.

The 1838 law was based in a particular professional arbitrage. Many psychiatrists resented that the law created a privileged pathway for the prefecture into the hospitals, but within the asylum, psychiatrists would enjoy significant autonomy. As an 1839 ordinance implementing the law decreed, "The treatment of madness requires very specific care . . . that requires that a doctor can order, with a certain independence, all measures that he deems appropriate to return the *malade* to reason."[32] French psychiatrists were notably shielded from oversight by the professionals that were a nuisance to their Anglo-Saxon colleagues: judges. In over a dozen attempted reforms across a century and a half, liberal members of the National Assembly sought to expand the role of the judiciary. As one deputy decried, the 1838 law "destroyed the judicial guarantees" that were the "basis . . . of individual liberty"[33] in France. These efforts went nowhere, victims of the weak judiciary and ferocious opposition from the Ministry of the Interior (which wanted to preserve the prerogatives granted to its prefectures). The definition of what kind of patient was serviceable thus depended on ongoing negotiations between psychiatry and state administration, care and control. Rights were largely left out.

The dramatic decline of rates of involuntary care with the advent of sectorization was not just a win for *malades*. It helped psychiatrists parry demands for social control and concerns about civil rights. In 1970, a local official wrote to the Ministry of Health complaining that "multiple crimes . . . are committed each year by *malades* prematurely placed at liberty." The ministry replied that, in fact, sectorization had "significantly reduced the medical-legal acts [crimes] committed by *malades* leaving psychiatric hospitals"[34] through intensive follow-up and surveillance. In 1978, the Union of Hospital Psychiatrists defeated a legislative proposal for systematic hearings to approve hospitalizations (modeled on California's Lanterman-Petris-Short Act), arguing this would "lead to a significantly heavier procedure" at a time when only 12 percent of admissions were involuntary anyway.[35] This was the heyday of sectorization, in which psychiatrists could credibly argue they were creating a mostly voluntary system that ensured both social control and care based on patients' status as *malades* rather than a judicial determination of dangerousness.

Chapter 5 will chart how this equilibrium broke down at the turn of the twenty-first century based on three factors. First, the central state began pushing for psychiatry to assume greater responsibility for caring for people whose dangerousness, delinquency, or deviancy was more evident than their pathology. Second, *secteurs* themselves struggled to provide voluntary treatment for *malades*, pushing rates of involuntary treatment upward. Third, in the culmination of a long battle from patients' advocates, assisted by pressure from European institutions, the judiciary finally entered the fray. Under a constitutional court ruling, from 2011 onward, judges would decide whether control and care outweighed the right to move freely. Suddenly, to be serviceable to psychiatry, patients would have to be both treatable *malades* and rights-bearing citizens.

Chapter 6 will draw on observations of over one hundred hearings about whether a hospitalized patient would leave the hospital or remain interned. Far from working to get patients out, judges largely embraced helping psychiatrists render refractory patients serviceable. The guide produced by the National School of the Magistrature gives some direction about what that means. It states, in bold font, that for patients, "the first right = the right to care" (underlining theirs). It goes on, "The first goal of treatment without consent is to provide care to a person who suffers."[36] Judges faced patients who struggled against the identity *malade* that had been imposed upon them and worked to push them back into that very same bureaucratic kind. A new conception of what *malades* could be, and the relative roles of psychiatrists and jurists, emerged from this resistance. Serviceable patients were suffering citizens who could minimally consent to care in the *secteurs.* Doing so was not just in their best interest. It actualized their right to health—a right that psychiatrists and jurists (if not patients) defined as more fundamental than a fleeting desire to leave the hospital and go home.

*Chapter Five*

# THE RISE OF RIGHTS AND THE SPECTER OF CONTROL

The cry of the Collective of 39 was still echoing eight years later. But while in 2008 it was a howl of rage and resistance, by 2016 it sounded like loss and lament.

Nothing inspired more anguish among my interviewees than Nicolas Sarkozy's infamous speech at the psychiatric hospital Érasme—a first for a president of the Republic—on December 2, 2008. The impetus was a stabbing of a student in the streets of Grenoble the previous month. The perpetrator was a patient with a history of violent behavior who had nonetheless escaped from the local facility.[1] After praising the work done by psychiatric clinicians as "indispensable to society," Sarkozy pivoted to questioning some deeply held tenets of that work. He lectured, "The hope of returning [a patient] to normal life should not always supersede the protection of our fellow citizens," adding that "potentially dangerous *malades* need to be subjected to particular surveillance, in order to block them from acting [on that dangerousness]."[2] He promised millions of euros for security cameras and seclusion rooms in hospitals, tracking bracelets for patients on temporary furlough, and an expansion of hypersecure Units for Difficult *Malades*. For Sarkozy, serviceable patients were those who were tightly controlled—and for whom rights and care were secondary.

That's when the Collective of 39, a newly assembled band of psychiatrists and nurses committed to the most idealistic version of sectorization, released its cry "against the securitarian night." In a petition that gathered several thousand signatories, it "refused with force" the "ideology that stigmatizes, restrains, isolates, and mistreats the most diminished of citizens." The right-wing president, in their eyes, was "amalgamating madness and social dangerousness, a calculated assimilation of mental illness and delinquency" in order to "justify . . . unacceptable security measures."[3] The collective called instead for a return to "hospitality toward madness," which could only happen if psychiatry was recognized as "caring for the person, not just an illness." The collective was the vanguard of an uprising that mobilized protests and strikes across the French mental health system. The resistance notched some successes, helping block some of Sarkozy's most repressive proposals. But rates of involuntary treatment kept going up, locks grew more ubiquitous, and mechanical restraints became pervasive on unruly wards.

And that's why the meetings of the Collective of 39, which I attended in 2016, oscillate between organizing to defend a more humanist psychiatry and mourning a model that already seemed dead. The group assembled after-hours in a Parisian *secteur*'s short-term crisis center, in a shared activity room with a small patient-run commissary and a chart announcing key principles of institutional psychotherapy. The meeting opens with a gray-bearded, self-described Freudian psychoanalyst from a *secteur* for children explaining, "What we share is pain. It's a pain that we felt in response to the speech from Sarkozy, which brought us from apathy to doing something."

"We can blame Sarkozy," declares a nurse wearing one pin advertising his union and another for the French communist party, "but the collective brought us together because of something we had been feeling for a long time."

The meeting bounces between despondency about psychiatry's "turn to security" and any number of other concerns. There was, of course, the "extreme neoliberalism" that was leaving *secteur* outpatient Clinics understaffed; a Ministry of Health that was trying to "normalize everything with protocols" and seeking the "total destruction of the *secteur*;" and the rising use of the label "handicap" for autism, which "rejects that it is an illness, something you can work on. [Instead], you can't treat it, it's permanent."

The conversation eventually circles back to the official topic of the night: a recently released report from the General Controller of Places of Deprivation of Liberty, a government oversight body, on the use of restraints and seclusion in psychiatric hospitals. The report argued that for the 25,000 patients subjected to these measures in 2014, restraints and seclusion had been "banalized" by a "political discourse of security that stigmatized the crazy person not for her suffering but for her dangerousness."[4] This time, the collective was of the same mind as the regulators, releasing a statement declaring that "this degrading practice had once almost disappeared . . . [but] today in France, we are locking in, immobilizing, attaching, strapping people . . . [and] the strap that binds is killing the human connection that heals."[5]

It's worth noting that many of the members of the collective worked in hospital units that practiced involuntary treatment. I spoke to psychiatrists among them who regularly wrote medical certificates that provided the legal justification for internment. But they truly believed this constraint was in the service of care. In their eyes, this was nothing like using force for control and convenience in a diminished system. Thus, it is no surprise that the collective's communiqué blamed, alongside Sarkozy, a broader "managerial and bureaucratic grip" that was "dissolving" the ability of medical teams to "search for humane solutions to calm a patient."

The collective's adversaries, however, were not just in the ministry. Philippe Bichon, the gray-haired, sandal-clad psychiatrist at the private psychiatric hospital *La Borde*, bemoans the negative reaction to the communiqué he encountered: "A lot of professionals responded poorly to what we wrote. They said, 'You debate, you talk, but you're practically retired. You have no idea what's happening on the ground.' "

The older child psychiatrist sighs and adds, "It's true. When I talk to my nurses about this, they say, 'Doctor, these patients aren't like before. They're users of multiple drugs, precarious, dangerous . . . There's nothing we can do but restrain them.' The nurses are afraid too, and they feel that we are blaming them!"

"People are scared, no doubt!" declares Bichon. "They're scared from a lack of training, they're scared they'll lose their jobs, and they're scared because of the hatred of madness in society as a whole."

A young nurse is less forgiving: "The people tying up patients need to learn to take some responsibility. I'm ashamed to have some of these nurses as my colleagues. I had to convince them that we should take the patients out [of the hospital] for an activity at least once a month, that they should even address people by their name . . . That's why I come here, to be with others who see the same things and want to change them."

No easy answers were forthcoming because they went deeper than just one malignant president. As part I of this book showed, *secteurs* were being deluged with requests to treat people with addictions, criminal justice contact, or troubling behaviors. In part II, we saw how the existing system that the collective was defending left many *malades* interned in institutions whose hospitality toward madness petered out years ago. As a result of both trends, the patients that public psychiatrists had in front of them really did seem too disruptive, too hostile, or simply too sick to be serviceable for the kind of voluntary care that was ideally the heart of the *secteur* system. These pressures pushed up the use of restrictive practices that had faded (but not disappeared) in previous decades.

This chapter traces an intense period of conflict over involuntary treatment. We'll revisit the *secteur* I observed in part 1 as well as the Police Infirmary to see what made patients seem so unserviceable to public psychiatry. These are the background conditions for policy debates that implicated the autonomy of health professionals, the prerogatives of state administration, and—in a sudden intrusion sparked by a 2010 appellate ruling—the responsibility of judges. Underlying this was a rift about what to make of *malades* who rejected treatment: Should they be seen as diseased persons deserving care, deviants requiring control, or citizens with a right to refuse both? In chapter 6, we will watch lawyers, judges, and psychiatrists attempt to refashion recalcitrant *malades* into suffering citizens, serviceable enough to restore a fragile balance between care, control, and rights.

## WHEN THE REAL *MALADES* ARE DANGEROUS

The triumph of voluntary care in French psychiatry was short-lived (figure 5.1). In 2002, *Le Figaro* sounded the alarm about a striking turnaround from the nadir of involuntary hospitalization in the 1980s: "no less than 60,000 people in France are interned each year, a record in Europe . . . and a 60 percent increase in ten years." Hospitalizations were, it added, "the only instance where one can be deprived of liberty without the intervention of a judge."[6] The ongoing harm to the credibility of psychiatry, which had made voluntary care both the metric of its own success and a key argument for its autonomy from law and the state, was clear. The *Mediateur de la République*, a regulatory body, wrote the Ministry of Health in 2005 noting that the number of hospitalizations, which was "largely superior to

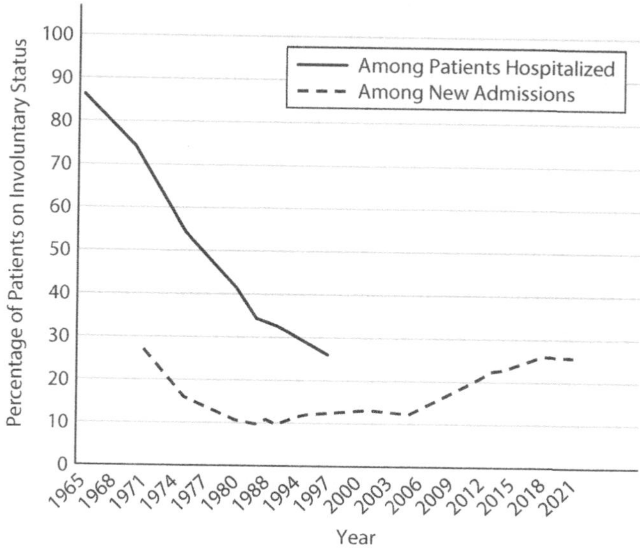


FIGURE 5.1 Involuntary hospitalizations, 1965–2021. *Source*: Mediateur de la république, "Hospitalisation sans consentement en raison de troubles mentaux," November 18, 2005, *DGS 2009/037/3*.

comparable countries like Italy or the United Kingdom . . . suggests that the French health system suffers from major dysfunctions."[7]

Why were *secteurs*, once able to transform resistant, potentially disruptive *malades* into serviceably compliant, cooperative ones, now struggling to do so? Psychiatrists themselves blamed a range of factors. Doctor Mailhol, who we met in chapter 3, explained that "convincing a patient that it's useful to be hospitalized takes time to speak, to listen . . . to engage in a process of therapeutic alliance. . . . When you don't have time, you ask the family [to sign a third-party demand for involuntary hospitalization], and voilà."[8] The exploding caseloads that constricted clinical time was one factor; another was the closure of beds. One spokesperson for a psychiatrists' union decried in *Le Monde* in 2005, "We are being forced to release patients who are still far too fragile, in order to free up beds," leading to readmissions.[9] As the number of hospitals shrunk, an involuntary hospitalization was becoming the emergency room clinician's best bet for accessing the remainder.[10]

But the real driver I want to focus on here is not changes in the services that *secteurs* offered but the perceived transformations in whom they were serving. Doctor Kuorio commented that they were facing an "augmentation of drug use, and greater precarity among patients . . . social as well as psychiatric problems that are really aggravating situations." At the same time, she noted a broader societal belief that "hospitalization in psychiatry is going to resolve the problems of people who are not doing well," and whose behavior—driven by illness or not—was bothering neighbors, mayors, or business owners.[11] In the next two sections, I'll unpack these two points: that *malades* were more dangerous and that the system was being pressured to serve dangerous people who were not *malades*.

One day, I sped through the spare corridor of one of the *secteur*'s fifteen-bed units, where patients in hospital pajamas paced restlessly and aimlessly, to attend a weekly team meeting upstairs. I had interviewed the head of the unit, Doctor Clech, a few days prior about her niche within the *secteur*. She explained, "I'm responsible for a unit where virtually every patient is involuntary. It's almost exclusively patients who don't want care, who are there for serious behavioral problems and psychosis. . . . I'm the one who goes to get our patients from prison, for example." This specialization emerged in response to a changing pool of *malades*: "There was a point where [Doctor Delignon] and I realized we were having more and more patients who had killed someone or tried to, and it was a real challenge, and so I decided to specialize in it because these are the patients that made the other doctors afraid."

That trepidation was widespread. The *secteur's* head nurse, Guilhem, had watched the unit transform across a thirty-year career. Heavier locks, emergency call buttons, and seclusion rooms had come to replace the specially trained (and typically male) nurses that used to contain patients. "These days, the young nurses arrive and discover a reality that is very complicated," he told me. "They [nurses] show up, they're agitated, and they're struggling to control their emotions . . . in front of a situation that is much more violent [than it used to be]."

During the unit team's meeting, Doctor Clech is multitasking, scribbling the medical certificates necessary to prolong involuntary hospitalizations. The nurses report that, in the last week, there have been four new patients admitted. One was brought back by police after he escaped from the ward, and another was a returning patient who had been hospitalized for thirteen years, discharged, and then "decompensated" (had a relapse). The center of the discussion, however, is a male patient in his forties who has arrived after being found too ill to be prosecuted for a serious violent crime. He's currently in an isolation room.

"This is a patient who is going to spend his whole time here attacking the institution," Doctor Clech observes.

Nurse Guilhem nods, "He needs a very strict structure."

"I agree," Doctor Clech adds, "but everyone needs to understand that won't necessarily protect us. We're going to have him for a long time . . . The only thing that can protect us is working together as a team."

Nurse Guilhem emphasizes the patient's lack of a horizon beyond the hospital: "For some patients, we can envision them going to a [disability] structure in Belgium or something, but for him, there is no alternative. And he has a potential for dangerousness that, even with treatment, is almost entirely intact."

The team then discusses drawing up a contract for care that will be signed by the doctors, the head nurse, and the patient. Doctor Clech solicits the advice of the nurses, noting, "You have an experience that is much closer to the patient than ours."

Marianne, a nurse who looked to be in her early twenties, offers, "We're thinking he should stay in isolation for at least three weeks."

"No, we should leave it open, don't make the end point clear. Just tell him there will be an evaluation every week. Not an interview, an evaluation," Doctor Clech emphasizes.

"And as for his living conditions, are we thinking hospital gown? What if he wants a sweater?" Julie, another young nurse, adds.

"No outside clothes. And no visits, no telephone calls," Clech declares.

"How about a prayer rug?" The patient is a devout Muslim.

"That, yes. And he can have a Koran," Doctor Clech concedes. "Let's keep an eye out for anything else he requests from the library. It could provide some insights."

The tone felt admittedly harsh. Nurse Guilhem, the grizzled veteran, cuts in, "We should remember, he's suffering."

"He's 'suffering' from a serious psychiatric pathology with perverse manifestations," Doctor Clech shoots back.

"What about restraints?" Julie queries.

"We can be clear in the contract: If he gets physically agitated, he's going to be restrained."

Marianne has a last request: "We were also thinking the contract should say 'administration' of treatment rather than 'distribution.'" (The former term implied that the nurses would be delivering his treatment in injectable form, whether the patient wanted it or not.)

"Exactly," Doctor Clech confirms, "He needs to know we're not going to let up on care." She closes by reminding the team that no nurse should visit him alone. "Protect him and us; that's the goal, and to keep this up over the long term."

They quickly move to another arrival: a homeless patient hospitalized after he threatened a cashier. Nurse Guilhem notes, "He's going to pose problems. We've got him on serious medication, and he's still awake."

Before we can discuss the patient, however, Doctor Clech has to cut the meeting short—"There are three patients waiting outside my office, and one is very manic."

When I followed up with Doctor Clech, I think she could tell I was taken aback by the restrictive measures, like isolation, involuntary medication, and severed communication, that her team was imposing. It's not just me who is concerned: Both government agencies like the General Controller for Places of Deprivation of Liberty and groups like the Collective of 39 have lamented how the use of restraints in some hospitals has become reflexive and automatic. A *Le Monde* investigation found one individual had been strapped down four hundred times; it concluded with an editorial calling for the abolition of such coercive measures.[12] All this outrage had helped spark the provision in a 2016 Law of Modernization of Our Health System defining restraints as "practices of last resort" that could be used only to prevent "immediate harm" for a "limited time."[13]

Doctor Clech understood the intention but was frustrated: "Do you think that we're tying up patients for pleasure?. . . . I understand that this is something that should be regulated, and we need to explain what we're doing. . . . But the legislature is manifestly functioning in a reality that is not our own, which is that we have patients that are extremely violent. One year ago, we had a nurse who was almost killed. Thirty seconds more [before other staff arrived], she would have been dead. It was a patient who we knew was dangerous. He was restrained, and I said he needed to be restrained, and the nurse went to detach him—alone. . . . This is difficult work. It's not easy to go home at night." Necessary or not, French researchers have argued that such coercive measures offer a "training in violence" to those subjected to them, which ricochets back to personnel, other patients, and persons themselves.[14]

There was one qualification that Doctor Clech wanted to emphasize: "Talking about a 'dangerous patient' doesn't mean anything. What I work on is psychiatric dangerousness—the anxiety or delirium that makes a patient dangerous at a given moment. But my job is not to work on the [person] who decides to kill someone for no reason." This was a distinction I heard repeatedly. When I asked Doctor Mairesse, the head of the Paris Police Infirmary, how his psychiatrists evaluated "dangerousness," he cautioned:

> This notion of "dangerousness" is something you're reproducing from English. But when I write medical certificates [for an involuntary hospitalization], I write "dangerous state." Dangerousness is a quality inherent to the person; that's for a nonpsychiatric criminal, a bandit, a gangster, a personality structure that leads us to say someone's dangerousness is permanent . . . But with mental illnesses, there are periods that lead to dangerous states, and which treatment is going to make disappear. . . . It's going to be transitory because it is going to be cared for.

Real *malades* were falling more and more into dangerous states because they were poorer and more isolated. For lack of resources, time, and personnel, the *secteurs* were having a harder and harder time pulling them out of those states. But these were patients who were potentially serviceable to psychiatry; they could be properly treated by the *secteurs*, even if right now they weren't. The problem was that there was a whole other population that, in their eyes, couldn't be treated at all.

## WHEN THE DANGEROUS AREN'T REAL *MALADES*

That psychiatric hospitals would be instrumentalized for social control was a reality built into the dual-track model for internments by the 1838 Law of Madmen. It allowed for hospitalization based on a need for treatment but also at the demand of the prefecture based on behavior that "troubled public order." Yet just as psychiatry resisted informal societal pressures to take charge of a wider range of social problems, it has a decades-long history of pushing back against attempts to expand this latter pathway. For example, in 1983, the Ministry of Justice proposed creating a new mechanism for court-ordered hospitalization for "delinquents with mental abnormalities."

The Union of Hospital Psychiatrists countered that "psychiatry should not be considered a tool for the control of social dangerousness."[15]

But the state didn't necessarily need new legislation. Hospitalizations demanded by the prefecture (known as "placement by office" in the 1838 law) already allowed, as a major report by two psychiatrists on involuntary treatment released in 1997 put it, "the authorities of the state to put to the side a person whose behavior . . . goes against social norms and for which neither family, nor the social system have found a solution. . . . Psychiatric hospitals have become a 'landfill' to intern people that we can no longer tolerate outside."[16]

The psychiatrists at the Police Infirmary in Paris saw themselves as trying to hold the line. "We know how this one is going to turn out," Doctor Laulaire tells me, as she flips through the dossier of a thirty-six-year-old Algerian immigrant. A hotel manager called the police when he was found drunk in the lobby; when they arrived, he told them he was a "violent schizophrenic" and wanted to leave so he could go to Bordeaux and "rip the neck out of a guy who owes me money." He admitted to the intern, who did a quick evaluation when he arrived the night before, that he used to be a heroin addict. He claims he kicked the habit—by drinking more. "He's doing great!" Doctor Laulaire laughs.

The man stumbles in. His head is drooping, and his eyes are partly closed. It's hard to know whether it's a hangover, medication, or both. Doctor Laulaire attempts some basic introductory questions and gets only mumbling as a response. "Were you drunk when they picked you up?"

"No," the man slurs.

"That's not what your toxicology test showed."

"I drank a couple of bottles . . . Can I get some valium?" the man queries.

"You love it all—alcohol, benzodiazapenes, methadone," Laulaire lectures. "You know taking those together can kill you?"

The man seems to be waking up a bit. He starts struggling against the restraints binding him. "Don't get angry," Laulaire cautions. "You know, yesterday you did a bit of *n'importe quoi*. Do you think you could use a little treatment to help with your addictions?"

"I'm fine."

"That's true. You're doing great," she opines, sarcastically. "But you're going to need to quit these antics if you want to stay out of prison."

Doctor Laulaire closes the interview and doesn't mention that the man is going to be picked up by the police later that day, additional antics or not.

Her certificate declares that he is a "psychopath" with "multiple addictions" but "no psychiatric dangerousness."

This decision rested on a sharp distinction between psychopaths and psychotics, through which psychiatrists pulled the principles of bounding into decision making about involuntary care.[17] In some cases, however, these categories were so contested that they could not neatly separate bureaucratic kinds as intended.

On another morning, I trail Doctor Fournier, who comes in several times a week when he's not writing prescriptions at a nearby prison (although he's constantly threatening to retire and move to Las Vegas, Nevada). When he walks in, the intern hands him a dossier. Doctor Fournier looks at the front page, and stops: The patient, a thirty-seven-year-old white man, is a known quantity. In fact, he's been incarcerated fifteen times, most recently, for threatening people at a café with a knife. A few days prior, the police had transferred him to the Police Infirmary, saying that his mental state was not compatible with jail; a doctor at the infirmary said that it was and sent him back; the prefecture then brought in a hired-gun expert psychiatrist who, after a ten-minute evaluation in the man's cell, reiterated that it wasn't—so now, the Infirmary, again.

"Is there a drug test in here?" Fournier asks.

"Yeah, he was positive for everything," the intern replies.

Doctor Fournier had already conducted a court-ordered evaluation of the patient in 2010 to see whether he could be prosecuted; Fournier had said yes. "He's basically just an addict," he explains.

The intern is a bit more sympathetic: "It turns out he's been followed off and on in a *secteur*. I got them on the phone, and they think there might be a chronic psychosis underneath all the drugs."

When the man is marched in by a nurse and security guard, his face is puffy, like it's recently collided with something hard. He slurs his words and seems on the verge of listing out of his chair. "Do you know why you were sent here?" Doctor Fournier asks.

"Because I'm a *malade*," the man states. This is a rare admission at the Police Infirmary and one that typically implies a person is not actually a *malade*. "I have schiz . . . schizo . . . schizophrenia," he adds.

"And this 'schizophrenia' manifests itself how?" the doctor asks. The man sits up and makes a motion of grasping at things hovering in the air around him. "That's not schizophrenia," Fournier clarifies. Fournier spends a few futile minutes trying to get the man to admit taking the drugs that the toxicology results show in his system. "What should we do with you?" he muses.

"I'd like to leave," the man proffers.

"Well, that's not going to happen," Fournier announces.

"So I'm going back to jail, then?" the man queries.

Fournier picks up the report from the psychiatrist who saw the man in jail: "No, you're *not* because another doctor said you can't be held responsible for your crimes." He dramatically throws the papers onto the desk. "I personally think you have no business being in a psychiatric hospital." He closes, "The nurses will let you know my decision later today."

With the man gone, Fournier muses aloud: "We're in a bind here, so we'll send him to the hospital for more observation." But under which status? The "placement by office" pathway would put him in the hospital on the basis of his risk to the public order. This would also give the prefect a say over when he leaves. Fournier notes: "If I do that, he'll be stuck there [in the hospital] for the rest of his life." The state appears to have already decided it's psychiatry, not prison, that is best positioned to contain him. Doctor Fournier walks the other hospitalization pathway. He will intern him based on his need for treatment and the "imminent peril" he poses to himself. This is in clear contradiction with Doctor Fournier's own assessment that he doesn't really need psychiatric treatment. It will give his colleagues in the hospital, unenthusiastic about his arrival on their unit, a larger say in when he leaves.

The medical certificate he writes is a study in passive aggression: "The patient presents neither delirium, nor hallucinations, nor disassociation, nor issues of mood, nor psychiatric dangerousness." However, "given that there seem to be disagreements between psychiatrists, I propose further observation."

I ask Doctor Mairesse, the head of the Police Infirmary, about the case. "We can't win when we're fighting everyone"—the judges, the police, or the elected officials who want to see certain problematic persons interned—"and, eventually, because they're a human being and not a can of peas to be passed around, we give in."

There's one rosy read of what happens at the Police Infirmary, one almost certainly not shared by patients themselves or the regulators who have roundly critiqued it. From one perspective, it's the pinnacle of public service, offering care even to those who can't even find their way to a Clinic. As Mairesse's predecessor once wrote, the Police Infirmary is for patients "who are outside the limits and outside the criteria of the *secteurs*. . . . Hopeless, relapsing, ruined feet, their clothes as worn out as their minds, floating in the vapors of alcohol or the smoke of hashish, rapidly deteriorating in the gutters of the metro."[18] It is the last thread of the safety net, in a moment where "the rights of *malades* are in the air, but not in the sense of a right to be *malade*."[19] But the doctors of the Police Infirmary were convinced that the right of *malades* to get (involuntary) care in a hospital and not a prison meant keeping those not categorized as *malades* in prisons rather than hospitals.

Yet even mental health professionals can't agree on how to draw these distinctions. In Doctor Clech's unit, some nurses thought their new patient was too much of a psychopath to be healed; before Doctor Fournier's evaluation, a psychiatric expert and a doctor at the Clinic thought that, beneath a dysfunctional personality, there was a treatable pathology. One nurse, who had watched the changing *secteur* population across a decades-long career, admitted to a growing sense of disconnect between populations and institutions: "We have people [patients in the hospital] who might be better taken care of in prison, and maybe in prison there are people who would be better off in the hospital."

The confusion was accentuated because, alongside the binaries of delinquent/*malade* and dangerous person/dangerous state, other identities were in play. The French state doesn't (officially) see race. I do. Of the seventy-two individuals I saw evaluated at the Police Infirmary, 43 percent were of North African origin and 24 percent were Black; over half were born outside France. *Malade*, if you recall, never officially had a race or gender. But it's hard to believe that an increasingly nonwhite and foreign patient pool didn't put into question some of the assumptions that category carried: a deservingness of care (whether wanted or not), for example, or a need to protect a *malade* from a harsh society, which might outweigh the need to protect society from a *malade*. In any case, for the professionals on the wards or in the Police Infirmary, the reality was stark: These were not patients who could be rendered serviceable to the psychiatric system voluntarily.[20]

## CONFUSING HEALTH AND REPRESSION UNDER SARKOZY

These underlying transformations of the public psychiatric system were difficult enough on their own. Politicians, in mental health professionals' eyes, were only making the situation worse.

At least some elected officials saw the rise in the rates of involuntary treatment as a cause for concern—and as a warrant to call psychiatrists to heel. In 2004, National Assemblymember Georges Hage from the Community Party filed a resolution for a parliamentary inquiry, noting that the increase was a "situation of manifest danger for the rights of man." The interchanges around the proposal were revealing. Hage told the assembly, "It is important to be conscious of the fact that an . . . [involuntary hospitalization] is first and foremost a measure of deprivation of liberty." A centrist deputy retorted, "We regret the use of the term . . . 'psychiatric internment' [in the call for an inquiry] . . . Far from a measure of internment and sanction, hospitalization without consent . . . is a measure of constraint justified by the specificity of some mental illnesses, given their denial of illness and refusal of care."[21]

The resolution was defeated, a sign that, for most politicians, events that year suggested the real problem was that psychiatry was too lax. On December 17, 2004, a former patient who had been released with minimal surveillance returned to the hospital and decapitated a nurse and aide. The Drama of Pau (the city where it took place) was followed closely by a patient-on-patient strangling in Pas-de-Calais, a dead patient found inside a hospital unit in Albi, a stabbing at a Clinic in Saint-Maur-des-Fossés, and a nurse bound and gagged in Var. All signs pointed toward "degradation in the conditions of work in psychiatry, increasing risks for caregivers as well as *malades*," as *Le Monde* reported.[22]

The minister of health responded by announcing a moratorium on the closure of psychiatric hospital beds and commissioning a report on "care for patients susceptible to being dangerous."[23] He used the occasion of Pau to recommend a range of measures to reorganize and refinance the *secteurs*, which public psychiatrists had been requesting for years. The proposals reflected the assumption that the best approach to *malades* who might be in a dangerous state was to treat the malady rather than control the dangerousness. One author of the report, psychiatrist Alain Lopez, told me, "One of our theses was that the more you focus on security [over delivering care], the more you increase the danger . . . But the ideology of the moment was to multiply barbed wire."

Indeed. The minister of the interior at the time, Nicolas Sarkozy, commissioned his own report. It lambasted the health system for its "insufficient consideration . . . of the security of persons and the preservation of public order."[24] In a move that, intentionally or unintentionally, was sure to fuel the worst fears of psychiatry, Sarkozy rolled some of the report's recommendations into a broader "Law on the Prevention of Delinquency" (itself a response to riots in the suburbs of Paris in 2005).[25] Among other provisions, the law would limit psychiatrists' ability to allow hospitalized patients to leave on temporary furloughs, create a national database (accessible to police) of people subject to hospitalization, and require that all patients whose condition "troubled public order" or "placed others at risk" be interned exclusively via request of the prefecture. This would curtail the discretion of psychiatrists, who previously could choose whether to request the approval of the prefecture for a hospitalization *or* use the alternative pathway based on the need for treatment (which, in the case above, Doctor Fournier leveraged to preserve psychiatrists' autonomy in deciding when to discharge a patient). In presenting his plan before the National Assembly, Sarkozy insisted that "it is up to the representative of the state, and not only doctors," to decide on hospitalization.[26]

The response to the proposed law was virulent. "Sarkozy raised a huge amount of emotion in psychiatry," one psychiatrist told me, "because he considered the *malade* as a dangerous person, which was a true rupture with the whole approach since the 1960s." The Union of Hospital Psychiatrists declared that it "refused this amalgamation between delinquency and mental illness" and called for a strike.[27] Another group of psychiatrists distributed hundreds of stamps that could add a message to the bottom of each prescription declaring oneself a "psychiatrist opposed to Sarkozy's Law on Delinquency."

It's important to recognize what was *not* at issue in these acrimonious debates. In the first iteration of the 1965–1967 *Journées psychiatriques* conference that set out the principles of sectorization, psychiatrist Hubert Mignot offered a plenary speech on "the legislative problem" (which had been basically the same since 1838). He noted, "Mental illness can make the person affected by it . . . incapable of deciding to get care . . . To prevent the disastrous consequences of this absence of care, we are generally in agreement that it is legitimate that this decision can be taken by others." As such, it is "normal and necessary that the legislature determine with exact precision under what conditions . . . this care can be given . . . in order to ensure . . . the defense of the mentally ill person." If the legislature could define these conditions, though, their application "could only be based on technical considerations." It was up to the doctor "to determine the patient is no longer able to formulate a valid judgment" about treatment.[28] When the final 1967 plenary of the conference called—with 80 percent of those in attendance voting in favor—for the abolition of the law of 1838, they were in no way demanding the abolition of involuntary treatment.[29] Rather, they wanted decisions about hospitalization to rest entirely in the hands of psychiatrists.

The battle with Sarkozy, forty years later, was also more about the autonomy of psychiatrists to impose hospitalization than the autonomy of patients to escape it. Psychiatrists also unsurprisingly resented that practices they saw as primarily medical were being rolled into a law on public safety and punishment. They reiterated that "only a global vision and actions taken on the [public psychiatric] system in its entirety . . . will be effective" because "the quality of care remains the best tool for prevention of violence in our field."[30] The minister of health apparently felt the same way; the archives reveal the minister's growing frustration at being left out of discussions of a law that had six articles pertaining to psychiatry.[31] In the face of growing resistance, which threatened to derail the entire legislation, Sarkozy withdrew the articles in February 2007.[32]

One year later, Sarkozy (now president) made the infamous speech inside a psychiatric hospital that provoked the Cry of the 39. His words still stung in 2016. "President Sarkozy made an amalgam between schizophrenia and criminality," Doctor Clech lamented, "and now when we tell parents their child is schizophrenic, they ask, 'Is he going to kill someone?'" Even without legislative reform, however, the attention (and millions of euros in financing) Sarkozy directed toward hospital security had its effect. Doctor Laulaire, the forensic psychiatrist who worked at the Police Infirmary, recounted, "When I started my residency at [psychiatric hospital], nothing was closed. And little by little, I saw them install barriers everywhere, bars on the windows, you needed a badge to get in anywhere. It was really shocking."

Looking through the archives, it's clear that opposition to Sarkozy hinged on the same series of symbolic boundaries we have seen throughout this chapter: between *malades* and delinquents, care and control, health professionals and state administrators. But herein lay the scariest part of Sarkozy's turn toward security and dangerousness. He wasn't just envisioning a dystopian future for psychiatry; he was describing a dystopian present. Those symbolic boundaries had quite clearly broken down already in practice. Clinicians might vehemently deny that their *malades* were criminals, but few contested a much circulated (if methodologically imperfect) 2006 study that claimed 35 percent of French prisoners had a serious mental illness.[33]

Meanwhile, rates of involuntary treatment kept rising, even though Sarkozy's reforms to ease the process of internments had failed. The events in Pau and Grenoble were exceptional but testified to a patient population that psychiatry was struggling to render serviceable for treatment. With conditions in overcrowded hospitals worsening, some psychiatrists welcomed the money Sarkozy promised for improving security and tightening surveillance of dangerous *malades*.[34] If Sarkozy seemed to be "confusing repression for health," as one editorial put it, [35] psychiatric teams on the ground were themselves increasingly confused about whether they themselves were providing care, imposing repression, or both.

## JUDICIAL INTRUSION

In 2010, Sarkozy came back with a new proposal for psychiatry that picked up many of the provisions from the failed 2007 reform.[36] Perhaps the most controversial was a new tool, the "program of care" (*programme de soins*). These measures would obligate a patient to accept treatment outside a hospital, with the threat of readmission for noncompliance. Similar proposals had been mooted by some psychiatrists since the 1960s, and they had a certain logic to them: Just as care in general was moving to the community, so, too, should constraint.[37] UNAFAM (the family organization) endorsed the new programs as not just encouraging their loved ones to comply with treatment but also creating an obligation for overwhelmed *secteurs* to provide that treatment diligently.[38] Given their suspicion of anything Sarkozy touched, however, psychiatric professional organizations unsurprisingly declared their opposition. Once the possibility of extending constraint outside hospital walls was opened, one union wrote, it would "become something banal . . . a rule, and this will lead us [psychiatrists] to become social controllers."[39] The battle lines were, needless to say, predictable.

Nonetheless, a piece of the 2010 proposal's euphemistic title—Law on the Rights and Protection of People Who Are the Object of Psychiatric Care and of Modalities of Their Care—suggested something else was afoot. While the law's provisions on rights were derisory,[40] they spoke to their gradual intrusion into a debate long polarized between care and control.

The shift was visible by 1990, when the legislature finally reformed the 1838 law. While it left the basic architecture intact (particularly, the two-track system of involuntary hospitalization and its limited role for judges), it did insist that patients had a "right to respect of [their] dignity."[41] Henceforth, hospital patients would be entitled to receive mail, vote, and practice their religion. The law also, for the first time, formally established a legal status for truly voluntary psychiatric hospitalizations. This provision may have paradoxically increased involuntary hospitalizations: Because it banned placing voluntary patients in locked wards or in isolation—practices that had been used informally in a void of legal oversight—it pushed teams to convert some voluntary patients to an involuntary status.[42]

The 1990 law also created a new body, the Department Commissions of Psychiatric Hospitalizations (later renamed *Commissions départementales de soins psychiatriques*, replacing "Hospitalizations" with "Care"), which would review hospitalizations that lasted beyond a year, periodically inspect facilities, and receive and respond to patient complaints. In practice, these commissions were dominated by psychiatrists and garnered little interest or support from the ministry.[43] I actually sat in on a commission meeting in 2017. The team of six sped through about one hundred dossiers to make sure medical certificates were signed by the right person. We opened one letter from a patient decrying the "unconscionable scandal" of his hospitalization; the psychiatrist declared the patient was in a state of "total delirium" and explained to all present that the treatment the man was objecting to—electroshock—was entirely justified. Still, the commission was another small step toward greater oversight of psychiatric decisions.

The patient above noted that he had sent a copy of his letter to the General Controller for Places of Deprivation of Liberty (*Contrôleur general des lieux de privation de liberté*), in addition to the commission. This new independent regulator had been created in 2007 after France signed the UN Convention Against Torture. The controller was focused initially on prisons, but the mandate included psychiatric hospitals. Their first visit to such a facility, one controller told me, was "extremely tense. The head of the hospital's medical commission said, 'There's no need for you to be regulating involuntary hospitalization, there's no real deprivation of liberty here.'" But when the head controller saw the decrepit state of the hospital's isolation rooms, the lack of easy access to a toilet on the wards, and the systematic removal of patients' personal affairs and replacement with pajamas, he declared, "Prisons would never accept these conditions." The Controller has subsequently become one of the most aggressive actors denouncing "carceral conditions" (or worse) in psychiatric facilities.[44] These developments created a new challenge for rendering patients serviceable. Teams not only needed to deliver care and maintain control but also to do so in ways that were procedurally correct in the eyes of the proliferating number of agencies looking over their shoulders.

The one set of actors who still largely weren't gazing disapprovingly at the *secteurs'* ad hoc approach to patients' rights and dignity were judges. Under the 1838 law, patients actually could request that a judge review their internment. But given that there was no mechanism to ensure that they were informed of this right, they almost never did.[45] The absence of systematic judicial review pushed France steadily further from international norms. From 1950 to 2007, France was the target of one-third of all complaints concerning psychiatry lodged with the European Court of Human Rights, which had been strongly recommending "judiciarization" since the 1980s.[46] Many of these cases emanated from the *Group Information Asiles* (GIA), a litigious group of ex-patients that could trace its heritage back to the *Group d'information sur les prisons*, an organization born from the uprisings of 1968 in France and of which Michel Foucault was a notable member.[47]

The GIA benefited from a broader awakening of the quiescent French judiciary. This included the introduction of a new system of constitutional review in 2008, under pressure from European institutions.[48] In 2010, the GIA seized on this opportunity to file a "Question of Constitutional Priority" challenging France's laws on involuntary hospitalization. They argued internments infringed on fundamental rights to privacy, bodily integrity, and freedom of movement. In her argument before the court, Corine Vaillant, the GIA's lawyer, denounced that "this is the only case in France where a person can find themselves deprived of liberty . . . without intervention of judicial authorities. . . . [Current law] gives absolute power to doctors . . . who, in the name of the health of a person . . . restrict the liberties of individuals without any external control."[49] The court concurred: the need to ensure "the protection of health" and the "prevention of troubles to the public order" had to be tempered by "the protection of rights and constitutional principles." They decreed that, going forward, all hospitalizations would need to be reviewed by a judge within fifteen days. Judges would now go from reviewing less than 1 percent of hospitalizations, in the rare instances patients asked for them, to tens of thousands a year.[50] Patients' rights would not be just a matter of distant regulation by bodies like the Departmental Commissions and General Controller but a regular, systemic collision between psychiatry and the law.

This judicial intrusion came in the middle of the ongoing heated debate over Sarkozy's proposed law, in which judges had been playing essentially no part. André Bitton, one of the ringleaders' of the GIA's "judicial putsch," described his group as having achieved the constitutional court's ruling "against medical advice, against public powers, against the ample majority of psychiatric corporations [unions], and even against the judicial corporations that did not want judicial controls . . . except in a very minority fashion."[51] Nonetheless, in a joint communication, UNAFAM, FNAPSY (the National Federation of Patients in Psychiatry), and key professional organizations all "salute[d] the decision of the Constitutional Council on the necessity of reinforcing guarantees to protect the liberties of people cared for without consent," which were particularly important given the "insufficient guarantees" made in the law proposed by Sarkozy and currently under review.[52] By 2011, if the idea that psychiatrists would be the sole decision maker on hospitalizations was no longer plausible, psychiatrists could now propose "substitut[ing] the judge for the representative of the State or prefecture, as is the case in most European countries."[53] In effect, these organizations viewed judges as a potential lever for curtailing psychiatry's role in policing public order, allowing it to refocus involuntary hospitalization on individuals who might be dangerous but were, above all, *malades*.

Yet the constitutional court's ruling favored Sarkozy in an oblique way. Its decision meant that the entire legal architecture of France's mental health system, in place since 1838, would collapse on August 1, 2011—with uncertain consequences for thousands of people currently interned. Groups like the Collective of 39 continued to denounce the proposed law, which still included provisions to reinforce the role of the prefectures and to introduce involuntary care outside the hospital. Political opposition buckled, however. The parliamentary majority, one senator explained, voted for it "without enthusiasm" but "in the spirit of responsibility," even though "*malades* would not find any improvement in their care" as a result.[54] The law was finally promulgated on July 5, 2011.

## CONCLUSION: SEARCHING FOR A NEW EQUILIBRIUM

2012 brought the end of Sarkozy's presidency, but not the end of the heated debates over the role of psychiatry in maintaining public order that he had stoked. Professional organizations used the occasion of a new socialist government to call for revisiting the 2011 law. But when members of the Collective of 39 and sympathizers met with the new minister of health to request the full "abrogation" of the 2011 law, they were disappointed. Denys Robiliard, a member of the National Assembly charged with revisiting the law, told me, "We decided we didn't want to relight the bonfires of Antony [the city where Sarkozy gave his speech], to restart with a divisive approach . . . for which psychiatrists and above all *malades* would pay the price." There's something deeper here than mere political arbitrage. As Robiliard wrote in a report to the Assembly, "One should show some humility in the face of the stability of the texts that regulate this delicate matter. . . . There is an inherent difficulty to reforming the architecture of a measure that rests on a delicate equilibrium between issues of equal importance: health, guarantees of liberties, and security."[55]

A modest reform authored by Robiliard passed in 2013, with little dissent. It removed a provision that created extra hurdles to ending the hospitalization of people in hyper-secure Units for Difficult *Malades*, shortened the waiting period for the intervention of judges to twelve days, and eliminated one of the time-consuming certificates psychiatrists had to fill out (on the eighth day of a hospitalization).[56] But it didn't touch the role of the prefecture. As Robiliard himself confessed to me, "There are socialists who are extremely security-focused, including the prime minister," for whom leaving an avenue open for the state to demand hospitalization remained appealing. A blatant example came in 2017, when the interior minister called to "mobilize psychiatric hospitals against the terrorist menace." He wanted involuntary hospitalizations to target people on the "*Fichier S*," or the country's Islamic radicalization watchlist.[57] In short, the original balance of the 1838 law—in which both psychiatrists and the state got a say in who went in and who went out of the hospital—might now have to give a say to a third party, judges. But a definitive resolution of the fragile balance between care, control, and rights was difficult to determine from above.

There's an ideal kind of *malade* that could help reconcile these competing demands. When a patient embraces the need to take medication diligently outside the hospital, they have accepted the most modern care the psychiatric system has to offer. If they learn to monitor their own symptoms and detect an impending relapse, they are exercising self-control in a way that assuages risk-conscious public authorities. And insofar as they are active participants in treatment, they are rights-bearing subjects in a way that asylum patients never were.

This ideal, needless to say, did not describe an important subset of *secteur* patients at the time of my fieldwork (if it ever did). Then again, states rarely actually expect people to act as perfectly self-governing subjects.[58] They do need people, however, to be *serviceable*: That is, bureaucratic kinds need to engage with public agencies in ways at least minimally satisfactory to under-resourced institutions and overextended professionals.[59] As I found in New York, the seemingly opposing forces of care, control, and rights could converge when patients performed as "compliant calculators": actors who, even through a haze of psychosis, could bargain over medication compliance in open court. In so doing, their right to have their choices respected in the treatment process was valorized, something resembling care was delivered, and control was assured (at least until they were discharged and disappeared).

If the ways that judges could render patients serviceable were evident to me based on my time in the United States, it wasn't obvious to actors in France. The whole point of the legal advocacy of groups like GIA was to have judges rule that a large proportion of patients were *unserviceable* for further hospitalization. Professionals' fear of the reform was real. Michel, the hospital director I cited at the beginning of part III, recounted that preparing for the August 2011 start date for judicial hearings required that he cut short his usually sacrosanct summer vacation. Everyone, he admitted, was out of sorts: "If you look at the context in which the law was implemented—at one point, very security-focused . . . saying 'we're going to intern everyone,' and at the same time, paradoxically, 'we're going to exercise a [judicial] control that is going to permit people to get out, we're going to verify what you, psychiatrists, have been doing, tranquilly, for two hundred years'—it was hard to understand." Given French psychiatry's self-understanding as a nationally distinctive discipline, it was not auspicious, as several Parisian practitioners wrote in a professional journal, that the law "is adapting the body of Napoleonic legislation to foreign laws, whose spirit is Anglo-Saxon, giving oversight of a doctor to a jurist."[60] For anyone resistant to the Americanization of French psychiatry, August 1, 2011, was a "pre-announced catastrophe."[61]

The first weeks were complicated, Michel admitted: "At the beginning, we had judges lifting measures of hospitalization, and we just didn't understand it. We really had to try to make sense of how the judges were arriving at their decisions." Higher-level debates raged on, driven by the reality of more *malades* in rupture with their treatment, more delinquents being pushed onto the *secteurs*, and more rights restrictions imposed every year.[62] Yet by 2016, when I conducted my fieldwork, there really did seem to be a new balance on the ground. A new arbitrage between law, medicine, and administration was possible, as I will show in chapter 6, because judges found a way to render patients into a new kind of serviceable subject: *suffering citizens*. For them, involuntary care was a way of actualizing the most fundamental right of a *malade*, that of ongoing solidarity from the psychiatric system. Control was a helpful side effect.

*Chapter Six*

# JUDGING SUFFERING CITIZENS

On one spring day in 2017, the judge of liberties and detentions assigned to handle the hospital cases for the week has found a middle ground on a thorny question: judicial attire. He is wearing a jurist's black robe, but it is unbuttoned. A flannel shirt and jeans are visible underneath. The white tie, which judges usually pull tightly around their neck, hangs loosely to the side.

You could argue that he has reconciled two competing visions of his role. In parliamentary hearings held as part of an evaluation of the 2011 reform to France's laws around involuntary treatment, representatives of the magistrates' union told the National Assembly that the standard jurists' wear would "scare" those hospitalized into thinking that they were being interrogated or condemned. For patients' rights advocates, though, a "black robe and not a white blouse" would show that those appearing before the judge were not just *malades* but rights-bearing citizens—or, as some lawyers referred to them, *judicables*.[1] Both perspectives recognized that it wasn't just the continuation of an individual's hospitalization at play at a hearing but their overarching social status in the eyes of the state.

Today's sartorially ambivalent judge presides over a room that, while in the heart of an old asylum, is now under the jurisdiction of the Ministry of Justice. He sits next to a clerk. Each has a computer displaying the medical certificates and admission decisions for the cases before them. The patients sit at the other side of the judge's desk, with the lawyer assigned for this half-day's hearings to the side. There are ten chairs in the back that—along with a door left slightly ajar—testify to the public character of the hearings. The chairs are typically unoccupied; the public is a solitary sociology student. A half-dozen patients wait outside with the nurses who have accompanied them from hospitals around the city.

A man in his mid-sixties shuffles in. The judge fires off an introduction: "You've been hospitalized without your consent, at the demand of a third party. The law in France requires that, after twelve days, a magistrate rules on whether the hospitalization can continue. I've read the recommendation from your medical team, but I'd like to know what you think."

Not getting an immediate response, he presses, "Would you like for your hospitalization to continue, or not?"

The man speaks slowly, and angrily, "No. I want it to stop. But I know it doesn't matter."

The judge responds, "Have you brought up your desire to leave with the medical team?"

"Of course," the man retorts, adding a dismissive, "Pfff."

The judge turns to the lawyer: "Maître, do you have anything to add?"

The lawyer sifts through some papers. "I have not found any irregularities in his dossier, but it's clear that monsieur would like to go home."

The judge turns back to the judiciable, "Okay, I'm going to deliberate on this, and you'll get a decision this afternoon. I wish you a good recovery!"

When the man leaves, the judge rapidly dictates a decision to the clerk: "The medical opinion says that he is stabilized . . . [but] . . . there persists nonetheless a certain ambivalence in the recognition of his troubles and his adhesion to treatment . . . [so] consolidation is necessary before envisioning withdrawing the measure of constraint."

The subject of the next hearing is younger. He was hospitalized at the demand of a representative of the state under the law's criteria of "grave risk to the security of persons or public order." If, in the psychiatric parlance used in the medical certificates, the previous man was "laconic," this one is "logorrheic." He launches into an explanation of why he tried to beat down the door of a business associate he claimed owed him 150,000 francs (a tall order, given the replacement of the franc with the euro fifteen years prior). The man announces, "The person who is my so-called doctor, who didn't see me for six months, said that I was in rupture with my treatment.

He's collaborating with my parents against me. This is abusive, unjust, and shameful."

The judge proposes, "Did you try going back to the Clinic, to maybe figure out a treatment that would work better for you?"

The man replies, "I don't like it there. The people there are real crazies." The man declares that he doesn't want his attorney to talk, and so the hearing ends.

The decision notes that man "presents a delirium, primarily of a persecutive type. . . . He does not critique his behavioral problems and does not understand their pathological character. . . . He is opposed to care. . . . The continuation of the measure of complete hospitalization is thus ordered."

The next woman walks in. For the first time, the lawyer presents an assertive case. "This medical recommendation is from a doctor who didn't even examine her. It states that she's so mute that they 'cannot fully evaluate her symptoms.' This is in irregularity; there is no basis for this hospitalization. I have some jurisprudence . . ." He hands the judge a handwritten page quoting several articles of the Code of Public Health (*Code de la santé publique*).

The judge turns to the woman. "If I let you go, will you continue your care on the outside?"

She shakes her head.

"Has this hospitalization helped you, at all?"

She shakes her head again, pauses, then suddenly expounds: "I am a writer. I sing. I make poems. I want to be free!"

The decision notes that "the patient has already been hospitalized in this same setting and her medical situation is known to her team." As such, "the fact that Madame has been almost mute is not an obstacle to identifying her need for a full-time hospitalization."

The judge hears twelve cases this morning. The circumstances that brought these individuals to the hospital range from suicide attempts provoked by work stress to deliria prompted by an abandonment of antipsychotic medications. The judge authorizes the hospital to keep all twelve. He is not far from the norm: six years after the law required that judges authorize any hospitalization lasting longer than twelve days, and again after six months, 91.2 percent of requests to continue hospitalizations are granted.[2]

A critical observer will lament how quickly patients' complaints were put aside by an ill-attired judge and ill-prepared attorneys. In that respect, France's new judicial controls resemble the "degradation rituals" characterized by US scholars of commitment hearings in the 1960s.[3] At the very least, they speak to a French justice system where restricted resources and a rising workload hollow out solemn constitutional guarantees.[4] But we should recognize that those black robes, unbuttoned or not, are doing more than just abdicating their responsibility to protect the rights of vulnerable citizens. The law, notes Pierre Bourdieu, is never inert; instead, it is "the quintessential form of symbolic power" that, in its pronouncements, "creates the things named."[5]

In this chapter, I propose a middle ground between depictions of legal impotence and omnipotence. Judges and lawyers cannot make patients into the rights-bearing but treatment-accepting *malades* that might be the ideal subjects of the psychiatric system. But they can, in many cases, create a minimally serviceable version of it. Through hearings, hospitalized individuals become bearers of a modicum of procedural protections. But they are also pushed to accept a narrow conception of their rights as citizens as, above all, a right to medical care. In the face of patients who exercised their rights in less-than-ideal ways, judges redefined their own role. They ceded power back to psychiatrists and thus allowed the bureaucratic kind of patient-*malade* to dominate over the new status of citizen-judiciable that judges were supposed to elevate.

## A COURTROOM WITHOUT CONFLICT

The hearings instituted by the 2011 law were designed to take the form of what the French call a "contradictory debate." Policymakers decided to confer the mission to judges of liberties and detentions, whose bread and butter was ruling on the undoubtedly contested cases of continued incarceration for migrants and detainees.[6] Patients were guaranteed access to a lawyer, and the hospital or prefecture could (although usually did not) send a lawyer to oppose them. Of course, the greatest guarantee of an adversarial process would presumably be the patients themselves, who would oppose hospitalizations imposed against their will.

Yet it often seemed as if neither the judge, nor the lawyer, nor even the patients were playing their role. One hearing was for a nineteen-year-old white man who was hospitalized after a psychotic break where he accused his family of a plot to poison him. He walks in, wearing flip flops and a track suit. The judge launches into a rote description of the procedure. She explains, "You're here because you were hospitalized without your consent."

"No, no," the man cuts in. "When my grandma took me to the emergency room, I agreed with the hospitalization."

"Well, it's not you who signed the paper. But how are things going now?"

"It's good," he replies.

"You're feeling better?"

"Yes."

"I'm glad to hear that," the judge elaborates, "but your doctor thinks you should stay a bit longer, so you can have a better situation after discharge."

"That's fine. I'm very worried about what happened. Don't put me on the street." He then makes an orthogonal comment about helping to sweep the hospital grounds. "It's important to protect the planet," he closes.

The judge then asks the attorney for her observations. She replies, "He's pretty much said everything. He's a young man, this is his first hospitalization, and all the medical certificates say it's necessary for him to stay in the hospital. And he thinks it's doing good for him."

"You've really calmed down," the judge interjects approvingly, adding, "You're going to get my decision in the afternoon in writing, but I'll tell you now that you're going to stay."

The man nods, but then insists, "I'd like to be able to go outside more. And when am I going to leave?"

The judge ignores the first comment. She then explains, "I don't decide when your hospitalization will end. It's the doctor who decides." The judge declares au revoir and the judiciable shuffles out.

Before observing hearings, I would have assumed scenes like this would be vanishingly rare. After all, aren't involuntary hospitalizations by definition something a person does not want? But one in ten judiciables didn't offer any opposition whatsoever. There are some good reasons this might be the case (and many bad ones, which we'll get to later). After twelve days, some had connected with their medical team, come to appreciate the treatment offered to them, and found the hospital a welcome respite from a hostile world outside. Research consistently finds that someone's formal legal status upon entrance to a hospital matters less to their experience than their perception of coercion inside.[7] For those judiciables that took their treatment, could wear street clothes, and stayed out of isolation, that coercion could seem pretty minimal.

Another, larger subset of patients came in agreeing, more or less, with their hospitalization but voicing complaints about it. They contested heavy medication dosages, uncomfortable beds, or other patients haranguing them for cigarettes. In its momentous ruling, the French constitutional council declared that hospitalization without a hearing violated Article 66 of the Constitution, which guaranteed freedom of movement. But the court did not accept plaintiffs' argument that it also infringed on a right to privacy and bodily integrity. As a result, the conditions of hospitalization were placed outside the bounds of hearings, as shown by the judge's rapid dismissal of the man's desire to spend more time on the hospital grounds (protecting the planet, in his own small way).

What really stymied adversarial hearings, however, was lawyers' own failure to advocate on behalf of their clients. One sixty-nine-year-old white woman walks in slowly, a nurse holding her arm; she is gaunt and her white hair unkempt. According to her medical certificates, her depression now has "psychotic features" and has sparked deepening anorexia. The judge asks, in a gentle voice, how her hospitalization is going.

The woman responds in a hushed tone: "It's been difficult . . . I have problems in my life . . . It's difficult to walk . . . My intestines don't function."

"Are you doing a little a little better now that you're here?" the judge nudges.

"Nothing helps, and I didn't choose to be here."

"Maybe you could help explain why things aren't going better?"

"No, it's too complicated, we don't have the time."

The judge turns to the lawyer. "As you can see, Madame is not sure what she wants," the lawyer hesitantly recounts. She fidgets. She's done her homework and found a procedural issue in the dossier. "I wrote out some conclusions," she continues, "but I'm not going to give them to you [the judge] because, well, I think it's important she remains here, given her state. She's not going to stay in the hospital forever, but . . ."

"It's not going to fix me," her client protests.

"Yes, but if you stay, it'll help you," her lawyer responds.

After a few more interchanges, the hearing ends.

I spoke with the judge in an adjacent break room afterward. She told me, "I've been a judge for twenty-four years . . . and I have a good relationship with lots of psychiatrists. I basically think, in France, they do a good job taking care of people. I trust them." She went on, "Even if that lawyer had found a real problem, I would have found a way to keep her [the woman] in the hospital. The right to be alive is more important than the right to liberty. That woman, she'd die in a day."

Plenty of lawyers felt the same way. That same day, I spoke to the lawyer who had declined to provide her written conclusions. I described the more adversarial hearings I observed in the United States. She looked aghast: "That sounds awful. These are people in psychic suffering, they are vulnerable, and you put them in a room with all those people looking at them, and they'll crumble." She went on, "I'm not going to be one to get someone out if they are just going to commit suicide. I'm sorry, I want to sleep tonight." That afternoon, a patient—perhaps having watched too many dubbed episodes of *Law & Order*—stood up at the beginning of a hearing and raised his right hand, as if he was going to be sworn in. "Relax, we're not in America here," the lawyer said as she tugged him back into his chair. Policymakers envisioned contentious hearings; on the ground, jurists were imagining something different. Judges and lawyers violated professional norms of vigorous representation based on the claim that hospitalized judiciables were simply not the same kind of client as a detained migrant or defendant.

Cases where judiciables wouldn't fight their hospitalizations and lawyers didn't argue against them colored judges' perceptions of the value of the hearings writ large.[8] For some judges, this was a "different type of law" because it was useless law. One told me:

> When there's a new law, the first thing that a magistrate does is ask the question: "Why is there a need for a judge?". . . . A judge is someone who is there to resolve a conflict, and make a decision based on divergent interests . . . But often in these cases [psychiatry], there's no conflict. The people come to tell me, "Yeah, voilà, I was hospitalized . . ." but often we realize that they come [to the hearing] because they have to, because they've been summoned, because there's a law imposed on them. The profound interest of the thing [the hearing], I don't see it.

This sense of futility was a product of the architecture of France's new hearing system. In New York, involuntarily hospitalized patients see a judge only if they ask to (although specialized lawyers help facilitate the request).[9] The 20 percent or so of involuntary hospitalized patients who make it to a hearing really want out. But French hearings are systematic for everyone after twelve days. Courts were destined to be faced with a mass of would-be litigants who had already been rendered serviceable by the psychiatric system on its own.

## FIGHTING OVER FORM

One could try to be a bit forgiving toward these not-very-contentious judges and lawyers by recalling the circumstances under which the 2011 law was implemented. Hearings were introduced thanks to the actions of a tiny group of ex-patients and trailblazing lawyers. They entered into a political knife fight between psychiatry and the state, within which the judiciary had been sidelined since 1838 (during the reign of King Louis Philippe I, for reference). Judges' unions stated that they supported playing a greater role in concept but decried an absence of resources to handle a growing caseload.[10] Lawyers regretted that the local bar seemed completely unprepared. "When the law passed there was no system set up to pay for the lawyers who were covering hearings [for patients who couldn't hire their own, which is to say, nearly all of them],"[11] Raphael Mayet, a lawyer in Versailles, told me. "Some of us said we'd do them anyway, but it was a crazy bet; we didn't even know if we were going to get paid!" Now there isn't any doubt about remuneration, but as another lawyer, Elena, explained to me after a dozen hearings, "Honestly, at 300 euros for a day's work, I'm doing this basically as activism." As we will see in this section, this activism could make for more contentious hearings. But it did so by putting the accent on procedural issues. This left medical control of patients circumscribed but still dominant.

In 2013, Mayet and a few dozen others created a new association called Lawyers, Rights, and Psychiatry. They share new jurisprudence and gripe about their torpid colleagues. I joined Mayet in Versailles for a training he put on for a handful of new lawyers in 2017. He opened by insisting on the gravity of the matter: "This is a major issue of individual liberty. . . . A person who is hospitalized can be under conditions that are much stricter than those for detainees. For example, [in a hospital] you can be put in isolation without a TV or radio, with no right to go outside. In detention, even if you're in a disciplinary block, there are moments of recreation and the length is limited." To my surprise, however, he quickly dismissed what I might have guessed would be the heart of lawyers' arguments: "You can, of course, contest the underlying justification of the measure [of hospitalization]. Is it really necessary? Really indispensable?" But, for him, fighting against the idea that a *malade* needed psychiatric care was an uphill battle: "Once the person is diagnosed as schizophrenic or bipolar, they've gone into a box, and it's difficult to get out."

The training emphasized instead how lawyers should challenge a hospitalization based on a Byzantine array of procedural issues: the appropriate time frame for notification of the judge, the presence of an ID card identifying the signatory of a third-party demand, whether a patient was given a physical examination within forty-eight hours, if the paperwork was legible ("this might seem obvious, but it's definitely not systematic!"), and whether certificates were written by authorized doctors ("sometimes it's an intern who signs or, in the countryside, a doctor brought in from another country who is not yet permitted to work as a psychiatrist in France"). Et cetera, et cetera: one report documented one hundred such potential "mistakes of form."[12] Mayet was endorsing a long-running strategy of legal advocates for the mad in France that involved not contesting madness at all.[13] The rights might be fundamental, but the strategy was to "search for a little stupid thing" to protect them, as Mayet told me over lunch afterward. In my own coding, the arguments used by lawyers that called into question psychiatric expertise largely focused on procedural issues (table 6.1).

I shadow Elena, who is part of the same association as Mayet, a few weeks later. She's unsparing: "I'm from Spain. We were under a dictatorship for forty years. I think when it comes to rights, we're still more advanced than in France." By way of example, she recounted, "I went to one hearing where the judge was in a hoodie, and he didn't even write down my arguments."

She was using procedural irregularities to challenge that complacency. One of her clients is a twenty-three-year-old white woman who came to her hearing dressed to impress, with a pressed skirt, blouse, and makeup. The judge explains, "You're here because you were hospitalized at the demand of a third party . . ."

TABLE 6.1
Arguments made by lawyers against involuntary hospitalization*

| **Arguments emphasizing usefulness or success of treatment** | | **Arguments challenging psychiatric expertise** | |
|---|---|---|---|
| Willing to take treatment | 46% (22) | Procedural | 32% (15) |
| Can return to work/family outside | 29% (14) | Lack of information/justification | 21% (10) |
| Not severe/improving | 27% (13) | Alternative explanation for behavior | 10% (5) |
| Not dangerous | 17% (8) | Side effects | 8% (4) |

* Analysis based on all hearings in which the attorneys made an argument or statement in favor of release of the patient; $n = 47$.

"That's right; it was my father," she interjects, before launching into a rapid-fire narrative: "So I was hospitalized in 2015, after a suicide attempt. Actually, I was a victim of sexual abuse, from my mother, who threatened me, although I didn't bring a complaint to the police in the end. But I did look into various associations that provide help to victims." She lists three, spelling out each letter by letter. "I then spent one year going to a psychotherapy institute for adolescents."

Before she starts spelling its name, the judge cuts in, "And did you get medication there?"

"Yes, I took Zoloft and then Seroplex [two antidepressants]." The judge starts asking her about her experience with the medications, but the woman keeps talking: "So then I started going to the Clinic, I saw doctor [name]." She spells it out. "But the doctor told me to leave, so I went to a shelter in Lyon, but it was a bit chaotic."

The judge attempts to get in a word: "So things were really not going well for you."

"But then my friend paid for a hotel"—she gives the name, letter by letter—"it was 189 euros per night, but there were some issues with the room cleaning, eventually the police came, they took me to the emergency room, they tied me up, and my dad decided to hospitalize me."

The judge is evidently trying to move things along: "Do you think you need the hospitalization?"

The woman states confidently: "Yes, I needed to get away from my family problems."

"And how are you feeling now?"

"Great. And that's why I'm just asking you for one thing today: to leave. The *secteur* is going to find me housing, and I can't deal with the food here anymore."

The judge and the woman have a few minutes of back and forth where he tries to convince her it's still a bit early for discharge. Looking exasperated, he passes the baton to the lawyer, Elena.

"There's an issue in this dossier, which is that when I looked last night, there was no document confirming my client was notified of her hospitalization. A document from the doctor stating that she was initially too sick to be notified suddenly appeared this morning."

"So the documents are all there," the judge parries.

Elena cites the relevant portion of the Code of Public Health, and insists, "This is not resolved by the magical appearance of a document. The lack of notification violates French law and the European Convention. It's a serious infringement."

The woman is now crying. "I want to go. I wasn't even able to vote in the second round of the election [France's presidential election had taken place in the week prior]."

The judge looks annoyed, "There was a delay in notification because the doctors did not think you were in a state to receive the notification. The procedure seems right to me. You're not stabilized. These things take time."

The woman sobs, "It's been so long, it's twelve days already."

The judge tells her she'll receive her notification later but adds, "Remember you can appeal." He stumbles, "But only if my ruling goes against you." The writing is on the wall.

When the woman leaves, Elena confronts the judge: "I can't believe you're going to dismiss this. We don't have any reason to think she wasn't well enough to be notified."

"Look, I'm not a doctor, so if the medical information says she couldn't receive the notification, that's it. Voilà." The judge let me view his conclusions, which stated, among other things, "No harm to the patient has been established by any delayed notification."

That line is important. Judges could discard these procedural errors by declaring them harmless, regardless of a patient's certainty that they had, in fact, been harmed.[14] Judge Léonhard, who was one of the first judges to take on the new hospitalization hearings in 2011, told me, "So imagine it's a third-party demand for hospitalization, but it turns out the third party is someone who works for the hospital. . . . That's an irregularity, no question. Does that cause harm to the rights of the patient? Well, the consequence of this irregularity is that the person was hospitalized, they received care. Is that a harm? I'm not so sure." Not all judges see this the same way. In the first year after systematic hearings went into effect, judges ended forty-three internments at Sainte Anne's Hospital in Paris for the kinds of procedural issues for which Mayet was training lawyers.[15] But Judge Léonhard told me—proudly—that subsequently the judges had learned to pick up the phone and remind psychiatrists to dot their I's and cross their T's on their medical certificates. "It's absurd for the judges to be telling one of the parties how to win," Raphael Mayet griped. Still, it's an approach that makes sense when the goal is to create a serviceable subject who has procedural rights that should be respected but that don't block them from receiving care (whether they want it or not).[16]

I actually did see one hospitalization that was ended for a procedural reason. It was the exception that proved the rule: that judges are not there to create unserviceable subjects who have too many rights to be treated. This case was an appeal after a judge had ordered the release of a patient because the patient's notification of the admission decision lacked a date and time. In her written argument to the appellate court, the district attorney wrote: "The patient was immediately informed of his rights. The notification document for the initial decision of admission is in the dossier of the judges and has the signature of the patient. However, the section 'date and location' has not been filled in . . . Such an omission is a pure formality and can be explained by the difficulty of getting a patient in a state of health that was extremely degraded to sign."

The patient himself had declined to attend and thus missed a somewhat nitpicky hearing. His lawyer, Axel, admits that "the patient was informed . . . but the forms do not have any date allowing us to show such information . . . The hospital cannot therefore certify that the decision was notified with the delay required by the health code."

The district attorney then intervenes: "The fact is that, yes, there's no date, no one is arguing with that. But unless you are suspicious of some kind of fraud, it's evident that the decision was notified. No one has the capacity to do these things perfectly. Imagine that moment, with someone who is very sick, agitated. You can understand that the team forgot."

The judge, speaking largely to himself, replies, "Yes, yes, the absence doesn't automatically nullify the hospitalization. But it isn't in conformity with the code."

The judge seems to be leaning in favor of the justiciable, but a third lawyer, representing the hospital, then intervenes: "It's totally counterproductive to imply that the hospital is acting in bad faith. We work with the means that we have. The patient is not at all alert, he's not clear about anything. . . . Given his health, I believe that this would be prejudicial to let him out." She then adds, to everyone's surprise, "He's homeless and he doesn't even want to leave. The psychiatrist didn't provide a medical certificate for today because monsieur is taking his treatment voluntarily. I emailed him [the psychiatrist] three times, but he said it didn't matter anymore."

Axel, the patient's lawyer, perks up, "Wait! There's no recent medical certificate in this dossier?"

The judge seizes on the same point, "Yes . . . according to the code, there should be a new medical certificate before the hearing for appeal." He then observes, "But if the hospital doesn't even want to keep him in an involuntary hospitalization anyway, what am I actually deciding here?"

If the reader is lost by this point, don't worry; the judge was, too. The appeals court ultimately ruled to liberate the justiciable from a measure of constraint that had already ended.

These hearings at times merited the harsh epithets coined by sociolegal scholars: "ceremonial charades . . . without substance" or "hollow law."[17] But procedural advocacy cannot be entirely discounted. Nearly one in ten hospitalizations is indeed ended by a judge, most frequently because the hospital did not file paperwork in time for a hearing on day twelve.[18] This is not trivial. A timely hearing creates pressure on the hospital to discharge if the medical justification for it is questionable. And as the young woman whose case was recounted above reminded us, a lot can happen in twelve days (including a presidential election).

Fighting over formality did discipline psychiatry. But it didn't insist that patients were anything other than *malades*. As one lawyer reminded me, "A serious defense does not stop the person from being cared for . . . It's just that a deprivation of liberty should be procedurally correct." He insisted, "Ninety-five percent of the people admitted in psychiatry, they belong there."

## LISTENING TO PROZAC PRESCRIBERS

The psychiatrists to which the lawyers deferred did not attend these hearings. They're not even a party to them. In theory, they provide an expert opinion in a struggle between patients and the hospital administrators (and, in the case of what is now called "psychiatric care at the demand of a representative of the state" [once referred to as "hospitalization by office"], the prefecture) who have formally ordered the hospitalization. Physicians nonetheless dominated from afar.

One of the boldest assertions of medical power was to declare patients "nonpresentable." In 2012, some courtrooms sat empty as psychiatrists pronounced that 100 percent of their patients were too unstable to make the trip to the *Palais de justice*.[19] Some judges fought back by lifting hospitalizations for patients who didn't appear.[20] Follow-up legislation in 2013 partly resolved the problem by pushing hospitals to hand over a room to the Ministry of Justice to hold hearings on-site. About one-quarter of patients were still absent, however, from the hearings I observed. It rarely appeared that they had refused to come. Psychiatrists' explanations were sometimes pretty compelling. One wrote that the patient was at "high risk of escape . . . put in isolation due to delirious decompensation, risky behavior, and physical agitation." Other times, they boldly asserted that care trumped rights: "[Patient] is capable of presenting herself but . . . this would imply an excessive stimulation which risks perturbing the dynamic of clinical amelioration taking place." In any case, if the patient wasn't there, no one could question whether those descriptions were accurate.

Even if patients were present, however, they were fighting an uphill battle against a medical expertise to which judges readily deferred.[21] "As to whether the treatment is justified," one judge told me, "neither we [judges] nor lawyers are doctors . . . How a person is going to be cared for, that's a medical decision."[22] One judge's decision for a twenty-nine-year-old woman read that the patient "presents a mediocre contact with agitation, tachypsychia and logorrhea, dissociative delirium, discordant, very little construction, persecuted and megalomaniacal; poor understanding with morbid rationalization." Either judges were hiding a much more sophisticated understanding of psychiatric terminology than they let on, or they were copying and pasting from the medical certificates written one, three, and six days after hospitalization. I directly observed the latter: One judge filled in most of her decisions for the afternoon's cases during her lunch break beforehand.[23]

Judge Pierraud really did seem to know more than most of her colleagues. When one patient told her that, rather than being hospitalized, she'd like to see a psychoanalyst, Pierraud counseled, "Be careful. In France, basically anyone who has been analyzed and taken a course can say they're one. They're not doctors" (true). In another case, a lawyer articulated her concern about a patient who "is going to be transferred to [other hospital] for something called 'electroconvulsive therapy.'" Pierraud disabused the lawyer that the treatment resembled the images of it in *One Flew Over the Cuckoo's Nest*: "It's actually been shown to be very effective for deep depression" (also true, although there are still plenty of good reasons—including serious and enduring side effects—for patients to refuse it). Judge Pierraud was one of the only judges who delivered her decisions, which systematically maintained hospitalizations, directly to patients. "I like to do it because I think it has a pedagogical value," she explained, "to really emphasize the importance of treatment."

In two hearings I attended later that week, Pierraud went beyond deferring to medicine. She actively promoted it. I joined the lawyer for her initial meeting with a client, a white woman in her sixties who had been hospitalized as an "imminent peril" to herself. The lawyer asks her client if she knows why she's here.

"Yes, because I was hospitalized under constraint. Do you know why?"

The lawyer shuffles her papers. "Let me check . . . It says you stopped your treatment."

"*Who* said that?" the woman shoots back.

"—And, sadly, it also says you have delirious ideas and a paranoid sense of persecution . . . Sometimes the psychiatrists use words that are difficult to understand," the attorney states sympathetically.

I struggle to follow the woman's subsequent narrative, which hinges on the idea that both her neighbors and others on the metro are mocking her. "They were going to knock down my door and make me jump out the window," she insists, "but the fire department came first and brought me to the hospital." The interview does yield one important point: that the woman was followed by a private psychiatrist, but she was not informed she had a right to contact him.

When the hearing begins, the woman continues her tale of persecution—"They laugh at me like I have the head of a clown"—and muses about whether "the police are in on this also."

Judge Pierraud lets these comments pass by. "You've been treated a long time for these . . . troubles?"

"Yes, but Seroquel [an antipsychotic] is not recommended for people my age, so I asked to diminish and stop my treatment. These have the most side effects of any drugs!"

"All medicines have secondary effects, but the question is whether the primary effect outweighs them," the judge lectures. She then leans in, "When you don't take your drugs, what happens? You come back to the hospital!"

"I don't like the hospital!" the woman exclaims.

"You are in a vicious cycle here. No one likes having health problems, but we deal with it."

The woman insists, "I used to weigh eighty-seven kilos on these meds."

The lawyer cuts in to affirm, "It's true, she's had serious side effects."

"I'm not going to make decisions based on the medical observations of a lawyer," Judge Pierraud states dismissively. She goes on, "It's like diabetes. You have to take a treatment every day for your whole life. It's not fun, it's not easy, but you accept it and move on."

"These drugs are contraindicated for thrombosis," the woman flails.

"Then talk to your doctor. There would be research on that if it were true. If they gave these medicines to you, it's because they evaluated the risks and benefits." Pierraud declares, "Look, we're not advancing here" and turns to the lawyer. When the attorney raises her concerns about the notification of the right to contact an outside doctor, the judge replies, "I can't be looking over every doctor's shoulder all the time." She tells the woman, "Officially, you're going to learn this at the end of the day, but I'm going to keep you here, with the hope that you can leave with a solid care plan that limits your side effects." The woman starts raising concerns about her apartment (whose door really might have been broken down by the fire department), but Judge Pierraud waves her out.

Michel Foucault wrote that an earlier era where society dialoged with madness has given way to a "monologue of reason about madness," which could "only have come into existence in . . . silence" on the part of the mad themselves.[24] Judge Pierraud actually held long hearings and tolerated extended digressions. Her pedantic explanations still seemed like a monologue. These endless admonitions to take medications were something I saw among judges in New York, too. In both places, they elided real questions about their efficacy and side effects. But French judges went beyond demanding treatment compliance: They imposed the identity of *malade* itself.

At another hearing, a rail-thin, seventy-four-year-old white woman, who looks like she could be ninety, shuffles in. Judge Pierraud's tone is soft: "To start with, let's hear about how your hospitalization is going."

"It's not going well. The people in the unit are young, of different origins [races], and have different problems," the woman explains. She's arguably a victim of the downsizing of hospital units, which means the *secteurs* that used to have separate units for the aged-and-depressed and young-and-psychotic have had to consolidate everyone on the same ward. "It's really military style. It's adapted to the young *malades* but I don't understand why I'm being treated in the same fashion."

Judge Pierraud lets out a supportive sigh: "But is the hospitalization doing at least some good for you?"

"I've been drugged for years now, and I keep getting worse," the woman responds. She explains that her husband was recently treated for cancer, and that she's been waiting to hear whether the tumor has made an anticipated return.

"That's a very anxious situation," the judge replies, "and I know you think you have a normal response to objective conditions, but the doctors say you're in a severe depression and you don't see the pathological dimension of it. Most treatments for depression don't even work within twelve days, so it's normal if you don't feel better yet. It's a chemical thing."

"We haven't even talked about why I came here," the woman states, referencing a threat of suicide she made after a conflict with her children over their future inheritance

"That's because there are troubles that are exogenous and endogenous. Everyone has difficulties, but not everyone gets depressed." Judge Pierraud reproduces, exactly, the dividing lines between depression as a malady and depression as a trouble I saw operative in both the *secteur* and the Disability Office. She then announces that, given that the woman was on the illness side of the binary, she is going to stay.

"This was useless," the woman huffs.

"No, it wasn't. You still got to talk to me. But it's normal that you're staying here. When people go into the hospital, it's for a good reason."

These cases are emblematic of "sanism," which discounts the perspectives and experiences of the mad in the name of paternalist protection.[25] But Pierraud also subtly shifted these hearings out of the register of control and into that of care. She copied a medical certificate into her decision describing the woman's "sadness, moral injury, devaluation of the future, a sentiment of incurability and indignity . . . anxious ruminations and a sense of being condemned . . . ideas of death." These are concerning observations, but it certainly did not suggest either of these women posed an imminent risk to society. Judge Pierraud's decisions seemed motivated not just by an abdication to psychiatric expertise but also by confidence in medicine itself: of the capacity of hospitalization and treatment to alleviate suffering that, to her, seemed very real. From this perspective, it was logical to give doctors more time to do their work—and, as you will see in the next section, to convince patients to agree to measures that would nonetheless remain involuntary.

## CULTIVATING CONSENT

Only about 20 percent of hospitalized persons articulated a complete opposition to any form of psychiatric care or categorically rejected the label of "mentally ill." Far more common were individuals who were "ambivalent" about treatment—a term that appeared over and over again in medical certificates. This characterization was borne out in the uncertain and contradictory ways judiciables expressed their views in hearings. As the lectures about the value of treatment and the need to recognize depression as an illness recounted above showed, judges assumed they could appeal to a residual rationality to transform ambivalence into a serviceable commitment to care.

Yet what happened when these lectures actually worked? Perhaps the trickiest cases for judges were not those of all-out opposition but those of all-out acceptance. Some patients insisted that they were fully consenting to care and thus were ready to be treated voluntarily. Judge Léonhard described the tension this posed: "[Ruling to continue a hospitalization] is an infringement on the constitutional right to consent to care . . . But then you're in a hearing, and you're really dragged into it because you have someone under constraint who tells you, 'Of course, I'm going to take my treatment.' It's complicated . . . We [judges] really have to puzzle out, 'is this [consent] valid?'" The French public health code clearly states that "no medical act and no treatment can be practiced without free and clear consent."[26] But we will see that there's a difference between giving consent and being *able* to give consent, one which gave judges wiggle room to extend involuntary treatment in ways that met the needs of the *secteurs*.

I accompanied one lawyer, Axel, to a day's worth of hearings in a jurisdiction outside Paris. Our first meeting is with a thirty-five-year-old white woman. She walks in confidently, wearing smart professional attire. Axel leafs through her dossier and declares, "There are several irregularities here, but I'd like to hear from you first."

"The problem was that all my memories of sexual abuse from childhood were coming at once, and I was overwhelmed. I actually came to the hospital at the recommendation of my psychotherapist," she recounts, after she made a half-hearted attempt to overdose on medication. She affirms, "I needed the hospitalization. I wasn't eating. But now I'm eating again. I still haven't gone outside in two weeks. I would like something less restrictive [a voluntary hospitalization]."

"And were you taking a treatment already?" Axel clarifies.

"Yes, Zoloft [an antidepressant], for a few years. I can take that outside, but I want to stay [in the hospital]." But she goes on, "The problem is that I think the doctors are getting my diagnosis wrong"—they've claimed she's psychotic, she thinks she's suffering from trauma—"and when I told them that, they lost it."

Axel is looking at a copy of a medical certificate, in which the psychiatrist explains, "She is persuaded of her delusions of having been assaulted. She believes she is persecuted. She is banalizing her suicide attempt and is ambivalent about care." When she confronted them about her diagnoses, they determined she posed a "risk of aggression" and placed her in an isolation room.[27]

Axel stops reading: "This is ridiculous. This medical certificate is pretty excessive."

Through all this, she's still asking to stay. On the paperwork informing her of her hospitalization without consent, she wrote, "I refuse to be hospitalized under constraint because I want to be hospitalized freely and because I take my treatment. I would like to see a psychiatrist specialized in trauma."

That is her line in the hearing, too: She repeats "I wanted to be here. But it has become too restrictive." She'd like to transfer to a private hospital or at least leave for a few hours to see her therapist, for example.

"The doctor thinks that an involuntary hospitalization is necessary because of an ambivalence toward care and a degraded relationship with the medical team," the judge declares.

"I haven't changed," the woman ripostes.

Axel intervenes: "She's voluntarily at the hospital. She's taking her treatment. I'm not going to read the code [the Code of Public Health], but all of this is incoherent. She feels she is fragile and wants to be cared for. There's just no motivation for an involuntary hospitalization here."

After Axel raises a few procedural issues, the judge offers the last word to the woman, who reiterates, "I want to stay in the hospital, but with the doctor of my choice."

In truth, the judge had the last word. He rules that she had "not fully accepted the gravity of her suicide attempt" as shown by her insistence on seeing a private doctor and not a *secteur* psychiatrist. Accepting treatment meant not just recognizing that she had a pathology and needed professional care. That treatment needed to come from the *secteur*. Without that realization on the part of the patient, it was, the judge wrote, "impossible [for her] to consent to care."

That term—"impossible to consent"—merits an aside. In 1999, a French delegation attended meetings in which the Council of Europe was developing a series of recommendations on psychiatry and the rights of citizens. The council was planning to advise that national legislation should limit hospitalizations to when "the person in question does not consent to their placement [in a hospital]" but suffers from a mental illness that puts them or others in danger.[28] The French delegation expressed its concern that this choice of criteria "is not in keeping . . . with the respect for consent which is one of the fundamental principles of French law." The French recommended instead that the recommendations refer only to people who are "afflicted by mental troubles that render consent impossible." This distinction is medically dubious but legally essential. Determining whether someone is consenting (such as freely entering into a contract) is a judicial matter. But whether someone is *capable* of consenting is a medical determination. In theory, a French citizen's consent (or lack thereof) to care is always respected; involuntary hospitalization can take place only when a person is so sick that a doctor (not a judge) concludes there's no consent to be given or withheld at all.

This still doesn't quite get at why psychiatrists would insist on continuing hospitalization for a person who says that they're doing better and eager to continue treatment on the outside. After all, the psychiatrists I interviewed universally regretted the pileup of acutely ill patients in emergency rooms waiting for the beds that these recovering individuals were occupying. Nor does the letter of the law explain why judges spent so much time cultivating consent that they would then discard.

Consider the case of a twenty-three-year-old woman born in North Africa. She had been placed in foster care as a child but had been reunited with her mother. She was hospitalized after she stopped her medication for schizophrenia and came to the *secteur*'s day hospital having smoked a joint. The judge asks her how the hospitalization is going.

"It's going really well," she replies in a chipper tone. "I've had some time to rest, to take some distance. As you know, I had a bit of a crisis, but I was going to the day hospital every day, and I'd like to return."

"There's two problems with that," the judge says, "which is that you have a mental pathology and diabetes, and both require a strict treatment. Apparently, you didn't follow up."

"It's true, it was dumb," the woman replies ruefully. "I got sick of taking the pills, morning and night. But I'm sorry."

"I'm sorry for *you*," the judge reflects, before declaring, "The doctors say it's a bit early for you. They want to make sure your follow-up care is ready. Are you willing to stay?"

"No, I have a plan, I've got a boyfriend, and I'm going to stay with him. He lives right next to the Clinic. This was supposed to be a quick hospitalization," she elaborates.

"The last time it [the hospitalization] was six months," the judge notes, and adds, "And this time you really think you're ready to leave after twelve days?"

"I'm not going to the street," she insists, "I have my boyfriend, I have the day hospital . . . I never even stopped going there. Here, I'm just sleeping all day. It's boring."

The judge turns to the attorney, who asserts, "These medical certificates are not conclusive. There's no mention of her being in danger. It's only speaking about her issues in the past. They say that a meeting with the mother first is necessary to ensure good follow up care, but that's not a criterion for an involuntary hospitalization—"

The judge cuts him off, "It seems like this therapeutic project has not been discussed enough. You need to figure out how care can be put in place and followed. You were in the hospital for six months, and you came back quickly. . . . I prefer to be prudent here."

The woman protests, "I'm solid, really. I'm twenty-three. I'm an adult. I have things to do, I want to see my friends."

"I understand your desire to leave, you feel ready, but you're still fragile. I'm trying to protect you. Your friends would want you to be treated."

The judge's decision maintaining her hospitalization conceded that there had been a "positive evolution" but that it "needed to be consolidated, in order to give doctors the time necessary to construct a structured project of departure." As some judges told me, these orders were not just authorizations but admonitions: In a context of shortening hospital stays, hospital administrators should give psychiatrists time to do their work.

The greatest "ambivalence" in these cases was not the patients' stated interest in treatment but their psychiatrists' confidence in that statement. Here, the contrast with the United States is stark. In New York, hospital administration and insurance generally demanded discharge as soon as a person had achieved a bare sliver of stability. That might be achieved by not articulating any plan to commit suicide for a full twenty-four hours. When that person left, they'd go to an organizationally distinct outpatient clinic with a different medical team. While hospital clinicians certainly would prefer that patients comply with their treatment on the outside, it wasn't exactly their problem if they didn't.

The challenge for the *secteur*s is different. The system was designed on the assumption that, as its architects declared in the 1960 Circular on *sectorization*, it was "indispensable that the *malade* leaving the psychiatric hospital finds at the [outpatient clinic] the same doctor."[29] The authors imagined the advantage therein would come from the fact that "no one more than the hospital psychiatrist is interested in avoiding useless hospitalizations." The logic also applies in reverse. Because a patient remains the responsibility of a *secteur* psychiatrist (or one of their colleagues) after a hospitalization, they also have a strong interest in avoiding useless discharges insofar as a person might come back quickly.

"Consent," writes Roi Livne, based on his research on palliative-care clinicians, entails transforming a patients' "volatile and possibly momentary feelings" about end-of-life care into a "fixed and solid" acceptance of death.[30] *Secteur* psychiatrists might idealize a fixed and solid acceptance of an identity as a *malade*, but they recognized it was often unrealistic. They still needed serviceable consent, which meant some basic acquiescence to the core responsibility of anyone in the bureaucratic kind *malade*: maintaining an ongoing relationship with psychiatry. Achieving it in the hospital was crucial because, once the patient was in the community, the *secteur*'s ability to nurture consent would be curtailed by the very limited time that could be dedicated to a given patient.[31]

In this process, judges could play a useful role. French psychiatrists of a psychoanalytic persuasion have long insisted that they should deliver treatment only in response to a "demand."[32] If not from the patient themselves, this could come from the family member who signs the paperwork for a hospitalization or, in the case of psychiatric care at the demand of a representative of the state, the prefect. Yet these third parties have become unreliable: isolated patients more and more often have no family to sign, and the demands of the prefecture appear suspiciously more focused on control than care. Judges have now stepped in to fill the "deficit of moral authority" sapping state institutions facing a precarious and skeptical populace.[33] "It's helpful to not be the only authority behind the maintenance of the hospitalization," one psychiatrist told me, "and to show that it's society, not the doctor, who requested it."[34]

The benefits were not just for psychiatrists' own self-conception. It allowed psychiatrists to tell their patients that it was the judge who was imposing the hospitalization (leaving out that judges invariably did so on the basis of psychiatrists' medical certificates). This displacement of responsibility, several interviewees insisted, helped maintain the relationship of trust and collaboration that a forced hospitalization invariably threatened. Preserving that relationship was essential for making patients serviceable to long-term care in the community.

## POLICING ORDER BY TREATING SUFFERING

Despite broader social narratives that associated involuntary hospitalization with the social control of violent individuals, the previous pages in this chapter have shown this misrepresents the majority of people being forced into the category *malade*. Indeed, three-quarters of the hearings I observed were for hospitalizations that were based on need-for-treatment criteria. These evoked the old justification for involuntary commitment, parens patriae, or the state's obligation to care for individuals who are too depressed, suicidal, or psychotic to do it for themselves. It was, as we have seen, relatively easy to paint imposed medical care as a way of actualizing these suffering citizens' rights. But the remainder of cases originated in another rationale for civil commitment: the state's police power, or its prerogative to preserve public order.[35] Debates over the appropriate use of *Soins psychiatrique sur décision d'un représentant de l'État* (SPDRE, Psychiatric Care at the Demand of a Representative of the State) have been so contentious precisely because these measures blur the line between healing the sick and policing the deviant. Whether these patients were considered serviceable for *secteur* psychiatry, then, was much more open to debate.

SPDRE hearings were treacherous for the psychiatric expertise that has invariably won the day, at least so far in this chapter. For one thing, the patients under SPDRE that I observed were far more likely to be male and nonwhite, and thus were more likely to trigger cultural associations of dangerous delinquents than deserving *malades*. The criteria for an SPDRE—a mental illness that "compromises the security of persons or seriously infringes on public order"—are written in the register of law, not medicine. Even judges who told me they were usually disinterested in hearings for psychiatric patients saw their value here: "These hearings are useful because, effectively, it [SPDRE] is very close to detention [in a criminal matter]: an organism of the state exercises power for public security. . . . 'Public order' is something that we know well, and there's usually a real debate [at the hearing] about it." Judges could be brought in not just automatically after twelve days, but also to adjudicate a disagreement between a treating psychiatrist (who wanted to release a patient) and the prefecture (who wanted to keep them).

In truth, the most dramatic-seeming cases of SPDREs provoked the least discussion. I observed hearings for individuals whose medical certificates reported them as having threatened to decapitate siblings, sought to abduct and rape a child, tried to force their way through security at the Parisian airport, shouted that they were a member of the Islamic State and were going to detonate themselves, or smashed a police car and spat on the officers. Judges accepted these versions of events without question. They instead asked banal questions about how a judiciable was feeling before ruling, rapidly, to keep them in.

There were more marginal cases, however. I shadowed Elena—a member of the Lawyers Rights and Psychiatry group and introduced above—as she represented a twenty-year-old man who migrated alone from Mali as a teenager. He explained that he was at the *Gare du Nord* train station when police discovered a suspicious package. They began stopping and searching pedestrians. (It's probably not by chance that they stopped a young Black man.[36]) They found an illegal knife on him and took him to a holding cell. "I live in a migrant shelter, I need it to defend myself," he explains, as Elena nods. The police then said his protestations against being incarcerated (which they apparently perceived as delusional) were "not compatible with being in a holding cell" and asked the prefecture to have him hospitalized.

"Then you don't even really have a psychiatric problem! And you definitely weren't disrupting public order," Elena exclaims, sounding incensed. That was indeed the issue: The man had actually had his twelfth-day hearing the week prior, but the judge had been unable to make a decision and called for an additional psychiatric evaluation. That evaluation stated that "the pathological character of his condition and his necessity for care remain unknown." Elena editorializes, "That's pretty curious."

When the hearing begins, the judge actually lets the man recount his story in detail. The man insists that he needs to leave the hospital to return to his job at a bakery, which provides the remittances supporting his parents in Mali. He avows, "I have nothing to do with psychiatry"—this is his first hospitalization—and that "these medications are making me weird."

"Okay, you've told me that you want to stop," the judge closes, before asking Elena, "Are there any arguments on the merits, maître?"

Elena attacks the expert evaluation: "It looks to me like it's just copied and pasted from the medical certificates. The medical evaluation says he's 'calmed down' and his delirium has been 'diminished,' even if it also says he has 'anosognosia' [a lack of insight into his condition]. It says this 'could' compromise the public order, but that's not what is required in the code. This is absolutely not enough to justify the prefecture's action [SPDRE]."

What was striking was how much the decision punted on the one issue about which the judge could have asserted their professional prerogative: whether carrying a (hidden) knife in a train station "seriously infringes on public order." Instead, his written conclusion reframed the debate in psychiatric, not legal, terms: the "risk of infringement on public order is characterized by a vast state of delirium. . . . with interpretive and hallucinatory mechanisms . . . [and] with a pathological character that [the judiciable] has only partially understood." What made him a risk to public order for the police was that he had a knife and protested being in a holding cell; what made him serviceable to psychiatry, however, was that these behaviors could be redefined as treatable psychic suffering, even if the diagnosis remained vague.

Activist lawyers like Elena accused judges of hiding behind flimsy medical evaluations because they were afraid of legal consequences if they released someone who really was violent. "I can tell you, there were six thousand patients released last year, and there were not six thousand murders," Raphael Mayet, the lawyer in Versailles, told me, "and in any case, I've never heard of a case being brought against a judge for letting someone go." But even taken at face value, this fear is a weak explanation for judicial behavior, at least outside a small subset of cases. Only a portion of SPDRE hospitalizations were in response to serious threats against others. "Troubles of public order" were often just that: patients throwing laundry out of windows in apartment buildings, walking naked down the street, or climbing atop the main statue in *Place de la République*. Involuntary psychiatric treatment was not a direct tool of the police state. It was a way of displacing social problems for which the police claimed they had no other solution.

One thirty-nine-year-old white woman really did appear to have posed more problems for the police responsible for protecting the public order than the public order per se. She requested to see the judge because she's in a program of care: a legal obligation to accept treatment on an outpatient basis under threat of rehospitalization. These programs were introduced—to much rancor—in the 2011 reform. They quickly became a ubiquitous tool for *secteur* psychiatrists seeking to liberate hospital beds by discharging patients whose commitment to care was shaky.[37] The prefecture also frequently insisted on these programs as a condition for release.[38] There's certainly merit to some psychiatrists' caution that these programs created a risk of "extending coercive treatment for an indefinite period,"[39] especially because they aren't subject to automatic judicial review.[40] That seems to be exactly the concern bringing the woman here.

This is not a typical case. The woman is accompanied by a private attorney; the prefecture has sent its own representative. Perhaps feeling a sense of gravity, the judge walks slowly through an explanation of the procedure, before asking the woman to speak.

"I have an obligation to follow this program," the woman explains, her eyes red and looking very tired, "even though I consider it completely disproportionate to my situation. It's bad for me."

"What is the program?" the judge asks.

"It's a neuroleptic injection every fourteen days at the Clinic. It's a true ordeal every time. They leave me in a terrible state. They affect my memory, my concentration, my ability to speak. I am trying to work and to study, but this is destroying my social situation. I am having to take sick days all the time because I am too tired."

"So I understand that this treatment is hard for you," the judge offers, but then sternly adds, "But I imagine they had a reason for this. They don't impose things like this for pleasure."

The woman is struggling to speak. "I don't accept that my life should be destroyed as a result of this! It's been ten months I've been doing this [the program of care]." The judge allows the conversation to wade deep into the woman's educational and professional trajectory. As the woman recounts a series of false starts on new careers in communications, advertising, and the arts, the judge recommends she read a book, *Trop intelligent pour être heureux* (*Too Intelligent to Be Happy*).

The woman's lawyer thanks the judge for "giving her some time" before explaining that "we need to go back to the origins of the case." The inception was repeated trips to the prefecture to file noise complaints. The police eventually reached the limits of their patience and brought her to the emergency room, where she was diagnosed with "incoherent and delirious ideas of persecution" and hospitalized under an SPDRE. She appealed her hospitalization and was released on a program of care. "I want to insist on a vicious cycle here," the lawyer emphasizes, in which the woman's opposition to involuntary treatment at each step became evidence of her need for it. The lawyer hired an outside expert, who concluded that she is "not refusing care but just wants to be involved in the decision. . . . Her psychic fragility is not of concern to the prefecture. She presents no risk of public order."

The lawyer for the prefecture has been looking steadily more frustrated. When it's her turn, she sharply interjects, "I've had this file for a year, and since then, she's been in complete opposition. . . . We're hearing one thing today, but when you look at what's written [in the certificates], she's denying any pathology. . . . Usually, when we're talking about ending a program, it's because the patient is fully participating, no problem, no risk of noncompliance. So let's recenter the debate: Does she need care or not?"

The woman's lawyer cuts in, "It's not that at all. The question is whether this entire circuit was justified. . . . She didn't threaten anyone. There is no complaint from the neighbors. She is the one who went to commissariat, and the police were the ones who 'detected suffering' and had her hospitalized."

"What we need to know is if she will take her medication on her own. . . . Even Madame's own expert describes her as 'fragile.' When this is the case, I have to do something," the prefecture's lawyer responds.

"Enough!" the judge declares and turns to the woman to say, "You need to understand that we're not in a penal situation here. It's not about guilt." She addresses the room: "What we have here is woman who isn't doing well, and we need to figure out what is best for her. That is the spirit that will guide my decision." The judge ultimately decided to ask for an additional expert evaluation.

The willingness of the prefecture to send a lawyer, pay for multiple outside evaluations, and fight for her continued involuntary treatment on appeal suggests that there was more at issue than the woman's well-being. But these problematic cases, which did not fit neatly into the bureaucratic kind of "criminal," needed to be reframed to fit within the overarching logic of French public psychiatry, which focused on providing care that protected a person, above all, from their own pathology. In this case, the expertise came back confirming that the woman could, and would, accept oral treatment voluntarily. The judge ended the program of care. The patient could no longer be treated involuntarily, albeit only because she had been rendered serviceable for outpatient *secteur* care.

Foucault argued that French psychiatry, as it consolidated into a medical discipline in the nineteenth century, closely allied itself with a state obsessed with security. It embraced the "notion of danger" in order to "transform an act of assistance into a phenomenon of protection."[41] Yet hearings sometimes did the opposite. They took problematic situations that had arrived in psychiatry based on concerns about danger and social protection, and reframed hospitalization as a form of assistance. But in modestly regulating a state administration that envisioned involuntary hospitalization as a tool for social control, they sidelined patients' advocates and lawyers' insistence that it was, above all, a restriction of civil liberties.

## CONCLUSION: REFRAMING RIGHTS

Elena was exasperated. She had been up all night combing through the dossiers that the clerk had sent her—far, far too late in the day—for this afternoon's hearing. She wrote her conclusions in detail, pointing to the precise requirements of the Code of Public Health that a missing signature or incomplete medical justification violated. She coached her clients and fought hard in the hearings. All for naught. The judge left every patient in the hospital. "I don't know at what point a person [one of Elena's clients] lost their status as a citizen. Is it when she became sick? When she was hospitalized? . . . We lose our rights the same time we lose our minds. But those are two independent things—we can keep our rights and lose our minds," she fumed.

France is a laggard. As one group of French sociologists wrote, the "judiciarization" of involuntary care in 2011 was "slow" (decades after the United States), "inevitable" (given European mandates), and "embarrassing" (in the gaping holes it left regarding patients' rights).[42] Even with a massive mobilization of judicial resources to oversee psychiatry, France's rate of involuntary hospitalization has continued its inexorable rise.[43] It is now well above the median for developed countries (figure 6.1).[44] As I argued in chapter 5, this rise in constraint is probably more sociologically than legally determined: It is a function of the changing profiles of psychiatric patients, the diminished capacity of psychiatry to respond to them effectively, and a vicious cycle by which steadily more disaffected patients are met with firmer and firmer constraint. Judges legitimated this rise, rendering patients serviceable

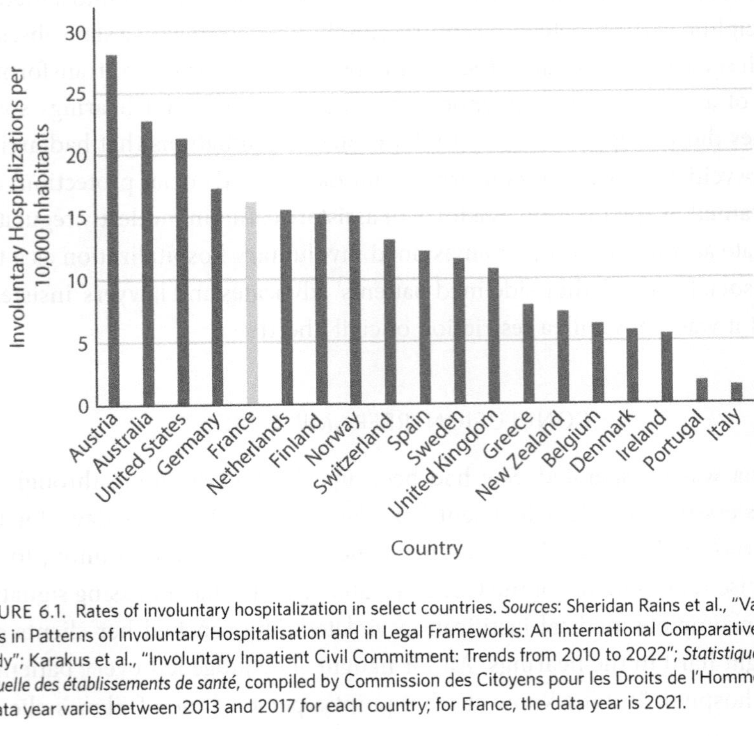


FIGURE 6.1. Rates of involuntary hospitalization in select countries. *Sources*: Sheridan Rains et al., "Variations in Patterns of Involuntary Hospitalisation and in Legal Frameworks: An International Comparative Study"; Karakus et al., "Involuntary Inpatient Civil Commitment: Trends from 2010 to 2022"; *Statistique annuelle des établissements de santé*, compiled by Commission des Citoyens pour les Droits de l'Homme.
* Data year varies between 2013 and 2017 for each country; for France, the data year is 2021.

by confirming that constraint was minimally procedurally compliant in a context of tightening national and international norms.

One reason the judicial intrusion into French psychiatry has had such a muted effect may be that, quite simply, many judges and lawyers didn't see involuntary treatment as a bad thing. As Judge Pierraud told me after a day of lecturing judiciables about the merits of treatment, "The people we saw today, they were all really not doing well. They're here to get care. A lot of them are going to leave in a few days, so there's no reason to lift the hospitalization. The idea of the sane person who's trapped by psychiatry, that's something that's in novels, but not something I see here." She went on, "I've read Foucault. I get there's a tension in a democratic society between safety and liberty. . . . When I do hearings for detainees [in jail], I see some situations that are pretty marginal [i.e., lacking justification]. I let people go all the time. But I don't think that's what we're doing in psychiatry."

Judges effectively abdicated their own power in order to defer to psychiatrists as the real judges of the need for care. They could tell that themselves they did so based on high-minded ideals that would be less available to, say, a judge in New York, where "social rights" (an entitlement to medical care or housing, for example) do not exist alongside civil rights. Judge Léonhard told me, "There are two infringements to rights [in involuntary hospitalizations]: individual liberty and consent to care. Those are constitutional rights. . . . For the law to permit such an infringement on such important rights, there has to be another right that is as important to justify it. . . . That's the right to protection of health. The law says, clearly: if there's someone who needs care, she's not able to demand it, then I, the state, will substitute for her and organize involuntary care." From her perspective, lawyers like Elena were wrong: Citizens can keep their rights and lose their minds as long as "rights" mean the paternalistic protection of a nominally benevolent state. Reclassifying patients as suffering citizens not only reinforced their identification as *malades*; it also reconfirmed psychiatric jurisdiction over them.

No one should be let off the hook here. Courtroom practices ranged from disrespectful to shameful, as evidenced by a judge's unbuttoned robe or by a lawyer scrolling through text messages while her client described the most traumatic moment of his life. Judges probably were leaving some patients in the hospital based on false stereotypes about people with mental illness as dangerous.[45] Psychiatrists were firing off medical certificates for patients whose internment was more about the *secteur*'s convenience than medical necessity. Judge Pierraud's dismissal of Foucault's idea that psychiatry can be an instrument of social control was too glib: As chapter 5 showed, the French interior ministry and its local prefectures have jealously guarded their prerogative to use hospitals to manage the most vexing marginal people.

This chapter has shown, however, that professional perceptions of the hearings reflect their actual content, that is, the reality of how *malades* grasped (or not) the new rights afforded them. While a subset of patients looked like the ones I saw in New York—potentially threatening and adamantly resistant—*most* patients really did appear, as one judge wrote, as "above all, people who suffer."[46] Their complaints were more often about the nature of care (an excess of restrictions on circulating in the hospital or an overly heavy medication dosage) than the principle of needing care itself. After the 2011 reform, they were only legally serviceable if a judge approved their hospitalization. From a medical point of view, most of them were already on their way to being serviceable outpatients—not self-governing, independent subjects, but people for whom *secteur* care was more or less likely to stick, at least for a time.

The result of these dynamics was, in a way, parallel to what we saw in part II of this book. When faced with the difficulty of reclassifying chronic *malades* as people with psychic handicaps, the tendency was for one system of social protection—the one for disabilities—to retreat, leaving them to the *secteurs*. When conducting hearings for patients who, on the whole, looked less like the dangerous madmen conjured up by Sarkozy and more like a mass of suffering (and, admittedly, occasionally delinquent or disruptive) *malades*, judges withdrew from claiming jurisdiction over this bureaucratic kind. Black robes hid behind white coats, control was redefined as care, and rights kept the same meaning they had had since the 1960s: a right, above all, to whatever services the *secteurs* were offering.

# CONCLUSION

## Beyond *Malades*

When I conducted my observations in 2015 and 2016, I heard almost unanimous worries about lengthening waits for outpatient care in the *secteurs*; insufficient places in the disability system to make up for hospital beds that were closing; and looming cuts to personnel everywhere, from the clinics to the courts. I followed up with Doctor Delignon, the head psychiatrist of the *secteur* where I conducted my fieldwork, toward the end of my sojourn. I asked about her expectations for the future. She sighed, "We used to see our patients more often, now less. We used to fight to have funds for a new project, now we are just fighting not to lose them. Next, I don't know what we're going to be fighting for. Voilà, that's where we are. It's difficult."

It was, as she perhaps realized, the calm before the storm. Soon, a slow decline would become a free fall. In 2018, I revisited the hospital where her *secteur* was located. The grounds were calm and well-tended, the high stone wall around them muffling the frenzied noise of the city outside. A flyer on a bulletin board advertised a patient support group and a monthly meeting dedicated to the "Pleasure of Reading [Jacques] Lacan." (Such reading is not, in my experience, pleasurable, but then again, I never attended the group.) Then I saw them: painted outlines of nurses on the pavement, as if I were visiting a murder scene. I looked up to see a banner hung from one of the wards, declaring, "Hospital at the end of its breath" (figure C.1).

FIGURE C.1. Image of a protest, in the form of a chalk outline, on the grounds of a psychiatric hospital. *Source*: Author.

Indeed, according to *Le Monde*, France's public psychiatric system in 2018 was subject to "economic asphyxiation."[1] The newspaper varied the descriptors in a series of articles, but they all went in the same direction: the *secteurs* were "hell" and being "massacred" by budget cuts.[2] This was leading to a "profound depression"[3] and "great suffering,"[4] for professionals as well as patients. In Rouvray, seven psychiatric nurses went on a hunger strike underneath a banner giving the middle finger to the Regional Health Authority (or, according to them, the "Regional Authority for the Restriction of Care"), declaring that "the psychiatric hospital is cracking up."[5] In Le Havre, staff camped on top of an overflowing emergency room, broadcasting the message, "Welcome to the Hospital of Shame."[6] That year, the National Assembly issued a new report on psychiatry. The deputies who authored it ditched the usual staid prose to declare that the public psychiatric system was "bordering on implosion." The *secteurs* were "inefficient and ineffective," resulting in a "catastrophic care."[7]

It's striking that for all the debates about the ideal system of the future that have crisscrossed this book—should we focus on a bounded group of real *malades* or scale up treatment to address mental health; put the accent on autonomy or protection; prioritize rights, control, or care?—the assessment of the present was remarkably similar. Almost no one I interviewed would disagree that the system was providing "too late diagnoses, insufficient prevention and early intervention, ruptures in the trajectory of care, excessive use of involuntary hospitalization, unreliable returns to social and professional life . . . As the number of people in suffering rises without ceasing, French psychiatry is waiting to be cared for."[8]

With respect to the chalk-outline images of the nurses I encountered, the culprit to many was clear: a center-right government presided over by Emmanuel Macron that was more committed to making France into a "start-up nation" than one with decent public services. Gaia, one of the *secteur* psychologists who worked beside Doctor Delignon, lamented, "The public medical system in France is dying, and at the level of the state, there's no one to defend it. There's always fewer staff, fewer beds, so our working conditions demand we give a lot of ourselves for financial remuneration that is pretty minimal relative to our training. . . . And so for our patients, I wonder where they have to go to be treated properly. . . . We're leaving patients in the street while private clinics are opening." While eight thousand beds in the public system had closed since 2008, the private sector—for which psychiatry was the most profitable medical discipline—was expanding.[9] Sometimes, they were taking over the very buildings that the public system had abandoned. Rarely were they serving the same patients.[10] "They're always recruiting," Gaia, the psychologist, noted.

Frustrated with the way a lack of resources forced them to deliver care that they themselves knew was substandard, more and more professionals were "throwing in the sponge [towel]," according to the head of the Union of Hospital Psychiatrists.[11] By 2023, nearly one-quarter of psychiatric positions in the *secteurs* were empty.[12] Even with an emergency injection of new funds, clinics struggled to find nurses willing to work there.[13] The situation will get worse. One-quarter of French psychiatrists are over the age of sixty-five. Psychiatry is one of the least-demanded specialties among French medical students: In 2019, nearly one in five residency positions went unfilled.[14] "If you want to really do psychiatry, you need human relations," one nurse told me, "and if you have only minimal personnel, you just become a distributor of medications. It creates frustration and violence"—which in turn means fewer humans to relate in the future.

Neoliberalism is a perennial boogeyman. Austerity is guilty of the wrongs attributed to it. Public services could almost always do with more money. Making budget cuts the primary source of all ills certainly appeals to me. It would allow me to keep my faith in the fundamental soundness of the state-led, public welfare model I went to France to study in the first place. But a diagnosis fixated on funding requires a bit of contextualization. In the 2010s, psychiatry's budget grew more slowly than that for health care in general, but it still rose roughly in line with inflation.[15] In response to those dire headlines and irate protesting nurses in 2018 (a time christened the "Springtime of Psychiatry"), the state injected a 32 percent budgetary increase into the proverbial arm of public psychiatry from 2020 to 2023.[16] But when another parliamentary mission delved deep into the situation in 2024, it concluded that, billions of euros later, public mental health care remained in "profound crisis" with "systemic failings and dysfunctions."[17]

In the decade since I conducted my primary fieldwork (and at the time this book went to press), I have struggled with what to make of these dire portrayals. We should be careful about narratives of "crisis," recognizing that they are never neutral descriptors but always arguments that we prioritize one set of issues and solutions over others. References to a psychiatric system in crisis go back decades. Perhaps, even, as one French university psychiatrist wrote, "psychiatry is in a permanent state of crisis" because of the "complexity of the functioning of the brain" and, as such, the difficulty of treating it.[18] But as I have reconnected with some of my key informants in the final stages of writing this book, I have been convinced that the contemporary crisis in France is indeed deep. It is not a media construction or political instrument. The crisis goes beyond the failed implementation of a model that is fundamentally sound. This concluding chapter is my attempt to grapple with that uneasy recognition.

## TROUBLE IN THE GARDEN

Faced with a relentless stream of negative portrayals and depressing predictions, I decided to end every interview with a simple question: "What works well in France?" It often provoked an abrupt pause, an uncomfortable rupture in a prototypically French litany of complaints. Then it seemed like my informants remembered where I was from, and an answer came to them. "Well, I don't know about *the United States*, but here we have public psychiatry, the *secteurs*, that permits people to have care—even if it's late, even if it could be better. In another system, those people might not have access. We need to keep that." It wouldn't be particularly revealing if this praise of the *secteurs* came from one of the old-guard psychiatrists (say, Doctor Mailhol) who had a hand in setting them up. But the above quote came from a management consultant working for the government agency responsible for improving health system performance. A ministry official who had spent our interview trashing public psychiatry for clinging to psychoanalysis and delivering poor quality care conceded, "There is an honor to French psychiatry, which is to be everywhere and to be free, to receive every person sent to it." Only about 20 percent of my interviewees actually worked in the *secteurs*, but half of my sample evoked the *secteurs* and the access to care they (theoretically) provided as the system's strong point.

If I were to sit down with a piece of paper and sketch the outlines of an ideal mental health system, the contours would look like the system in France.[19] I would start with robust public financing.[20] This is obvious but not automatic: as the introduction to this book suggested, "It was no mean feat . . . to make madness 'a matter of state' "[21]—or at least, a matter of the caring wing of the state (and not the responsibility of the police or prison system). For all the justified complaints about budgets, mental health in France, as psychiatrist Alain Lopez writes, "benefits from an important effort of collective solidarity."[22] Although we should be cautious about whether the data are entirely comparable, France spends the largest proportion of its health budget (15 percent) on mental health of any country reporting data to the World Health Organization. That is twice the level of the United States (figure C.2).

That funding finances a system that is public in both statute and ethos. Precisely because the mad are subject to stigma and prejudice, ensuring they have access to care demands more than just giving them health insurance. Carefully delineated criteria (like those I saw in California or Lille) might seem like a smart way to allocate scarce resources, but they're easy to twist to keep out clients who might be expensive or unpleasant. By contrast, the *secteur*, a single institution responsible for a given territory, created, as one psychiatrist explained to me, "a quasi-legal obligation" to provide a minimum floor of care to everyone with a serious mental illness.

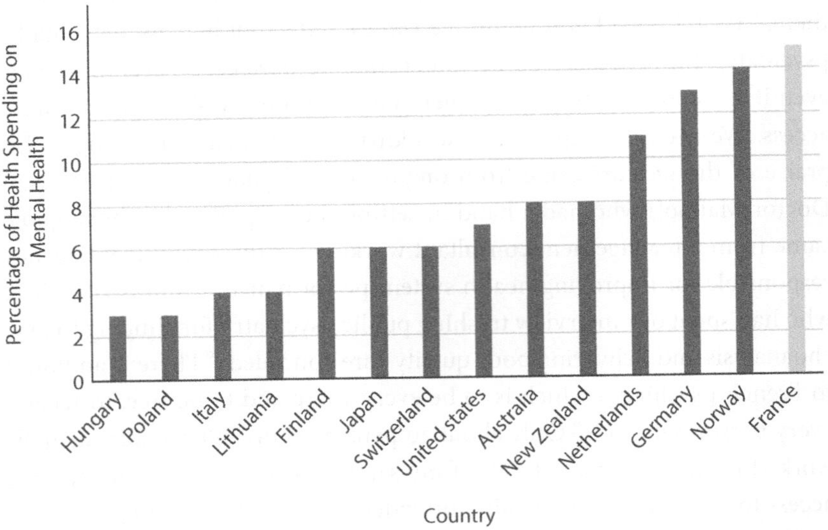


FIGURE C.2. Mental health spending as a proportion of overall health spending, by country. *Source*: World Health Organization, *Mental Health Atlas 2020*, World Health Organization, published October 8, 2021, https://www.who.int/publications/i/item/9789240036703.

With or without that obligation, the spirit of French professionals I interviewed was that the noblest exercise of their occupation was in working with the sickest patients. Public mental health workers in France saw themselves like oncologists; many psychiatrists in the United States appear to view themselves more like cosmetic surgeons. The attempts by French professionals to cleave "mental illness" and "mental health" through practices of bounding is too neat to account for the complexity of human suffering. But systems with limited resources need to set priorities. With its ongoing commitment to the (problematic) category of *malades*, France has done much better than the United States, where resources seem pulled invariably toward the worried well or visibly (but not necessarily pathologically) disruptive.

In my view, it was equally logical to link inpatient and outpatient care, as the *secteurs* do. The original sin of deinstitutionalization in the United States was the rapid abandonment into the community of the people previously abandoned in the back of the state hospitals. US architects of deinstitutionalization designed a system as if hospitalization was completely unnecessary. Yet hospitalization remains part of the trajectory of people with the most serious illnesses—it's just that psychiatric hospitals have become a lucrative private enterprise that have little obligation to coordinate with the public outpatient teams that work with their barely stabilized patients on discharge.[23] The heavy French reliance on long hospitalizations is an enormous problem. But so long as the system relies on hospitalization in some cases, those expensive and restrictive sojourns should be in the service of a comprehensive, integrated, and long-term therapeutic strategy. To that end, sectorization built in, from the start, a mandate that the mental health system address social as well as medical needs, with the understanding that more "general" welfare programs might exclude *malades*. In France, responsibility for meeting those needs has passed from the asylums to the *secteurs*, to the disability system, but it has always rested somewhere.

Perhaps the strongest contrast was captured in the simplest quote, this one from Gaia, the *secteur* psychologist. "What is the strong point of the French system?" I queried, and she responded, "That it exists. The clinic exists, the disability office exists, national insurance exists." I've presented the US system as a kind of distorted mirror to France. But there's an alternative view: The comparison makes no sense because the United States has no system. There is no overarching logic of allocation, no bureaucratic kind for people with mental illness, no coherent vision of what makes a patient serviceable for hospital discharge or ready for an autonomous life in the community.[24] France has a system. There is a theory behind it, one based on real historical reflection about the character and needs of *malades*. It binds together, loosely, the host of government agencies responding to people with mental illness. As psychiatrist Alain Lopez writes, "Seen from the sky, the landscape designed by [sectorization] appears calm, carefully organized, ordered in the style of the French garden. . . . No territory untended. . . . Sometimes complicated but obeying a strict geometry planned by the architect-gardeners."[25]

"Closer to the ground," Lopez admits, "the 'psycho-paradise' loses its elegant colors."[26] Theory has to confront practice.[27] And in practice, the beautiful model doesn't work—for any of the core challenges analyzed in this book. For all the supposed integration of inpatient and outpatient care in the *secteur* system, one-quarter of French patients have not had any follow-up within two months of a hospital discharge. This rate is much higher than that in the United Kingdom, Germany, Italy, Poland, or Belgium.[28] As for autonomy, the Economist Intelligence Unit ranked

France twentieth out of thirty countries for its integration of people with serious mental illnesses into a "full life" in the community.[29] In 2017, a UN Special Rapporteur on the rights of people with disabilities concluded her visit to France by decrying the way the country clung to institutions that "segregate and isolate individuals from their communities, deny their choice of and control over living and support arrangements, and significantly restrict their day-to-day decisions."[30] When it comes to rights, the picture is dire. Patients are far more likely to be subjected to isolation and restraints than in many other European countries (where, in some cases, these measures have been abolished).[31]

This book has pointed to complex arbitrages around (imposed) care versus civil rights, protection versus independence. Yet at many points in history, the mad have been offered none of the above. It's the potential worst-case scenario that looms fearsomely over contemporary debates in France.

## THEORY AND PRAXIS

How do we turn a system that works in theory into one that works in practice? I embarked on this project with a strong set of theoretical priors of my own. I assumed that the distinctive balance of rights, care, and control that differentiated the French public mental health system from its US counterpart would be the outcome of classification struggles. The key players would be state administrators pushing certain categories down the transmission belt, which would clash with the categories that emerge from the interprofessional shoving match on the ground. Yet my framework left out a third, crucial factor: the population of *malades* themselves. As I saw in every field site, they constantly violated bureaucratic divisions between maladies and troubles; they exposed the contradictions in public policy by engaging with disability benefits in ways that sharply diverged from the expectations of administrators and advocates; they sometimes refused to offer the cooperation and consent that the *secteur* system required for them to be serviceable—and, I should note, they rarely presented the kind of dangerousness that would lend any truth to the discourse of dangerousness promulgated by partisans of hard-edged social control, like Nicolas Sarkozy. This book's argument has thus had to account for the often hidden human reality that resists, even in the absence of a visible antipsychiatric movement of the kind documented in Italy or the United States. The landscape-architects of the proverbial French psychiatric garden must do the same.

As the case of psychic handicap and the evolution of the disability system showed particularly sharply, the constant jostling of *malades* against the categories imposed on them has been, on its own, a motor for adapting policy and professional practices to match. The next step for reformers, however, is to incorporate preemptively and explicitly the people most directly concerned by public psychiatry into the organization of the system. Since a 2002 Law on the Rights of *Malades* (which covered the entire health system, not just psychiatry), the participation of the public in French social policy has advanced through the inclusion of patients in the management committees of hospitals and greater support for national users' associations.[32] Still, when it comes to user participation, the mental health system lags behind. Only in September 2023 did the state introduce a questionnaire to gather patients' own opinions on their hospitalizations.[33]

One promising transformation has been the gradual incorporation of "peers" into treatment teams. People with lived experience carry with them a new capacity to connect to patients and an orientation that pushes medical teams to focus on strengths and the possibility of recovery, not just chronicity and symptoms.[34] There's been a flourishing of terms to describe these actors: "peer mediators," "peer aids," "professional peers," "peer practitioners," and "persons with lived experience."[35] Most of these appellations were dreamed up by reform-minded professionals, like Jean-Luc Roelandt in Lille, to try to legitimize peers as professionals alongside nurses, social workers, and psychiatrists. But I'm struck by the demand of a group of service users who wanted to be recognized as "citizen-experts," a name that they insisted "distinguishes them from 'expert users' or 'expert patients' . . . because citizenship assumes their inclusion . . . in society as actors fully engaged in the mechanisms of democracy, and contributing to the decision-making process."[36] The coordinator for one department's planning process for mental health, which had actively incorporated these citizens into every working group, explained, "They're really the guardians of the temple. . . . We see in the meetings that when they explain what they need, it cuts off debates that are more ideological or political, it runs around all the power games" between different factions of psychiatry.

Consider how citizen expertise could bring a new perspective on one of the most entrenched debates in French psychiatry. For decades, university- and neurobiologically-inclined psychiatrists have been trying to shift hospital care away from the old asylums, now rebaptized "specialized hospital centers," into multidisciplinary general hospitals.[37] The hope is that, in doing so, they will finally establish psychiatry as a prestigious medical specialty, founded on scientifically validated treatments. Arrayed against them are practitioners who see dedicated psychiatric hospitals as bastions of a distinctive and autonomous discipline, anchored in institutional psychotherapy and psychoanalysis. (Plus, several insisted, the green spaces around the old asylums make for a more pleasant place to perambulate than sterile hospital corridors.)

When I raised this debate with the president of an association for people diagnosed as bipolar, she immediately pivoted to something more practical. Once someone is identified as a *malade*, no matter what kind of hospital they are at, professionals "think about our soul and our psychic problems, but they have a tendency to forget about our bodies." Her concerns about *physical* care for patients with *mental* illnesses is well-founded: Life expectancy for people with serious mental illness is a shockingly low sixty years in France.[38] Yet moving care to general hospitals, she told me, did not solve the problem in her case because the stigma against mentally ill patients continues among somatic doctors even when psychiatry is just down the hallway. So some citizen-experts have proposed bringing generalist doctors into the clinics, allowing same-day psychiatric and medical consultations. This would extend the model of low-barrier access and universal coverage on which the *secteurs* were founded to heal patients' bodies alongside their spirits.

Citizen expertise could point out, in advance, the potential pitfalls of well-meaning reforms. Now, in theory, the main legislative changes charted by this book had been given a stamp of approval by psychiatric patients. In practice, this meant that Claude Finkelstein, the head of the national organization representing users of psychiatry, signed off on communiqués authored by weightier associations like UNAFAM, representing parents. But it's clear that no one really asked, prior to the 2005 reform to the disability system, whether service users wanted to pursue their desire for autonomy through the label of "psychic handicap." As I could see in my observations at the disability office, had they asked, the answer might have been no. As Finkelstein told me,

"The day that we have a meeting at the disability office, we're going to get up, get dressed, put on a tie, and say 'We can do everything' and the person at the disability office, they're not going to try to understand if it's just to show that we're still human or because we are really able to do all those things." There are clearly ways that disability office evaluations could be improved: focusing on strengths or conducting assessments at sites that do not require a self-identification of disability to access (like the public employment agency or housing for people recently brought in from the street).

Ultimately, though, what users emphasized was that the rights to social services that the disability system offers should not be secondary to and contingent upon psychiatric care. Claude Deutsch, from Advocacy France, told me his shock when he was invited by the state disability agency after the 2005 reform to a group to elaborate best practices around psychic handicap: "It was flagrant: they said, 'there's a new paradigm,' but the first subject they wanted to talk about was . . . medical treatment. And very last, social life." Interventions like Housing First or Accompanied Employment, which have had tiny pilots in France, focus on meeting basic needs for a roof or a paycheck first, without requiring participants to be medicated or wholly without symptoms. They only subsequently use housing and work as a way to build connections that later bring people into treatment. "We want work and a roof, not another evaluation," one service user remarked to me.

A broader rethink would reimagine who exactly will render chronic *malades* autonomous. From the therapeutic clubs of institutional psychotherapy onward, French policy has almost always imagined autonomy as something developed from the top down. These initiatives largely ignore independence that is being built from the bottom up. As Sasha Warren, a scholar, activist, and founder of a Hearing Voices Network in Minnesota in the United States, notes, even where there is "no mass movement of the mad as mad," people nonetheless "organize themselves wherever they talk openly about their pain and strengths, meet in group homes or on street corners, exchange cigarettes or secrets . . . [They] organize themselves in every psych ward, every clubhouse, and every asylum in the world."[39] One successful bridging of state-sanctioned and user-led organizing has been the spread of groups of mutual assistance (*groupes d'entraide mutuelle*), of which there are now 690 in France.[40] These were originally conceived of us sites of social exchange, but this vision lacks ambition. These groups should be authorized to apply for financing to provide some of the services currently assigned only to professional associations via the disability office, like launching small-scale shared cooperative housing or providing services for helping with activities of daily life (for example, shopping or hygiene).

The judicial reviews of involuntary hospitalization were one of the most flagrant sites of discord between theory and practice. Nearly everyone I interviewed saw them as ethically essential in principle and mostly useless in reality. In the United Kingdom, patients have been asked to help design psychiatric hospital wards (more colorful walls, a 'zany zone' to let off steam without going into isolation[41]); why not ask users to reimagine hearings in France? That could start with recognizing, as a participant in the *Group Information Asile* noted to me, the marked devaluation implied by the fact that judges are asked to verify the detention of a criminal defendant after only forty-eight hours, while patients in psychiatry wait twelve days. For all the flaws of the US mental health system, I saw a better model in New York: one where specially trained lawyers meet with patients upon their admission, negotiate with psychiatrists to find an agreement that avoids legal constraint, and demand a hearing when no accord is forthcoming. Refocusing the work of judges on instances of real conflict will make their role clearer and—one hopes—help correct their shameful disinvestment in the procedure.

The best way to address the problems with judicial hearings, however, is to have far fewer of them. Pioneering French researchers have already shown how psychiatric advanced directives—documents that specify a person's preferences for how to be treated, who to contact, and where to take them in the event of a crisis—can lead to dramatic reductions in involuntary treatment. This is especially true when the documents are filled in with the collaboration of peers (not psychiatrists), who are both better able to understand the intimate needs of other people living with mental illnesses and share what works for them.[42] These documents can help answer questions that are unanswerable at the level of all *malades* at once. Should judges wear street clothes, to emphasize that patients are not before the court to be judged, or black robes, to highlight that the subjects of the hearings are judiciables whose concerns merit the full solemnity of the law? Because taking on and off a robe is the matter of a few seconds, we could let each person specify in advance.

Many of my interlocuters emphasized that none of these transformations was possible without a profound change in a professional culture that prioritizes paternalist protection over horizontal engagement. Culture does not simply drift; it must be pushed. As Philippe Maugiron, a person with experience being treated in the French mental health system and who now trains other peer workers, put it, "The future, it's users who are going to go inside the services, influence the professionals and slowly modify the practices of care so that they're more in line with their needs and that will take into account their experiences." Maugiron wanted to emphasize, however, how difficult it is to "superimpose knowledge that we have a hard time qualifying and attaching to 'legitimate knowledge' because the real question, it's the legitimacy and hierarchization of knowledge within the teams."

What Maugiron captured, I think, is that participation—whether a citizen-expert in a working group or a peer aid in a *secteur* team—means little without power.[43] I don't mean "power" in the sense of the most sanitized vision of "empowerment," which often refers to training individuals to master their own symptoms; I mean power *over* the system. One citizen-expert who lived with bipolar disorder was tapped to colead a working group focused on prevention and destigmatization in her departmental mental health planning project. She told me, "The fact of being a coleader [of the group] alongside a psychiatrist, with a big group around the table . . . was what allowed me to finally say, 'Yes, I've recovered.' . . . it was all about power." Such a transformation is no doubt a moral imperative. But as I hope I've shown throughout the book, it's also the best way to harness the constant movement of *malades*, who have never really acted in line with what the category implies about them, and use it to create a system that actually matches the people it serves.

## BRINGING THE BUREAUCRATIZED BACK IN

States make people. This statement is both jarring from a lay perspective and a truism from a sociological one. States wrangle infinitely complex human variations and cram them into population categories as diverse as "domestic violence victim," "missing person," or "Hispanic."[44] Professionals craft new populations as well; when clinicians think they are elaborating a new diagnosis, like "multiple personality disorder," they are inadvertently fabricating new people who fit into it. Ian Hacking's theory of human kinds is precisely about how experts create new possibilities for how people exist in the world, such that "classifications and our classes [of people] conspire to emerge hand in hand."[45] His framework is powerful because it is dynamic. The making of new populations is not just a matter of top-down imposition or professional-to-professional classificatory combat; it is one where human kinds are constantly forcing modifications to the categories applied to them. I've swapped in the modifier "bureaucratic" to help us think more precisely about the kinds that states create, and the way bureaucratic kinds in turn transform states. I'll highlight three key distinctions.

In Hacking's world, new classifications can emerge almost as fast as a new printing of the *Diagnostic and Statistical Manual*, and they disappear once professionals decide to start using a new diagnostic code. "*Fugeur*" (a person departing on inexplicable pathological voyages) and "multiple personality disorder" were once the human kinds du jour, but they rapidly fell out of favor.[46] The bureaucratic kind *malade* has, in contrast, had remarkable staying power, enduring through profound changes to psychiatric nosography (like the declining importance of psychoanalysis), the invention of new medications, and a dramatic cultural change that has reclassified a host of experiences and psychological states under the rubric of "mental health."

In part 1 of this book, I examine how states identify bureaucratic kinds through an analysis of a distinctive approach to identifying *malades*: "bounding." This classificatory approach, I argue, was persistent (despite high-level attempts to displace it) because state categories are not just figments of experts' conceptual imagination; they are embedded throughout the administrative apparatus. In France, bounding is rooted in the underdevelopment of epidemiology, the historical deference to professional judgment in regulation, and an approach to funding mental health care that favored categorical rationing over fine-grained rationalization of care. By juxtaposing "bounding" against "scaling" (and pointing to how scaling seems to have permeated the US mental health system), I hope this book can push forward comparative research on the distinctive ways that states delineate, demarcate, and designate their subjects.[47]

In part II of this book, I asked how states transform (or fail to transform) bureaucratic kinds. Again, the story here is more complex than that told by Hacking, for whom "transformation" usually came through some kind of therapy or treatment. States care, but they also punish, rehabilitate, discipline, and educate. Increasingly, they try to do so all at once. As I point out, one feature of bureaucratic kinds is a set of expectations for how those in a bureaucratic kind relate to the state itself: the manner in which they ask for benefits, participate in programs, and provide necessary information. Insofar as sociologists have redefined the state as a many-handed entity, the way these expectations cohere or conflict is a crucial question that can only be answered by studies that examine how the same population is palmed off from one agency to another.[48]

The admittedly very particular case of psychic handicap points to an underexamined challenge in transforming bureaucratic kinds. Scholars have frequently analyzed morally and politically charged debates over the direction of change for certain categories of people (consider, for example, conflicts over whether welfare reform should approach recipients as cheats to be punished or victims to be paternalistically redirected[49]). In the French case, however, we see that even politically and morally consensual reforms can face their own difficulties. After all, nearly all my informants in France described greater autonomy as a desirable goal and recognized that in the current context a label of "disability" was crucial for cultivating it. The 2005 reform that introduced psychic handicap nonetheless foundered in a morass of logical and practical contradictions. The state expected different things from different bureaucratic kinds, disabled and *malade*, while also presuming the same people would act as if they belonged to both categories simultaneously. This incoherence may actually be a core part of the contemporary experience of marginalized people in navigating complex social welfare systems. In the criminal justice system, for example, public defenders may ask their clients to be deferential and passive, while the courts that mandate people to therapeutic rehabilitation programs might ask for an active pursuit of self-reliance.[50]

Bureaucratic kinds are distinctive not just in the ways they are identified and change, but also in the degree to which membership in them is involuntary. While people placed in the human kinds of interest to Hacking didn't necessarily choose to be diagnosed with conditions like "multiple personality disorder," many of us can avoid the scientists and medical professionals Hacking focused on if we want to. But human kinds administered by the state—conscripted soldier, say, or minor in the child protective system—are not optional. Involuntary hospitalization, which we examined in part III, is an exemplary case of how the coercive power of the state can be harnessed toward cramming recalcitrant subjects into a bureaucratic kind that they are actively refusing.

Toward what end? Social theorists like Nikolas Rose have envisioned a brave new world in which people are "governed through freedom": Society's demand for policing marginalized people can be reconciled with the state's limited resources and new civil rights protections only by making people into self-governing subjects.[51] This would appear like a fantastical ideal to the *secteur* professionals I interviewed, for whom *malades* seemed indefinitely destined to need an occasional arm-twist to stay in care. A different set of scholars have argued more recently that states' aspirations of social control, particularly in places like California where where mass incarceration has (temporarily) lost support but a dramatic expansion of the welfare state is deemed impossible, have been defined down.[52] Harm reduction programs like syringe exchanges, sanctioned homeless encampments, or mental health programs content to respect clients' choices to refuse treatment and (sometimes literally) rot away reflect a new, de minimis approach to the "tolerant containment" of disorder

I have offered "serviceability" as a middle ground between images of an omnipotent disciplinary state and of one withered into begrudging, if not benevolent, toleration. It starts from the recognition that what modern states most demand from bureaucratic kinds is that they keep moving: Welfare-to-work recipients need to be progressing to the next level of a retraining program; addicts should be stepping down to a less intensive level of treatment; inmates should be preparing for release to a halfway house. Serviceability captures the minimum level of cooperation for "people-processing" institutions to keep processing.[53] In the hospitalization hearings I observed in Paris, that meant patients performing a more-than-skin-deep consent to a long-term relationship with psychiatry, even if it rarely took the form of a firm acceptance of the identity of *malade*. But serviceability depends on context-specific regulations and resource limitations. In New York, serviceability meant compliance—not in the sense of long-term, self-administered medication but a willingness to swallow resistance to swallowing pills for just a few more days until discharge.[54] States may not be able to impose social control through a unified, all-encompassing web of surveillance and discipline, but as the mad can attest, they haven't given up on it either. Instead, control stems from the aggregation of more localized attempts to garner just enough collaboration from recalcitrant subjects to pass them along to the next bureaucracy.

That's the three-part story of how states make bureaucratic kinds. What about how bureaucratic kinds remake states? I've argued that bringing bureaucratic kinds into our analysis helps solve two analytic problems in the study of street-level bureaucracies (focused on a horizontal shoving match) and the fabrication of new classifications in state policy (the transmission belt). The existing research on public servants on the ground points to perpetual chaos via never-ending processes of "burden shuffling," "people exchanging," or "institutional offloading."[55] While I saw this anarchy up close in ethnographic research in both the United States and France, what struck me as a comparative scholar when I zoomed out was that ubiquitous practices of shuffling, exchanging, and offloading added up to completely divergent trajectories for people living with serious mental illnesses in the two countries. When evaluators in the disability office decided an applicant was too sick to benefit from a program, law enforcement officers brought someone to the police infirmary after deeming them too disruptive to be placed in jail, or judges threw up their hands claiming they lacked the jurisdiction or expertise to challenge psychiatrists' restrictions on patients' rights, the result was the same: people were funneled back to the *secteurs*. Even in the face of professional practices that look like signs of conflict and fragmentation, the bureaucratic kind of *malade* holds the distinctively French response to madness together, even in the face of winds blowing (often from across the Atlantic) pushing it in a different direction. By contrast, I have argued that the absence of any true state-recognized identity for people with chronic, disabling mental illness in the United States facilitates this same population's aimless inter-agency itinerancy between emergency rooms, shelters, jails, and the street.

I'll extend this idea of the power of bureaucratic kinds to give direction to the shoving match by drawing on Elizabeth Chiarello's study of the professional scrum—pharmacists, pain doctors, district attorneys, police officers—jockeying over how to respond to the opioid epidemic in the United States. She initially expected to find health-care and enforcement professionals "at an impasse," a perpetual standoff as to whether opioid users are patients to be cared for or criminals to be policed.[56] Yet she arrived at a striking conclusion: Health-care professionals had largely embraced "policing patients" as a core part of their mission. As I had in France, she too found a tacit agreement that limited the endless bureaucratic shuffle. She argues that pharmacists and physicians had been enlisted as enforcers after receiving from the criminal-legal system what she calls a "Trojan horse technology"[57]: databases of patients' prescription histories. These were sold to them as a tool for making responsible and legally compliant decisions about dispensing opioids but facilitated monitoring and flagging heavy users to law enforcement. A solution developed in response to the particular challenges faced by law enforcement, when "gifted" to another set of professionals to solve a different set of problems, can facilitate collaboration between them.

But police aren't just sending *solutions* to health-care professionals; they're also creating the *problem*, that is, a population of people in (psychic and physical) pain seeking drugs. The oversized criminal justice system in the United States produces enormous amounts of suffering.[58] It starves social and medical services of the resources to address it. It then deprives people of other tools to numb their hurt beyond legal or illegal opioids. In short, when they get in front of health-care professionals, many ostensible patients don't look like the kinds of patients these professionals have been trained to treat; rather, they've been made to resemble the bureaucratic kind, criminals, they've been socialized to stigmatize and exclude. Professional responses thus appear coordinated, despite a lack of direct collaboration, because they are adapting their practices to the same category of problematic people the state itself has created.

Bureaucratic kinds are thus a kind of glue in two senses. They bind together agencies and bureaucracies that may never actually interact with one another by traveling between them, bearing the imprint of past attempts at care or control. Professionals may have their own distinct mandates, professional ethos, and toolkits for intervention, but they are ultimately expected to act on the same human raw material. But glue does not just stick; it immobilizes. In the case of the US response to the opioid crisis, the crafting of a population so marginalized as to have no licit way to survive is—through no fault of the people within it—a thorny challenge for reforms. As I've seen in California, it is in no small part because of the perceived difficulties in transforming "criminal addicts" into "reformed, self-reliant substance users" (in a context where robust supports and welfare programs remain absent) that calls are growing to use involuntary psychiatric treatment to compensate for the diminished control exercised by the criminal-legal system. The looping that the elaboration of new bureaucratic kinds sparks, as classifications, classifiers, and the classified all adapt to one another, means that social policy is never static; but it can create a tight knot that even well-meaning public policy cannot easily untangle.

Sunmin Kim offers another illustrative example of the unintended, enduring effects of past state classificatory efforts in his meticulous study of the Dillingham Commission, a Congressionally-mandated investigation of immigration conducted from 1907 to 1911. The Commission concluded, as its backers intended, that recent waves of Southern and European migrants were of a fundamentally different racial character than native-born whites and merited exclusion. But the Commission also produced a host of "unruly facts" that undermined its own conclusions: on the ground, immigrant subjects "mobilized against the attempts to study them; other times, they just said too much, providing answers that investigators did not anticipate or appreciate."[59] Bright lines the commission sought to draw between "races or peoples" were impossible to draw in practice; populations supposedly locked into a state of immutable difference were actually assimilating at a rapid clip. The unanticipated findings of the Commission, while glossed over in its policy recommendations, provided subsequent ammunition for pro-immigrant advocates to argue that Southern and European immigrants could, in fact, become white.

Kim, then, has uncovered another example of looping, whereby an attempt to more carefully demarcate the category "white" to include only Western or Northern Europeans inadvertently expanded it—in a way that, decades later, doubtlessly buttressed the political power of an enlarged white majority while continuing to reinforce their sharp differentiation from non-white groups. As in my case, it points to the analytical utility of extending looping beyond instances where groups overtly mobilize to change the categories applied to them (as, for example, is the case of autistic people attempting to reclassify the condition as an example of "neurodiversity") toward the more "unruly" ways that "innovations in governance" can emerge in the absence of any "purposeful coordination" or a "mastermind."[60] Policymakers and street-level professionals never make kinds of people *de novo*; instead, they are constantly trying to catch up to populations that have been created by their predecessors, and which invariably slip out of the state's many hands.

## UNTYING THE KNOTS

We finish this book back at the (in)famous Parisian police infirmary. While this site didn't wind up being a major part of this book, as I write this conclusion, I'm reminded of how clearly the human consequences of the failings I've documented snap into focus there. It's where the power of *malade* to control and contain the mad is most visible. But it's precisely at this apex of bureaucratic classification that we see how the system becomes unglued.

The man, a thirty-seven-year-old migrant born in Algeria, has been here before. His dossier is enormous, filled with the notes from fourteen prior passages through the police infirmary. He's here today because the police followed a trail of blood leading away from a broken window—sign of an abortive break-in—and found him crumpled in an alleyway. Tracking down his *secteur* wasn't hard. The medical resident informs Doctor Montero, who'll be conducting his evaluation, that the man had last been hospitalized the year prior when an expert determined that he could not be judged for a violent robbery, committed at the command of the voices in his head. "As I heard from the *secteur*," the intern reports, "he's delirious all the time, even with treatment." The *secteur* released him on a program of care a few months later, but even with the legal mandate to come in to the Clinic, he quickly fell off its radar screen.

The man comes in and flops into his chair. He looks around. "Why are there so many people? I don't talk in front of so many people," he asserts.

"What bothers you about all these people? Do you want to talk about something intimate?" Doctor Montero asks, smoothly.

The man repeats: "I'm not going to talk. None of this is my problem."

"You don't want to participate in the decision about what is going to happen to you?" Doctor Montero counters, leaving the meaning of "participate" vague.

"You are incompetent dogs, let me sleep," the man pushes back.

"Do you think that attitude might be why you're incarcerated and hospitalized? You prefer that the police and psychiatrists make all the decisions for you? You are an adult."

Doctor Montero turns to the intern, trying to assess if the man had been more open to talking the day prior.

The man continues: "I don't control anything in my life," explaining that decisions are taken by cameras implanted in his eyes and microphone in his mouth. "You tell me I'm schizophrenic, but you don't do anything to take these devices out of my head." Doctor Montero starts another question, and the man cuts him off, "I've told you all these stories fifty times in this stupid institution. I have no place in prison. I have no place in the hospital."

"What is your place, then?" Doctor Montero queries.

"Dead."

The interview is over. Doctor Montero turns to the resident: "You can see here that the psychosis has developed to the point where he has no more interest in the exterior, he has become an object. And the *secteur* has tried just about everything," he sighs. Doctor Montero is weighing sending him back to jail, the first step to him being judged and potentially incarcerated. "You can understand why sometimes we declare someone like this responsible [i.e., capable of being prosecuted]. Psychiatry can't control him, so we hope that the law does. Right now, he has no responsibility and therefore no subjectivity."

Sending him back to the criminal justice system would, paradoxically, align decision making with high-minded principles. "People with psychic troubles are citizens with the same rights as the rest of the population called 'healthy,'" writes psychiatrist Jean-Luc Roelandt, "and responsibility is one of those rights."[61] The earliest French psychiatrists, wrote one another commentator, recognized that "the loss of reason is never complete in a *malade mental* . . . [They] are never a person who, as a result of their troubles, has their humanity cut off."[62] An exemption from that most basic requirement of citizenship—answering for our acts—would sever that humanity.

Doctor Montero hesitates, he deliberates, he decides. It will be another involuntary hospitalization. Montero spends most of his time working in a day hospital with chronic *malades*. There, they're still trying to hang on to some principles of institutional psychotherapy; he likes the idea of *malades* participating in the life of the institution, but to do that, you have to be in the right institution. So this patient is going back to the institution purpose built for *malades*, the *secteur*. It hasn't exactly been a good place for him, but it's the *correct* place in the sense that he belongs in the category it administers. For the diagnosis, Doctor Montero writes "discordant delirium," adding a novel designation to a file already rife with them. He laughs: "I know that's not in the *DSM*. I could just write 'schizophrenia.'" But it's clear what really matters: he's a *malade*.

It's not the worst identity that's been imposed on the mad. *Malade* emerged alongside an promise of treatment. This was, in most cases, a more hopeful bureaucratic fate than being thrown into the poorhouse or chained like an animal. Imagining madness as an illness that touches subjectivity, but does not negate it, reminds us that people with mental illness have inner lives, which the switch to behavioral health and a single-minded focus on public disruption or excessive service use in the United States seems to ignore. Denying illness, when the result is that people are incarcerated in the name of rendering them responsible, does not feel like a promising path to social incorporation. But *malade* does not have space in it for full citizenship. Forging another bureaucratic kind, one that focuses less on making order out of disordered persons, and more on respecting both their rights and differences, while honoring their need for support and solidarity, remains the real challenge for creating a new mental state.

# ACKNOWLEDGMENTS

Qualitative researchers live off the goodwill of their research subjects. I was lucky to find literally hundreds of people willing to share their time and knowledge with me. Most of my direct interlocutors in France must remain anonymous, but if you are reading this, and you took the time to answer an email, sit down for an interview, or let me observe your work (and pose many naïve questions) for months at a time, thank you. I will dare to mention Isabelle Billard, Clément Bonnet, Pascal Cacot, Alice Casagrande, Tim Graecen, Cécile Leca, Alain Lopez, Guénaëlle Jegu, Vassilis Kapsambélis, Eric Mairesse, Philippe Maugiron, Marion Primevert, and Roselyne Touroude as meriting a *grand merci*. I am also grateful to Jean-Paul Brière in the Ministry of Health and Marie-Odile Safon at *l'Institut de recherche et documentation en économie de la santé* for their help in accessing archival materials.

I was fortunate to have had the help of academic mentors Neil Fligstein, Armando Lara-Millán, and Thomas Laqueur during my time at UC Berkeley. Michael Burawoy somehow escaped any formal institutional responsibility for this book but did not escape me; we miss you. Carolyn Clark, Anne Meyer, Catherine Norton, and Tamar Young variously let me cry in their offices, helped me when I got locked out of mine, and generally made the department a livable place for the extended adolescence of graduate school. While I won't list every other emerging scholar who supported me along the way, special thanks must go to Lindsay Berkowitz, Dani Carrillo, Martin Eiermann, Jason Ferguson, Ian Gray, Chris Herring, Andrew Jaeger, Matty Lichtenstein, Noémie MP, Manuel Rosaldo, Jason Scott, Caleb Scoville, Josh Seim, Mary Shi, and Rebecca Tarlau. This research was only possible with the generous support of the Berkeley Empirical Legal Studies Fellowship, Institute for International Studies, the Institute for European Studies, the Georges Lurcy Foundation, and the Chateaubriand Fellowship.

When I arrived in France, I learned that there was another scholar, Isabel Perera, who was on the same fellowship and who was also comparing the French and US mental health systems. This was initially a source of panic, but it quickly became an enormously useful collaboration. I hope I can someday match the rigor of Isabel's thinking. There's no academic interlocutor who deserves more thanks than Tonya Tartour. Tonya: I still can't believe that Doctor Sleepy nodded off during our meeting, and I definitely owe you an apology for making you listen to that "is psychiatry a discipline like any other?" question at the end of every interview. Tonya jumped into a crucial book workshop, alongside Baptiste Brossard, Aurélien Éberhardt, Neil Gong, and Nicolas Henckes in December 2024. Numerous opportunities to present pieces of this work to French specialists helped me sharpen the argument. Particular gratitude to Remy Ponge and the *Laboratoire interdisciplinaire pour la sociologie économique*, Gisèle Sapiro at the *Centre européen de sociologie*, Mathias Millet at the *Université de Poitiers*, and Frederic Viguier and Dennis Bogusz at the New York University (NYU) Institute of French Studies. The MaxPo Center at SciencesPo and Olivier Godechot afforded a much-appreciated academic shelter at key moments.

For the final push in completing the manuscript, the NYU-Paris campus and the Global Research Initiative Fellowship, overseen by the wonderful Nathalie Gicquel, were indispensable. Jeff Manza helped make that stay happen. Big thanks also go to Eric Schwartz at Columbia, who still believed in the project when one-half of it (the US case) abruptly disappeared, and Alyssa Napier for carrying it through. Crucial pinch hitting for finalizing the manuscript came from Marlène Bouvet, Nick Rekenthaler, and Sasha Warren. The junior faculty at NYU have also been incredible; a shoutout goes to Guillermina Altomonte, Linsey Edwards, Nahoko Kameo, Carly Knight, B. K. Lee, Ravaris Moore, Simone Zhang, and Maria Abascal (honorary junior). I received additional advice on this manuscript from David Garland; he may have actually saved the project!

My longtime adviser Marion Fourcade deserves a paragraph of her own. There are so many moments when she could have cut me loose but instead caught me mid-fall. These moments start the night before I committed to Berkeley for graduate school and include a café in Paris, where I announced that I wanted to study the management of mental illness (a far cry from proposed research on climate change), and a phone call when I let her know that my fieldwork had, in large part, fallen apart. Her comments on my written work were always incisive; her guidance in my career trajectory was indispensable. Even six years after I graduated, she accepted the task of reading through the introduction one more time. I just hope this book lives up to all the time and effort you gave to make it possible.

For more extra-academic support, I am indebted to Dylan Alban, Nick Antipa, Kristina Cohen, Elizabeth Cruikshank, Sylvia Herbert, Sam Leachman, Tolan Thornton, Mia Tsui, Eti Valdez-Kadinsky, and Alia Whitney-Johnson. Thank you to Jordan Bubin for literally everything. Additional organizational thanks go to UAW 2865, the PUB, WCBC, RMO (thanks, especially, to Ryan for the "Theory and Praxis" idea used in the conclusion), the Citadel, *les pièces rapportées*, the Woolsey Mammoths, and the Friday Night Toddler Dance Party crew. My parents helped me bear many of the emotional burdens of this process and never let it seem like a burden themselves (the Mourad family carried its fair share of the weight, as well). Marie knows better than anyone what my downward academic trajectory would have looked like without her. Elias, Lydia, and Julien make everything worth it.

I dedicate this book to Sara and John.

# METHODOLOGICAL APPENDIX

"This isn't the [United] States. Not everyone is walking around with their Starbucks here. If you can't offer a coffee to a *malade*, don't drink it in front of him."

The admonishment felt a little absurd. I was sitting at the Police Infirmary, sipping a coffee (in a reusable mug, not a Starbucks cup, I'll note). Doctor Fournier had just wrapped up an evaluation of a man who had been brought in by the police. This "presumed *malade*," as the infirmary team called them, had been dispatched to the hospital. It was not a convivial scene. A burly nurse and guard loomed over the man throughout the evaluation. And here I was, getting reproached because I had been drinking my coffee off to the side, between scribbling field notes. The man's wrists were in mechanical restraints, so it would have been hard to drink coffee even had I been considerate enough to offer. But I wasn't that considerate.

By that point, I had been in a France for a year. I had sat in on dozens of triage meetings at the Clinic, completed my pseudo-internship at the disability office, and served as the public witness to dozens of hospitalization hearings. But there were still cultural codes I was unwittingly trespassing. That's the core methodological story of this book: of the scholarly benefits and risks of stumbling between field sites with little sense of what I would find, of asking confused questions in a strong accent, and of grappling constantly with the sense that things rarely seemed quite the way that the published literature—or my own intuitions as an US citizen—suggested they should be.

## CONSTRUCTING THE OBJECT

"You have to start by constructing your object," my wise and wonderful adviser Marion Fourcade (channeling the methodological precepts of both Emile Durkheim and Pierre Bourdieu), told me. She could have said, "You have to read the literature," which would be the standard advice to anyone trying to nail down a research topic. But that's not what she told me, and the distinction was essential. Reading the literature before going into the field is about abstraction: of understanding what your case is a case of and how it will help fill a gap in our generalizable knowledge of the world. To construct your object is to dig deep into particulars. This meant pouring over dozens of government reports, legislative analyses, and administrative statistics to understand what the French mental health system really was and how it compared to other countries.

That process was very frustrating. I initially envisioned building on multinational studies of the organization of mental health care. They have used as dependent variables the number of beds in psychiatric hospitals or antidepressant usage and considered their relationship to welfare regimes or health systems.[1] Constructing a coherent cross-national dataset on public mental health services quickly felt futile. Germany, for example, seems like a necessary case for any analysis of Western psychiatric systems. At the time I was putting together my prospectus, the country had 15 psychiatrists per 100,000 people according to the World Health Organization—fewer than France, and about the same as in the United States. The Organisation for Economic Co-operation and Development pegged the number at 27, which is more than any country save Switzerland. If you don't know German, you can't dig into internal national data to figure out which data point is right. Belgium and Japan have an astounding number of psychiatric beds per capita. But as an informant reminded me, a bed is a mattress: Raw counts tell us very little about what actually happens to the people sleeping in them. I do use cross-national data in this book, but it is suggestive and descriptive rather than analytical and explanatory.

Thus, constructing my object mostly meant relentlessly comparing the mental health systems in France and the United States on as many metrics as I could find. Some were dead ends. I tried to figure out if there were more people with serious mental illnesses in one country or the other and concluded that definitions were too inconsistent to tell us much.[2] "Which system works better?" is a legitimate question, but no comparative study has sought to answer whether French or US citizens with schizophrenia experience fewer symptoms or a higher quality of life.[3] These roadblocks pushed me to rethink "people with severe mental illness" not as a group that is more or less accurately measured in epidemiological studies (and whose trajectories I could track) but as one that is constituted through classification in specific institutional settings that differ systemically (and, to a degree, quantifiably) between countries. In that respect, at least one thing was clear: This population in France was being constructed through their passage through psychiatric hospitals, whereas in the United States, hospitals were secondary to homeless shelters, nursing homes, or jails.

Understanding why required not just analyzing decision making ("Are French clinicians quicker to resort to hospitalization?") but asking why the country has so many more hospital beds in the first place. This book is built on an extensive review of primary source documents dating back to the 1960s. More recent government reports and plans are available online; others I accessed in hospital libraries, in government archives, or through copies provided by retired policymakers or professionals. The French Statistical Yearbooks (*Annuaires statistiques de la France*) were invaluable for assembling historical data on the number of patients served by *secteurs* and availability of disability services. The archives of the Ministry of Health were also a rich source of information for understanding interministerial debates over whether involuntary treatment was primarily about care or control. I also reviewed over 500 newspaper articles with headers mentioning psychiatry in *Le Monde* (from the 1960s onward) and *Libération* and *Figaro* (which are available online starting in the 1990s). Constructing my object was an ongoing process: New acronyms, policies, and historical references came up constantly in field observations and interviews. Each often necessitated a new voyage back into primary sources. It has continued in the years since I left the field and is part of what gives me some confidence that the differences between the United States and France remain stark, even if the steady Americanization of the French system (read: more time spent in prison and in the street for *malades*, more training on the *Diagnostic and Statistical Manual* (*DSM*) and neurobiology for psychiatrists) is evoked ad infinitum.

That construction also involved constant dialog with research I conducted in the United States from 2015 to 2022. That included observations of an outpatient clinic and visits to a range of residential facilities for so-called gravely disabled patients unable to meet their basic needs in California, and nearly two hundred commitment hearings in New York. These medical, social, and judicial agencies faced dilemmas around care, control, and rights similar to their French counterparts, but they offered radically different responses. I also interviewed nearly three hundred stakeholders in California and sixty in New York. If anything, these states' mental health systems—robustly financed and professionally equipped compared to other states—were likely closer to what I saw in France than had I conducted my research in the proverbial US heartland. Recognizing the complete absence of any concept parallel to *malades*, which might capture a whiff of underlying consensus on who the objects of public mental health care actually were and the right balance of competing imperatives in responding to them, was key to developing this book's argument. I've made the unconventional choice to include snippets of ground-level data to pull these cases out of the shadows so readers can see the contrast for themselves.

## SOULLESS ETHNOGRAPHY

As I see it, there are two good reasons to do ethnography. One is that it plunges us into the worlds of our informants, giving us the visceral understanding of their daily routines and frustrations that can only come from experiencing them together. Compelling ethnography is driven by its characters, presented not as simplified typologies but as irreducibly complex and incommensurable individuals. This is undoubtedly the approach that produces the riveting ethnographic classics that made me embrace the method in the first place.

The other reason to do ethnography is more banal: It allows us to gather data we couldn't get any other way. This book leans on the second justification. My starting assumption was that the actual categories used by professionals in deciding who to treat, who to allocate benefits to, and who to control would differ from those emphasized in the literature (namely, diagnosis) or enumerated in official policies and plans. An administrative dataset might identify a relationship between patient characteristics and orientation outcomes, but it couldn't reveal the cognitive heuristics, clinical arguments, or shortcuts that professionals used to link the two.

Because the range of institutions that care for and control people with severe mental disorders is extensive, I had to be strategic. Based on preliminary interviews, I chose the Clinic, the Disability Office, and the judicial hearings for involuntary hospitalizations as the key decision points in a person's trajectory through public psychiatry and its intersection with the social and judicial systems. I also conducted observations at the Police Infirmary in Paris as another site at the boundary between medicine and law. The role of these date in this book is secondary, however, for reasons of both space and representativity. The infirmary is unique, and many informants gasped with concern that I would say anything about French psychiatry on the basis of a place that has been so roundly criticized.

My observations were targeted. I attended meetings to discuss new and difficult clients in the Clinic, evaluations by the multidisciplinary team and departmental review committee in the Disability Office, and involuntary hospitalization hearings. The basic unit of analysis was each person discussed: 260 new patients at the Clinic (in addition to 79 emergency cases), 297 applicants in the Disability Office, and 107 judicial controls. I also attended staff meetings at the Clinic, trainings at the Disability Office, and continuing legal education courses for lawyers working with psychiatric patients. In my time in France, I visited dozens of health and housing providers, observed a series of meetings for the formation of a new municipal mental health council, attended public information events, and interloped at assemblies of five activist groups.

This book will not win an ethnographic arms race when it comes to hours spent in the field. I have tried to offer a sense of the trajectories and motivations of the professionals I follow. But I'm not giving readers a full sense of why I trusted the snap judgments of Doctor Delignon at the Clinic, couldn't help but share Anne's enthusiasm for *doing something* to help the applicants at the Disability Office (no matter how messy their application), and felt Elena's visceral disappointment when judges ignored her meticulously documented legal arguments. I really *like* many of these people. Still, I have written a book that makes the state seem like a "cold monster"[4] rather than, in most (but, of course, not all) cases, an amalgam of well-meaning professionals who could have a higher salary and more prestige doing something other than serving people with schizophrenia.

Allow me to offer a few defensive comments about this approach. My ethnography is written in short snippets, often presented with little detail on the backstories that brought a person in front of the professionals classifying them. This brevity captures something important. In modern states, enormously consequential "biographical torquing"[5]—the sudden shift from being a detained criminal to a hospitalized *malade*, for example—can happen in minutes or seconds based on information that is scant and incomplete. My depictions reflect this reality: I often knew exactly as much about a given case as key decision makers did.

Focusing primarily on meetings or hearings, divided neatly into discrete cases, had other advantages. First, in all my primary sites, I had access to documentary traces: the typed summaries of new patients in the Clinic, application materials in the Disability Office, and judges' written conclusions (all entered into my field notes with vigorous scrubbing of identifying details). For an ethnographer conducting research in a foreign language, without the affordances that would be provided by being able to voice record interactions, these documents provided invaluable assurances that I was capturing key information correctly. Administrative data were helpful for identifying if and how the cases I observed were representative of the total range of clients served by a given institution. For example, the Disability Office in Paris provided a summary of the benefits they granted in 2014 and 2015. This confirmed that both the mix of cases I saw and their outcomes were relatively representative of the tens of thousands of applications they processed in a given year.

Second, a study of cases allowed me to make counts. I tallied demographic information when available. Important findings emerged from basic math. For example, professionals at the Clinic saw themselves as primarily treating real *malades*, but their meetings were mostly occupied with figuring out what to do with the 80 percent or so of new patients who did *not* have psychosis. I also developed my own categories to quantify the reasoning professionals used in making decisions in each site. This helped me realize, for example, that "still in care" was an argument frequently used at the Disability Office to deny professional retraining to people with a psychic handicap, but it was almost never evoked for other disabled people. I do not think that ethnographers should fetishize statistics or subject our observations to significance tests. But we probably should count when we can because it helps us avoid an understandable tendency to pay attention to the dramatic and revealing cases while leaving to the side the routine cases that make up the majority of professional work.

Third, there was an ethical justification to my restrained ethnographic approach. Toward the end of my observations at the Clinic, I interviewed a group of nurses who mentioned in passing that I should join them for some initial intake interviews. In fact, I consciously had not asked to participate in direct interactions between providers and their patients. In a field where therapy is relational, introducing a third party (especially a foreigner) could disturb an interactive process that took priority over my own data collection.

Ethnography is a useful research tool. It's also a disruptive one. I felt this acutely in the times when I encountered directly people with mental illness: observing information-gathering interviews at the Disability Office or meetings between lawyers and clients, for example. This was true even though these individuals agreed to my presence. Field research has costs for both practitioners and subjects. For that reason, I'm happy to have done only as much as seemed essential to substantiate the claims in this book.

## INTERVIEWING AT ITS LIMITS

Qualitative interviews were not just an auxiliary to ethnography but a coequal part of the project. The final tally—193 in total[6]—feels, in retrospect, both impossibly large[7] (certainly, it will be difficult to replicate without the limited administrative and family responsibilities I had in graduate school) and insufficient. I pursued interviews across multiple avenues. First, I sought to interview the people working in my three field sites; second, I reached out to people working in similar sites (other Clinics, for example, or Disability Offices elsewhere in the capital region); third, I contacted representatives of national advocacy groups, professional organizations, and state officials working in relevant agencies and ministries at the municipal, regional, and national level. A breakdown of my interviewees' domains of work and professions is provided in table A.1.

This aggregate number of interviews nonetheless feels insufficient because the respondents are distributed across a drove of institutions. For any given site (say, protected workshops) I might only have a handful of respondents. I was so scattered because, like a good relational researcher,[8] I sought to interview professionals in all the agencies, structures, and programs that were in interaction with my ethnographic field sites. This turned

TABLE A.1
Interview domains and professions

| Domain | | Profession | |
|---|---|---|---|
| *Secteur* | 38 | Psychiatrist | 52 |
| Advocacy or professional organization | 31 | Administrator/politician | 32 |
| Government—health | 30 | Psychologist/educator | 26 |
| Departmental Disability Office | 22 | Generalist doctor | 17 |
| Disability provider | 20 | Lawyer/judge | 14 |
| Government—disability/social | 17 | Facility director | 11 |
| Law/courts | 16 | Social worker | 10 |
| Government—municipal | 10 | Researcher | 9 |
| Research | 9 | Nurse | 8 |
| | | Service User/advocate | 6 |
| | | Other | 8 |
| **Total** | **193** | | |

out to be impossible. To do this for the Clinic, for example, would have required speaking to the generalist doctors, private psychiatrists, and university psychologists referring patients; the municipal social workers with whom the *secteur* social workers traded cases; the probation officers or judges who surveilled some *malades*; and the police who helped the nurses rehospitalize them. In the end, mental health is not a field with easily defined boundaries in the Bourdieusian sense (if any fields really are). I ultimately confined myself to pursuing interviews primarily with actors for whom engaging with the adult public psychiatric system was a primary responsibility while recognizing that these limits were somewhat arbitrary.

Interviews lasted between thirty minutes and two-and-a-half hours; I conducted nearly all of them in person except for a handful of follow-up conversations in 2021 via Zoom. I developed separate questionnaires depending on the profession and organizational context of each interviewee. To create some coherency and consistency, I tried to close each interview with the same series of questions about the weak/strong points of the system, the specificity of mental illness/psychiatry within medicine, the goals of treatment, views on key reforms or impending legislation, and the terminology used to describe people with mental illness. These general questions helped reveal how widely a conception of *malades* and the primacy of the *secteur* psychiatry in responding to them was shared.

I leaned heavily on interviews, and thus a method that has been heavily critiqued. Colin Jerolmack and Shamus Khan argue that "talk is cheap" because "explanations generated by interview data . . . can only reveal actors' justifications for actions that take place in unobserved contexts (the past or the future)."[9] I found interviews with the same people I was observing as a crucial way to get quick feedback on emerging hypotheses about what was happening and, as a foreign interloper, to elicit clarification for things I did not fully understand. I agree with Kathleen Gerson and Sarah Damaske that we should treat "behavior and mental states" as "distinct and equally consequential aspects" of professionals' lives.[10] That is, the fact that Disability Office professionals believed people with psychic handicaps deserved access to all the benefits available to other disabled people but frequently disqualified them from those very benefits in practice points to an inconsistency that the research subjects had to manage, and not one the researcher needs to explain away.

Limiting qualitative research to the directly observable and interactional risks confining researchers to a microsociology of private actors. I certainly would have enjoyed sitting in on meetings between the minister of health and heads of the French regional health authorities, but getting someone in the minister's cabinet to describe them to me in a confidential interview was an excellent and more realistic alternative. Much street-level bureaucratic work happens at the level of screens. It is solitary. Such work is not interactive in the way that some ethnographers privilege. In general, I am convinced that the study of power and of the state requires more methodological eclecticism than the full ethnographic immersion sociologists have taken as their gold standard, applied most frequently to marginalized groups or those with a low public profile, allows.

I analyzed my three sources of qualitative data (archives, interviews, and observations) in the software program *Dedoose*. I gradually elaborated five hundred codes, which I applied to twelve thousand units of text (take that, big data!). More artisanal methods ("just reread your field notes!") would have left me lost in a sprawling mess of heterogenous data and topics. While I did not use the more sophisticated affordances of data analysis software—much less the Artificial Intelligence-assisted coding that appeared at the end of my research—I found the overview of my dataset that these tools could offer indispensable. That is, although I asked no questions that included the term, in over one thousand excerpts, participants mentioned *malades*.

## REPRESENTATIVITY, REPRESENTATION, AND REFLEXIVITY

I close this methodological appendix with a few comments on case selection, generalization, and my own positionality.

Is this a book about France or Paris? My initial, overly ambitious plan was to conduct field research in sites *outside* the capital. This might have allowed me to identify truly national patterns in patient trajectories and classification practices as opposed to findings that reflected more localized resource availability or professional particularities. This vision foundered against both logistical challenges and the difficulty of identifying where exactly would be more representative than Paris. In the end, I settled on confining my core field sites to the city while supplementing them with interviews and site visits outside. My study was interested in the extent to which three key reforms (rationalizing reorganizations of psychiatry that culminated in 2016, the refoundation of the disability system in 2005, and the introduction of judicial hearings for involuntary hospitalizations in 2011) transformed the trajectories of people with severe mental illness. Analyzing field sites in Paris allowed me to study the place where actors thought these reforms had the greatest chance of success, given the intense scrutiny of government actors, concentration of advocacy organizations, and greater resources for psychiatry.[11] The fact that all three ran up against the resistance created by the way the population of *malades* had previously been constituted, in my reading, buttresses my general argument about that durability of patterns of institutional responses to mental illness.

Once I had settled on Paris, I faced what I expected to be the difficult challenge of gaining access to my field sites. Or, not. Doctor Delignon invited me to observe triage meetings after an initial interview; Arthur asked me to sign a confidentiality agreement with the Disability Office but subsequently gave me wide leeway; involuntary hospitalization hearings were technically public. The head judge of liberties and detention in Paris encouraged me to check with the clerk beforehand and then just show up, which I did. My sense was that the French operated on a principle of inter-professional trust; they took their work seriously and expected that I took the ethics of sociological research seriously as well. My fieldwork also took place prior to the implementation of the General Data Protection Regulation in the European Union, which no doubt would have made some forms of data collection more complicated. I have noted multiple times when I believe I benefited from a perception that I was unthreatening: a young foreign researcher in over his head. I was, of course, not any foreigner but a white man from the United States with a prestigious university pedigree. It helped.

There was one door I did not try to open. From the beginning, I conceptualized this as a study of professionals, not patients (with the exception of a handful of service users who had also assumed advocacy roles). The literature with which I was engaging provided some justification for this choice. Studies of state classification and street-level bureaucrats typically enter the field from the administrative side. Some work on how patient, client, or citizen resistance transforms the state has done so without delving into why individuals find these classifications objectionable.[12]

To be honest, my motivations were more personal. I had doubts about my capacity to manage complex interactions with vulnerable people in an ethical fashion in a foreign language. And as a person who has struggled with depression (including during the long, gray Parisian winter of 2015 and 2016), I concluded that maybe secondhand exposure to the suffering treated (or, in some cases, engendered) by the mental health system was enough.

A few months after I completed my fieldwork, I found myself in an emergency room in Northern California. Shortly after the staff psychiatrist informed me that I was staying and a psych tech watched me strip down and change into hospital pajamas, someone (and, really, I have no idea who they were) came to inform me of my rights and restrictions. The most important of these was that I would not be able to purchase a handgun for the next five years. I thought of how profoundly this reflected the pathologies of the US mental state (losing access to a personal arsenal never much figured into French discussions of patients' rights). I made what I thought was a decent joke about how if only we could put everyone on a seventy-two-hour emergency hold, we'd have no more problems with gun violence. The person who came to inform me of my rights didn't crack a smile. Like the patient described in the preface, whose sage insights about cross-national variation in mental health systems received no acknowledgment in the courtroom, I was now just a crazy person, saying crazy shit.

I wish I had the emotional fortitude, language skills, and courage to gather more testimonials from the mad, revealing the wisdom of people who have had to live within the category *malade*. I don't think their absence is fatal to my theoretical argument, but it does suggest that this book is leaving the most important stories of what's happening in the French mental health system untold.

# CHRONOLOGY

1838—The Law of Madmen obligates each French department to maintain an asylum. Establishes a two-track model for involuntary hospitalization based either on a need for treatment or on a threat to the public order.

1940—François Tosquelles, a Catalan refugee, arrives at Saint Alban's hospital. In the following years, he helps develop institutional psychotherapy, which seeks to heal the sick by healing the hospital.

1942—Insufficient rations and political indifference under the Vichy regime lead to the deaths of around one-third of asylum patients.

1958—The state changes the references to "madmen" in the public health code to *malades*.

1960—An administrative *circulaire* inaugurates a policy of sectorization, by which the country will be divided into territories of around seventy thousand inhabitants with a single public psychiatric team assigned to provide prevention, treatment, and rehabilitation.

1965–1967—At the *Journées psychiatriques* conference, the luminaries of French *secteur* psychiatry debate who should be served in the new public system. They evince a fear of making psychiatry's ambit too broad and call for focusing on the *malades* currently in asylums.

1974—After a series of *circulaires* attempting to push sectorization forward, the state declares that "further expansions of the number of beds in psychiatric hospitals can no longer be tolerated." Deinstitutionalization begins in France; while beds disappear, however, no public hospitals close.

1975—The Law in Favor of Handicapped Persons gives bureaucratic status to "inadapted" children, "mutilated" soldiers, and "invalid" workers as disabled persons. While not formally excluded from the law, psychiatrists successfully resist the creation of new structures in the disability system for long-term psychiatric patients.

1985—The *secteurs* are formally inscribed into law. Hospitals receive a global budget, which they can distribute between inpatient and outpatient *secteur* services.

1990—First major reform of the Law of 1838. It officially establishes a statute for voluntary hospitalization and creates new mechanisms for overseeing involuntary care (although it does not expand the role of judges). Nonetheless, rates of involuntary hospitalization increase.

1990s—The central state begins focusing intensively on extended psychiatric hospitalizations as a core problem, to which the expansion of housing in the medical-social (disability) system is seen as the solution.

2001—UNAFAM, a parents' organization, issues its white paper claiming that people with mental illnesses have been denied the right to be recognized as disabled. Meanwhile, a national plan calls for shifting attention from a narrow group of mental illness to broader issues of mental health.

2002—A law regarding health democracy emphasizes the participation of citizens in the health system and the necessity of informed consent for all medical care. The participation of people with mental illness, however, remains marginal, and psychiatric hospitalization is an important exception to the expectation of consent.

2005—The Law for the Equality of Rights and Opportunities, Participation, and Citizenship for Disabled Persons expands disability benefits and creates a new system of disability offices focused on promoting autonomy, in line with a person's life project. The law recognizes an alteration of psychic functions as a potential origin of a disability.

2006—Interior Minister Nicolas Sarkozy includes articles seeking to increase the prefecture's control over psychiatric hospitalizations in a proposed law on crime and delinquency. He withdraws the proposed articles in the face of professional resistance.

2008—After a murder committed by an escaped patient, Nicolas Sarkozy, now president, delivers a speech in a psychiatric hospital calling for intensified surveillance of dangerous *malades*. The Collective of the 39 issues its rallying cry against this "securitarian turn."

2010—In response to a suit brought by the *Group information asile*, an antipsychiatry group, the Constitutional Court rules that France's involuntary hospitalization laws are invalid because they do not include universal review by judges.

2011—Systematic hearings after fifteen days for involuntary psychiatric hospitalizations are introduced; judges go from reviewing a few thousand hospitalizations a year to tens of thousands.

2013—A reform under a new socialist government reduces the wait time after an involuntary hospitalization to see a judge to twelve days. The law largely leaves in place new security-focused measures introduced under President Sarkozy.

2016—The Law of Modernization of Our Health System reaffirms the *secteur* as the building block of the public psychiatric system, but the law attempts to integrate psychiatric hospitals more fully into the medical system writ large. The law also contains new regulations on the use of mechanical restraints and seclusion.

2019—The so-called springtime of psychiatry includes widespread strikes and hospital occupations by psychiatric professionals. It leads to an emergency injection of funds and a new interministerial delegate for mental health and psychiatry. Bed closures and a loss of professionals in the public sector continues.

2025—Mental health is declared the "grand national cause" of the year by the Prime Minister. Critics lament that the information campaign and publicity tied to this declaration do not address gaps in care for people with severe conditions.

# NOTES

## PREFACE

1. There is a rich literature on the history of French psychiatry that informs this book (even if it is not cited), but it rarely takes us past the mid-twentieth century. See, for example, Jan Goldstein, *Console and Classify: The French Psychiatric Profession in the Nineteenth Century* (Cambridge University Press, 1987); Jessie Hewitt, *Institutionalizing Gender: Madness, the Family, and Psychiatric Power in Nineteenth-Century France* (Cornell University Press, 2020); Camille Robcis, *Disalienation: Politics, Philosophy, and Radical Psychiatry in Postwar France* (University of Chicago Press, 2021); Sherry Turkle, *Psychoanalytic Politics: Jacques Lacan and Freud's French Revolution*, 2nd ed. (Guilford Press, 1992).
2. Lise Demailly and Michel Autès, *La politique de santé mentale en France: Acteurs, instruments, controverses* (Armand Colin, 2012); Pauline Rhenter, "De l'institutionelle au contractuel: Psychiatrie publique et politiques de Santé Mentale en France (1945–2003)" (PhD diss., Université Lumière Lyon 2, 2004); Livia Velpry, *Le Quotidien de la psychiatrie: Sociologie de la maladie mentale* (Armand Colin, 2008).
3. Benoît Eyraud, *Protéger et rendre capable* (Eres, 2013); Nicolas Henckes, "La politique du handicap psychique: Familles, psychiatres et état face à la chronicité des maladies mentales, des années 1960 aux années 1980," *DREES/MiRe-Convention de Recherche N° 08-2547*, 2011, https://hal.archives-ouvertes.fr/file/index/docid/769756/filename/Henckes_2011_Rapport_MiRe.pdf; Florence Weber, *Handicap et dépendance: Drames humains, enjeux politiques* (Éditions Rue d'Ulm, 2011).
4. Delphine Moreau, "Contraindre pour soigner? Les tensions normatives et institutionnelles de l'intervention psychiatrique après l'asile" (PhD diss., Écoles des hautes études en sciences sociales, 2015); Frédéric Mougeot, *Le travail des infirmiers en hôpital psychiatrique* (Érès, 2019); Tonya Tartour, "L'administration du

désordre: Gouverner l'hôpital psychiatrique depuis les années 1980" (PhD diss., Sciences Po Paris, 2021).

5. Marlène Bouvet, "Réenchanter les Déprimé.Es: Une sociologie de la thérapie en clinique privée" (PhD diss., École nationale supérieur, 2023); Ivan Garrec, "Trouble dans les émotions: enquête sur l'éxistence sociale du 'trouble de la personnalité borderline' en France" (PhD diss., École doctorale Érasme, 2024), https://theses.fr/2024PA131068.

## INTRODUCTION

1. Quoted in Andrew Scull, *Madness in Civilization* (Thames & Hudson, 2015), 32.
2. Michel Foucault, *The History of Madness*, ed. Jean Khalfa, trans. Jonathan Murphy (Routledge, 2006), 148.
3. William Salmon (1686), quoted in Andrew Scull, *The Most Solitary of Afflictions: Madness and Society in Britain, 1700–1900* (Yale University Press, 2005), 49. The same was true of nineteenth-century Japan, where rules around the management of the mad were grouped with those on loose animals wandering into cities. Sasha Warren, *Storming Bedlam: Madness, Utopia, and Revolt* (Common Notions Press, 2024), 19.
4. The intermingling of the mad with other marginalized populations in the poorhouses of the Anglo-Saxon world and *Hôtels Dieux* in France is documented by Michael B. Katz, *In the Shadow of the Poorhouse: A Social History of Welfare in America*, Tenth Anniversary Edition (Basic Books, 1996); Robert Castel, *The Regulation of Madness: The Origins of Incarceration in France*, trans. W. D. Halls (Polity Press, 1988).
5. Phillipe Pinel, "A Treatise on Insanity," in *From Madness to Mental Health*, ed. Greg Eghigian (Rutgers University Press, 2010), 100.
6. Dora B. Weiner, "Philippe Pinel in the Twenty-First Century," in *History of Psychiatry and Medical Psychology*, ed. Edwin R. Wallace and John Gach (Springer, 2008).
7. Marcel Gauchet and Gladys Swain, *La pratique de l'esprit humain: l'institution asilaire et la révolution démocratique* (Gallimard, 1980), 206.
8. Quoted in H. Beaudouin and J. L. Beaudouin, "La conception du 'service ouvert' (ou service libre) face à face avec sa carence juridique," *L'information psychiatrique*, no. 1/3 (1967): 39.
9. Castel, *The Regulation of Madness*, 4.
10. Roy Porter, *A Social History of Madness: The World Through the Eyes of the Insane* (Plume, 1989), 19.
11. Andrew T. Scull, *Social Order/Mental Disorder: Anglo-American Psychiatry in Historical Perspective* (University of California Press, 1989), 88.
12. Note that a parallel eugenics movement in the nineteenth and early twentieth century seeking to eliminate the mad through sterilization did, in fact, treat them as subhuman. Robert A. Nye, *Crime, Madness, & Politics in Modern France: The Medical Concept of National Decline* (Princeton University Press, 1984).
13. Isabelle von Bueltzingsloewen, *L'hécatombe des fous: La famine dans les hôpitaux psychiatriques français sous l'Occupation* (Flammarion, 2007), 250–51.

14. Subcommittee on Mental Health, *The Dilemma of Mental Commitments in California* (California State Legislature, 1966), 13.
15. Lion Murard and François Fourquet, *Histoire de la psychiatrie de secteur ou le secteur impossible?* (Recherches, 1975), 191–92.
16. Adrianna Bagnall and Gil Eyal, "Forever Children and Autonomous Citizens: Comparing the Deinstitutionalizations of Psychiatric Patients and Developmentally Disabled Individuals in the United States," in *50 Years After Deinstitutionalization: Mental Illness in Contemporary Communities*, ed. Brea L. Perry (Emerald, 2016).
17. Marion Leboyer and Pierre-Michel Llorca, *Psychiatrie: L'état d'urgence* (Fayard, 2018), 46.
18. Marcel Jaeger, *Le désordre psychiatrique: Des politiques de la santé mentale en France* (Payot, 1981), 11–12. Teresa Scheid makes a similar point: "part of the reason for the dearth of a coherent mental health policy is disagreement over the nature of the problem." Teresa L. Scheid, "Competing Institutional Demands: A Framework for Understanding Mental Health Policy," *Social Theory & Health* 6, no. 4 (2008): 292, https://doi.org/10.1057/sth.2008.12.
19. President's New Freedom Commission on Mental Health, *Achieving the Promise: Transforming Mental Health Care in America* (US Government Publishing Office, 2003), 3.
20. Owen Whooley, *A Mad Mess: Community Mental Health in Crisis* (University of Chicago Press, 2026).
21. Lisa Davis et al., "Deinstitutionalization? Where Have All the People Gone?," *Current Psychiatry Reports* 14, no. 3 (2012): 259–69, https://doi.org/10.1007/s11920-012-0271-1.
22. Leboyer and Llorca, *Psychiatrie*, 20.
23. Jean Ayme, *Chroniques de la psychiatrie publique: A travers l'histoire d'un syndicat* (Érès, 1995), 9.
24. Elisabeth Roudinesco, *Jacques Lacan & Co.: A History of Psychoanalysis in France, 1925–1985*, trans. Jeffrey Mehlman (University of Chicago Press, 1990), 105.
25. Contrôleur général des lieux de privation de liberté, *Rapport d'activité* (Dalloz, 2015), 61.
26. As of 2009 only 1.08 percent of patients at the Police Infirmary contacted an attorney during their stay. Betty Brahmy et al., *Rapport de visite: Infirmerie psychiatrique de la préfecture de police à Paris* (Contrôleur général des lieux de privation de liberté, 2009), 26.
27. You could phrase this as "the sorting state," but as Morgan and Orloff point out, the formula "the [X] state" has been used with dozens of modifiers. I'm reluctant to add another. See Kimberly J. Morgan and Ann Shola Orloff, *The Many Hands of the State: Theorizing Political Authority and Social Control* (Cambridge University Press, 2017), 2.
28. Pierre Bourdieu, *On the State* (Polity, 2015); Margot Canaday, *The Straight State: Sexuality and Citizenship in Twentieth-Century America* (Princeton University Press, 2009); Armando Lara-Millán, *Redistributing the Poor: Jails, Hospitals, and the Crisis of Law and Fiscal Austerity* (Oxford University Press, 2021); Mara Loveman, *National Colors: Racial Classification and the State in Latin America* (Oxford University Press, 2014).

29. Michael Lipsky, *Street-Level Bureaucracy: Dilemmas of the Individual in Public Service*, 30th Anniversary Edition (Russell Sage Foundation, 2010); Josh Seim, *Bandage, Sort, and Hustle: Ambulance Crews on the Frontlines of Urban Suffering* (University of California Press, 2019); Catherine Sirois, "Contested by the State: Institutional Offloading in the Case of Crossover Youth," *American Sociological Review* 88, no. 2 (2023): 350–77, https://doi.org/10.1177/00031224231160297.
30. Liat Ben-Moshe et al., eds., *Disability Incarcerated: Imprisonment and Disability in the United States and Canada* (Palgrave Macmillan, 2014); Rob Wipond, *Your Consent Is Not Required: The Rise in Psychiatric Detentions, Forced Treatment, and Abusive Guardianships* (Ben Bella Books, 2023).
31. See, for example, John Carson, *The Measure of Merit: Talents, Intelligence, and Inequality in the French and American Republics, 1750–1940* (Princeton University Press, 2007); Frank Dobbin, *Forging Industrial Policy: The United States, Britain, and France in the Railway Age* (Cambridge University Press, 1994); Marion Fourcade, *Economists and Societies: Discipline and Profession in the United States, Britain, and France, 1890s to 1990s* (Princeton University Press, 2009); Lynn Payer, *Medicine and Culture* (Penguin, 1988); Abigail Cope Saguy, *What Is Sexual Harassment? From Capitol Hill to the Sorbonne* (University of California Press, 2003); David Wilsford, *Doctors and the State: The Politics of Health Care in France and the United States* (Duke University Press, 1991).
32. Contrary to this point, several commentators have argued there is a weak relationship between mental health systems and social policy more broadly. See, for example, Mick Carpenter, "'It's a Small World': Mental Health Policy Under Welfare Capitalism Since 1945," *Sociology of Health & Illness* 22, no. 5 (2000): 602–20, https://doi.org/10.1111/1467-9566.00222; David Mechanic and David A. Rochefort, "Deinstitutionalization: An Appraisal of Reform," *Annual Review of Sociology* 16 (1990): 301–27.
33. Simon Goodwin, *Comparative Mental Health Policy: From Institutional to Community Care* (SAGE, 1997).
34. John F. Kennedy, *Special Message to the Congress on Mental Illness and Mental Retardation.* (Office of the President of the United States, 1963), http://www.presidency.ucsb.edu/ws/?pid=9546.
35. Ministère de la santé publique et de la population, *Circulaire du 15 Mars 1960 relative au programme d'organisation et d'équipement des départements en matière de lutte contre les maladies mentales* (Le ministre de la santé publique, 1960), 12.
36. Ministère de la santé publique et de la population, *Circulaire du 15 Mars 1960 relative au programme d'organisation*, 1.
37. These ideas were informed by visits by psychiatrists from one country to the other as well as their joint participation in international conferences. Nicolas Henckes, "Narratives of Change and Reform Processes: Global and Local Transactions in French Psychiatric Hospital Reform After the Second World War," *Social Science & Medicine* 68, no. 3 (2009): 511–18, https://doi.org/10.1016/j.socscimed.2008.10.032.
38. Andrew T. Scull, *Decarceration: Community Treatment and the Deviant*, 2nd ed. (Polity Press, 1984).
39. Alex V. Barnard, *Conservatorship: Inside California's System of Coercion and Care for Mental Illness* (Columbia University Press, 2023).

40. On the way the French reformed, rather than replaced, psychiatric hospitals, see Benoît Eyraud and Livia Velpry, "Le secteur psychiatrique: Une innovation instituante?," *Socio-Logos* 7 (2012): 1–12; Nicolas Henckes, "Reforming Psychiatric Institutions in the Mid-Twentieth Century: A Framework for Analysis," *History of Psychiatry* 22, no. 2 (2011): 164–81, https://doi.org/10.1177/0957154X11401867.
41. Ministère de la santé publique et de la population, *Circulaire du 15 Mars 1960 relative au programme d'organisation*, 2.
42. On the logic behind this choice, see Michel Audisio, *La psychiatrie de secteur: Une psychiatrie militante pour la santé mentale* (Éditions Édouard Privat, 1980).
43. Ministère de la santé publique et de la population, *Circulaire du 15 Mars 1960 relative au programme d'organisation*, 13. The Circulaire was actually released the same day as another document on modernizing—not closing—hospitals. See Ministère de la santé publique et de la population, *Circulaire du 15 Mars 1960 relative au plan directeur des hôpitaux psychiatriques anciens* (Le ministre de la santé publique, 1960).
44. Gil Eyal et al., *The Autism Matrix* (Polity, 2010), 2.
45. Magali Coldefy and Sarah E. Curtis, "The Geography of Institutional Psychiatric Care in France 1800–2000: Historical Analysis of the Spatial Diffusion of Specialised Facilities for Institutional Care of Mental Illness," *Social Science & Medicine* 71, no. 12 (2010): 2117–29, https://doi.org/10.1016/j.socscimed.2010.09.028.
46. For one famous example, see Albert Deutsch, *The Mentally Ill in America*, 2nd ed. (Columbia University Press, 1949).
47. Bueltzingsloewen, *L'hécatombe des fous*, 56.
48. Bueltzingsloewen, *L'hécatombe des fous*, 81.
49. Bueltzingsloewen, *L'hécatombe des fous*, 99.
50. Polemics aside, the current consensus is that the Vichy regime took some modest measure to alleviate the famine in late 1942. Jean-Pierre Azéma, *Mission sur le drame que les personnes handicapées mentales ou malades psychiques ont connu dans les hôpitaux psychiatriques et les hospices Français entre 1941 et 1945* (Ministère de la Défense, 2015).
51. Murard and Fourquet, *Histoire de la psychiatrie de secteur*, 101.
52. Camille Robcis, *Disalienation: Politics, Philosophy, and Radical Psychiatry in Postwar France* (University of Chicago Press, 2021).
53. Isabelle Billiard, *Santé mentale et travail: L'émergence de la psychopathologie du travail* (La Dispute, 2001), 101.
54. Alain Lopez, *La psychiatrie dans la tourmente* (Hygée, 2023), 8.
55. Eric Favereau, "Jean Oury, Fou des Fous," *Libération*, June 27, 1998, http://www.liberation.fr/societe/1998/06/27/jean-oury-74-ans-psychiatre-n-a-jamais-cesse-de-saint-alban-a-la-borde-de-vouloir-soigner-l-hopital-_239972.
56. Robcis, *Disalienation*, 40.
57. Eugene Bardach, *The Skill Factor in Politics: Repealing the Mental Commitment Laws in California* (University of California Press, 1972), 101. For a less flippant articulation, see Comptroller General of the United States, *Returning the Mentally Disabled to the Community* (US Government Printing Office, 1977), A5.
58. Roudinesco, *Jacques Lacan & Co.*, 101.
59. Vassilis Kapsambelis, "Cinquante ans après: La crise du secteur," in *Le souci de l'humain: Un défi pour la psychiatrie*, ed. Colette Chiland et al. (Érès, 2010), 441.

See also Sandra Jacqueline, "Les politiques du patient en pratique : Psychanalyse et psychopharmacologie à l'hôpital," *Politix* 73, no. 1 (2006): 83–108, https://doi.org/10.3917/pox.073.0083.

60. Isabel M. Perera, *The Welfare Workforce: Why Mental Health Care Varies Across Affluent Democracies* (Cambridge University Press, 2025).
61. Gerald N. Grob and Howard H. Goldman, *The Dilemma of Federal Mental Health Policy: Radical Reform or Incremental Change?* (Rutgers University Press, 2006).
62. Perera, *The Welfare Workforce.*
63. It is worth noting that French psychiatrists had separate unions for public and private psychiatrists, while public psychiatry was dissolved into a professional organization dominated by private practitioners in the United States. Isabel M. Perera, "Interest Group Governance and Policy Agendas," *Governance* 35, no. 3 (2022): 869–86, https://doi.org/10.1111/gove.12615.
64. François Alfandari, "Le syndicalisme à l'heure de la transformation de la psychiatrie: Des militants CGT à l'hôpital psychiatrique du Vinatier (Lyon, années 1960–1970)," *Genèses* 107, no. 2 (2017): 82–105, https://doi.org/10.3917/gen.107.0082.
65. As one 1976 report noted, the asylums had the "advantage of being situated outside of urban areas, and favor the creation of employment in rural zones." Cour des comptes, *L'Organisation de la Lutte Contre les Maladies Mentales* (1976), 595.
66. Erwan Alix, "Six graphiques pour mesurer la situation de la psychiatrie en France," *Ouest France*, April 26, 2023, https://www.ouest-france.fr/sante/psycho/six-graphiques-pour-mesurer-la-situation-de-la-psychiatrie-en-france-011657ac-debc-11ed-8876-51122d90141b.
67. Pierre Bourdieu, *Distinction* (Harvard University Press, 1984). This framework has already been applied productively to study conflicts between diagnostic approaches in psychiatry by Michael Strand, "Where Do Classifications Come From? The DSM-III, the Transformation of American Psychiatry, and the Problem of Origins in the Sociology of Knowledge," *Theory and Society* 40, no. 3 (2011): 273–313, https://doi.org/10.1007/s11186-011-9142-8.
68. Bourdieu, *On the State*, 9, 166. This claim of the state's central role as an organ of classification is developed in Fourcade, *Economists and Societies*; Damon Mayrl and Sarah Quinn, "Defining the State from Within: Boundaries, Schemas, and Associational Policymaking," *Sociological Theory* 34, no. 1 (2016): 1–26, https://doi.org/10.1177/0735275116632557; Brian Steensland, "Cultural Categories and the American Welfare State: The Case of Guaranteed Income Policy," *American Journal of Sociology* 111, no. 5 (2006): 1273–1326, https://doi.org/10.1086/ajs.2006.111.issue-5.
69. Pierre Bourdieu, "Rethinking the State: Genesis and Structure of the Bureaucratic Field," trans. Loic J. D. Wacquant and Samar Farage, *Sociological Theory* 12, no. 1 (1994): 1–18, https://doi.org/10.2307/202032.
70. The "Frenchness" of Bourdieu's theory of the state is emphasized in Steven Loyal and Stephen Quilley, "The Particularity of the Universal: Critical Reflections on Bourdieu's Theory of Symbolic Power and the State," *Theory and Society* 46, no. 5 (2017): 429–62, https://doi.org/10.1007/s11186-017-9298-y.
71. Eugen Weber, *Peasants into Frenchmen: The Modernization of Rural France, 1870–1914* (Stanford University Press, 1976).

72. Matthew Norton, "Classification and Coercion: The Destruction of Piracy in the English Maritime System," *American Journal of Sociology* 119, no. 6 (2014): 1537–75, https://doi.org/10.1086/676041; Canaday, *The Straight State*; Sadia Saeed, "Religion, Classification Struggles, and the State's Exercise of Symbolic Power," *Theory and Society* 50, no. 2 (2021): 255–81, https://doi.org/10.1007/s11186-020-09415-z.
73. Bourdieu, "Rethinking the State," 1. In fairness, in Bourdieu's own empirical examination of bureaucracy, he emphasized precisely the "indeterminacy or uncertainty" of practices vis-à-vis formal regulations. Pierre Bourdieu, *The Social Structure of the Economy*, trans. Chris Turner (Polity, 2005), 130.
74. Bourdieu, *On the State*, 10. See also Paul Starr, "The Sociology of Official Statistics," in *The Politics of Numbers*, ed. Paul Starr and William Alonso (Russel Sage Foundation, 1987).
75. Mara Loveman, "The U.S. Census and the Contested Rules of Racial Classification in Early Twentieth-Century Puerto Rico," *Caribbean Studies* 35, no. 2 (2007): 79–113.
76. Yehenskel Hasenfeld et al., "The Welfare State, Citizenship, and Bureaucratic Encounters," *Annual Review of Sociology* 13, no. 1 (1987): 387–415; Lipsky, *Street-Level Bureaucracy*; Jeffrey Prottas, *People Processing: The Street-Level Bureaucrat in Public-Service Bureaucracies* (Lexington Books, 1979).
77. Vincent Dubois, *La vie au Guichet: Relation administrative et traitement de la misère*, 2nd ed. (Economica, 2003); Joe Soss et al., *Disciplining the Poor: Neoliberal Paternalism and the Persistent Power of Race* (University of Chicago Press, 2011); Celeste Watkins-Hayes, *The New Welfare Bureaucrats: Entanglements of Race, Class, and Policy Reform* (University of Chicago Press, 2009).
78. Emily Adlin Bosk, "Between Badness and Sickness: Reconsidering Medicalization for High Risk Children and Youth," *Children and Youth Services Review* 35, no. 8 (2013): 1212–18, https://doi.org/10.1016/j.childyouth.2013.04.007; Kerry Dobransky, "The Good, the Bad, and the Severely Mentally Ill: Official and Informal Labels as Organizational Resources in Community Mental Health Services," *Social Science & Medicine* 69, no. 5 (2009): 722–28.
79. On "discipling," "punishing," or "regulating," the poor, see Soss et al., *Disciplining the Poor*; Loïc Wacquant, *Punishing the Poor: The Neoliberal Government of Social Insecurity* (Duke University Press, 2009); Frances Fox Piven and Richard Cloward, *Regulating the Poor: The Functions of Public Welfare* (Vintage, 2012).
80. Seim, *Bandage, Sort, and Hustle*; Chris Herring, "Complaint-Oriented Policing: Regulating Homelessness in Public Space," *American Sociological Review* 84, no. 5 (2019): 769–800, https://doi.org/10.1177/0003122419872671; Lara-Millán, *Redistributing the Poor*; Barnard, *Conservatorship*; Sirois, "Contested by the State."
81. Kim Hopper et al., "Homelessness, Severe Mental Illness, and the Institutional Circuit," *Psychiatric Services* 48, no. 5 (1997): 659–65, https://doi.org/10.1176/ps.48.5.659.
82. Morgan and Orloff, *Many Hands*; Didier Fassin, *At the Heart of the State* (University of Chicago Press, 2015).
83. The parochialism of theorizing contemporary poverty governance in this way reminds us that, as punk legends NOFX put it, "Outside of California, it's foreign policy."

84. Ian Hacking, "The Looping Effects of Human Kinds," in *Causal Cognition: A Multidisciplinary Approach*, ed. Dan Sperber et al. (Oxford University Press, 1995), 352.
85. Hacking, "The Looping Effects of Human Kinds," 360.
86. See also Daniel Navon, *Mobilizing Mutations: Human Genetics in the Age of Patient Advocacy* (University of Chicago Press, 2019).
87. Hacking, "The Looping Effects of Human Kinds," 380. On Hacking's somewhat frustrating unwillingness to define his concepts clearly, see Baptiste Brossard, "Why Mental Disorders Flourish and Wither: Extending the Theory of Ecological Niches," *Social Science & Medicine* 237 (2019): 112445, https://doi.org/10.1016/j.socscimed.2019.112445.
88. Hacking, "The Looping Effects of Human Kinds," 370. This is a long-running insight within the so-called labeling theory of mental illness. T. J. Scheff, "The Labelling Theory of Mental Illness," *American Sociological Review* 39, no. 3 (1974): 444–52, https://doi.org/10.2307/2094300.
89. Hacking, "The Looping Effects of Human Kinds," 370.
90. Eyal et al., *The Autism Matrix*; Daniel Navon and Gil Eyal, "Looping Genomes: Diagnostic Change and the Genetic Makeup of the Autism Population," *American Journal of Sociology* 121, no. 5 (2016): 1416–71, https://doi.org/10.1086/684201; Catherine Tan, *Spaces on the Spectrum: How Autism Movements Resist Experts and Create Knowledge* (Columbia University Press, 2024).
91. Ian Hacking, *Rewriting the Soul: Multiple Personality and the Sciences of Memory* (Princeton University Press, 1998), 239.
92. Nancy Scheper-Hughes and Anne M. Lovell, "Breaking the Circuit of Social Control: Lessons in Public Psychiatry from Italy and Franco Basaglia," *Social Science & Medicine* 23, no. 2 (1986): 159–78, https://doi.org/10.1016/0277-9536(86)90364-3; Michael Staub, *Madness Is Civilization* (University of Chicago Press, 2011); Warren, *Storming Bedlam*.
93. Nick Crossley, *Contesting Psychiatry: Social Movements in Mental Health* (Routledge, 2006); Phyllis Vine, *Fighting for Recovery: An Activists' History of Mental Health Reform* (Beacon Press, 2022).
94. There is a recent exception: the success of a small group of ex-patients in convincing the French constitutional court to obligate hearings on involuntary hospitalizations in 2010. I discuss this in part III.
95. Claude Quétel, *Histoire de la folie* (Tallandier, 2012), 530. See also Sherry Turkle, *Psychoanalytic Politics: Jacques Lacan and Freud's French Revolution*, 2nd ed. (Guilford Press, 1992), 144.
96. Robert Castel, *La gestion des risques: De l'anti-psychiatrie à l'après-psychanalyse* (Minuit, 1981), 35.
97. Robcis, *Disalienation*, 6.
98. Ayme, *Chroniques de la psychiatrie publique*, 13.
99. Bruno Latour, *Laboratory Life: The Construction of Scientific Facts*, with Steve Woolgar and Jonas Salk (Princeton University Press, 1979), 260.
100. Fourcade, *Economists and Societies*, 14.
101. Fourcade, *Economists and Societies*, 14.
102. Alain Ehrenberg, "La plainte sans fin: Réflexions sur le couple souffrance psychique/santé mentale," *Cahiers de recherche sociologique*, nos. 41–42 (2005): 17–41; Nikolas

Rose, "Disorders Without Borders? The Expanding Scope of Psychiatric Practice," *BioSocieties* 1, no. 4 (2006): 465–84, https://doi.org/10.1017/S1745855206004078.

103. Kerry Dobransky, *Managing Madness in the Community: The Challenge of Contemporary Mental Health Care* (Rutgers University Press, 2014); Benoît Eyraud, *Protéger et rendre capable* (Eres, 2013).
104. Michael Dudley et al., *Mental Health and Human Rights: Vision, Praxis, and Courage* (Oxford University Press, 2012); Jeppe Oute and Susan McPherson, "Conflict and Antagonism Within Global Psychiatry: A Discourse Analysis of Organisational Responses to the UN Reports on Rights-Based Approaches in Mental Health," *Sociology of Health & Illness* 46, no. 3 (2024): 473–94, https://doi.org/10.1111/1467-9566.13717.
105. Tineke Broer and Martyn Pickersgill, "Targeting Brains, Producing Responsibilities: The Use of Neuroscience Within British Social Policy," *Social Science & Medicine* 132 (2015): 54–61, https://doi.org/10.1016/j.socscimed.2015.03.022; Castel, *La gestion des risques*; Nikolas Rose, "Governing Risky Individuals: The Role of Psychiatry in New Regimes of Control," *Psychiatry, Psychology and Law* 5, no. 2 (1998): 177–95.
106. Nicolas Henckes, "Schizophrenia Infrastructures: Local and Global Dynamics of Transformation in Psychiatric Diagnosis-Making in the Twentieth and Twenty-First Centuries," *Culture, Medicine, and Psychiatry* 43, no. 4 (2019): 548–73, https://doi.org/10.1007/s11013-019-09636–7; Andrew Lakoff, *Pharmaceutical Reason: Knowledge and Value in Global Psychiatry* (Cambridge University Press, 2006); Ethan Watters, *Crazy Like Us: The Globalization of the American Psyche* (Free Press, 2011).

## PART I. BETWEEN SICKNESS AND HEALTH

1. Sukanta Saha et al., "A Systematic Review of the Prevalence of Schizophrenia," *PLoS Med* 2, no. 5 (2005): e141, https://doi.org/10.1371/journal.pmed.0020141;In Pescosolido et al.'s worldwide survey of stigma, an average of 92 percent of people across sixteen different countries stated, in response to a vignette describing someone with schizophrenia, that the person should go to a mental health professional. Bernice A. Pescosolido, Tait R. Medina, Jack K. Martin, and J. Scott Long, "The 'Backbone' of Stigma: Identifying the Global Core of Public Prejudice Associated with Mental Illness," *American Journal of Public Health* 103, no. 5 (2013): 855, https://doi.org/10.2105/AJPH.2012.301147.
2. U.S. Department of Health and Human Services, *Health, United States*, no. 78–1232 (US Government Printing Office, 1978), 73.
3. France Meslé and Jacques Vallin, "La population des établissements psychiatriques: Évolution de la morbidité ou changement de stratégie médicale?," *Population* 36, no. 6 (1981): 1041, https://doi.org/10.2307/1532324. Of course, many of the people in asylums did not have schizophrenia, and many people with schizophrenia remained in the community, often cared for by their families.
4. Michael Staub, *Madness Is Civilization* (University of Chicago Press, 2011), 37.
5. Sherry Turkle, *Psychoanalytic Politics: Jacques Lacan and Freud's French Revolution*, 2nd ed. (Guilford Press, 1992).

6. Allan V. Horwitz and Gerald N. Grob, "The Troubled History of Psychiatry's Quest for Specificity," *Journal of Health Politics, Policy and Law* 41, no. 4 (2016): 521–39, https://doi.org/10.1215/03616878-3620797.
7. French estimates claim around 2 percent of the population suffers from a "serious" psychiatric condition, although longitudinal epidemiology is less developed than in the United States. Christine Chan Chee et al., "État des lieux de la surveillance de la santé mentale en France," *Santé publique* 23, no. 6 (2012): 11–29.
8. Nikolas Rose, *Powers of Freedom: Reframing Political Thought* (Cambridge University Press, 1999); Whitney L. Duncan, "Psicoeducación in the Land of Magical Thoughts: Culture and Mental-Health Practice in a Changing Oaxaca," *American Ethnologist* 44, no. 1 (2017): 36–51, https://doi.org/10.1111/amet.12424; Rémy Ponge, "D'un enjeu politique à un problème personnel: L'individualisation de la réparation des souffrances psychiques liées au travail," *Revue française de sociologie* 61, no. 3 (2020): 435–63, https://doi.org/10.3917/rfs.613.0435.
9. Alain Ehrenberg, "La plainte sans fin: Réflexions sur le couple souffrance psychique/santé mentale," *Cahiers de Recherche Sociologique*, nos. 41–42 (2005): 18.
10. Peter Conrad, *The Medicalization of Society: On the Transformation of Human Conditions into Treatable Disorders* (Johns Hopkins University Press, 2007); Allan V. Horwitz and Jerome C. Wakefield, *The Loss of Sadness: How Psychiatry Transformed Normal Sorrow into Depressive Disorder* (Oxford University Press, 2007); Annemarie Goldstein Jutel, *Putting a Name to It: Diagnosis in Contemporary Society* (Johns Hopkins University Press, 2011).
11. Sherry Glied and Richard G. Frank, "Economics and the Transformation of the Mental Health System," *Journal of Health Politics, Policy and Law* 41, no. 4 (2016): 541–58, https://doi.org/10.1215/03616878-3620809.
12. Valérie Paris et al., *Des comptes de la santé par pathologie: Un prototype sur l'année 1998*, (Direction de la recherche, des études, de l'évaluation et des statistiques, 2002). The most recent figure is from the 2020 World Health Organization Mental Health Atlas.
13. Teresa L. Scheid, *Tie a Knot and Hang On: Providing Mental Health Care in a Turbulent Environment* (Transaction Publishers, 2004).
14. Stella R. Quah, "Rationalization," in *Encyclopedia of Health, Illness, Behavior, and Society*, ed. Stella R. Quah et al. (Wiley-Blackwell, 2014), 2, https://doi.org/10.1002/9781118410868.wbehibs019.
15. Some scholars and activists have rejected this implicit setup that there are never sufficient medical resources to treat all the people who could at least theoretically benefit from care. My argument does not dismiss that a hyperabundant, barrierless medical system could exist, but it does assume that these dilemmas are inevitable within our existing political and economic system. Beatrice Adler-Bolton and Artie Vierkant, *Health Communism* (Verso, 2022); Donald W. Light and David Hughes, "Introduction: A Sociological Perspective on Rationing: Power, Rhetoric and Situated Practices," *Sociology of Health & Illness* 23, no. 5 (2001): 551–69, https://doi.org/10.1111/1467-9566.00265.
16. I use "logic" here in the sense of "epistemic logics," as elaborated by Stefan Vogler. In the case of the evaluation of sexuality of criminal defendants and asylum seekers, epistemic logics serve as "institutionalized ways of knowing . . . giv[ing] rise to different legal conceptions of sexuality, what counts as evidence of sexuality, and how sexuality will be measured and assessed." Bounding and

scaling similarly reflect different background assumptions about how mental illness should be conceptualized and measured, and whether it is best assessed through professional judgment or more "objective" tools. Stefan Vogler, *Sorting Sexualities: Expertise and the Politics of Legal Classification* (University of Chicago Press, 2021), 10.

17. Christopher G Hudson, "Behavioral Mental Health: An Emerging Field of Service or an Oxymoron?," *Social Work* 63, no. 1 (2018): 27–36, https://doi.org/10.1093/sw/swx048.
18. On the rise of a continuum approach in post–World War II American psychiatry, see Gerald N. Grob, *From Asylum to Community: Mental Health Policy in Modern America* (Princeton University Press, 1991), 18.
19. The fixation on time-limited care in the United States is documented in Kerry Michael Dobransky, *Managing Madness in the Community: The Challenge of Contemporary Mental Health Care* (Rutgers University Press, 2014); Lorna A. Rhodes, *Emptying Beds: The Work of an Emergency Psychiatric Unit* (University of California Press, 1991).
20. They are thus tools for what Marion Fourcade calls "ordinalization." Marion Fourcade, "Ordinalization," *Sociological Theory* 34, no. 3 (2016): 175–95, https://doi.org/10.1177/0735275116665876.
21. Howard Padwa, "Oral History: Martha Long," February 2, 2010, http://histpubmh.semel.ucla.edu/sites/default/files/oral_histories/ae4dd9bf_Long_Web_Version_Final.pdf.
22. John R. Elpers, "Public Mental Health Funding in California, 1959 to 1989," *Psychiatric Services* 40, no. 8 (1989): 803, https://doi.org/10.1176/ps.40.8.799.
23. Karen de Sá, "Mental Health Spending Creating Haves and Have-Nots in California," *Contra Costa Times*, June 26, 2011, https://www.mercurynews.com/2011/06/25/mental-health-spending-creating-haves-and-have-nots/.
24. Direction générale de la santé, *Plan psychiatrie et santé mentale, 2011–2015* (Ministère du travail, de l'emploi et de la santé, 2012), 42, http://www.sante.gouv.fr/plan-psychiatrie-et-sante-mentale-2011-2015.html.
25. Other studies have also shown a contrast between a French reliance on expert judgments and an American emphasis on quantitative criteria. Theodore M. Porter, *Trust in Numbers: The Pursuit of Objectivity in Science and Public Life* (Princeton University Press, 1996); John Carson, *The Measure of Merit: Talents, Intelligence, and Inequality in the French and American Republics, 1750–1940* (Princeton University Press, 2007).

## 1. THE BOUNDARIES OF "SANTÉ-MENTALISME"

1. Eric Piel and Jean-Luc Roelandt, *De la psychiatrie vers la santé mentale*, Rapport de Mission (Ministre de l'Emploi et de la Solidarité, 2001), 6.
2. Nicolas Daumerie et al., *The WHO Recommendations and Mental Health in France: The Real and Tacit Instrumentalisation of the Instrument* (KNOWandPOL, 2009), 17.
3. As an official from the High Commission for the Future of National Insurance told me, "For us, the objective is to avoid people going to the hospital . . . And for that, Jean-Luc Roelandt's *secteur* is the model."

4. Direction de la recherche, des études, de l'évaluation et des statistiques, *Les dépenses de santé en 2017: Résultats des comptes de la santé* (2017), 76.
5. Jean-Luc Roelandt et al., "Community Mental Health Service: An Experience from East Lille, France," *Journal of Mental Health and Human Behaviour* 19, no. 1 (2014): 10, https://doi.org/10.4103/0971-8990.143884.
6. "Pôle Remois (51 ZR4)," *Établissement public de santé mentale de la Marne*, retrieved July 6, 2021, https://www.epsm-marne.fr/toute-notre-offre-2/psychiatrie-adultes/pole-remois-51-zr4/.
7. More discussion of this approach can be found in Baptiste Brossard, "L'organisation sociale des 'hasards heureux': Qu'est-ce qu'un soin en psychiatrie?," *Sociologie du Travail* 55, no. 1 (2013): 1–19.
8. Andrew T. Scull, *Social Order/Mental Disorder: Anglo-American Psychiatry in Historical Perspective* (University of California Press, 1989), 242; Gil Eyal et al., *The Autism Matrix* (Polity, 2010), 38; Simon Dinitz and Nancy Beran, "Community Mental Health as a Boundaryless and Boundary-Busting System," *Journal of Health and Social Behavior* 12, no. 2 (1971): 101, https://doi.org/10.2307/2948516.
9. Ministère de la santé publique et de la population, *Circulaire du 15 Mars 1960 relative au programme d'organisation et d'équipement des départements en matière de lutte contre les maladies mentales* (Le ministre de la santé publique, 1960), 14.
10. Ministère de la santé publique, *Circulaire du 15 Mars 1960*, 2.
11. Quoted in Jean Ayme, *Chroniques de la psychiatrie publique: A travers l'histoire d'un syndicat* (Érès, 1995), 443.
12. Henri Ey, "Exposé du Secrétaire Générale de l'évolution psychiatrique," in *Livre blanc de la psychiatrie française*, vol. 2 (Éditions Édouard Privat, 1966), 10.
13. Ey, "Exposé du Secrétaire Générale," 9.
14. "Les institutions et l'organisation de secteurs psychiatriques," in *Livre blanc de la psychiatrie française*, vol. 2 (Éditions Édouard Privat, 1966), 51.
15. Lion Murard and François Fourquet, *Histoire de la psychiatrie de secteur ou le secteur impossible?* (Recherches, 1975), 476.
16. Michel Audisio, *La psychiatrie de secteur: Une psychiatrie militante pour la santé mentale* (Éditions Édouard Privat, 1980), 244.
17. "Les institutions et l'organisation de secteurs psychiatriques," 36.
18. Murard and Fourquet, *Histoire de la psychiatrie de secteur*, 219.
19. Ey, "Exposé du Secrétaire Générale," 10.
20. Nicolas Henckes, "Mistrust of Numbers: The Difficult Development of Psychiatric Epidemiology in France, 1940–80," *International Journal of Epidemiology* 43, Suppl. 1 (2014): i50, https://doi.org/10.1093/ije/dyu116.
21. As one psychiatrist characterized it, "We've arrived at a complete mixing of types [of patients], extremely shocking for new arrivals, but which has quickly been very well tolerated by nearly all *malades*." Note that in this "complete mixing of types," everyone is still a *malade*. Murard and Fourquet, *Histoire de la psychiatrie de secteur*, 493.
22. Wendy Nelson Espeland and Michael Sauder, "Rankings and Reactivity: How Public Measures Recreate Social Worlds," *American Journal of Sociology* 113, no. 1 (2007): 1–40, https://doi.org/10.1086/517897.
23. Ségolène Neuville, "Cap sur la santé mentale," Cérémonie d'ouverture du premier village santé mentale en France, Ministère des affaires sociales et de la santé,

Paris, France, May 10, 2016), https://sante.gouv.fr/IMG/pdf/discours_de_segolene_neuville_-_sante_mentale_10052016.pdf.

24. A comparative analysis by the European Union also concluded France deemphasized the promotion of mental health in favor of a focus on addressing mental illness. Chiara Samele et al., *European Profile of Prevention and Promotion of Mental Health* (European Commission, 2013), 188.
25. Graham Thornicroft et al., "Global Pattern of Experienced and Anticipated Discrimination Against People with Schizophrenia: A Cross-Sectional Survey," *The Lancet* 373, no. 9661 (2009): 408–15, https://doi.org/10.1016/S0140-6736(08)61817-6.
26. Paul Benkimoun and Sandrine Blanchard, "Le ministre délégué à la santé présente un plan sur la santé mentale en conseil des ministres," *Le Monde*, November 15, 2001.
27. This changed in 2021, when the state introduced a new program, "Mon soutien psy," which reimbursed a limited number of sessions for people with mild-to-moderate conditions. Critics argued that it was, in reality, pirating resources that should have been going to serve more severe patients in the *secteurs*. "'Mon soutien psy' ne répond pas à une exigence de qualité des soins, mais à une logique économique," *Le Monde*, June 5, 2025, https://www.lemonde.fr/idees/article/2025/06/05/mon-soutien-psy-ne-repond-pas-a-une-exigence-de-qualite-des-soins-mais-a-une-logique-economique_6610593_3232.html.
28. Marie-Aude Poisson et al., *Les parcours des personnes en psychiatrie et santé mentale: Première approche* (L'Agence Nationale d'Appui à la Performance des Établissements Sanitaires et Médico-Sociaux, 2015), 15.
29. Direction générale de la santé, *Plan psychiatrie et santé mentale, 2005–2008* (Comité technique national de suivi du plan « psychiatrie et santé mentale », 2005), 8, https://sante.gouv.fr/IMG/pdf/bilan_2007.pdf.
30. B. Kouchner, *Plan Santé Mentale: L'usager au centre d'un dispositif à rénover* (Ministre de l'emploi et de la solidarité, 2001), 33.
31. Allan V. Horwitz and Jerome C. Wakefield, *The Loss of Sadness: How Psychiatry Transformed Normal Sorrow into Depressive Disorder* (Oxford University Press, 2007). The "bereavement exclusion" is the only exception.
32. Xavier Briffault et al., *Le dépression: En savoir plus pour en sortir* (Institut national de prévention et d'éducation pour la santé, 2007), 25.
33. J. Alonso et al., "Psychotropic Drug Utilization in Europe: Results from the European Study of the Epidemiology of Mental Disorders (ESEMeD) Project," *Acta Psychiatrica Scandinavica*, no. 420 (2004): 55–64, https://doi.org/10.1111/j.1600-0047.2004.00331.x.
34. Maryvonne Briot, *Rapport sur le bon usage des médicaments psychotropes*, N° 422 (Office parlementaire d'évaluation des politiques de santé, 2006), 58.
35. Organisation for Economic Co-operation and Development (OECD) Health Stat, 2024, "Pharmaceutical Market," retrieved January 10, 2025, https://data-explorer.oecd.org/.
36. Ruth Brauer et al., "Psychotropic Medicine Consumption in 65 Countries and Regions, 2008–19: A Longitudinal Study," *The Lancet Psychiatry* 8, no. 12 (2021): 1071–82, https://doi.org/10.1016/S2215-0366(21)00292-3.
37. Sandrine Blanchard, "Pourquoi les Français consomment toujours plus de psychotropes," *Le Monde*, September 7, 2004, https://www.lemonde.fr/archives/article

/2004/09/06/pourquoi-les-francais-consomment-toujours-plus-de-psychotropes_378001_1819218.html.

38. Another clear example of this is French child psychiatrists' reluctance to prescribe Ritalin; as of 2014, rates of consumption were one-fifteenth those in the United States. Manuel Vallée, "The Countervailing Forces Behind France's Low Ritalin Consumption," *Social Science & Medicine* 238 (2019): 112492, https://doi.org/10.1016/j.socscimed.2019.112492.
39. Spending on prevention in mental health, as of 2017, was "negligible." Direction de la recherche, *Les dépenses de santé en 2017*, 154.
40. For more on how the critique of the "psychologization of existence" has come from mental health professionals themselves, see Samuel Lézé, *L'autorité des psychanalystes* (Presses universitaires de France, 2010), 32.
41. Antoine Lazarus and Hélène Strohl, *Une souffrance qu'on ne peut plus cacher* (Délégation interministérielle à la ville et au développement social urbain, 1995), 8.
42. Lazarus and Strohl, *Une souffrance qu'on ne peut plus cacher*, 18.
43. Laurence Follea, "Dans un 'Livre Blanc': Les psychiatres français dénoncent le traitement psychiatrique des problèmes sociaux," *Le Monde*, June 9, 1994.
44. Nicole Dubré-Chirat and Sandrine Rousseau, *Rapport sur la prise en charge des urgences psychiatriques*, N° 714 (Assemblée Nationale, 2024), 151, https://www.assemblee-nationale.fr/dyn/17/rapports/cion-soc/l17b0714_rapport-information.pdf.
45. Centre collaborateur OMS, *Les conseils locaux de santé mentale: État des lieux* (CCOMS Lille, 2018).
46. The ambivalence of French mental health professionals in the face of profound precarity mixed with real suffering is also examined in Isabelle Coutant and Jean-Sébastien Eideliman, "Listening to Suffering: The Treatment of Mental Fragility at a Home for Adolescents," in *At the Heart of the State*, ed. Didier Fassin (University of Chicago Press, 2015).
47. For a broader discussion of attempts to rationalize psychiatric financing, see Sylvie Biarez, "Une politique publique: La santé mentale (1970–2002)," *Revue française d'administration publique* 3, no. 111 (2004): 517–31; Lise Demailly and Michel Autès, La politique de santé mentale en France: Acteurs, instruments, controverses (Armand Colin, 2012); Tonya Tartour, "L'administration du désordre: Gouverner l'hôpital psychiatrique depuis les années 1980" (PhD diss., Sciences Po Paris, 2021).
48. Magali Coldefy and Charlène Le Neindre, *Les disparités territoriales d'offre et d'organisation des soins en psychiatrie en France: D'une vision segmentée à une approche systémique*, N° 558 (Institut de recherche et documentation en économie de la santé, 2014), 22–23.
49. See Daniel Benamouzig, *La santé au miroir de l'économie: Une histoire de l'économie de la santé en France* (Presses universitaires de France, 2005); Bruno Palier, *Gouverner la sécurité sociale: Les réformes du système français de protection sociale depuis 1945* (Presses universitaires de France, 2005).
50. I give more detail on these efforts in Alex V. Barnard, "A Discipline Like No Other: Marginalized Autonomy and Institutional Anchors in French Public Psychiatry (1945–2016)," *Comparative Studies in Society and History* 66, no. 3 (2024): 643–72, https://doi.org/10.1017/S0010417524000070.

51. Pierre-André Juven, "'Des trucs qui rapportent': Enquête ethnographique autour des processus de capitalisation à l'hôpital public," *Anthropologie & santé*, no. 16 (May 2018), https://doi.org/10.4000/anthropologiesante.2860.
52. Marion Leboyer and Pierre-Michel Llorca, *Psychiatrie: L'État d'Urgence* (Fayard, 2018), 266.
53. Claire Bélart and Olivier Dembinski, "Les nouveaux outils de géstion en psychiatrie," in *La politique de santé mentale en France: Acteurs, instruments, controverses*, ed. Lise Demailly and Michel Autès (Armand Colin, 2012), 162.
54. Jean-Marie Rolland, *Rapport sur la tarification à l'activité dans les établissements de santé*, N° 3265 (Assemblée Nationale, 2006), 21.
55. These practices of strategic subversion of managerial tools are not limited to doctors; psychiatric nurses in France have also been key to this resistance. Frédéric Mougeot, *Le travail des infirmiers en hôpital psychiatrique* (Érès, 2019).
56. In 2022, the global budget was reformed to take into partial account the populations served, the volume of activity, innovation, and quality. The extent of its practical effects were unclear when this book went to press. Ministère du travail, de la santé, et des solidarités, *Santé mentale et psychiatrie: État d'avancement* (Ministère du travail et des solidarités, 2024), 94, https://sante.gouv.fr/IMG/pdf/feuille_de_route.sante-mentale-psychiatrie-2024.pdf.
57. Alain Lopez and Gaëlle Turan-Pelletier, *Organisation et fonctionnement du dispositif de soins psychiatriques, 60 ans après la Circulaire du 15 Mars 1960*, N°2017-064R (Inspection générale des affaires sociales, 2017).
58. Pierre Bourdieu, "Rethinking the State: Genesis and Structure of the Bureaucratic Field," trans. Loic J. D. Wacquant and Samar Farage, *Sociological Theory* 12, no. 1 (1994): 1, https://doi.org/10.2307/202c32.
59. "L'organisation des soins psychiatriques," in *Livre blanc de la psychiatrie française*, vol. 2 (Éditions Édouard Privat, 1966), 38.
60. A report from 1981 estimates that *secteurs* served about 1.8 percent of the adult population; in 1993, the figure was only 1.7 percent. François Zambrowski, *Moderniser et diversifier les modes de prise en charge de la psychiatrie française* (Ministre de la Solidarité, de la Santé, et de la Protection Sociale, 1986), 151; Pierre Joly, *Prevention et soins des maladies mentales* (Conseil economique et social, 1997). For the most recent figure, see Cour des comptes, *Les parcours dans l'organisation des soins en psychiatrie*, Rapport public thématique (Cour des comptes, 2021).
61. This distinction between "rationing" and "rationalization" could also be articulated as the distinction between explicit, rules-based rationing and implicit mechanisms based on professional judgment. David Mechanic, "Dilemmas in Rationing Health Care Services: The Case for Implicit Rationing," *BMJ* 310, no. 6995 (1995): 1655–59, https://doi.org/10.1136/bmj.310.6995.1655.

## 2. RATIONING FOR REAL *MALADES*

1. This process of verifying addresses is a controversial one. It creates the possibility for unhoused individuals to be passed around in a game of psychiatric hot potato. It's nonetheless one of the few apparently legitimate ways for *secteurs* to limit the influx of new patients.

2. This figure excludes *secteurs* for incarcerated individuals and for children.
3. Livia Velpry, *Le quotidien de la psychiatrie: Sociologie de la maladie mentale* (Armand Colin, 2008), 83.
4. Robert Castel, *The Regulation of Madness: The Origins of Incarceration in France*, trans. W. D. Halls (Polity Press, 1988), 150.
5. Didier Fassin and Richard Rechtman, *The Empire of Trauma: An Inquiry into the Condition of Victimhood* (Princeton University Press, 2009), 115. See also Stephanie Lloyd, "Morals, Medicine and Change: Morality Brokers, Social Phobias, and French Psychiatry," *Culture, Medicine, and Psychiatry* 32, no. 2 (2008): 279–97, https://doi.org/10.1007/s11013-008-9092-4.
6. This use of typologies, rather than formal diagnostic categories, is documented for French psychiatrists in other settings, like treating sexual offenders. Eléonore Rimbault, "Killing Two Birds with One Stone: Mandatory Therapy and the Prevention of Sex Crime in France," *Culture, Medicine, and Psychiatry* 49, no. 1 (2025): 304–27, https://doi.org/10.1007/s11013-024-09882-4.
7. This modality of hospitalizations, *soins psychiatrique sur décision d'un représentant de l'État* (psychiatric care by decision of a representative of the state) is discussed in more detail in chapter 5. It allows a person to be hospitalized when they pose an "imminent risk for the security of persons" or pose "grave troubles for the public order." *Code de santé publique*, article L3213-1, retrieved May 9, 2025, https://www.legifrance.gouv.fr/codes/article_lc/LEGIARTI000028016871.
8. Pierre-André Juven, "'Des trucs qui rapportent': Enquête ethnographique autour des processus de capitalisation à l'hôpital public," *Anthropologie & santé*, no. 16 (May 2018), https://doi.org/10.4000/anthropologiesante.2860.
9. Mougeot documents how psychiatric hospital nurses, rather than dividing finite clinical time equally among a rising number of cases, invest heavily in a subset of them. Frédéric Mougeot, *Le travail des infirmiers en hôpital psychiatrique* (Érès, 2019), 111.
10. Eviatar Zerubavel, "Lumping and Splitting: Notes on Social Classification," *Sociological Forum* 11, no. 3 (1996): 424.
11. One study found that 19 percent of patients in one sample of *secteurs* had schizophrenia, 4 percent had bipolar, 21 percent had depression, and 56 percent had "neuroses," a psychoanalytic category nominally in official disuse. Erik A. Sauleau et al., "Approche géographique du recours aux soins en santé mentale," *Journal de gestion et d'économie médicales* 31, no. 7 (2014): 506.
12. In France, professionals often treated suicidality and depression as separate phenomena. This mirrors national policy, which differentiates the two and suggests that the former is not necessarily pathological.
13. Pierre-Yves Baudot, "L'invention des délais: Pourquoi l'administration doit-elle répondre dans les temps?," *Politiques sociales et familiales* 119, no. 1 (2015): 11, https://doi.org/10.3406/caf.2015.3067.
14. Alain Ehrenberg, "La plainte sans fin: Réflexions sur le couple souffrance psychique/santé mentale," *Cahiers de recherche sociologique*, no. 41–42 (2005): 29.
15. See also Céline Borelle, "'C'est uniquement social': Sur la production d'un dualisme social/psychiatrique en sciences sociales et dans le travail ordinaire de la psychiatrie," *Politix* 117, no. 1 (2017): 201–22, https://doi.org/10.3917/pox.117.0201.

16. François Chapireau, *Les recours aux soins spécialisés en santé mentale*, N° 533 (Direction de la recherche, des études, de l'évaluation et des statistiques, 2006), 2. In surveys of public perceptions, French people frequently used "crazy" and "mentally ill" as substitutable, and distinguish both from depression. Jean-Luc Roelandt et al., "Représentations sociales du 'fou', du 'malade mental' et du 'dépressif' en population générale en France," *L'encéphale* 36, no. 3 (2010): 7–13.
17. Thierry Trémine, "Y-a-t-il une identité de la psychiatrie française ?," in *Psychiatrie française/psychiatrie en France*, ed. Frédéric Rouillon (Springer, 2012), 2.
18. One study argued French clinicians resist prescribing antidepressants for mood disorders among homeless people on the assumption that the patients' mood disorders are reactive to their social condition. G. Fond et al., "Prescription of Potentially Inappropriate Psychotropic Drugs in Homeless People with Schizophrenia and Bipolar Disorders. Results from the French Housing First (FHF) Program," *Progress in Neuro-Psychopharmacology & Biological Psychiatry* 89 (March 2019): 84–89, https://doi.org/10.1016/j.pnpbp.2018.08.024.
19. This is the opposite of what Bouvet found in her study of private psychiatric hospitals, where doctors invested more in cases in which patients' depression was tied to external events. This may reflect the different orientation of private and public psychiatrists, or the fact that higher-status private patients may have external factors deemed more interesting than poverty and precarity. Marlène Bouvet, "Réenchanter les déprimé.es: Une sociologie de la thérapie en clinique privée" (PhD diss., École nationale supérieur, 2023).
20. See also Velpry, *Le quotidien de la psychiatrie*, 100.
21. Private psychiatrists protest that private hospitals (which are now one-third of psychiatric beds in France) take 40 percent of cases of bipolar disorder and 60 percent of acute depression reimbursed by national insurance. Marion Leboyer and Pierre-Michel Llorca, *Psychiatrie: L'état d'urgence* (Fayard, 2018), 88. On the other hand, one national study claimed that 83 percent of people with schizophrenia were cared for in public hospitals. Magali Coldefy and Clément Nestrigue, *La variabilité de la prise en charge de la schizophrénie dans les établissements de santé en 2011*, N° 206 (Institut de recherche et documentation en économie de la santé, 2015), 1–8.
22. Statistics on rates of renouncing care in France vary depending on the phrasing of questions. In one study of recipients of the *revenu de solidarité active* (RSA), a minimum income, 18 percent claimed they had not consulted a doctor for reasons of cost. Muriel Moisy, *État de santé et renoncement aux soins des bénéficiaires du RSA*, N° 882 (Direction de la recherche, des études, de l'évaluation et des statistiques, 2014). We should not pretend these statistics show France has anywhere near the problems with access to care as the United States.
23. Elizabeth Chiarello, *Policing Patients: Treatment and Surveillance on the Frontlines of the Opioid Crisis* (Princeton University Press, 2024), 130.
24. Assurance Maladie, "Psychiatres et Neuro-Psychiatres Libéraux," accessed January 29, 2026, https://www.assurance-maladie.ameli.fr/sites/default/files/2024_fiche_psychiatres-et-neuro-psychiatres-liberaux.pdf.
25. For a similar case of how French professionals' identities as public servants depend on their "positive discrimination" in favor of the most severe cases, see

Carine Vassy, "Categorisation and Micro-Rationing: Access to Care in a French Emergency Department," *Sociology of Health & Illness* 23, no. 5 (2001): 615–32, https://doi.org/10.1111/1467-9566.00268.

26. Martine Barres, *L'action de la psychiatrie pour l'accès et le maintien dans le logement des personnes vivant avec des troubles psychiques en Île-de-France* (Agence régionale de santé, 2016), 14. This report claimed that some teams refused third-party referrals entirely.
27. Body mass index is a notoriously problematic measure, but 14.2 is well below the normal range of 18.5–24.9.
28. Although I never heard the *secteur* team refer to a patient as "borderline" (i.e., having borderline personality disorder), their skepticism here of a (female) patient whose challenges were attributed primarily to personality mirrors that documented by Ivan Garrec, "Trouble dans les émotions: Enquête sur l'éxistence sociale du 'trouble de la personnalité borderline' en France" (PhD diss., École doctorale Érasme, 2024).
29. See Angèle Christin, *Comparutions immédiates: Enquête sur une pratique judiciaire* (La Découverte, 2008), 168; Ana Marques et al., "Des murailles de papier: La contrainte aux soins en ambulatoire," *Revue française des affaires sociales*, no. 6 (2016): 57–74.
30. Similar resistance is documented in Thomas Le Bianic, "Certified Expertise and Professional Responsibility in Organizations: The Case of Mental Health Practice in Prisons," *Sociological Review* 59, no. 4 (2011): 803–27, https://doi.org/10.1111/j.1467-954X.2011.02029.x; Fabrice Fernandez and Samuel Lézé, "Finding the Moral Heart of Treatment: Mental Health Care in a French Prison," *Social Science & Medicine* 72, no. 9 (2011): 1563–69, https://doi.org/10.1016/j.socscimed.2011.03.013.
31. It is worth noting that no patients were identified as being transgender. That may seem implausible, but my observations in 2016 came *before* the explosion of awareness of and identification as transgender in the latter part of the decade.
32. For more on this debate, see Terrence D. Hill and Belinda L. Needham, "Rethinking Gender and Mental Health: A Critical Analysis of Three Propositions," *Social Science & Medicine* 92 (2013): 83–91, https://doi.org/10.1016/j.socscimed.2013.05.025.
33. Mission nationale d'expertise et d'audit hospitalier, *L'organisation des centres médico-psychologiques* (Centre medico psychologique, 2008), 99. A 2020 report on medical-psychological centers makes no mention of this topic. Stéphanie Dupays and Julien Emmanuelli, *Les centres médico-psychologiques de psychiatrie générale et leur place dans le parcours du patient*, nos. 2019-090R (Inspection générale des affaires sociales, 2020), 132.
34. On the homogenization of treatment in French *secteurs*, see Julia Legrand, "L'injonction ou l'injection? Prescriptions de médicaments et reconfigurations contemporaines du pouvoir psychiatrique," *Genèses* 127, no. 2 (2022): 11–32, https://doi.org/10.3917/gen.127.0011.
35. Michel Barnier, "La santé mentale, grande cause nationale 2025," *Gouvernemente*, October 10, 2024, https://www.info.gouv.fr/actualite/la-sante-mentale-grande-cause-nationale-2025.
36. "Santé mentale grande cause nationale 2025: Ne pas oublier les soins psychiatriques!," *Santé Mentale*, September 25, 2024, https://www.santementale.fr/2024/09/sante-mentale-grande-cause-nationale-2025-ne-pas-oublier-les-soins-psychiatriques/.

37. Luc Bronner, "Les crises aiguës de la psychiatrie publique," *Le Monde*, January 11, 2025, https://www.lemonde.fr/societe/article/2025/01/10/les-crises-aigues-de-la-psychiatrie-publique-des-services-pepites-coexistent-avec-des-endroits-d-ou-tout-espoir-est-absent_6490744_3224.html.
38. Vincent Faustine, "Covid-19: La 'vague psychiatrique' monte," *Le Monde*, July 13, 2020, https://www.lemonde.fr/sante/article/2020/07/11/tous-les-voyants-sont-au-rouge-apres-le-covid-19-la-vague-psychiatrique-attendue-a-la-rentree_6045900_1651302.html.
39. Caroline Fiat and Martine Wonner, *Rapport en conclusion des travaux de la mission relative à l'organisation de la santé mentale*, N° 2249 (Assemblée Nationale, 2019), 74.
40. Fiat and Wonner, *Rapport en conclusion des travaux de la mission relative à l'organisation de la santé mentale*, 76.
41. Eric Favereau, "Psychiatrie: Un système sous contention," *Libération*, January 8, 2019, https://www.liberation.fr/france/2019/01/08/psychiatrie-un-systeme-sous-contention_1701720/.

## PART II. FROM CHRONICITY TO AUTONOMY

1. Quoted in Marcel Gauchet and Gladys Swain, *La pratique de l'esprit humain: L'institution asilaire et la révolution démocratique* (Gallimard, 1980), 75.
2. Albert Deutsch, *The Mentally Ill in America*, 2nd ed. (Columbia University Press, 1949), 150.
3. François Chapireau, unpublished data received via personal communication November 2015.
4. Gil Eyal et al., *The Autism Matrix* (Polity, 2010), 81.
5. Quoted in Benoît Majerus, "A Chemical Revolution as Seen from Below: The 'Discovery' of Neuroleptics in 1950s Paris," *Social History of Medicine* 32, no. 2 (2019): 395, https://doi.org/10.1093/shm/hkx113.
6. John F. Kennedy, *Special Message to the Congress on Mental Illness and Mental Retardation.* (Office of the President of the United States 1963), http://www.presidency.ucsb.edu/ws/?pid=9546.
7. Quoted in Nicolas Henckes, "Reshaping Chronicity: Neuroleptics and Changing Meanings of Therapy in French Psychiatry, 1950–1975," *Studies in History and Philosophy of Biological and Biomedical Sciences* 42, no. 4 (2011): 438, https://doi.org/10.1016/j.shpsc.2011.05.004.
8. Joseph P. Morrissey and Howard H. Goldman, "Care and Treatment of the Mentally Ill in the United States: Historical Developments and Reforms," *Annals of the American Academy of Political and Social Science* 484 (1986): 12–27; David Mechanic and David A. Rochefort, "Deinstitutionalization: An Appraisal of Reform," *Annual Review of Sociology* 16 (1990): 301–27.
9. Javier Auyero, *Patients of the State: The Politics of Waiting in Argentina* (Duke University Press, 2012), 9. See also Spire Alexis, *Accueillir ou reconduire: Enquête sur les guichets de l'immigration* (Éditions Raisons d'Agir, 2008); Vincent Dubois, *La vie au guichet: Relation administrative et traitement de la misère*, 2nd ed. (Economica, 2003).

10. Brian J. McCabe, "Ready to Rent: Administrative Decisions and Poverty Governance in the Housing Choice Voucher Program," *American Sociological Review* 88, no. 1 (2023): 86–113, https://doi.org/10.1177/00031224221131798; Joe Soss et al., *Disciplining the Poor: Neoliberal Paternalism and the Persistent Power of Race* (University of Chicago Press, 2011); Celeste Watkins-Hayes, *The New Welfare Bureaucrats: Entanglements of Race, Class, and Policy Reform* (University of Chicago Press, 2009).
11. Alain Ehrenberg, "L'institution de l'autonomie ou le nouvel esprit du soin," *Rhizome* 83, no. 2 (2022), 14, https://doi.org/10.3917/rhiz.083.0012.
12. David Pettinicchio, *Politics of Empowerment: Disability Rights and the Cycle of American Policy Reform* (Stanford University Press, 2019).
13. This tension, between protection of those deemed incapable and the promotion of autonomy is elegantly elaborated in the case of guardianship by Benoît Eyraud, *Protéger et rendre capable* (Eres, 2013).
14. Ian Hacking, "The Looping Effects of Human Kinds," in *Causal Cognition: A Multidisciplinary Approach*, ed. Dan Sperber et al. (Oxford University Press, 1995), 352.
15. Sue E. Estroff, *Making It Crazy: An Ethnography of Psychiatric Clients in an American Community* (University of California Press, 1981); Dan Lewis et al., *Worlds of the Mentally Ill: How Deinstitutionalization Works in the City* (Southern Illinois University Press, 1991).
16. Committee on Psychiatry and the Community, *The Chronic Mental Patient in the Community* (Group for the Advancement of Psychiatry, 1978), https://www.ourgap.org/resources/the-chronic-mental-patient-in-the-community; Martin Fleishman, "Board and Care Homes 1984: Return of the House Call," *Psychiatric Annals* 15, no. 11 (1985): 654–60, https://doi.org/10.3928/0048-5713-19851101-08; H. Richard Lamb, "Young Adult Chronic Patients: The New Drifters," *Psychiatric Services* 33, no. 6 (1982): 465–68, https://doi.org/10.1176/ps.33.6.465.
17. Comptroller General of the United States, *Returning the Mentally Disabled to the Community* (US Government Publishing Office, 1977), 5.
18. Steering Committee on the Chronically Mentally Ill, *Toward a National Plan for the Chronically Mentally Ill* (US Department of Health and Human Services, 1980), 1–6.
19. Andrew Scull, "A New Trade in Lunacy: The Recommodification of the Mental Patient," *American Behavioral Scientist* 24, no. 6 (1981): 741–54, https://doi.org/10.1177/000276428102400602; Phil Brown and Elizabeth Cooksey, "Mental Health Monopoly: Corporate Trends in Mental Health Services," *Social Science & Medicine* 28, no. 11 (1989): 1129–38, https://doi.org/10.1016/0277-9536(89)90005-1.
20. In his study of high-end private mental health services in Los Angeles, for example, Neil Gong shows the absence of long-term housing; the identity of rich-but-chronically-ill is, in effect, unthinkable. Neil Gong, *Sons, Daughters, and Sidewalk Psychotics: Mental Illness and Homelessness in Los Angeles* (University of Chicago Press, 2024), 95.
21. Nora Jacobson and Dianne Greenley, "What Is Recovery? A Conceptual Model and Explication," *Psychiatric Services* 52, no. 4 (2001): 483, https://doi.org/10.1176/appi.ps.52.4.482.
22. Quoted in Gaëlle Giordano and Samuel Neuberg, *Parcours de vie, parcours de soins: Évaluer le coût des prises en charge entre services d'accompagnement et secteurs psychiatriques* (École Normale Supérieur, 2014), 11.

23. Martine Aubry, *Plan d'action pour le développement de l'autonomie des personnes handicapées dans leur milieu de vie ordinaire* (Secrétaire d'État à la santé et aux handicapés, 1999), 1–2.
24. I elaborate this argument theoretically in Alex V. Barnard, "Bureaucratically Split Personalities: (Re)Ordering the Mentally Disordered in the French State," *Theory and Society* 48, no. 5 (2019): 753–84, https://doi.org/10.1007/s11186-019-09364-2.
25. Of course, in a social model, disability is not fixed at all because impairment is actually created by a maladapted but malleable external environment. Michael Oliver, *The Politics of Disablement: A Sociological Approach* (Palgrave Macmillan, 1990). In practice this is not how French disability offices see disability.
26. Ian Hacking, *Rewriting the Soul: Multiple Personality and the Sciences of Memory* (Princeton University Press, 1998), 21.

## 3. A HANDICAPPED REVOLUTION

1. Jeannine Verdes-Leroux, *Le travail social* (Les Editions de Minuit, 1978).
2. The requested benefit was the Benefit for the Compensation of Handicap, discussed in chapter 4. It can't actually be used to substitute for an *aide à domicile*, so the doctor's demand was unlikely to pan out (as Sarah told him).
3. Secrétariat d'État chargé des personnes handicapées et de la lutte contre l'exclusion, *Stratégie quinquennal de l'évolution de l'offre médico sociale: Volet handicap psychique* (Ministère des affaires sociales et de la santé, 2016), 4.
4. Gil Eyal et al., *The Autism Matrix* (Polity, 2010), 3.
5. François Chapireau, unpublished data, received through personal communication November 2015.
6. Isabelle von Bueltzingsloewen, *L'hécatombe des fous: La famine dans les hôpitaux psychiatriques français sous l'Occupation* (Flammarion, 2007), 236.
7. Georges Lanteri-Laura, "La chronicité dans la psychiatrie moderne française: Note d'histoire théorique et sociale," *Annales. Histoire, Sciences Sociales* 27, no. 3 (1972): 548–68, https://doi.org/10.3406/ahess.1972.422522.
8. Quoted in Marion Leboyer and Pierre-Michel Llorca, *Psychiatrie: L'état d'urgence* (Fayard, 2018), 395.
9. Nicolas Henckes, "Reshaping Chronicity: Neuroleptics and Changing Meanings of Therapy in French Psychiatry, 1950–1975," *Studies in History and Philosophy of Biological and Biomedical Sciences* 42, no. 4 (2011): 436, https://doi.org/10.1016/j.shpsc.2011.05.004.
10. Catherine Barral, "Disabled Persons' Associations in France," *Scandinavian Journal of Disability Research* 9, nos. 3–4 (2007): 214–36, https://doi.org/10.1080/15017410701680506.
11. Cour des comptes, *L'organisation de la lutte contre les maladies mentales* (Cour des comptes, 1976), 596.
12. Pierre Romien, "À l'origine de la réinsertion professionnelle des personnes handicapées: La prise en charge des invalides de guerre," *Revue française des affaires sociales*, no. 2 (2005): 229–47.
13. C. Lasry and M. Gagneux M, *Bilan de la politique en direction des personnes handicapées* (Rapport au Ministre de la solidarité nationale, 1983).

14. Jean-François Bauduret and Marcel Jaeger, *Rénover l'action sociale et médico-sociale: Histoires d'une refondation*, 2nd ed. (Dunod, 2005), 24.
15. Pierre Bourdieu, *On the State* (Polity, 2015), 9.
16. Quoted in François Chapireau, "Le handicap psychique," in *L'encyclopédie médico-chirurgicale* (Elsevier, 2016), 5.
17. République Française, *Loi N° 75-534 du 30 Juin 1975 d'orientation en faveur des personnes handicapées* (1975), https://www.legifrance.gouv.fr/loda/id/JORFTEXT000000333976.
18. Jean Ayme, *Chroniques de la psychiatrie publique: A travers l'histoire d'un syndicat* (Érès, 1995), 298.
19. Jean-Pierre Martin, *Psychiatrie dans la ville: Pratiques et clinique de terrain* (Erès, 2000), 152.
20. Nicolas Henckes, "La politique du handicap psychique: Familles, psychiatres et état face à la chronicité des maladies mentales, des années 1960 aux années 1980," *DREES/MiRe–Convention de Recherche N° 08-2547*, May 2011, 119, https://hal.archives-ouvertes.fr/file/index/docid/769756/filename/Henckes_2011_Rapport_MiRe.pdf.
21. Henckes, "La politique du handicap psychique," 8.
22. François Chapireau, "Le handicap psychique: La construction sociale d'un nouveau trouble spécifiquement français," *Socio-logos*, no. 9 (2014): 7.
23. Right before the 2005 reform, nearly a quarter of recipients of the disability allocation were classified as having a psychiatric condition. Jean-Marie Chanut et al., *L'AAH, un minimum social destiné aux adultes handicapés*, N° 344 (Direction de la recherche, des études, de l'évaluation et des statistiques, 2004).
24. Doctor Mailhol's explanation for deinstitutionalization, centering the new availability of welfare payments to the disabled, is congruent with the explanation given for the United States in Andrew T. Scull, *Decarceration: Community Treatment and the Deviant*, 2nd ed. (Polity Press, 1984).
25. E. Belliard, "L'hôpital psychiatrique en 1986 et ses récents bouleversements," *Confrontations psychiatriques*, 32 (1990): 89.
26. Camille Robcis, *Disalienation: Politics, Philosophy, and Radical Psychiatry in Postwar France* (University of Chicago Press, 2021), 77.
27. Eric Favereau, "Jean Oury, fou des fous," *Libération*, June 27, 1998, http://www.liberation.fr/societe/1998/06/27/jean-oury-74-ans-psychiatre-n-a-jamais-cesse-de-saint-alban-a-la-borde-de-vouloir-soigner-l-hopital-_239972.
28. Lion Murard and François Fourquet, *Histoire de la psychiatrie de secteur ou le secteur impossible?* (Recherches, 1975), 164.
29. Favereau, "Jean Oury, fou des fous."
30. Jean Nves Nau, "La clinique psychiatrique de la borde fait face à de nouvelles difficultés," *Le Monde*, April 3, 1991.
31. Bruno Forestier et al., "L'avenir des CHS passe-t-il par le médico-social?," in *Évaluation et organisation des soins en psychiatrie*, ed. Alain Lopez (Éditions Frison-Roche, 1994), 251.
32. Jean-Yves Barreyre et al., "Les patients séjournant au long cours dans les services de psychiatrie adulte en Île-de-France," *Vie Sociale* 3 (2003): 46.
33. Eric Piel and Jean-Luc Roelandt, *De la psychiatrie vers la santé mentale* (Rapport de Mission. Ministre de l'Emploi et de la Solidarité, 2001), 234.

34. Direction de l'hospitalisation et de l'organisation des soins, "Éléments d'analyse des inadéquations de prise en charge en hospitalisation complète en psychiatrie et des besoins de développement d'une offre sociale et médico-sociale adaptée dans le champ social et médico-social," 2008, *DGOS 2014/011/3*.
35. Union nationale des amis et familles des malades mentaux, *Le livre blanc des partenaires de santé mentale France, associations d'usagers de la psychiatrie, de soignants et de responsables du social dans la cité* (2001).
36. Occasional critiques are still published by psychoanalytically oriented psychiatrists. Philippe Amarilli, "Psychiatrie de secteur et handicap psychique," *L'information psychiatrique* 94, no. 5 (2018): 347–53; Valérie Boucherat-Hue et al., "La notion de handicap psychique: Un levier politicosocial 'à la française'!," *L'information psychiatrique* 87, no. 8 (2011): 668–76.
37. Michel Charzat, *Pour mieux identifier les difficultés des personnes en situation de handicap du fait de troubles psychiques et les moyens d'améliorer leur vie et celle de leurs proches* (Ministère de la Famille, a l'Enfance et aux personnes Handicapées, 2002), 18, 47.
38. Neil Gong, *Sons, Daughters, and Sidewalk Psychotics: Mental Illness and Homelessness in Los Angeles* (University of Chicago Press, 2024), 112.
39. Anne Waldschmidt, "Disability Policy of the European Union: The Supranational Level," *Alter* 3, no. 1 (2009): 8–23, https://doi.org/10.1016/j.alter.2008.12.002.
40. Francis Kessler, "Handicap: Le grand chantier," *Le Monde*, September 17, 2002.
41. *Le Monde*, "Le handicap demeure une cause majeure d'exclusion," May 25, 2000.
42. Jacques Chirac, *Discours de le président de la république devant le conseil national consultatif des personnes handicapées* (Présidence de la République, 2002), https://www.jacqueschirac-asso.fr/archives-elysee.fr/elysee/elysee.fr/francais/interventions/discours_et_declarations/2002/decembre/fi001873.html.
43. Astrid de Larminat, "Une année pour changer le regard sur le handicap," *Le Figaro*, February 4, 2003.
44. Andrew Power et al., "Active Citizenship and Disability in France," in *Active Citizenship and Disability: Implementing the Personalisation of Support*, edited by Allison S. DeFranco, Andrew Power, and Janet E. Lord (Cambridge University Press, 2014).
45. *Le Monde*, "L'union nationale des amis et parents de personnes handicapées mentales (Unapei) va déposer une pétition," March 20, 2002.
46. Astrid de Larminat, "Les parcours du combattant des fauteuils roulants," *Le Figaro*, September 17, 2003.
47. Chirac, *Discours de le président de la république*.
48. Union nationale des amis et familles des malades mentaux, "Communiqué de Presse: Le handicap psychique enfin reconnu," *Archives institut de recherche et de documentation en économie de la santé*, 2002.
49. Activists involved in drafting the law have written entire histories of it without a single reference to UNAFAM. Jean-Claude Cunin, *Le handicap en France: Chroniques d'un combat politique* (Dunod, 2008).
50. République Française, *Loi N° 2005-102 pour l'égalité des droits et des chances, la participation et la citoyenneté des personnes handicapées* (2005), https://www.legifrance.gouv.fr/affichTexte.do?cidTexte=JORFTEXT000000809647&categorieLien=id.

51. Ian Hacking, "Making Up People," in *The Science Studies Reader*, ed. Mario Biagioli (Routledge, 1999), 165. For a convincing demonstration of this claim in the case of anorexia, see Ethan Watters, *Crazy Like Us: The Globalization of the American Psyche* (Free Press, 2011), chap. 1.
52. UNAFAM, *Le livre blanc des partenaires de santé mentale France*, 12.
53. On the way psychic handicap emerged from political arbitration rather than scientific delineation, see Aude Béliard and Jean-Sébastien Eideliman, "Aux frontières du handicap psychique: Genèse et usages des catégories médico-administratives," *Revue française des affaires sociales*, no. 1 (January 26, 2010): 99–117.
54. Gaëlle Giordano and Samuel Neuberg. *Parcours de vie, parcours de soins: Évaluer le coût des prises en charge entre services d'accompagnement et secteurs psychiatriques* (École Normale Supérieur, 2014), 19.
55. Agence régionale de santé, *Projet régional de santé: Schéma d'organisation médico-social* (Île-de-France, 2011), 89. I want to emphasize that this vision of intellectual and developmental disabilities vastly underestimates these individuals' capacity to develop, change, and live rich and full lives. Adrianna Bagnall-Munson, "How to Become an Adult," *Contexts* 20, no. 3 (2021): 10–15, https://doi.org/10.1177/15365042211035327; Allison C. Carey, *On the Margins of Citizenship: Intellectual Disability and Civil Rights in Twentieth-Century America* (Temple University Press, 2009).
56. Florence Vallade, "Le problème public de l'autisme dans la presse française," *Alter* 10 (2016): 266, https://doi.org/10.1016/j.alter.2016.05.001. See also Brigitte Chamak, "Autism and Social Movements: French Parents' Associations and International Autistic Individuals' Organisations," *Sociology of Health & Illness* 30, no. 1 (2008): 76–96, https://doi.org/10.1111/j.1467-9566.2007.01053.x.
57. République Française, *Loi No 96-1076 du 11 Décembre 1996 modifiant la loi No 75-535 du 30 Juin 1975 relative aux institutions sociales et médico-sociales et tendant à assurer une prise en charge adaptée de l'autisme*, 1996, https://www.legifrance.gouv.fr/jorf/id/JORFTEXT000000746537.
58. In 2013, militant psychiatrists of a Lacanian persuasion declared, "Today it's autism, but the risk is inevitable of a generalization of this method [a transfer of responsibility to the disability system] . . . Tomorrow, it will be a plan for bipolar disorder or schizophrenia." Collectif 39, 2013, "Pour un autre plan autisme 2013: Pour le retrait de la recommandation de l'HAS sur l'autisme," retrieved May 25, 2017, http://www.hospitalite-collectif39.org/?POUR-UN-AUTRE-PLAN-AUTISME-2013#sp1.
59. Chapireau, "Le handicap psychique."
60. Charzat, *Pour mieux identifier les difficultés*, 25.
61. Jean-François Chossy, *Rapport sur le projet de loi pour l'égalité des droits et des chances, la participation et la citoyenneté des personnes handicapées*, N° 1991 (Assemblée Nationale, 2004), 37.
62. As one commentator put it, "While [psychiatric] care under constraint exists, not compensation under constraint." Jean-Yves Barreyre and Carole Peintre, *Handicap des origines psychiques et évaluations des situations: Volet 2. Synthèse de la phase "terrains"* (Caisse nationale de solidarité pour l'autonomie, 2009), 27.
63. On the lack of an equivalent to the category of "psychic handicap" internationally, see Chapireau, "Le handicap psychique: La construction sociale;" Philippe Auvergnon,

"Approche juridique du handicap psychique: Les enjeux d'une définition en droit social," *Alter* 6, no. 4 (2012): 255–66.

64. Kimberly J. Morgan and Ann Shola Orloff, eds., *The Many Hands of the State: Theorizing Political Authority and Social Control* (Cambridge University Press, 2017).
65. Patricia Fernández-Kelly, *The Hero's Fight: African Americans in West Baltimore and the Shadow of the State* (Princeton University Press, 2015).
66. Eyal et al., *The Autism Matrix.*
67. James Scott, *Seeing Like a State* (Yale University Press, 1998), 8.
68. Bourdieu, *On the State*, 4.
69. Nicolas Marquis, "Making People Autonomous: A Sociological Analysis of the Uses of Contracts and Projects in the Psychiatric Care Institutions," *Culture, Medicine, and Psychiatry* 46, no. 2 (2022): 265, https://doi.org/10.1007/s11013-019-09624-x.
70. Guillermina Altomonte and Adrianna Bagnall Munson, "Autonomy on the Horizon: Comparing Institutional Approaches to Disability and Elder Care," *Theory and Society* 50, no. 6 (2021): 935–63, https://doi.org/10.1007/s11186-021-09434-4.
71. Marie-Aude Poisson et al., *Les parcours des personnes en psychiatrie et santé mentale: Première approche* (L'Agence Nationale d'Appui à la Performance des Établissements Sanitaires et Médico-Sociaux, 2015), 9.
72. L'agence nationale de l'évaluation et de la qualité des établissements et services sociaux et médico-sociaux (ANESM), *Spécificités de l'accompagnement des adultes handicapés psychiques* (ANESM, 2016), 11. The term "parcours" is used thirty-three times in the law of 2005. Alain Ehrenberg, "L'institution de l'autonomie ou le nouvel esprit du soin." *Rhizome* 83, no. 2 (2022): 19, https://doi.org/10.3917/rhiz.083.0012.

## 4. DESIGNATING DISABILITY, ENABLING INDEPENDENCE

1. Paul Blanc, *Maisons départementales des personnes handicapées* (Sénat, 2005), 11.
2. Pierre Bourdieu, *The State Nobility: Elite Schools in the Field of Power*, trans. Lauretta Clough (Polity Press, 1996), 376.
3. Nationwide, Disability Offices processed 4.5 million requests from 1.7 million people in 2020. Sécretaire d'État en chargé des personnes handicapées, *Feuille de route: MDPH 2022* (Sécretaire d'État en chargé des personnes handicapées, 2020), 6.
4. On the treatment en masse of demands in Disability Offices, see Pierre-Yves Baudot, "L'invention des délais: Pourquoi l'administration doit-elle répondre dans les temps?," *Politiques sociales et familiales* 119, no. 1 (2015): 11, https://doi.org/10.3406/caf.2015.3067; Marie-Christine Bureau et al., "La traduction de la demande d'aide sociale: Les cas du handicap et de l'insertion des jeunes," *Revue française d'administration publique* 145, no. 1 (2013): 175–88; Louis Bertrand et al., "Situating Disability: The Recognition of 'Disabled Workers' in France," *Alter* 8, no. 4 (2014): 269–81, https://doi.org/10.1016/j.alter.2014.09.006.
5. In one survey, 87 percent of Disability Offices said that psychic handicap was the most difficult disability to evaluate. Claudine Berr et al., *Enquête quantitative sur les modes d'évaluation et de traitement des demandes de compensation du handicap par les MDPH* (Haut conseil de la santé publique, 2014), 24.

6. On the contested history of this idea—which nonetheless is taken as a given in contemporary psychiatric practice—see Neil Gong, "'That Proves You Mad, Because You Know It Not': Impaired Insight and the Dilemma of Governing Psychiatric Patients as Legal Subjects," *Theory and Society* 46, no. 3 (2017): 201–28, https://doi.org/10.1007/s11186-017-9288-0.
7. Élodie Picolet et al., "Agir vers son rétablissement avec un handicap psychique: Un parcours de reconnaissance(s)," *Revue française des affaires sociales*, no. 1 (2021): 193, 197, https://doi.org/10.3917/rfas.211.0189.
8. Edward D. Berkowitz and Larry DeWitt, *The Other Welfare: Supplemental Security Income and U.S. Social Policy* (Cornell University Press, 2013).
9. Because, while they proposed continuing to attribute the allocation, they were lowering her "level" of disability from 80 percent to 50–79 percent. It is a weird set of categories and not really worth explaining.
10. Josh Seim, *The Welfare Assembly Line: Public Servants in the Suffering City* (University of California Press, 2026).
11. Yehenskel Hasenfeld et al., "The Welfare State, Citizenship, and Bureaucratic Encounters," *Annual Review of Sociology* 13, no. 1 (1987): 401.
12. Caisse nationale de solidarité pour l'autonomie, *Une réforme tarifaire pour faciliter les parcours des personnes handicapées accompagnées par les services ou accueillies dans les établissements médico-sociaux* (Caisse nationale de solidarité pour l'autonomie, 2017), 2.
13. Vincent Dubois, *La vie au guichet: Relation administrative et traitement de la misère*, 2nd ed. (Economica, 2003); Spire Alexis, *Accueillir ou reconduire: Enquête sur les guichets de l'immigration* (Éditions Raisons d'Agir, 2008).
14. See also Roger Gayton and Yann Boulon, "L'évaluation du handicap d'origine psychique et des besoins de compensation," *Revue française des affaires sociales*, no. 1 (2010): 129–35.
15. According to one dated statistical report, there are eight times as many denials of allocations for mood disorders as for schizophrenia. Elvire Demoly, *Les Demandeurs de l'AAH*, N° 640 (Direction de la recherche, des études, de l'évaluation et des statistiques, 2008), 3.
16. Ministère de la santé publique et de la population, *Circulaire du 4 Février 1958 portant organisation du travail des malades mentaux en traitement dans les hôpitaux psychiatriques* (Le ministre de la santé publique, 1958).
17. Bertrand et al., "Situating Disability," 273.
18. Caisse nationale de solidarité pour l'autonomie, *Troubles psychiques: Guide d'appui pour l'élaboration de réponses aux besoins des personnes vivant avec des troubles psychiques* (Paris, France, 2017), 88.
19. Fadéla Amara et al., *La prise en charge du handicap psychique* (Inspection générale des affaires sociales, 2011), 50.
20. Annie Le Houérou, *Dynamiser l'emploi des personnes handicapées en milieu ordinaire* (Assemblée Nationale, 2014), 24
21. Economist Intelligence Unit, *France Country Report: Political Leadership Is Needed to Build on Early Advances* (2015).
22. On the complex relationship between the public Disability Office and these private institutions, see Pierre-Yves Baudot and Anne Revillard, "Entre mobilisations et institutions: Les politiques des droits dans l'action publique," *Gouvernement et action publique* 4, no. 4 (2014): 9–33, https://doi.org/10.3917/gap.144.0009.

23. US Department of Justice, *Breaking Down Barriers to Employment of People with Disabilities* (blog post) October 14, 2015, https://www.justice.gov/archives/opa/blog/breaking-down-barriers-employment-individuals-disabilities.
24. Marcel Jaeger, *L'articulation du sanitaire et du social*, 3rd ed. (Dunod, 2012), 94.
25. This division is discussed in Isabelle Billiard, *Santé mentale et travail: L'émergence de la psychopathologie du travail* (La Dispute, 2001).
26. This idea that, in the *secteurs*, "autonomy passes necessarily through the establishment of acceptable relations with professionals," is detailed in Livia Velpry, *Le quotidien de la psychiatrie: sociologie de la maladie mentale* (Armand Colin, 2008), 178.
27. Éric Bocquet, *Rapport d'information au nom de la commission des finances sur les établissements et services d'aide par le travail*, N° 409 (Sénat, 2015), 9.
28. Christophe Baret, "Les établissements et services d'aide par le travail (ESAT) parviennent-ils à concilier objectifs économiques et missions médico-sociales?," *Revue interdisciplinaire management, homme & entreprise*, no. 2 (2012): 66–82, https://doi.org/10.3917/rimhe.002.0066.
29. Le Houérou, *Dynamiser l'emploi des personnes handicapées*, 5.
30. Amara et al., *La prise en charge du handicap psychique*, 3.
31. Marie-Cécile Renault, "Le handicap: Une priorité du gouvernement," *Le Figaro*, July 6, 2017.
32. This division is so strong that one government report recommended reclassifying people on long work stoppages for illnesses as "disabled" so that they could return to work. Xavier Darcos and Nadine Morano, *L'emploi: Un droit à faire vivre pour tous* (Ministre du Travail, des Rélations Sociales, de la Famille, de la Solidarité, et de la Ville, 2009).
33. At the turn of the century, 88 percent of places in the disability system were in private nonprofit facilities. Jean-François Bauduret and Marcel Jaeger, *Rénover l'action sociale et médico-sociale: Histoires d'une refondation*, 2nd ed. (Dunod, 2005), 67. I can find no recent statistics as this book goes to press.
34. Nicole Dubré-Chirat and Sandrine Rousseau, *Rapport sur la prise en charge des urgences psychiatriques*, N° 714 (Assemblée Nationale, 2024), 75, https://www.assemblee-nationale.fr/dyn/17/rapports/cion-soc/l17b0714_rapport-information.pdf.
35. Of people leaving a *foyer d'accueil médicalisé* (FAM) or a *maison d'accueil spécialisée* (MAS) in a given year for reasons other than death, about 10 percent go back to psychiatric hospitals. These statistics include all residents, not just those with psychic handicaps, so the proportion of that narrower population returning to hospitals is likely higher. Yara Makdessi and Bénédicte Mordier, *Les établissements et services pour adultes handicapés: Résultats de l'enquête ES 2010*, N° 180 (Direction de la recherche, des études, de l'évaluation et des statistiques, 2013), 274, 309.
36. Emmanuelle François, "De plus en plus de demandes pour une place en Belgique," *Ouest-France*, February 12, 2020.
37. Denis Piveteau et al., *"Zéro sans solution": Le devoir collectif de permettre un parcours de vie sans rupture, pour les personnes en situation de handicap et pour leurs proches* (Ministère des Affaires sociales, de la santé, et des Droits des femmes, 2014), 21. For more on how these initiatives focused on rationalizing the disability system rather than effectively guaranteeing rights—and largely left out long-term adult psychiatric hospitalizations—see Aymeric Mongy, "Les droits, masques de

la rationalisation gestionnaire? Processus de traduction des droits des personnes handicapées dans l'action publique départementale," *Droit et société* 113, no. 1 (2023): 91–110, https://doi.org/10.3917/drs1.113.0091.

38. Cour des comptes, *Les parcours dans l'organisation des soins en psychiatrie*, Rapport public thématique (Cour des comptes, 2021), 113.
39. Ian Hacking, "The Looping Effects of Human Kinds," in *Causal Cognition: A Multidisciplinary Approach*, ed. Dan Sperber et al. (Oxford University Press, 1995), 370.
40. Vanessa Bellamy and Thomas Bergeron, *312,000 Personnes sont accompagnées dans les établissements et services médico-sociaux pour adultes handicapés Fin 2018*, no.1247 (Direction de la recherche, des études, de l'évaluation et des statistiques, 2022).
41. See Emmanuelle Fillion et al., "Recenser et prévenir le handicap, plutôt que lutter contre les discriminations: Les référent.es handicap dans la fonction publique française," *Alter* 15, no. 1 (2021): 71–88, https://doi.org/10.1016/j.alter.2020.09.003.
42. Secrétariat d'État chargé des personnes handicapées et de la lutte contre l'exclusion, *Stratégie quinquennal de l'évolution de l'offre médico sociale: Volet handicap psychique* (Secrétariat d'État chargé des personnes handicapées et de la lutte contre l'exclusion, 2016).
43. The complex relationship individuals have with the label "psychic handicap" is detailed in Élodie Picolet et al., "Agir vers son rétablissement avec un handicap psychique: Un parcours de reconnaissance(s)," *Revue française des affaires sociales*, no. 1 (2021): 189–210; Anne M. Lovell et al., "Du handicap psychique aux paradoxes de sa reconnaissance: Éléments d'un savoir ordinaire des personnes vivant avec un trouble psychique grave," *Revue française des affaires sociales*, no. 1 (2010): 209–27.
44. National surveys show a similar underrepresentation of people with mental illnesses among people applying to Disability Offices. Frédérique Quidu and Pascale Roussel, "Liens entre troubles psychiques et recours aux dispositifs du champ du handicap en France," *Sante publique* 31, no. 3 (2019): 417–26.
45. Bruno Forestier et al., "L'avenir des CHS passe-t-il par le médico-social?," in *Évaluation et organisation des soins en psychiatrie*, ed. Alain Lopez (Éditions Frison-Roche, 1994), 259.
46. On the increasing weight hospitals in the disability sphere, see Magali Robelet, "Les transformations des modes de contrôle croisés entre associations et autorités publiques dans le secteur du handicap," *Revue française d'administration publique* 163, no. 3 (2017): 599–612, https://doi.org/10.3917/rfap.163.0599.
47. Nick Rekenthaler and Alex V. Barnard, "Chronic, Disruptive, or Resistant? Target Ecologies and the Medicalization of Homelessness in California," *Social Problems* 72, no 4 (2025): 1339–1354, https://doi.org/10.1093/socpro/spae019.

## PART III. BALANCING RIGHTS, CONTROL, AND CARE

1. For example, "medicine and psychiatry have been used as camouflage for attempts to identify and control groups that pose threats of one sort or another to law and order." Françoise Castel et al., *The Psychiatric Society*, trans. Arthur Goldhammer (Columbia University Press, 1982), 200.
2. Claude Quétel, *Histoire de la folie* (Tallandier, 2012), 530; Andrew T. Scull, *Social Order/Mental Disorder: Anglo-American Psychiatry in Historical Perspective* (University of California Press, 1989).

3. A similar change was effected in Great Britain with the 1774 Madhouse Act. Scull, *Social Order/Mental Disorder*, 147.
4. Robert Castel, *The Regulation of Madness: The Origins of Incarceration in France*, trans. W. D. Halls (Polity Press, 1988), 154.
5. Special Committee to Study Commitment Procedures, *Mental Illness and Due Process* (Cornell University Press, 1962), 3.
6. Ministère de la santé publique et de la population, *Circulaire du 15 Mars 1960 relative au programme d'organisation et d'équipement des départements en matière de lutte contre les maladies mentales* (Le ministre de la santé publique, 1960), 24.
7. Paul S. Appelbaum, *Almost a Revolution: Mental Health Law and the Limits of Change* (Oxford University Press, 1994), 29.
8. Quoted in Jean Ayme, *Chroniques de la psychiatrie publique: A travers l'histoire d'un syndicat* (Érès, 1995), 371.
9. Substance Abuse and Mental Health Services Administration, *Mental Health United States*, DHHS-ADM-85-1378 (US Department of Health and Human Services, 1985), 45.
10. Société l'évolution psychiatrique, "Conclusions: Résolutions adoptées par la société," in *Livre blanc de la psychiatrie française*, vol. 3 (Éditions Édouard Privat, 1967), 155.
11. François Zambrowski, *Moderniser et diversifier les modes de prise en charge de la psychiatrie française* (Ministre de la Solidarité, de la Santé, et de la Protection Sociale, 1986), 31. As they had argued with their claims about the persistence of long-term hospitalization, psychiatrists insisted that the remaining people interned involuntarily were there because they didn't really belong. A report in the 1970s, for example, claimed that these patients were "essentially [those with] dementia or senility," not *malades* with schizophrenia. Benoît Eyraud and Delphine Moreau, "Formes et régulations de l'enfermement psychiatrique: De la création de l'asile aux nouvelles unités sécurisées, l'exemple de l'hôpital du Vinatier," *Cultures & Conflits*, no. 90 (2013): 129.
12. Robert Castel, *La gestion des risques: De l'anti-psychiatrie à l'après-psychanalyse* (Minuit, 1981); Gilles Deleuze, "Postscript on the Societies of Control," in *Surveillance, Crime and Social Control*, ed. Clive Norris and Dean Wilson (Routledge, 2006); David Garland, *The Culture of Control* (University of Chicago Press, 2001); Nikolas Rose, "Governing Risky Individuals: The Role of Psychiatry in New Regimes of Control," *Psychiatry, Psychology and Law* 5, no. 2 (1998): 177–95.
13. Michael Dudley et al., *Mental Health and Human Rights: Vision, Praxis, and Courage* (Oxford University Press, 2012), vii.
14. Michael Dudley et al., "Human Rights Development: Provenance, Ambit and Effect," in *Mental Health and Human Rights: Vision, Praxis, and Courage*, ed. Michael Dudley et al. (Oxford University Press, 2012).
15. This distinction is also articulated in Ian Hacking, "Between Michel Foucault and Erving Goffman: Between Discourse in the Abstract and Face-to-Face Interaction," *Economy and Society* 33, no. 3 (2004): 277–302, https://doi.org/10.1080/0308514042000225671.
16. Erving Goffman, *Asylums: Essays on the Social Situation of Mental Patients and Other Inmates* (Anchor Books, 1961), 16.
17. Goffman, *Asylums*, 383.
18. Goffman, *Asylums*, 361, 367.

19. For more detail on these observations, see Tonya Tartour and Alex V. Barnard, "Démocratie sanitaire à New York: La participation dans le contrôle judiciaire des soins psychiatriques sans consentement," *Participations*, no. 3 (2018): 83–107, https://doi.org/10.3917/parti.022.0083.
20. Special Committee to Study Commitment Procedures, *Mental Illness and Due Process*, 7.
21. At the time, it was called the Mental Health Information Service.
22. "The New York Mental Health Information Service: A New Approach to Hospitalization of the Mentally Ill," Columbia Law Review, 67, no. 4 (1967): 672–715. https://doi.org/10.2307/1121084; Raj K. Gupta, "New York's Mental Health Information Service: An Experiment in Due Process," *Rutgers Law Review* 25, no. 3 (1970): 405–51.
23. Special Committee to Study Commitment Procedures, *Mental Illness and Due Process*, 14.
24. Bryan Nelson, "Bellevue Psychiatric: Tales of Despair," *New York Times*, September 20, 1983.
25. Arline Mathieu, "The Medicalization of Homelessness and the Theater of Repression," *Medical Anthropology Quarterly* 7, no. 2 (1993): 170–84, https://doi.org/10.1525/maq.1993.7.2.02a00030.
26. The State Commission on Quality of Care for the Mentally Disabled, *Strengthening Patient Advocacy: A Review of the Mental Health Information Service* (1980).
27. For debates on the true balance between medical care, administrative control, and social welfare embedded in the law of 1838, see Nicolas Henckes, "Un tournant dans les régulations de l'institution psychiatrique: La trajectoire de la réforme des hôpitaux psychiatriques en France de l'avant-guerre aux années 1950," *Genèses*, no. 76 (2010): 76–98.
28. Quoted in Quétel, *Histoire de la folie*, 277.
29. Quoted in Castel, *The Regulation of Madness*, 244.
30. Special Committee to Study Commitment Procedures, *Mental Illness and Due Process*, 286–87.
31. The law of 1838 "integrated [psychiatry] . . . into the apparatus of the state." Jan Goldstein, *Console and Classify: The French Psychiatric Profession in the Nineteenth Century* (Cambridge University Press, 1987), 276.
32. Quétel, *Histoire de la folie*, 292.
33. Quoted in Marcel Jaeger, *Le désordre psychiatrique: Des politiques de la santé mentale en France* (Payot, 1981), 57.
34. Ministère de la Santé, "Question Écrite N 3.921 A.N.,", January 21, 1970, *DGS 2009/037-1*
35. Ayme, *Chroniques de la psychiatrie publique*, 327.
36. École Nationale de la Magistrature, *Soins psychiatriques sans consentement* (École Nationale de la Magistrature, 2013).

## 5. THE RISE OF RIGHTS AND THE SPECTER OF CONTROL

1. Delphine Chayet, "Drame de Grenoble: L'élysée veut une réforme," *Le Figaro*, November 14, 2008, https://www.lefigaro.fr/actualite-france/2008/11/14/01016-20081114ARTFIG00276-drame-de-grenoble-l-elysee-veut-une-reforme-.php.

2. Nicolas Sarkozy, "Déclaration du président de la république sur la réforme de l'hôpital psychiatrique, notamment la prise en charge des patients à risque," Antony, France, December 2, 2008, https://www.vie-publique.fr/discours/173244-declaration-de-m-nicolas-sarkozy-president-de-la-republique-sur-la-re.
3. Collectif 39, *Charte contre la nuit sécuritaire*, December 15, 2008, https://www.collectifpsychiatrie.fr/?p=17.
4. Contrôleur général des lieux de privation de liberté, *Isolement et contention dans les établissements de santé mentale* (Dalloz, 2016), 5.
5. Collectif 39, "La sangle qui attache tue le lien humain qui soigne," September 21, 2015, https://www.hospitalite-collectif39.org/?NON-A-LA-CONTENTION.
6. Delphine de Mallevoue, "L'hôpital psychiatrique sous contraint," *Le Figaro*, October 17, 2002.
7. Mediateur de la république, "Hospitalisation sans consentement en raison de troubles mentaux," November 18, 2005, *DGS 2009/037/3*. Point of reference, of course, matters: France also had far *fewer* involuntary hospitalizations at this point than Germany. Hans Joachim Salize and Harald Dressing, "Epidemiology of Involuntary Placement of Mentally Ill People Across the European Union," *British Journal of Psychiatry* 184, no. 2 (2004): 163–68, https://doi.org/10.1192/bjp.184.2.163.
8. Psychiatric hospital clinicians' inability (or unwillingness) to listen to a constant stream of patient demands, in a context of limited resources and intensified turnover, is thoroughly documented in Sébastien Saetta et al., "'Pas de crise, soyez coopérative!': Les conditions de prise en compte de la parole des patient·e·s dans une unité psychiatrique," *Sciences sociales et santé* 41, no. 2 (2023): 5–29, https://doi.org/10.1684/sss.2023.0245.
9. Catherine Petitnicolas, "Les psychiatres appellent au secours," *Le Figaro*, January 19, 2005.
10. Nicole Dubré-Chirat and Sandrine Rousseau, *Rapport sur la prise en charge des urgences psychiatriques*, N° 714 (Assemblée Nationale, 2024), 99, https://www.assemblee-nationale.fr/dyn/17/rapports/cion-soc/l17b0714_rapport-information.pdf.
11. See also Pauline Rhenter, "Usages et mésusages de l'hospitalisation d'office," *Rhizome* 24 (October 2006), http://www.ch-le-vinatier.fr/orspere-samdarra/rhizome/anciens-numeros/rhizome-n24-elus-des-villes-et-sante-mentale/usages-et-mesusages-de-lhospitalisation-doffice-1951.html.
12. Luc Bronner, "'Il y en a combien qui souffrent comme cela depuis des années?': Enquête sur les patients attachés dans les hôpitaux psychiatriques," *Le Monde*, January 12, 2025, https://www.lemonde.fr/societe/article/2025/01/12/il-y-en-a-combien-qui-souffrent-comme-cela-depuis-des-annees-enquete-sur-les-patients-attaches-dans-les-hopitaux-psychiatriques_6493847_3224.html.
13. République Française, "Loi no. 2016-41 du 26 janvier 2016 de modernisation de notre système de santé," effective 2016, https://www.legifrance.gouv.fr/loda/id/JORFTEXT000031912641.
14. Frédéric Mougeot et al., "Apprendre (de) la violence à l'hôpital: Directives anticipées en psychiatrie et violence des soins," *Rhizome* 8081, no. 2 (2021): 27–28.
15. Jean Ayme, *Chroniques de la psychiatrie publique: A travers l'histoire d'un syndicat* (Érès, 1995), 408–409.

16. Hélène Strohl and Martine Clemente, *Rapport du group nationale d'evaluation de la loi du 27 Juin 1990*, N° 97081 (Inspection générale des affaires sociales, 1997), 44.
17. Note that "psychopath" does not have the same connotation: "The American psychopath [is] understood as the 'predator-murderer'. . . . The French psychopath has a trajectory of lack of affection and education . . . an institutional life that is chaotic . . . and a difficult relationship to the law." Jean-Louis Senon and Nemat Jaafari, "La loi du 25 Février 2008 relative à la rétention de sûreté: Ne faudrait-il pas clarifier et établir des priorités dans les rapports entre psychiatrie et justice ?," *L'information psychiatrique* 84, no. 6 (2008): 514.
18. Jacques Feillard, "La psychiatrie médico-légale, de l'expertise à la question des soins des malades dangereux," *Journal français de psychiatrie*, N° 19 (2005): 18.
19. Feillard, "La psychiatrie médico-légale," 17.
20. Isabelle Coutant makes a similar observation based on social class: More privileged adolescents have shorter hospitalizations (arguably having been rendered serviceable for community care much faster) than those from more precarious backgrounds, who tend to stay longer. Isabelle Coutant, *Troubles en psychiatrie: Enquête dans une unité pour adolescents* (La Dispute, 2012).
21. Briot, Maryvonne. *Rapport fait sur la proposition tendant à la création d'une commission d'enquête sur la progression du nombre d'internements psychiatriques en France*. N° 1598. Assemblée Nationale, 2004, 7.
22. Cécile Prieur, "Ministre des solidarités, de la santé et de la famille: 'Je veux donner un nouvel élan au secteur psychiatrique,'" *Le Monde*, February 5, 2005.
23. Ramiro Reira et al., *La prise en charge des patients susceptibles d'être dangereux*, N° 020 (Inspection générale des affaires sociales, 2006).
24. Chantal Mauchet et al., *Rapport sur les problèmes de securité liés aux régimes d'hospitalisation sans consentement*, N° 04-023-01 (Ministere de l'interieur, de la securité interieure et des liberties locales, 2004), 5.
25. République Française, "Loi n° 2007-297 du 5 mars 2007 relative à la prévention de la délinquance," effective 2007, https://www.legifrance.gouv.fr/loda/id/JORFTEXT000000615568.
26. *Audition de M. Nicolas Sarkozy, ministre d'état, ministre de l'intérieur et de l'aménagement du territoire, sur le plan national de prévention de la délinquance*, N° 54, with Commission des affaires culturelles, familiales, et sociales (Assemblée Nationale, 2006).
27. Syndicat des psychiatres des hôpitaux, *Á propos du projet de loi de prévention de la délinquance*, Communique de presse (2006), https://sip.sphweb.fr/2006/11/10/psychiatrie-et-projet-de-loi-de-pravention-de-la-dalinquance/.
28. H. Mignot, "Le problème législatif," in *Live blanc de la psychiatrie française* (Éditions Édouard Privat, 1965), 1:103, 104, 111.
29. Ayme, *Chroniques de la psychiatrie publique*, 127.
30. Syndicat des Psychiatres d'Éxercice Public, *Securité: Communiqué IDEPP* (2005), 11–12.
31. Bernard Durand, "Soins psychiatriques: Le retour de la contrainte et de la stigmatisation," *Les tribunes de la santé*, no. 32 (2011): 43–54.
32. Another bill, the Law Relative to Retention for Security, would allow indefinite detention of people who had served at least a fifteen-year prison sentence but continued to show "dangerousness characterized by a high probability of recidivism

because they suffer from a grave trouble of personality." Although it passed in 2008, psychiatrists largely refused to participate in the new centers charged with detaining and treating this population. Claude-Olivier Doron, "La rétention de sûreté: Vers un nouveau type de positivisme juridique?," *L'information psychiatrique* 84, no. 6 (2008): 536, https://doi.org/10.3917/inpsy.8406.0533.

33. Bruno Falissard et al., "Prevalence of Mental Disorders in French Prisons for Men," *BMC Psychiatry* 6, no. 1 (2006): 33, https://doi.org/10.1186/1471-244X-6-33.
34. Livia Velpry and Benoît Eyraud, "Confinement and Psychiatric Care: A Comparison Between High-Security Units for Prisoners and for Difficult Patients in France," *Culture, Medicine, and Psychiatry* 38, no. 4 (2014): 550–77, https://doi.org/10.1007/s11013-014-9400-0.
35. David Noël, "Psychiatrie: Sarkozy confond santé et répression," Section d'Hénin-Beaumont du Parti Communiste Français, December 12, 2008, http://www.lheninois.com/article-25551001.html.
36. These included reinforcing the role of the prefecture in authorizing (and blocking) temporary furloughs of hospitalized patients, creating a minimum seventy-two-hour observation period for any involuntary patient before they could be released, and establishing a lengthy process for releasing patients who had been in a secured Unit for Difficult *Malades*. Roselyne Bachelot-Narquin, *Projet de loi relatif aux droits et à la protection des personnes faisant l'objet de soins psychiatriques et aux modalités de leur prise en charge* (Assemblée Nationale, 2010).
37. Jean-Christophe Coffin, "'Misery' and 'Revolution': The Organisation of French Psychiatry, 1900–1980," in *Psychiatric Cultures Compared*, ed. Marijke Gijswijt-Hofstra et al. (Amsterdam University Press, 2005), 232.
38. Laetitia Clavreul, "Débat autour ses soins psychiatriques sous contrainte," *Le Monde*, April 20, 2010, https://www.lemonde.fr/societe/article/2010/04/20/debat-autour-des-soins-psychiatriques-sous-contrainte_1340052_3224.html.
39. Emmanuelle Chevallereau, "'Nous redoutons que les soins psychiatriques sans consentement deviennent la règle,'" *Le Monde*, May 11, 2011, https://www.lemonde.fr/societe/article/2011/05/11/nous-redoutons-que-les-soins-psychiatriques-sans-consentement-deviennent-la-regle_1520445_3224.html.
40. They included requiring that hospital teams collect patients' "observations about the decisions concerning them" and mandating that a departmental commission examine hospitalizations lasting more than one year.
41. For more detail, see Tonya Tartour, "L'administration du désordre: Gouverner l'hôpital psychiatrique depuis les années 1980" (PhD diss., Sciences Po Paris, 2021).
42. Benoît Eyraud and Delphine Moreau, "Formes et régulations de l'enfermement psychiatrique: De la création de l'asile aux nouvelles unités sécurisées, l'exemple de l'hôpital du Vinatier," *Cultures & Conflits*, no. 90 (2013): 117–34.
43. Alain Monnier and Jean-Paul Tachon, "Les commissions départementales de soins psychiatriques: Un pilier de la démocratie sanitaire à consolider," *L'information psychiatrique* 91, no. 6 (2015): 455–58. For example, the ministry ultimately stopped summarizing the commission reports, which provided one of the most reliable sources of statistics on involuntary hospitalizations. Today, the baton has been picked up by the Church of Scientology. I kid you not.
44. Bronner, "Il y en a combien qui souffrent comme cela depuis des années?"

45. I cannot find any reliable historical statistics on the frequency of these hearings. One magazine article in 1987 claimed that there were three hundred hearings for sixty thousand internments, or 0.5 percent. Olivier Guérin, "Le fou entre deux chaînes," *Justice*, N° 116–117 (October 1987): 11.
46. G. Niveau and J. Materi, "Psychiatric Commitment: Over 50 Years of Case Law from the European Court of Human Rights," *European Psychiatry* 22, no. 1 (2007): 59–67, https://doi.org/10.1016/j.eurpsy.2006.05.004.
47. Claire Martinez, "Systématisation de la judiciarisation des hospitalisations sous contrainte: Impact de l'action du Groupe Information Asiles" (MD diss., Université de Lille 2, 2016).
48. Mitchel de S.O.-l'E. Lasser, "The Judicial Dynamics of the French and European Rights Revolution," in *Consequential Courts: Judicial Roles in Global Perspective*, ed. Diana Kapiszewski et al. (Cambridge University Press, 2013); Pierre-Yves Baudot and Anne Revillard, "Entre mobilisations et institutions: Les politiques des droits dans l'action publique," *Gouvernement et action publique* 4, no. 4 (2014): 9–33.
49. Corine Vaillant, *Conclusions par avocat de la Groupe Information Asilés*, N° QPC 2010–71 (Conseil constitutionnel, 2010).
50. One study estimated that only 1 percent of involuntary hospitalizations were reviewed by a judge. Delphine Legohérel, *Étude sur les soins psychiatriques sans consentement* (Service de Documentation, des Études et du Rapport, Cour de cassation, 2014), 5, http://psychiatrie.crpa.asso.fr/IMG/pdf/2014-12-31-etude-sur-les-soins-sans-consentement-cour-de-cassation.pdf.
51. André Bitton, *Bulletin d'information trimestriel N°29* (Cercle de Réflexion et de Proposition d'Actions sur la psychiatrie, 2018), 13.
52. UNAFAM et al., *Communiqué: Usagers et professionnels saluent la décision du conseil constitutionnel renforcant la protection de la liberté individuelle des personnes hospitalisées sans consentement pour troubles mentaux* (2010).
53. Fédération de l'Aide à la Santé Mentale—Croix-Marine, *Communiqué de Presse* (2011).
54. Le Monde avec AFP, "Le sénat adopte le projet de loi sur l'hospitalisation d'office,"*Le Monde*, May 13, 2011, https://www.lemonde.fr/politique/article/2011/05/13/le-senat-adopte-le-projet-de-loi-sur-l-hospitalisation-d-office_1521848_823448.html.
55. Denys Robiliard, *Sur la proposition de loi relative aux soins sans consentement en psychiatrie*, Rapport d'Information, N° 1284 (Assemblée Nationale, 2013), 23.
56. Robiliard, *Sur la proposition de loi relative aux soins sans consentment en psychiatrie.*
57. David Gourion, "Terrorisme: ' Les psychiatres n'ont pas vocation à collaborer avec le ministère de l'intérieur,' " *Le Monde*, August 21, 2017, https://www.lemonde.fr/idees/article/2017/08/21/les-psychiatres-n-ont-pas-vocation-a-collaborer-avec-le-ministere-de-l-interieur_5174728_3232.html.
58. For discussion of the self-governing ideal and its inevitable failure, see Teresa Gowan and Sarah Whetstone, "Making the Criminal Addict: Subjectivity and Social Control in a Strong-Arm Rehab," *Punishment & Society* 14, no. 1 (2012): 69–93, https://doi.org/10.1177/1462474511424684; Kerwin Kaye, "Rehabilitating the 'Drugs Lifestyle': Criminal Justice, Social Control, and the Cultivation of Agency," *Ethnography* 14, no. 2 (2013): 207–32, https://doi.org/10.1177/1466138112457311; Allison McKim,

"'Getting Gut-Level': Punishment, Gender, and Therapeutic Governance," *Gender & Society* 22, no. 3 (2008): 303–23, https://doi.org/10.1177/0891243208317826.

59. Nicolas Marquis and Sophie Pesesse describe this as a search for patients who are "adequate." Nicolas Marquis and Sophie Pesesse, "De l'incertitude en santé mentale: Analyse de la prise de décision aux urgences psychiatriques," *Sciences Sociales et Santé* 39, no. 1 (2021): 43–67, https://doi.org/10.1684/sss.2021.0191.
60. A. Mondoloni et al., "Le péril imminent dans la loi du 5 Juillet 2011: Quelles implications sur les soins?," *L'encéphale* 40, no. 6 (2014): 472.
61. Guy Lefrand and Serge Blisko, *Rapport sur la mise en oeuvre de la loi N° 2011-803 du 5 Juillet 2011 relative aux droits et protection des personnes faisant l'objet des soins psychiatriques et aux modalités de leur prise en charge*, N° 4402 (Assemblée Nationale, 2012).
62. Magali Coldefy et al., *De l'hospitalisation aux soins sans consentement en psychiatrie: Premiers résultats de la mise en place de la loi du 5 Juillet 2011*, N° 222, (Institut de recherche et documentation en économie de la santé, 2017), 1–8.

## 6. JUDGING SUFFERING CITIZENS

1. Denys Robiliard and Denys Jacquat, *Rapport d'information en conclusion des travaux de la mission d'évaluation de la loi N° 2013-869 du 27 Septembre 2013 modifiant certaines dispositions issues de la loi N° 2011-803 du 5 Juillet 2011 relative aux droits et à la protection des personnes faisant l'objet de soins psychiatriques et aux modalités de leur prise en charge*, N° 4486 (Assemblée Nationale, 2017), 108.
2. Robiliard and Jacquat, *Rapport d'information en conclusion des travaux de la mission d'évaluation de la loi N° 2013-869*, 78. More recent statistics put the rate of judges confirming hospitalizations at 94 percent. Luc Bronner, "'Leurs paroles n'ont jamais aucun crédit': L'impossible dialogue entre les patients en psychiatrie et les juges," *Le Monde*, January 12, 2025, https://www.lemonde.fr/societe/article/2025/01/11/leurs-paroles-n-ont-jamais-aucun-credit-l-impossible-dialogue-entre-les-patients-en-psychiatrie-et-les-juges_6492179_3224.html.
3. Carol Warren, *The Court of Last Resort* (University of Chicago Press, 1982); Harold Garfinkel, "Conditions of Successful Degradation Ceremonies," *American Journal of Sociology* 61, no. 5 (1956): 420–24.
4. Lili Dao, "Hollow Law and Utilitarian Law: The Devaluing of Deportation Hearings in New York City and Paris," *Law & Society Review* 57, no. 3 (2023): 317–39, https://doi.org/10.1111/lasr.12665. See also Angèle Christin, *Comparutions immédiates: Enquête sur une pratique judiciaire* (La Découverte, 2008).
5. Pierre Bourdieu, "The Force of Law: Toward a Sociology of the Juridical Field," *Hastings Law Journal* 38 (1987): 838.
6. The alternative would have been to assign the matter to administrative judges, who would be expected to rule only on the procedural regularity of a hospitalization, not its justification.
7. Alicia Lucksted and Robert D. Coursey, "Consumer Perceptions of Pressure and Force in Psychiatric Treatments," *Psychiatric Services* 46, no. 2 (1995): 146–52.
8. Professionals engage in social control based on a perception of their entire caseload rather than on the features of individual cases. Robert M. Emerson, "Holistic Effects in Social Control Decision-Making," *Law & Society Review* 17, no. 3 (1983): 425–55.

9. Sheila Shea, "The Mental Hygiene Legal Service at 50: A Retrospective and Prospective Examination of Advocacy for People with Mental Disabilities," *Government, Law, and Policy Journal* 14, no. 2 (2012): 35–41.
10. Syndicat de la magistrature, *Observations sur l'application de la loi du 5 Juillet 2011 relative aux droits et à la protection des personnes faisant l'objet de soins psychiatriques et aux modalités de leur prise en charge*, February 2, 2012, https://psychiatrie.crpa.asso.fr/2012-02-02-Syndicats-de-magistrats-observations-sur-l-application-de-la-loi-du-5-juillet-2011.
11. One report stated that patients could not pay for their own lawyer in 95 to 98 percent of cases. Hélène Mauduit, "Soins sans consentement en psychiatrie: Magistrats et avocats favorables à moins de certificats," *Agence presse médicale*, February 22, 2013, https://psychiatrie.crpa.asso.fr/2013-02-22-Audition-des-representants-des-professionnels-par-la-mission-la-sante-mentale-et-psychiatrie?lang=fr.
12. Robiliard and Jacquat, *Rapport d'information en conclusion des travaux de la mission d'évaluation de la loi N° 2013–869*, 111.
13. Claire Martinez, "Systématisation de la judiciarisation des hospitalisations sous contrainte: Impact de l'action du Groupe Information Asiles" (MD diss., Université de Lille 2, 2016), 49.
14. In one study, two-thirds of decisions in cases with a procedural irregularity declared they did not cause harm. Delphine Legohérel, *Étude sur les soins psychiatriques sans consentement* (Service de Documentation, des Études et du Rapport, Cour de cassation, 2014), 81, http://psychiatrie.crpa.asso.fr/IMG/pdf/2014-12-31-etude-sur-les-soins-sans-consentement-cour-de-cassation.pdf.
15. Hélène Mauduit, "Soins sans consentement en psychiatrie: Plusieurs difficultés constatées sur les décisions de mainlevées," *Agence presse médicale*, June 13, 2013, https://psychiatrie.crpa.asso.fr/2013-06-14-APM-Soins-sans-consentement-en-psychiatrie-plusieurs-difficultes-constatees-sur-les-decisions-de-mainlevee?lang=fr.
16. A more recent study found that there are almost never judicial orders to end hospitalizations for administrative reasons in Paris, which suggests the success of legal-medical collaboration to ensure procedural conformity. R. Gousset et al., "Étude descriptive des mainlevées prononcées par le juge des libertés et de la détention au groupe hospitalier universitaire Paris psychiatrie & neurosciences du 1er Novembre 2017 au 31 Octobre 2018," *L'encéphale* 46, no. 6 (2020): 436–42.
17. Armando Lara-Millán and Nicole Gonzalez Van Cleve, "Interorganizational Utility of Welfare Stigma in the Criminal Justice System," *Criminology* 55, no. 1 (2017): 69; Dao, "Hollow Law and Utilitarian Law."
18. Robiliard and Jacquat, *Rapport d'information en conclusion des travaux de la mission d'évaluation de la loi N° 2013–869*, 78.
19. Guy Lefrand and Serge Blisko, *Rapport sur la mise en oeuvre de la loi N° 2011–803 du 5 Juillet 2011 relative aux droits et protection des personnes faisant l'objet des soins psychiatriques et aux modalités de leur prise en charge*, N° 4402 (Assemblée Nationale, 2012), 41.
20. Hélène Mauduit, "Psychiatrie: Crispations entre le Groupe Hospitalier Paul-Guiraud et le tribunal de Créteil sur les audiences de patients," *Dépêche APM*, March 16, 2012, h4p://goo.gl/5ch3h.

21. Scholars have not found this same level of deference of French judges toward experts in criminal cases. We can hypothesize that this reflects a strong, compartmentalized conception of each profession being dominant in its respective domain: health or justice. Ronan Palaric and Valérie Moulin, "Critères intervenant dans le choix de l'expert judiciaire, psychiatre ou psychologue, en France," *Annales Médico-Psychologiques, Revue Psychiatrique* 172, no. 7 (2014): 489–94, https://doi.org/10.1016/j.amp.2013.07.011; Jérôme Pélisse et al., *Des chiffres des maux et des lettres: Une sociologie de l'expertise judiciaire en économie, psychiatrie et traduction* (Armand Colin, 2012); Sébastien Saetta et al., "Les usages des expertises psy au procès d'assises et les définitions pratiques de la responsabilité," *Déviance et société* 34, no. 4 (2010): 647–69.
22. Judges' "insistence on their own incompetence" is documented by Benoît Eyraud, *Protéger et rendre capable* (Érès, 2013), 165–66.
23. Conversely, in the rare cases of judges ending hospitalizations, an absence of extensive medical documentation in the certificates appears determinative. R. Gousset et al., "La moindre argumentation des certificats médicaux accroît le risque de mainlevée," *L'encéphale* 49, no. 2 (2023): 165–73.
24. Michel Foucault, *The History of Madness*, ed. Jean Khalfa, trans. Jonathan Murphy (Routledge, 2006), xxviii.
25. Michael L. Perlin, "On Sanism," *SMU Law Review* 46, no. 2 (1992): 373–408.
26. Code de santé publique, L. 1111–4 al., 2 et 4, https://www.legifrance.gouv.fr/codes/article_lc/LEGIARTI000041721056.
27. This recourse to serious deprivations of liberty is common. One-third of involuntary hospitalized patients are subject to isolation at some point; one in ten is subject to mechanical restraints. Esther Touitou-Burckard et al., *Isolement et contention en psychiatrie en 2022: Un panorama inédit de la population concernée et des disparités d'usage entre établissements*, N° 286 (Institut de recherche et documentation en économie de la santé, 2024).
28. Direction générale de la santé, "Note pour Madame Chef du Bureau PS1," June 10, 1999, *DGS 2009/037-3*.
29. Ministère de la santé publique et de la population, *Circulaire du 15 Mars 1960 relative au programme d'organisation et d'équipement des départements en matière de lutte contre les maladies mentales* (Le ministre de la santé publique, 1960), 10.
30. Roi Livne, *Values at the End of Life* (Harvard University Press, 2019), 199.
31. Julia Legrand, "L'injonction ou l'injection? Prescriptions de médicaments et reconfigurations contemporaines du pouvoir psychiatrique," *Genèses* 127, no. 2 (2022): 11–32, https://doi.org/10.3917/gen.127.0011.
32. Caroline Guibet Lafaye, "L'hospitalisation sous contrainte: Une source de conflits normatifs," *Revue française des affaires sociales* 2 (2016): 38–55.
33. Isabelle Coutant and Jean-Sébastien Eideliman, "Listening to Suffering: The Treatment of Mental Fragility at a Home for Adolescents," in *At the Heart of the State*, ed. Didier Fassin (University of Chicago Press, 2015), 211.
34. Many interviewees said this is particularly true for a new modality of hospitalization created by the 2011 law, which allowed for hospitalization without a third-party demand when a person is in "imminent peril."
35. In 2021, 16.4 percent of involuntary psychiatric interventions were taken through the framework of a *Soins psychiatrique sur décision d'un représentant de l'État*

(SPDRE, Psychiatric Care at the Demand of a Representative of the State). The fact that the proportion of SPDREs was higher in the hearings I saw was unsurprising, given that these hospitalizations tend to last longer. Magali Coldefy et al., *Les soins sans consentement et les pratiques privatives de liberté en psychiatrie: Un objectif de réduction qui reste à atteindre*, N° 269 (Institut de recherche et documentation en économie de la santé, 2022).

36. On ubiquitous discrimination in French police officer stops, see Magda Boutros, "Legal Mobilization and Branches of Law: Contesting Racialized Policing in French Courts," *Law & Society Review* 56, no. 4 (2022): 623–45.
37. Gilles Vidon, Marie-Christine Hardy-Baylé, and Nadia Younès, "Quelle place pour les soins sans consentement en ambulatoire? À propos de l'enquête IDF sur les programmes de soins," *L'information psychiatrique* 91, no. 7 (2015): 602–607.
38. By 2021, there were 39,000 people in such programs, a striking 41 percent of all people subject to involuntary psychiatric measures that year. Coldefy et al., *Les soins sans consentement.*
39. Raphaël Gourevitch et al., "The Evolution of Laws Regulating Psychiatric Commitment in France," *Psychiatric Services* 64, no. 7 (2013): 611–12.
40. The French constitutional court determined that, because a person under a program of care could only be truly forced to take treatment upon returning to the hospital, no systematic review was necessary. Jean-Marc Panfili, *L'intervention du juge judiciaire dans les soins psychiatriques sans consentement: Analyse de la jurisprudence depuis la loi 5 Juillet 2011* (2016), https://psychiatrie.crpa.asso.fr/IMG/pdf/2016-12-31_analyse_de_la_jpdce_loi_du_05-07-2011_mise_a_jour.pdf.
41. Michel Foucault, *Psychiatric Power: Lectures at the College de France, 1973–1974*, ed. Jacques Lagrange, trans. Graham Burchell (Palgrave Macmillan, 2008), 220.
42. Ana Marques et al., "Les enjeux d'une judiciarisation tardive, inévitable et embarrassante," *L'information psychiatrique* 91, no. 6 (2015): 471–77.
43. Coldefy et al., *Les soins sans consentement.*
44. Luke Sheridan Rains et al., "Variations in Patterns of Involuntary Hospitalisation and in Legal Frameworks: An International Comparative Study," *The Lancet Psychiatry* 6, no. 5 (2019): 403–17, https://doi.org/10.1016/S2215-0366(19)30090-2; Mustafa Karakus et al., "Involuntary Inpatient Civil Commitment: Trends from 2010 to 2022," *Psychiatric Services* 76, no. 10 (2025): 861-866, https://doi.org/10.1176/appi.ps.20250024.
45. This is a delicate issue where key parties usually talk past each other. It is true that a range of studies show that people with mental illnesses, particularly psychosis, are more likely to commit acts of violence than similar individuals without such illnesses. It is also true that only a small proportion of people with mental illness act violently, our tools for prediction are poor, factors like poverty and past experience of victimization are more determinative, and people with mental illness themselves are particularly vulnerable to being recipients of violence. Sherry Glied and Richard G. Frank, "Mental Illness and Violence: Lessons from the Evidence," *American Journal of Public Health* 104, no. 2 (2014): e5–6, https://doi.org/10.2105/AJPH.2013.301710; Daniel Whiting et al., "Violence and Mental Disorders: A Structured Review of Associations by Individual Diagnoses, Risk Factors, and Risk Assessment," *The Lancet Psychiatry* 8, no. 2 (2021): 150–61, https://doi.org/10.1016/S2215-0366(20)30262-5.

46. Natalie Giloux and Marion Primevert, "La psychiatre et le juge dace à la protection de la personne dans les soins contraints," *Revue de droit sanitaire et social*, no. 6 (November–December 2015): 982.

## CONCLUSION

1. Le Monde, "Editorial: La psychiatrie, un secteur en profonde dépression," *Le Monde*, August 19, 2018, https://www.lemonde.fr/idees/article/2018/08/18/la-psychiatrie-un-secteur-en-etat-d-urgence_5343765_3232.html.
2. Daniel Zagury, "'La psychiatrie publique est devenue un enfer,'" *Le Monde*, June 12, 2018, https://www.lemonde.fr/idees/article/2018/06/12/la-psychiatrie-publique-est-devenue-un-enfer_5313233_3232.html.
3. Le Monde, "Editorial: La psychiatrie, un secteur en profonde dépression."
4. François Béguin, "La psychiatrie en grande souffrance," *Le Monde*, January 26, 2018, https://www.lemonde.fr/sciences/article/2018/01/26/le-grand-malaise-des-soignants-en-psychiatrie-on-a-le-sentiment-d-etre-maltraitant_5247248_1650684.html.
5. Aurore Esclauze, "A l'Hôpital du Rouvray, 'la situation devient critique' pour les grévistes de la faim," *Le Monde*, June 6, 2018, https://www.lemonde.fr/sante/article/2018/06/06/a-l-hopital-psychiatrique-du-rouvray-greve-de-la-faim-pour-des-moyens_5310386_1651302.html.
6. Mathieu Bellahsen and Rachel Knaebel, *La révolte de la psychiatrie: Les ripostes à la catastrophe gestionnaire* (La Découverte, 2020), 158.
7. Caroline Fiat and Martine Wonner, *Rapport en conclusion des travaux de la mission relative à l'organisation de la santé mentale*, N° 2249 (Assemblée Nationale, 2019), 27.
8. Catherine Vincent, "La très grande souffrance de la psychiatrie française," *Le Monde*, July 18, 2020, https://www.lemonde.fr/sante/article/2020/07/17/la-tres-grande-souffrance-de-la-psychiatrie-francaise_6046447_1651302.html.
9. Nicole Dubré-Chirat and Sandrine Rousseau, *Rapport sur la prise en charge des urgences psychiatriques*, N° 714 (Assemblée Nationale, 2024), 14, https://www.assemblee-nationale.fr/dyn/17/rapports/cion-soc/l17b0714_rapport-information.pdf.
10. Bellahsen and Knaebel, *La révolte de la psychiatrie*, 89.
11. Mattea Battaglia and Camille Stromboni, "Crise de l'hôpital: La difficile gestion des patients 'psy' aux urgences," *Le Monde*, September 1, 2024, https://www.lemonde.fr/societe/article/2024/09/01/crise-de-l-hopital-la-difficile-gestion-des-patients-psy-aux-urgences_6300755_3224.html.
12. Fédération Hospitalière de France, "Résultants de l'enquête FHF psychiatrie," 2023, https://www.fhf.fr/sites/default/files/2023-09/Enqu%C3%AAte%20psychiatrie_2023.pdf.
13. Ministère du travail, de la santé, et des solidarités, *Santé mentale et psychiatrie: État d'avancement* (Paris, France, 2024), 56, https://sante.gouv.fr/IMG/pdf/feuille_de_route.sante-mentale-psychiatrie-2024.pdf.
14. Dubré-Chirat and Rousseau, *Rapport sur la prise en charge*, 186.
15. From 2008 to 2018, public psychiatry's budget increased 12.7 percent, compared to inflation of 12.9 percent. Because health spending as a whole increased 22.9

percent, the discipline received a diminishing share of the budget (as well as losing ground relative to private psychiatric hospitals). Cour des comptes, *Les parcours dans l'organisation des soins en psychiatrie*, Rapport public thématique (Cour des comptes, 2021), 52.

16. Ministère du travail, de la santé, et des solidarités, *Santé mentale et psychiatrie*, 93.
17. Dubré-Chirat and Rousseau, *Rapport sur la prise en charge*, 9.
18. Thierry Trémine, "Y a-t-il une identité de la psychiatrie française?" in *Psychiatrie française/psychiatrie en France*, ed. by Frédéric Rouillon (Springer, 2012).
19. More detail on the strengths of the French system can be found in Isabel M. Perera and Alex V. Barnard, "Myths of Mental Health: Revelations from the French System for the United States," *Perspectives in Biology and Medicine* 64, no. 1 (2021): 103–18, https://doi.org/10.1353/pbm.2021.0008.
20. As Perera argues, the offer of mental health services depends particularly on public financing because of the inability of individuals with the most serious illnesses to pay for care and because of the historical unwillingness of private insurance companies to ensure parity with physical health care. Isabel M. Perera, "Is Psychiatry Different? An Economic Perspective," *The Lancet Psychiatry* 6, no. 4 (2019): 282–83.
21. Françoise Castel et al., *The Psychiatric Society*, trans. Arthur Goldhammer (Columbia University Press, 1982), 9.
22. Alain Lopez, *La psychiatrie dans la tourmente* (Hygée, 2023), 90.
23. Alex V. Barnard, *Conservatorship: Inside California's System of Coercion and Care for Mental Illness* (Columbia University Press, 2023).
24. Owen Whooley, *A Mad Mess: Community Mental Health in Crisis* (University of Chicago Press, 2026).
25. Lopez, *La psychiatrie dans la tourmente*, 85.
26. Lopez, *La psychiatrie dans la tourmente*, 86.
27. This reflects a certain French tendency to favor medical treatments that work in theory, regardless of their practical efficacy (see: the national enthusiasm for homeopathy). Lynn Payer, *Medicine and Culture* (Penguin, 1988).
28. Cour des comptes, *Les parcours dans l'organisation des soins en psychiatrie*, 63. The report compares French data to that found in Pablo Nicaise et al., "Healthcare System Performance in Continuity of Care for Patients with Severe Mental Illness: A Comparison of Five European Countries," *Health Policy* 124, no. 1 (2020): 25–36.
29. Economist Intelligence Unit, *France Country Report: Political Leadership Is Needed to Build on Early Advances* (2015).
30. Catalina Devandas-Aguilar, *End of Mission Statement by the United Nations Special Rapporteur on the Rights of Persons with Disabilities on Her Visit to France* (United Nations Human Rights, 2017).
31. Martha K. Savage et al., "Comparison of Coercive Practices in Worldwide Mental Healthcare: Overcoming Difficulties Resulting from Variations in Monitoring Strategies," *BJPsych Open* 10, no. 1 (2024): e26, https://doi.org/10.1192/bjo.2023.613.
32. In practice, however, the chairs for users in bodies like local councils of mental health continue either empty or filled by representatives of families. Centre collaborateur OMS, *Les conseils locaux de santé mentale: État des lieux* (CCOMS Lille, 2015), 5.
33. Dubré-Chirat and Rousseau, *Rapport sur la prise en charge*, 92.

34. Delphine Moreau and Christian Laval, "Care et Recovery: Jusqu'où ne pas décider pour autrui? L'exemple du programme 'Un Chez-Soi d'Abord,'" *Alter* 9, no. 3 (2015): 222–35.
35. Aurélien Troisoeufs, "Patients intervenants, médiateurs de santé-pairs: Quelles figures de la pair-aidance en santé ?," *Rhizome* 7576, no. 1 (2020): 27–36, https://doi.org/10.3917/rhiz.075.0027.
36. GHU Paris, "Projet territorial de santé mentale de Paris, 2021–2025" (GHU Paris, December 2020), 127, https://www.ghu-paris.fr/sites/default/files/media/downloads/PTSM%20Paris%20VFF.pdf.
37. Alex V. Barnard, "A Discipline Like No Other: Marginalized Autonomy and Institutional Anchors in French Public Psychiatry (1945–2016)," *Comparative Studies in Society and History* 66, no. 3 (2024): 643–72.
38. Catherine Ha et al., "Mortalité des personnes souffrant de troubles mentaux: Analyse en causes multiples des certificats de décès en France, 2000–2013," *Bulletin Épidémiologique Hebdomadaire* 23 (2017): 500–508.
39. Sasha Warren, *Storming Bedlam: Madness, Utopia, and Revolt* (Common Notions Press, 2024), 274.
40. Ministère chargé de la santé et de l'accès aux soins, *Santé mentale et psychiatrie: Mise en oeuvre de la feuille de route* (2025), 124, https://sante.gouv.fr/IMG/pdf/bilan_feuille_de_route.pdf.
41. Tom Heyden, "How Patients Might Design a Psychiatric Hospital," *BBC News*, May 13, 2014, https://www.bbc.com/news/blogs-ouch-27206405.
42. Aurélie Tinland et al., "Effect of Psychiatric Advance Directives Facilitated by Peer Workers on Compulsory Admission Among People with Mental Illness: A Randomized Clinical Trial," *JAMA Psychiatry* 79, no. 8 (2022): 752–59.
43. I am grateful to Keris Jän Myrick, a mighty peer advocate in California, for constantly reminding us that the three P's of recovery—people, place, and purpose—are nothing without a fourth P: power.
44. Paige L. Sweet, *The Politics of Surviving: How Women Navigate Domestic Violence and Its Aftermath* (University of California Press, 2021); Matthew Wolfe, "Policing the Lost: The Emergence of Missing Persons and the Classification of Deviant Absence," *Theory and Society* 51, no. 3 (2022): 511–41; G. Cristina Mora, "Cross-Field Effects and Ethnic Classification," *American Sociological Review* 79, no. 2 (2014): 183–210.
45. Ian Hacking, "Making Up People," in *The Science Studies Reader*, edited by Mario Biaglioli (Routledge, 1999), 165.
46. Ian Hacking, *Mad Travelers: Reflections on the Reality of Transient Mental Illnesses* (University Press of Virginia, 1998). For a convincing demonstration of this claim in a recent case, see Ethan Watters, *Crazy Like Us: The Globalization of the American Psyche* (Free Press, 2011), chap. 1.
47. An excellent step in this direction has already been taken by Luciana de Souza Leão, "Optics of the State: The Politics of Making Poverty Visible in Brazil and Mexico," *American Journal of Sociology* 128, no. 1 (2022): 1–46, https://doi.org/10.1086/719936.
48. Kimberly J. Morgan and Ann Shola Orloff, eds., *The Many Hands of the State: Theorizing Political Authority and Social Control* (Cambridge University Press, 2017).

49. Michael B. Katz, *The Undeserving Poor: America's Enduring Confrontation with Poverty* (Oxford University Press, 2013); Margaret R. Somers and Fred Block, "From Poverty to Perversity: Ideas, Markets, and Institutions over 200 Years of Welfare Debate," *American Sociological Review* 70, no. 2 (2005): 260–87.
50. Matthew Clair, *Privilege and Punishment: How Race and Class Matter in Criminal Court*, in *Privilege and Punishment* (Princeton University Press, 2020); Teresa Gowan and Sarah Whetstone, "Making the Criminal Addict: Subjectivity and Social Control in a Strong-Arm Rehab," *Punishment & Society* 14, no. 1 (2012): 69–93, https://doi.org/10.1177/1462474511424684.
51. Gilles Deleuze, "Postscript on the Societies of Control," in *Surveillance, Crime and Social Control*, edited by Clive Norris and Dean Wilson (Routledge, 2006); Neil Gong, " 'That Proves You Mad, Because You Know It Not': Impaired Insight and the Dilemma of Governing Psychiatric Patients as Legal Subjects," *Theory and Society* 46, no. 3 (2017): 201–28; Nikolas Rose, *Powers of Freedom: Reframing Political Thought* (Cambridge University Press, 1999).
52. Neil Gong, *Sons, Daughters, and Sidewalk Psychotics: Mental Illness and Homelessness in Los Angeles* (University of Chicago Press, 2024); Anthony DiMario, "To Punish, Parent, or Palliate: Governing Urban Poverty Through Institutional Failure," *American Sociological Review* 87, no. 5 (2022): 860–88.
53. Jeffrey Prottas, *People Processing: The Street-Level Bureaucrat in Public-Service Bureaucracies* (Lexington Books, 1979).
54. Alex V. Barnard, "Consent and Compliance: Serviceable Subjects in Involuntary Psychiatric Commitment Hearings in Paris and New York," *Law & Society Review*, 59, no. 4 (2025): 749–784.
55. Josh Seim, *Bandage, Sort, and Hustle: Ambulance Crews on the Frontlines of Urban Suffering* (University of California Press, 2019); Chris Herring, "Complaint-Oriented Policing: Regulating Homelessness in Public Space," *American Sociological Review* 84, no. 5 (2019): 769–800, https://doi.org/10.1177/0003122419872671; Armando Lara-Millán, *Redistributing the Poor: Jails, Hospitals, and the Crisis of Law and Fiscal Austerity* (Oxford University Press, 2021); Barnard, *Conservatorship*; Catherine Sirois, "Contested by the State: Institutional Offloading in the Case of Crossover Youth," *American Sociological Review* 88, no. 2 (2023): 350–77, https://doi.org/10.1177/00031224231160297.
56. Elizabeth Chiarello, *Policing Patients: Treatment and Surveillance on the Frontlines of the Opioid Crisis* (Princeton University Press, 2024), 78.
57. Chiarello, *Policing Patients*, 22.
58. Dora M. Dumont et al., "Public Health and the Epidemic of Incarceration," *Annual Review of Public Health* 33 (2012): 325–39.
59. Sunmin Kim, *The Unruly Facts of Race: The Politics of Knowledge Production in the Early Twentieth-Century Immigration Debate* (University of Chicago Press, 2026), 13.
60. Kim, *Unruly Facts of Race*, 223.
61. Jean-Luc Roelandt, "Pour en finir avec la confusion entre psychiatrie et justice, hôpital psychiatrique et prison, soins et enfermement," *L'information psychiatrique* 85, no. 6 (2009): 529.
62. Alain Lopez and Gaëlle Turan-Pelletier, *Organisation et fonctionnement du dispositif de soins psychiatriques, 60 ans après la Circulaire du 15 Mars 1960*, N° 2017-064R (Inspection générale des affaires sociales, 2017), 137.

# METHODOLOGICAL APPENDIX

1. Simon Goodwin, *Comparative Mental Health Policy: From Institutional to Community Care* (SAGE, 1997); Sigrun Olafsdottir, "Medicalizing Mental Health: A Comparative View of the Public, Private, and Professional Construction of Mental Illness" (PhD diss., Indiana University, 2007); Isabel M. Perera, *The Welfare Workforce: Why Mental Health Care Varies Across Affluent Democracies* (Cambridge University Press, 2025).
2. The closest to a reliable comparison comes from the World Mental Health Survey, which found that around 20 percent of US and French citizens will meet criteria for major depression at some point in their lives, a higher rate than in other developed countries. Ronald C. Kessler and Evelyn J. Bromet, "The Epidemiology of Depression Across Cultures," *Annual Review of Public Health* 34, no. 1 (2013): 119–38.
3. The European Schizophrenia Outcomes Study includes patients from ten countries, but results are aggregated. J. M. Haro et al., "The European Schizophrenia Outpatient Health Outcomes Study: Baseline Findings Across Country and Treatment," *Acta Psychiatrica Scandinavica* 107, no. S416 (2003): 7–15.
4. Didier Fassin, *At the Heart of the State* (University of Chicago Press, 2015), x.
5. Geoffrey C. Bowker and Susan Leigh Star, *Sorting Things Out: Classification and Its Consequences* (MIT Press, 1999).
6. The actual number of people I sat down with for interviews was closer to 220. An embarrassing number of interviews were lost because of sound issues (unexpectedly loud cafés!), a tape recorder I bought for my undergraduate thesis that decided to die with a dozen irretrievable files on it, and notes from unrecorded interviews that I waited to type up too late after the fact. I document these unflattering details in order to provide somewhat avuncular (and hopefully unneeded) advice to other novice researchers: If your interview isn't recorded and transcribed, you might as well not have done it at all when it comes time to write up your results a few years later.
7. The number of interviews, 193, puts this project at the upper end of published studies in sociology, according to one survey (the median number of interviews was fifty-five). Nicole M. Deterding and Mary C. Waters, "Flexible Coding of In-Depth Interviews: A Twenty-First-Century Approach," *Sociological Methods & Research* 50, no. 2 (2021): 708–39. Quantity and quality are not the same thing, of course.
8. Matthew Desmond, "Relational Ethnography," *Theory and Society* 43, no. 5 (2014): 547–79.
9. Colin Jerolmack and Shamus Khan, "Talk Is Cheap: Ethnography and the Attitudinal Fallacy," *Sociological Methods & Research* 43, no. 2 (2014): 186.
10. Kathleen Gerson and Sarah Damaske, *The Science and Art of Interviewing* (Oxford University Press, 2021), 71.
11. One strong exception to this claim appears to be judicial hearings, where the rate of releases by judges in Paris (1.5 percent) is way below the national average (8 percent). Gousset et al., "Étude descriptive des mainlevées prononcées par le juge des libertés et de la détention au Groupe Hospitalier Universitaire Paris Psychiatrie & Neurosciences du 1er Novembre 2017 au 31 Octobre 2018," *L'enchéphale* 46, no. 6 (2020): 436–44, doi:10.1016/j.encep.2020.01.008.

12. Daniel Navon and Gil Eyal, "Looping Genomes: Diagnostic Change and the Genetic Makeup of the Autism Population," *American Journal of Sociology* 121, no. 5 (2016): 1416–71, https://doi.org/10.1086/684201; Gil Eyal et al., *The Autism Matrix* (Polity, 2010); Mara Loveman, *National Colors: Racial Classification and the State in Latin America* (Oxford University Press, 2014).

# BIBLIOGRAPHY


Adler-Bolton, Beatrice, and Artie Vierkant. *Health Communism*. Verso, 2022.

Agence régionale de santé. *Projet régional de santé: schéma d'organisation médico-social*. Agence régionale de santé, 2011.

Alexis, Spire. *Accueillir ou reconduire: Enquête sur les guichets de l'immigration*. Éditions Raisons d'Agir, 2008.

Alfandari, François. "Le syndicalisme à l'heure de la transformation de la psychiatrie: Des militants CGT à l'hôpital psychiatrique du Vinatier (Lyon, années 1960–1970)." *Genèses* 107, no. 2 (2017): 82–105.

Alonso, J., M. C. Angermeyer, S. Bernert, et al. "Psychotropic Drug Utilization in Europe: Results from the European Study of the Epidemiology of Mental Disorders (ESEMeD) Project." *Acta Psychiatrica Scandinavica*, no. 420 (2004): 55–64.

Altomonte, Guillermina, and Adrianna Bagnall Munson. "Autonomy on the Horizon: Comparing Institutional Approaches to Disability and Elder Care." *Theory and Society* 50, no. 6 (2021): 935–63.

Amara, Fadéla, Danièle Jourdain-Menninger, Myriam Mesclon-Ravaud, and Gilles Lecoq. *La prise en charge du handicap psychique*. Inspection générale des affaires sociales, 2011.

Amarilli, Philippe. "Psychiatrie de secteur et handicap psychique." *L'information psychiatrique* 94, no. 5 (2018): 347–53.

Appelbaum, Paul S. *Almost a Revolution: Mental Health Law and the Limits of Change*. Oxford University Press, 1994.

Aubry, Martine. *Plan d'action pour le développement de l'autonomie des personnes handicapées dans leur milieu de vie ordinaire*. Secrétaire d'État à la santé et aux handicapés, 1999.

Audisio, Michel. *La psychiatrie de secteur: Une psychiatrie militante pour la santé mentale*. Éditions Édouard Privat, 1980.

*Audition de M. Nicolas Sarkozy, Ministre d'Etat, Ministre de l'intérieur et de l'aménagement du territoire, sur le Plan national de prévention de la délinquance.* N° 54. With Commission des affaires culturelles, familiales, et sociales. Assemblée Nationale, 2006.

Auvergnon, Philippe. "Approche juridique du handicap psychique: Les enjeux d'une définition en droit social." *Alter* 6, no. 4 (2012): 255–66.

Auyero, Javier. *Patients of the State: The Politics of Waiting in Argentina.* Duke University Press, 2012.

Ayme, Jean. *Chroniques de la psychiatrie publique: A travers l'histoire d'un syndicat.* Érès, 1995.

Azéma, Jean-Pierre. *Mission sur le drame que les personnes handicapées mentales ou malades psychiques ont connu dans les hôpitaux psychiatriques et les hospices français entre 1941 et 1945.* Ministère de la Défense, 2015.

Bachelot-Narquin, Roselyne. *Projet de loi relatif aux droits et à la protection des personnes faisant l'objet de soins psychiatriques et aux modalités de leur prise en charge.* Assemblée Nationale, 2010.

Bagnall, Adrianna, and Gil Eyal. "Forever Children and Autonomous Citizens: Comparing the Deinstitutionalizations of Psychiatric Patients and Developmentally Disabled Individuals in the United States." In *50 Years After Deinstitutionalization: Mental Illness in Contemporary Communities,* edited by Brea Perry. Emerald, 2016.

Bagnall-Munson, Adrianna. "How to Become an Adult." *Contexts* 20, no. 3 (2021): 10–15.

Bardach, Eugene. *The Skill Factor in Politics: Repealing the Mental Commitment Laws in California.* University of California Press, 1972.

Baret, Christophe. "Les établissements et services d'aide par le travail (ESAT) parviennent-ils à concilier objectifs économiques et missions médico-sociales ?" *Revue Interdisciplinaire Management, Homme & Entreprise,* no. 2 (2012): 66–82. https://doi.org/10.3917/rimhe.002.0066.

Barnard, Alex V. "Bureaucratically Split Personalities: (Re)Ordering the Mentally Disordered in the French State." *Theory and Society* 48, no. 5 (2019): 753–84.

——. *Conservatorship: Inside California's System of Coercion and Care for Mental Illness.* Columbia University Press, 2023.

——. "A Discipline Like No Other: Marginalized Autonomy and Institutional Anchors in French Public Psychiatry (1945–2016)." *Comparative Studies in Society and History* 66, no. 3 (2024): 643–72.

——. "Consent and Compliance: Serviceable Subjects in Involuntary Psychiatric Commitment Hearings in Paris and New York." *Law & Society Review,* 59, no. 4 (2025): 749–784.

Barnier, Michel. "La santé mentale, Grande cause nationale 2025." *Gouvernement,* October 10, 2024. https://www.info.gouv.fr/actualite/la-sante-mentale-grande-cause-nationale-2025.

Barral, Catherine. "Disabled Persons' Associations in France." *Scandinavian Journal of Disability Research* 9, nos. 3–4 (2007): 214–36.

Barres, Martine. *L'action de la psychiatrie pour l'accès et le maintien dans le logement des personnes vivant avec des troubles psychiques en Île-de-France.* Agence régionale de santé-Île-de-France, 2016.

Barreyre, Jean-Yves, Yara Makdessi, and Carole Peintre. "Les patients séjournant au long cours dans les services de psychiatrie adulte en Île-de-France." *Vie Sociale* 3 (2003): 37–75.

Barreyre, Jean-Yves, and Carole Peintre. *Handicap des origines psychiques et évaluations des situations: Volet 2. Synthèse de la phase "terrains."* Caisse nationale de solidarité pour l'autonomie, 2009.

Battaglia, Mattea, and Camille Stromboni. "Crise de l'hôpital: La difficile gestion des patients « 'psy' aux urgences." *Le Monde*, September 1, 2024. https://www.lemonde.fr/societe/article/2024/09/01/crise-de-l-hopital-la-difficile-gestion-des-patients-psy-aux-urgences_6300755_3224.html.

Baudot, Pierre-Yves. "L'invention des délais: Pourquoi l'administration doit-elle répondre dans les temps ?" *Politiques sociales et familiales* 119, no. 1 (2015): 5–18.

Baudot, Pierre-Yves, and Anne Revillard. "Entre mobilisations et institutions: Les politiques des droits dans l'action publique." *Gouvernement et action publique* 4, no. 4 (2014): 9–33.

Bauduret, Jean-François, and Marcel Jaeger. *Rénover l'action sociale et médico-sociale: Histoires d'une refondation.* 2nd ed. Dunod, 2005.

Beaudouin, H., and J. L. Beaudouin. "La conception du 'service ouvert' (ou service libre) face à face avec sa carence juridique." *L'Information Psychiatrique*, no. 1/3 (1967): 37–56.

Béguin, François. "La psychiatrie en grande souffrance." *Le Monde*, January 26, 2018. https://www.lemonde.fr/sciences/article/2018/01/26/le-grand-malaise-des-soignants-en-psychiatrie-on-a-le-sentiment-d-etre-maltraitant_5247248_1650684.html.

Bélart, Claire, and Olivier Dembinski. "Les nouveaux outils de géstion en psychiatrie." In *La politique de santé mentale en France: Acteurs, instruments, controverses*, edited by Lise Demailly and Michel Autès. Armand Colin, 2012.

Bellahsen, Mathieu, and Rachel Knaebel. *La révolte de la psychiatrie: Les ripostes à la catastrophe gestionnaire.* La Découverte, 2020.

Bellamy, Vanessa, and Thomas Bergeron. *312,000 Personnes sont accompagnées dans les établissements et services médico-sociaux pour adultes handicapés fin 2018.* N° 1247. Direction de la recherche, des études, de l'évaluation et des statistiques, 2022.

Belliard, E. "L'hôpital psychiatrique en 1986 et ses récents bouleversements." *Confrontations psychiatriques*, 32 (1990): 75–92.

Benamouzig, Daniel. *La santé au miroir de l'économie: Une histoire de l'économie de la santé en France.* Presses universitaires de France, 2005.

Benkimoun, Paul, and Sandrine Blanchard. "Le ministre délégué à la santé présente un plan sur la santé mentale en conseil des ministres." *Le Monde*, November 15, 2001.

Ben-Moshe, Liat, Chris Chapman, and Allison C. Carey, eds. *Disability Incarcerated: Imprisonment and Disability in the United States and Canada.* Palgrave Macmillan US, 2014.

Berkowitz, Edward D., and Larry DeWitt. *The Other Welfare: Supplemental Security Income and U.S. Social Policy.* Cornell University Press, 2013.

Berr, Claudine, Hélène Grandjean, Jean-François Mathé, and Virginie Halley des Fontaines. *Enquête quantitative sur les modes d'évaluation et de traitement des demandes de compensation du handicap par les MDPH.* Haut Conseil de la santé publique, 2014.

Bertrand, Louis, Vincent Caradec, and Jean-Sébastien Eideliman. "Situating Disability: The Recognition of 'Disabled Workers' in France." *Alter* 8, no. 4 (2014): 269–81.

Biarez, Sylvie. "Une politique publique: la santé mentale (1970–2002)." *Revue française d'administration publique* 3, no. 111 (2004): 517–31.

Billiard, Isabelle. *Santé mentale et travail: L'émergence de la psychopathologie du travail.* La Dispute, 2001.

Bitton, André. *Bulletin d'information trimestriel N° 29*. Cercle de Réflexion et de Proposition d'Actions sur la psychiatrie, 2018.

Blanc, Paul. *Maisons départementales des personnes handicapées*. Sénat, 2005.

Blanchard, Sandrine. "Pourquoi les Français consomment toujours plus de psychotropes." *Le Monde*, September 7, 2004, https://www.lemonde.fr/archives/article/2004/09/06/pourquoi-les-francais-consomment-toujours-plus-de-psychotropes_378001_1819218.html.

Bocquet, Éric. *Rapport d'information au nom de la commission des finances sur les établissements et services d'aide par le travail*. N° 409. Sénat, 2015.

Borelle, Céline. " 'C'est uniquement social'. Sur la production d'un dualisme social/psychiatrique en sciences sociales et dans le travail ordinaire de la psychiatrie." *Politix* 117, no. 1 (2017): 201–22. https://doi.org/10.3917/pox.117.0201.

Bosk, Emily Adlin. "Between Badness and Sickness: Reconsidering Medicalization for High-Risk Children and Youth." *Children and Youth Services Review* 35, no. 8 (2013): 1212–18.

Boucherat-Hue, Valérie, Pascale Peretti, and Bénédicte Courty. "La notion de handicap psychique: Un levier politicosocial 'à la française'!" *L'information psychiatrique* 87, no. 8 (2011): 668–76.

Bourdieu, Pierre. *Distinction*. Harvard University Press, 1984.

——. "The Force of Law: Toward a Sociology of the Juridical Field." *Hastings Law Journal* 38 (1987): 805–53.

——. "Rethinking the State: Genesis and Structure of the Bureaucratic Field." Translated by Loic J. D. Wacquant and Samar Farage. *Sociological Theory* 12, no. 1 (1994): 1–18.

——. *The State Nobility: Elite Schools in the Field of Power*. Translated by Lauretta Clough. Polity Press, 1996.

——. *The Social Structure of the Economy*. Translated by Chris Turner. Polity, 2005.

——. *On the State*. Polity, 2015.

Boutros, Magda. "Legal Mobilization and Branches of Law: Contesting Racialized Policing in French Courts." *Law & Society Review* 56, no. 4 (2022): 623–45.

Bouvet, Marlène. "Réenchanter les déprimé.es: Une sociologie de la thérapie en clinique privée." PhD diss., École nationale supérieur, 2023.

Bowker, Geoffrey C., and Susan Leigh Star. *Sorting Things Out: Classification and Its Consequences*. MIT Press, 1999.

Brahmy, Betty, Michel Clémot, Jacques Gombert, and Gino Necchi. *Rapport de visite: Infirmerie psychiatrique de la préfecture de police à Paris*. Contrôleur général des lieux de privation de liberté, 2009.

Brauer, Ruth, Basmah Alfageh, Joseph E. Blais, et al. "Psychotropic Medicine Consumption in 65 Countries and Regions, 2008–19: A Longitudinal Study." *Lancet Psychiatry* 8, no. 12 (2021): 1071–82.

Briffault, Xavier, Aude Caria, Claude Finkelstein, et al. *Le dépression: En savoir plus pour en sortir*. Institut national de prévention et d'éducation pour la santé, 2007.

Briot, Maryvonne. *Rapport fait sur la proposition tendant à la création d'une commission d'enquête sur la progression du nombre d'internements psychiatriques en France*. N° 1598. Assemblée Nationale, 2004.

——. *Rapport sur le bon usage des médicaments psychotropes.* N° 422. Office parlementaire d'évaluation des politiques de santé, 2006.

Broer, Tineke, and Martyn Pickersgill. "Targeting Brains, Producing Responsibilities: The Use of Neuroscience Within British Social Policy." *Social Science & Medicine* 132 (2015): 54–61. https://doi.org/10.1016/j.socscimed.2015.03.022.

Bronner, Luc. "Les crises aiguës de la psychiatrie publique." *Le Monde*, January 11, 2025. https://www.lemonde.fr/societe/article/2025/01/10/les-crises-aigues-de-la-psychiatrie-publique-des-services-pepites-coexistent-avec-des-endroits-d-ou-tout-espoir-est-absent_6490744_3224.html.

——. "'Il y en a combien qui souffrent comme cela depuis des années?' : Enquête sur les Patients Attachés dans les Hôpitaux Psychiatriques." *Le Monde*, January 12, 2025. https://www.lemonde.fr/societe/article/2025/01/12/il-y-en-a-combien-qui-souffrent-comme-cela-depuis-des-annees-enquete-sur-les-patients-attaches-dans-les-hopitaux-psychiatriques_6493847_3224.html.

——. "'Leurs paroles n'ont jamais aucun crédit': L'impossible dialogue entre les patients en psychiatrie et les juges." *Le Monde*, January 12, 2025. https://www.lemonde.fr/societe/article/2025/01/11/leurs-paroles-n-ont-jamais-aucun-credit-l-impossible-dialogue-entre-les-patients-en-psychiatrie-et-les-juges_6492179_3224.html.

Brossard, Baptiste. "L'organisation sociale des 'hasards heureux': Qu'est-ce qu'un soin en psychiatrie?" *Sociologie du travail* 55, no. 1 (2013): 1–19.

——. "Why Mental Disorders Flourish and Wither: Extending the Theory of Ecological Niches." *Social Science & Medicine* 237 (2019): 112445.

Brown, Phil, and Elizabeth Cooksey. "Mental Health Monopoly: Corporate Trends in Mental Health Services." *Social Science & Medicine* 28, no. 11 (1989): 1129–38.

Bueltzingsloewen, Isabelle von. *L'hécatombe des fous: La famine dans les hôpitaux psychiatriques français sous l'Occupation.* Flammarion, 2007.

Bureau, Marie-Christine, Barbara Rist, Léa Lima, and Christophe Trombert. "La traduction de la demande d'aide sociale: Les cas du handicap et de l'insertion des jeunes." *Revue Française d'administration publique* 145, no. 1 (2013): 175–88.

Caisse nationale de solidarité pour l'autonomie. *Troubles psychiques: Guide d'appui pour l'élaboration de réponses aux besoins des personnes vivant avec des troubles psychiques.* Dossier technique, 2017.

——. *Une réforme tarifaire pour faciliter les parcours des personnes handicapées accompagnées par les services ou accueillies dans les établissements médico-sociaux.* Caisse nationale de solidarité pour l'autonomie, 2017.

Canaday, Margot. *The Straight State: Sexuality and Citizenship in Twentieth-Century America.* Princeton University Press, 2009.

Carey, Allison C. *On the Margins of Citizenship: Intellectual Disability and Civil Rights in Twentieth-Century America.* Temple University Press, 2009.

Carpenter, Mick. "'It's a Small World': Mental Health Policy Under Welfare Capitalism Since 1945." *Sociology of Health & Illness* 22, no. 5 (2000): 602–20. https://doi.org/10.1111/1467-9566.00222.

Carson, John. *The Measure of Merit: Talents, Intelligence, and Inequality in the French and American Republics, 1750–1940.* Princeton University Press, 2007.

Castel, Françoise, Robert Castel, and Anne Lovell. *The Psychiatric Society.* Translated by Arthur Goldhammer. Columbia University Press, 1982.

Castel, Robert. *La gestion des risques: De l'anti-psychiatrie à l'après-psychanalyse*. Minuit, 1981.

——. *The Regulation of Madness: The Origins of Incarceration in France*. Translated by W. D. Halls. Polity Press, 1988.

Centre collaborateur OMS. *Les conseils locaux de santé mentale: État des lieux*. CCOMS Lille, 2015.

——. *Les conseils locaux de santé mentale: État des lieux*. CCOMS Lille, 2018.

Chamak, Brigitte. "Autism and Social Movements: French Parents' Associations and International Autistic Individuals' Organisations." *Sociology of Health & Illness* 30, no. 1 (2008): 76–96. https://doi.org/10.1111/j.1467-9566.2007.01053.x.

Chanut, Jean-Marie, Hélène Michaudon, and Anne Pla. *L'AAH, un minimum social destiné aux adultes handicapés*. N° 344. Direction de la recherche, des études, de l'évaluation et des statistiques, 2004.

Chapireau, François. *Les recours aux soins spécialisés en santé mentale*. N° 533. Études et Résultats. Direction de la recherche, des études, de l'évaluation et des statistiques, 2006.

——. "Le handicap psychique: La construction sociale d'un nouveau trouble spécifiquement français." *Socio-logos*, no. 9 (2014), https://doi.org/10.4000/socio-logos.2824.

——. "Le handicap psychique." In *L'encyclopédie médico-chirurgicale*, Elsevier, 2016.

Charzat, Michel. *Pour mieux identifier les difficultés des personnes en situation de handicap du fait de troubles psychiques et les moyens d'améliorer leur vie et celle de leurs proches*. Ministère de la Famille, a l'Enfance et aux personnes Handicapées, 2002.

Chayet, Delphine. "Drame de Grenoble: L'Élysée veut une réforme." *Le Figaro*, November 14, 2008. https://www.lefigaro.fr/actualite-france/2008/11/14/01016-20081114ARTFIG00276-drame-de-grenoble-l-elysee-veut-une-reforme-.php.

Chee, Christine Chan, Claire Gourier-Fréry, Romain Guignard, and François Beck. "État des lieux de la surveillance de la santé mentale en France." *Santé publique* 23, no. 6 (2012): 11–29.

Chevallereau, Emmanuelle. "'Nous redoutons que les soins psychiatriques sans consentement deviennent la règle.'" *Le Monde*, May 11, 2011. https://www.lemonde.fr/societe/article/2011/05/11/nous-redoutons-que-les-soins-psychiatriques-sans-consentement-deviennent-la-regle_1520445_3224.html.

Chiarello, Elizabeth. *Policing Patients: Treatment and Surveillance on the Frontlines of the Opioid Crisis*. Princeton University Press, 2024.

Chirac, Jacques. *Discours de le président de la république devant le conseil national consultatif des personnes handicapées. Présidence de la République*, 2002. https://www.jacqueschirac-asso.fr/archives-elysee.fr/elysee/elysee.fr/francais/interventions/discours_et_declarations/2002/decembre/fi001873.html.

Chossy, Jean-François. *Rapport sur le projet de loi pour l'égalité des droits et des chances, la participation et la citoyenneté des personnes handicapées*. N° 1991. Assemblée Nationale, 2004.

Christin, Angèle. *Comparutions immédiates: Enquête sur une pratique judiciaire*. La Découverte, 2008.

Clair, Matthew. *Privilege and Punishment: How Race and Class Matter in Criminal Court*. In *Privilege and Punishment*. Princeton University Press, 2020.

Clavreul, Laetitia. "Débat autour des soins psychiatriques sous contrainte." *Le Monde*, April 20, 2010. https://www.lemonde.fr/societe/article/2010/04/20/debat-autour-des-soins-psychiatriques-sous-contrainte_1340052_3224.html.

Coffin, Jean-Christophe. "'Misery' and 'Revolution': The Organisation of French Psychiatry, 1900–1980." In *Psychiatric Cultures Compared*, edited by Marijke Gijswijt-Hofstra, Harry Oosterhuis, Joost Vijselaar, and Hugh Freeman. Amsterdam University Press, 2005.

Coldefy, Magali, and Sarah E. Curtis. "The Geography of Institutional Psychiatric Care in France 1800–2000: Historical Analysis of the Spatial Diffusion of Specialised Facilities for Institutional Care of Mental Illness." *Social Science & Medicine* 71, no. 12 (2010): 2117–29. https://doi.org/10.1016/j.socscimed.2010.09.028.

Coldefy, Magali, Sarah Fernandes, and David Lapalus. *De l'hospitalisation aux soins sans consentement en psychiatrie: Premiers résultats de la mise en place de la loi du 5 Juillet 2011*. N° 222. Institut de recherche et documentation en économie de la santé, 2017.

Coldefy, Magali, Coralie Gandré, and Stéphanie Rallo. *Les soins sans consentement et les pratiques privatives de liberté en psychiatrie: Un objectif de réduction qui reste à atteindre*. N° 269. Institut de recherche et documentation en économie de la santé, 2022.

Coldefy, Magali, and Charlène Le Neindre. *Les disparités territoriales d'offre et d'organisation des soins en psychiatrie en France: D'une vision segmentée à une approche systémique*. N° 558. Institut de recherche et documentation en économie de la santé, 2014.

Coldefy, Magali, and Clément Nestrigue. *La variabilité de la prise en charge de la schizophrénie dans les établissements de santé en 2011*. N° 206. Institut de recherche et documentation en économie de la santé, 2015.

Collectif des 39. *Charte du Collectif des 39 Contre la Nuit Sécuritaire*. December 15, 2008. https://www.collectifpsychiatrie.fr/?p=17.

——. "La sangle qui attache tue le lien humain qui soigne." September 21, 2015. https://www.hospitalite-collectif39.org/?NON-A-LA-CONTENTION.

Committee on Psychiatry and the Community. *The Chronic Mental Patient in the Community. Group for the Advancement of Psychiatry (GAP)*, May 1978. https://www.ourgap.org/resources/the-chronic-mental-patient-in-the-community.

Comptroller General of the United States. *Returning the Mentally Disabled to the Community*. Washington, DC, 1977.

Conrad, Peter. *The Medicalization of Society: On the Transformation of Human Conditions into Treatable Disorders*. Johns Hopkins University Press, 2007.

Contrôleur général des lieux de privation de liberté. *Rapport d'activité*. Dalloz, 2015.

——. *Isolement et contention dans les établissements de santé mentale*. Dalloz, 2016.

Cour des comptes. *L'organisation de la lutte contre les maladies mentales*. Cour des comptes, 1976.

——. *Les parcours dans l'organisation des soins en psychiatrie*. Rapport public thématique. Cour des comptes, 2021.

Coutant, Isabelle. *Troubles en psychiatrie: Enquête dans une unité pour adolescents*. La Dispute, 2012.

Coutant, Isabelle, and Jean-Sébastien Eideliman. "Listening to Suffering: The Treatment of Mental Fragility at a Home for Adolescents." In *At the Heart of the State*, edited by Didier Fassin. University of Chicago Press, 2015.

Crossley, Nick. *Contesting Psychiatry: Social Movements in Mental Health*. Routledge, 2006.

Cunin, Jean-Claude. *Le handicap en France: Chroniques d'un combat politique*. Dunod, 2008.

Dao, Lili. "Hollow Law and Utilitarian Law: The Devaluing of Deportation Hearings in New York City and Paris." *Law & Society Review* 57, no. 3 (2023): 317–39. https://doi.org/10.1111/lasr.12665.

Darcos, Xavier, and Nadine Morano. *L'emploi: Un droit à faire vivre pour tous*. Ministre du Travail, des Rélations Sociales, de la Famille, de la Solidarité, et de la Ville, 2009.

Daumerie, Nicolas, Jean-Luc Roelandt, and Philippe Mossé. *The WHO Recommendations and Mental Health in France: The Real and Tacit Instrumentalisation of the Instrument*. KNOWandPOL, 2009.

Davis, Lisa, Anthony Fulginiti, Liat Kriegel, and John S. Brekke. "Deinstitutionalization? Where Have All the People Gone?" *Current Psychiatry Reports* 14, no. 3 (2012): 259–69. https://doi.org/10.1007/s11920-012-0271-1.

Deleuze, Gilles. "Postscript on the Societies of Control." In *Surveillance, Crime and Social Control*, edited by Clive Norris and Dean Wilson. Routledge, 2006.

Demailly, Lise, and Michel Autès. *La politique de santé mentale en France: Acteurs, instruments, controverses*. Armand Colin, 2012.

Demoly, Elvire. *Les demandeurs de l'AAH*. N° 640. Direction de la recherche, des études, de l'évaluation et des statistiques, 2008.

Desmond, Matthew. "Relational Ethnography." *Theory and Society* 43, no. 5 (2014): 547–79. https://doi.org/10.1007/s11186-014-9232-5.

Deterding, Nicole M., and Mary C. Waters. "Flexible Coding of In-Depth Interviews: A Twenty-First-Century Approach." *Sociological Methods & Research* 50, no. 2 (2021): 708–39. https://doi.org/10.1177/0049124118799377.

Deutsch, Albert. *The Mentally Ill in America*. 2nd ed. Columbia University Press, 1949.

Devandas-Aguilar, Catalina. *End of Mission Statement by the United Nations Special Rapporteur on the Rights of Persons with Disabilities on Her Visit to France*. United Nations Human Rights, 2017.

DiMario, Anthony. "To Punish, Parent, or Palliate: Governing Urban Poverty Through Institutional Failure." *American Sociological Review* 87, no. 5 (2022): 860–88. https://doi.org/10.1177/00031224221116145.

Dinitz, Simon, and Nancy Beran. "Community Mental Health as a Boundaryless and Boundary-Busting System." *Journal of Health and Social Behavior* 12, no. 2 (1971): 99–108. https://doi.org/10.2307/2948516.

Direction de la recherche, des études, de l'évaluation et des statistiques. *Les dépenses de santé en 2017: Résultats des comptes de la santé*. 2017.

Direction générale de la santé. *Plan psychiatrie et santé mentale, 2005–2008*. Comité technique national de suivi du plan « psychiatrie et santé mentale », 2005. https://sante.gouv.fr/IMG/pdf/plan_2005-2008.pdf.

——. *Plan psychiatrie et santé mentale, 2011–2015*. Comité technique national de suivi du plan « psychiatrie et santé mentale », 2012. https://sante.gouv.fr/IMG/pdf/Plan_Psychiatrie_et_Sante_Mentale_2011-2015.pdf.

Dobbin, Frank. *Forging Industrial Policy: The United States, Britain, and France in the Railway Age*. Cambridge University Press, 1994.

Dobransky, Kerry. "The Good, the Bad, and the Severely Mentally Ill: Official and Informal Labels as Organizational Resources in Community Mental Health Services." *Social Science & Medicine* 69, no. 5 (2009): 722–28.

——. *Managing Madness in the Community: The Challenge of Contemporary Mental Health Care*. Rutgers University Press, 2014.

Doron, Claude-Olivier. "La rétention de sûreté: Vers un nouveau type de positivisme juridique?" *L'information psychiatrique* 84, no. 6 (2008): 533–41. https://doi.org/10.3917/inpsy.8406.0533.

Dubois, Vincent. *La vie au guichet: Relation administrative et traitement de la misère.* 2nd ed. Economica, 2003.

Dubré-Chirat, Nicole, and Sandrine Rousseau. *Rapport sur la prise en charge des urgences psychiatriques.* N° 714. *Assemblée Nationale*, 2024. https://www.assemblee-nationale.fr/dyn/17/rapports/cion-soc/l17b0714_rapport-information.pdf.

Dudley, Michael, Derrick Silove, and Fran Gale. *Mental Health and Human Rights: Vision, Praxis, and Courage.* Oxford University Press, 2012.

Dudley, Michael, Derrick Silove, Fran Gale, and Winton Higgins, eds. "Human Rights Development: Provenance, Ambit and Effect." In *Mental Health and Human Rights: Vision, Praxis, and Courage*, edited by Michael Dudley et al. Oxford University Press, 2012.

Dumont, Dora M., Brad Brockmann, Samuel Dickman, Nicole Alexander, and Josiah D. Rich. "Public Health and the Epidemic of Incarceration." *Annual Review of Public Health* 33 (2012): 325–39.

Duncan, Whitney L. "Psicoeducación in the Land of Magical Thoughts: Culture and Mental-Health Practice in a Changing Oaxaca." *American Ethnologist* 44, no. 1 (2017): 36–51. https://doi.org/10.1111/amet.12424.

Dupays, Stéphanie, and Julien Emmanuelli. *Les centres médico-psychologiques de psychiatrie générale et leur place dans le parcours du patient.* Nos. 2019-090R. Inspection générale des affaires sociales, 2020.

Durand, Bernard. "Soins psychiatriques: Le retour de la contrainte et de la stigmatisation." *Les Tribunes de la santé*, no. 32 (2011): 43–54.

École Nationale de la Magistrature. *Soins psychiatriques sans consentement.* École Nationale de la Magistrature, 2013.

Economist Intelligence Unit. *France Country Report: Political Leadership Is Needed to Build on Early Advances.* 2015.

Ehrenberg, Alain. "La plainte sans gin: Réflexions sur le couple souffrance psychique/santé mentale." *Cahiers de recherche sociologique*, nos. 41–42 (2005): 17–41.

——. "L'institution de l'autonomie ou le nouvel esprit du soin." *Rhizome* 83, no. 2 (2022): 12–20. https://doi.org/10.3917/rhiz.083.0012.

Elpers, John R. "Public Mental Health Funding in California, 1959 to 1989." *Psychiatric Services* 40, no. 8 (1989): 799–804. https://doi.org/10.1176/ps.40.8.799.

Emerson, Robert M. "Holistic Effects in Social Control Decision-Making." *Law & Society Review* 17, no. 3 (1983): 425–55. https://doi.org/10.2307/3053588.

Esclauze, Aurore. "A l'hôpital du Rouvray, 'la situation devient critique' pour les grévistes de la faim." *Le Monde*, June 6, 2018. https://www.lemonde.fr/sante/article/2018/06/06/a-l-hopital-psychiatrique-du-rouvray-greve-de-la-faim-pour-des-moyens_5310386_1651302.html.

Espeland, Wendy Nelson, and Michael Sauder. "Rankings and Reactivity: How Public Measures Recreate Social Worlds." *American Journal of Sociology* 113, no. 1 (2007): 1–40. https://doi.org/10.1086/517897.

Estroff, Sue E. *Making It Crazy: An Ethnography of Psychiatric Clients in an American Community.* University of California Press, 1981.

Ey, Henri. "Exposé du secrétaire générale de l'évolution psychiatrique." In *Livre blanc de la psychiatrie française*, vol. 2. Éditions Édouard Privat, 1966.

Eyal, Gil, Hart Brendan, Emine Onculer, Neta Oren, and Natasha Rossi. *The Autism Matrix.* Polity, 2010.

Eyraud, Benoît. *Protéger et rendre capable*. Érès, 2013.
Eyraud, Benoît, and Delphine Moreau. "Formes et régulations de l'enfermement psychiatrique: De la création de l'asile aux nouvelles unités sécurisées, l'exemple de l'hôpital du Vinatier." *Cultures & Conflits*, no. 90 (2013): 117–34.
Eyraud, Benoît, and Livia Velpry. "Le secteur psychiatrique: Une innovation instituante?" *Socio-Logos* 7 (2012): 1–12.
Falissard, Bruno, Jean-Yves Loze, Isabelle Gasquet, et al. "Prevalence of Mental Disorders in French Prisons for Men." *BMC Psychiatry* 6, no. 1 (2006): 33. https://doi.org/10.1186/1471-244X-6-33.
Fassin, Didier. *At the Heart of the State*. University of Chicago Press, 2015.
Fassin, Didier, and Richard Rechtman. *The Empire of Trauma: An Inquiry into the Condition of Victimhood*. Princeton University Press, 2009.
Faustine, Vincent. "Covid-19: La 'vague psychiatrique' monte." *Le Monde*, July 13, 2020, https://www.lemonde.fr/sante/article/2020/07/11/tous-les-voyants-sont-au-rouge-apres-le-covid-19-la-vague-psychiatrique-attendue-a-la-rentree_6045900_1651302.html.
Favereau, Eric. "Jean Oury, fou des fous." *Libération*, June 27, 1998. http://www.liberation.fr/societe/1998/06/27/jean-oury-74-ans-psychiatre-n-a-jamais-cesse-de-saint-alban-a-la-borde-de-vouloir-soigner-l-hopital-_239972.
——. "Psychiatrie, un système sous contention." *Libération*, January 8, 2019, https://www.liberation.fr/france/2019/01/08/psychiatrie-un-systeme-sous-contention_1701720/.
Feillard, Jacques. "La psychiatrie médico-légale, de l'expertise à la question des soins des malades dangereux." *Journal français de psychiatrie*, 19 (2005): 17–18.
Fernandez, Fabrice, and Samuel Lézé. "Finding the Moral Heart of Treatment: Mental Health Care in a French Prison." *Social Science & Medicine* 72, no. 9 (2011): 1563–69. https://doi.org/10.1016/j.socscimed.2011.03.013.
Fernández-Kelly, Patricia. *The Hero's Fight: African Americans in West Baltimore and the Shadow of the State*. Princeton University Press, 2015.
Fiat, Caroline, and Martine Wonner. *Rapport en conclusion des travaux de la mission relative à l'organisation de la santé mentale*. N° 2249. Assemblée Nationale, 2019.
Fillion, Emmanuelle, Aude Lejeune, and Delphine Thivet. "Recenser et prévenir le handicap, plutôt que lutter contre les discriminations: Les référent.es handicap dans la fonction publique française." *Alter* 15, no. 1 (2021): 71–88. https://doi.org/10.1016/j.alter.2020.09.003.
Fleishman, Martin. "Board and Care Homes 1984: Return of the House Call." *Psychiatric Annals* 15, no. 11 (1985): 654–60. https://doi.org/10.3928/0048-5713-19851101-08.
Follea, Laurence. "Dans un 'livre blanc': Les psychiatres français dénoncent le traitement psychiatrique des problèmes sociaux." *Le Monde*, June 9, 1994.
Fond, G., A. Tinland, M. Boucekine, et al. "Prescription of Potentially Inappropriate Psychotropic Drugs in Homeless People with Schizophrenia and Bipolar Disorders. Results from the French Housing First (FHF) Program." *Progress in Neuro-Psychopharmacology & Biological Psychiatry* 89 (March 2019): 84–89. https://doi.org/10.1016/j.pnpbp.2018.08.024.
Forestier, Bruno, Patrick Rodriguez, and Marc Tonnet. "L'avenir des CHS passe-t-il par le médico-docial?" In *Évaluation et organisation des soins en psychiatrie*, edited by Alain Lopez. Éditions Frison-Roche, 1994.

Foucault, Michel. *The History of Madness*. Edited by Jean Khalfa. Translated by Jonathan Murphy. Routledge, 2006.

——. *Psychiatric Power: Lectures at the College de France, 1973–1974*. Edited by Jacques Lagrange. Translated by Graham Burchell. Palgrave Macmillan, 2008.

Fourcade, Marion. *Economists and Societies: Discipline and Profession in the United States, Britain, and France, 1890s to 1990s*. Princeton University Press, 2009.

——. "Ordinalization." *Sociological Theory* 34, no. 3 (2016): 175–95. https://doi.org/10.1177/0735275116665876.

François, Emmanuelle. "De plus en plus de demandes pour une place en Belgique." *Ouest-France*, February 12, 2020.

Garfinkel, Harold. "Conditions of Successful Degradation Ceremonies." *American Journal of Sociology* 61, no. 5 (1956): 420–24.

Garland, David. *The Culture of Control*. University of Chicago Press, 2001.

Garrec, Ivan. "Trouble dans les émotions: Enquête sur l'existence sociale du 'trouble de la personnalité vorderline' en France." PhD diss., École doctorale Érasme, 2024.

Gauchet, Marcel, and Gladys Swain. *La pratique de l'esprit humain: L'institution asilaire et la révolution démocratique*. Gallimard, 1980.

Gayton, Roger, and Yann Boulon. "L'évaluation du handicap d'origine psychique et des besoins de compensation." *Revue française des affaires sociales*, no. 1 (2010): 129–35.

Gerson, Kathleen, and Sarah Damaske. *The Science and Art of Interviewing*. Oxford University Press, 2021.

Giloux, Natalie, and Marion Primevert. "La psychiatre et le juge face à la protection de la personne dans les soins contraints." *Revue de droit sanitaire et social*, no. 6 (Novembre–Decembre 2015): 973–82.

Giordano, Gaëlle, and Samuel Neuberg. *Parcours de vie, parcours de soins: Évaluer le coût des prises en charge entre services d'accompagnement et secteurs psychiatriques*. École Normale Supérieur, 2014.

Glied, Sherry, and Richard G. Frank. "Economics and the Transformation of the Mental Health System." *Journal of Health Politics, Policy and Law* 41, no. 4 (2016): 541–58. https://doi.org/10.1215/03616878-3620809.

——. "Mental Illness and Violence: Lessons from the Evidence." *American Journal of Public Health* 104, no. 2 (2014): e5–6. https://doi.org/10.2105/AJPH.2013.301710.

Goffman, Erving. *Asylums: Essays on the Social Situation of Mental Patients and Other Inmates*. Anchor Books, 1961.

Goldstein, Jan. *Console and Classify: The French Psychiatric Profession in the Nineteenth Century*. Cambridge University Press, 1987.

Gong, Neil. "'That Proves You Mad, Because You Know It Not': Impaired Insight and the Dilemma of Governing Psychiatric Patients as Legal Subjects." *Theory and Society* 46, no. 3 (2017): 201–28. https://doi.org/10.1007/s11186-017-9288-0.

——. *Sons, Daughters, and Sidewalk Psychotics: Mental Illness and Homelessness in Los Angeles*. University of Chicago Press, 2024.

Goodwin, Simon. *Comparative Mental Health Policy: From Institutional to Community Care*. SAGE, 1997.

Gourevitch, Raphaël, Clara Brichant-Petitjean, Marc-Antoine Crocq, and François Petitjean. "The Evolution of Laws Regulating Psychiatric Commitment in France." *Psychiatric Services* 64, no. 7 (2013): 609–12.

Gourion, David. "Terrorisme : 'Les psychiatres n'ont pas vocation à collaborer avec le ministère de l'intérieur.'" *Le Monde*, August 21, 2017. https://www.lemonde.fr/idees/article/2017/08/21/les-psychiatres-n-ont-pas-vocation-a-collaborer-avec-le-ministere-de-l-interieur_5174728_3232.html.

Gousset, R., N. Alamowitch, C. Mache, and R. Gourevitch. "Étude descriptive des mainlevées prononcées par le juge des libertés et de la détention au groupe hospitalier Universitaire Paris Psychiatrie & Neurosciences du 1er Novembre 2017 au 31 Octobre 2018." *L'Encéphale* 46, no. 6 (2020): 436–42. https://doi.org/10.1016/j.encep.2020.01.008.

——. "La moindre argumentation des certificats médicaux accroît le risque de mainlevée." *L'encéphale* 49, no. 2 (2023): 165–73. https://doi.org/10.1016/j.encep.2022.03.008.

Gowan, Teresa, and Sarah Whetstone. "Making the Criminal Addict: Subjectivity and Social Control in a Strong-Arm Rehab." *Punishment & Society* 14, no. 1 (2012): 69–93. https://doi.org/10.1177/1462474511424684.

Grob, Gerald N. *From Asylum to Community: Mental Health Policy in Modern America*. Princeton University Press, 1991.

Grob, Gerald N., and Howard H. Goldman. *The Dilemma of Federal Mental Health Policy: Radical Reform or Incremental Change?* Rutgers University Press, 2006.

Guérin, Olivier. "Le fou entre deux chaînes." *Justice*, 116–117 (October 1987): 3–39.

Gupta, Raj K. "New York's Mental Health Information Service: An Experiment in Due Process." *Rutgers Law Review* 25, no. 3 (1970): 405–51.

Ha, Catherine, Elsa Decool, and Christine Chan Chee. "Mortalité des personnes souffrant de troubles mentaux : Analyse en causes multiples des certificats de décès en France, 2000–2013." *Bulletin épidémiologique hebdomadaire* 23 (2017): 500–508.

Hacking, Ian. "The Looping Effects of Human Kinds." In *Causal Cognition: A Multidisciplinary Approach*, edited by Dan Sperber, David Premack, and Ann James Premack. Oxford University Press, 1995.

——. *Mad Travelers: Reflections on the Reality of Transient Mental Illnesses*. University Press of Virginia, 1998.

——. *Rewriting the Soul: Multiple Personality and the Sciences of Memory*. Princeton University Press, 1998.

——. "Making Up People." In *The Science Studies Reader*, edited by Mario Biaglioli. Routledge, 1999.

——. "Between Michel Foucault and Erving Goffman: Between Discourse in the Abstract and Face-to-Face Interaction." *Economy and Society* 33, no. 3 (2004): 277–302. https://doi.org/10.1080/0308514042000225671.

Haro, J. M., E. T. Edgell, P. Frewer, J. Alonso, and P. B. Jones. "The European Schizophrenia Outpatient Health Outcomes Study: Baseline Findings Across Country and Treatment." *Acta Psychiatrica Scandinavica* 107, no. S416 (2003): 7–15. https://doi.org/10.1034/j.1600-0447.107.s416.4.x.

Hasenfeld, Yehenskel, Jane A. Rafferty, and Mayer N. Zald. "The Welfare State, Citizenship, and Bureaucratic Encounters." *Annual Review of Sociology* 13, no. 1 (1987): 387–415.

Henckes, Nicolas. "Narratives of Change and Reform Processes: Global and Local Transactions in French Psychiatric Hospital Reform After the Second World War." *Social Science & Medicine* 68, no. 3 (2009): 511–18. https://doi.org/10.1016/j.socscimed.2008.10.032.

——. "Un tournant dans les régulations de l'institution psychiatrique: La trajectoire de la réforme des hôpitaux psychiatriques en France de l'avant-guerre aux années 1950." *Genèses*, no. 76 (2010): 76–98.

——. "Reforming Psychiatric Institutions in the Mid-Twentieth Century: A Framework for Analysis." *History of Psychiatry* 22, no. 2 (2011): 164–81. https://doi.org/10.1177/0957154X11401867.

——. "Reshaping Chronicity: Neuroleptics and Changing Meanings of Therapy in French Psychiatry, 1950–1975." *Studies in History and Philosophy of Biological and Biomedical Sciences* 42, no. 4 (2011): 434–42. https://doi.org/10.1016/j.shpsc.2011.05.004.

——. "La politique du handicap psychique: Familles, psychiatres et état face à la chronicité des maladies mentales, des années 1960 aux années 1980." *DREES/MiRe-Convention de Recherche N° 08-2547* (May 2011). https://hal.archives-ouvertes.fr/file/index/docid/769756/filename/Henckes_2011_Rapport_MiRe.pdf.

——. "Mistrust of Numbers: The Difficult Development of Psychiatric Epidemiology in France, 1940–80." *International Journal of Epidemiology* 43, Supplement 1 (2014): i43–52. https://doi.org/10.1093/ije/dyu115.

——. "Schizophrenia Infrastructures: Local and Global Dynamics of Transformation in Psychiatric Diagnosis-Making in the Twentieth and Twenty-First Centuries." *Culture, Medicine, and Psychiatry* 43, no. 4 (2019): 548–73. https://doi.org/10.1007/s11013-019-09636-7.

Herring, Chris. "Complaint-Oriented Policing: Regulating Homelessness in Public Space." *American Sociological Review* 84, no. 5 (2019): 769–800. https://doi.org/10.1177/0003122419872671.

Hewitt, Jessie. *Institutionalizing Gender: Madness, the Family, and Psychiatric Power in Nineteenth-Century France*. Cornell University Press, 2020.

Heyden, Tom. "How Patients Might Design a Psychiatric Hospital." *BBC News*, May 13, 2014. https://www.bbc.com/news/blogs-ouch-27206405.

Hill, Terrence D., and Belinda L. Needham. "Rethinking Gender and Mental Health: A Critical Analysis of Three Propositions." *Social Science & Medicine* 92 (2013): 83–91. https://doi.org/10.1016/j.socscimed.2013.05.025.

Hopper, Kim, John Jost, Terri Hay, Susan Welber, and Gary Haughland. "Homelessness, Severe Mental Illness, and the Institutional Circuit." *Psychiatric Services* 48, no. 5 (1997): 659–65. https://doi.org/10.1176/ps.48.5.659.

Horwitz, Allan V., and Gerald N. Grob. "The Troubled History of Psychiatry's Quest for Specificity." *Journal of Health Politics, Policy and Law* 41, no. 4 (2016): 521–39. https://doi.org/10.1215/03616878-3620797.

Horwitz, Allan V., and Jerome C. Wakefield. *The Loss of Sadness: How Psychiatry Transformed Normal Sorrow into Depressive Disorder*. Oxford University Press, 2007.

Hudson, Christopher G. "Behavioral Mental Health: An Emerging Field of Service or an Oxymoron?" *Social Work* 63, no. 1 (2018): 27–36. https://doi.org/10.1093/sw/swx048.

Jacobson, Nora, and Dianne Greenley. "What Is Recovery? A Conceptual Model and Explication." *Psychiatric Services* 52, no. 4 (2001): 482–85. https://doi.org/10.1176/appi.ps.52.4.482.

Jacqueline, Sandra. "Les politiques du patient en pratique: Psychanalyse et psychopharmacologie à l'hôpital." *Politix* 73, no. 1 (2006): 83–108. https://doi.org/10.3917/pox.073.0083.

Jaeger, Marcel. *Le désordre psychiatrique: Des politiques de la santé mentale en France.* Payot, 1981.

——. *L'articulation du sanitaire et du social.* 3rd ed. Dunod, 2012.

Jerolmack, Colin, and Shamus Khan. "Talk Is Cheap: Ethnography and the Attitudinal Fallacy." *Sociological Methods & Research* 43, no. 2 (2014): 178–209. https://doi.org/10.1177/0049124114523396.

Joly, Pierre. *Prevention et soins des maladies mentales.* Conseil economique et social, 1997.

Jutel, Annemarie Goldstein. *Putting a Name to It: Diagnosis in Contemporary Society.* Johns Hopkins University Press, 2011.

Juven, Pierre-André. " 'Des trucs qui rapportent': Enquête ethnographique autour des processus de capitalisation à l'hôpital public." *Anthropologie & santé*, no. 16 (May 2018). https://doi.org/10.4000/anthropologiesante.2860.

Kapsambelis, Vassilis. "Cinquante ans après: La crise du secteur." In *Le souci de l'humain: Un défi pour la psychiatrie*, edited by Colette Chiland, Clément Bonnet, and Alain Braconnier. Érès, 2010.

Karakus, Mustafa, Victoria Nelson, Emma Scott, et al. "Involuntary Inpatient Civil Commitment: Trends from 2010 to 2022." *Psychiatric Services* 76, no.10: 861–866. https://doi.org/10.1176/appi.ps.20250024.

Katz, Michael B. *In the Shadow of the Poorhouse: A Social History of Welfare in America.* Tenth Anniversary Edition. Basic Books, 1996.

——. *The Undeserving Poor: America's Enduring Confrontation with Poverty.* Oxford University Press, 2013.

Kaye, Kerwin. "Rehabilitating the 'Drugs Lifestyle': Criminal Justice, Social Control, and the Cultivation of Agency." *Ethnography* 14, no. 2 (2013): 207–32. https://doi.org/10.1177/1466138112457311.

Kennedy, John F. *Special Message to the Congress on Mental Illness and Mental Retardation.* Office of the President of the United States, 1963. https://www.presidency.ucsb.edu/documents/special-message-the-congress-mental-illness-and-mental-retardation.

Kessler, Francis. "Handicap: Le grand chantier." *Le Monde*, September 17, 2002, https://www.lemonde.fr/archives/article/2002/09/17/handicap-le-grand-chantier_4258241_1819218.html.

Kessler, Ronald C., and Evelyn J. Bromet. "The Epidemiology of Depression Across Cultures." *Annual Review of Public Health* 34, no. 1 (2013): 119–38. https://doi.org/10.1146/annurev-publhealth-031912-114409.

Kim, Sunmin. *The Unruly Facts of Race: The Politics of Knowledge Production in the Early Twentieth-Century Immigration Debate.* University of Chicago Press, 2026.

Kouchner, B. *Plan Santé Mentale: L'usager au centre d'un dispositif à rénover.* Ministre de l'Emploi et de la Solidarité, 2001.

Lafaye, Caroline Guibet. "L'hospitalisation sous contrainte, une source de conflits normatifs." *Revue française des affaires sociales* 2 (2016): 38–55.

L'agence nationale de l'évaluation et de la qualité des établissements et services sociaux et médico-sociaux(ANESM). *Spécificités de l'accompagnement des adultes handicapés psychiques.* ANESM, 2016.

Lakoff, Andrew. *Pharmaceutical Reason: Knowledge and Value in Global Psychiatry.* Cambridge University Press, 2006.

Lamb, H. Richard. "Young Adult Chronic Patients: The New Drifters." *Psychiatric Services* 33, no. 6 (1982): 465–68. https://doi.org/10.1176/ps.33.6.465.

Lanteri-Laura, Georges. "La chronicité dans la psychiatrie moderne française: Note d'histoire théorique et sociale." *Annales histoire, sciences sociales* 27, no. 3 (1972): 548–68. https://doi.org/10.3406/ahess.1972.422522.

Lara-Millán, Armando. *Redistributing the Poor: Jails, Hospitals, and the Crisis of Law and Fiscal Austerity*. Oxford University Press, 2021.

Lara-Millán, Armando, and Nicole Gonzalez Van Cleve. "Interorganizational Utility of Welfare Stigma in the Criminal Justice System." *Criminology* 55, no. 1 (2017): 59–84. https://doi.org/10.1111/1745-9125.12128.

Larminat, Astrid de. "Une année pour changer le regard sur le handicap." *Le Figaro*, February 4, 2003.

——. "Les parcours du combattant des fauteuils roulants." *Le Figaro*, September 17, 2003.

Lasser, Mitchel de S.O.-l'E. "The Judicial Dynamics of the French and European Rights Revolution." In *Consequential Courts: Judicial Roles in Global Perspective*, edited by Diana Kapiszewski, Gordon Silverstein, and Robert A. Kagan. Cambridge University Press, 2013.

Latour, Bruno. *Laboratory Life: The Construction of Scientific Facts*. With Steve Woolgar and Jonas Salk. Princeton University Press, 1979.

Lazarus, Antoine, and Hélène Strohl. *Une souffrance qu'on ne peut plus cacher*. Délégation interministérielle à la ville et au développement social urbain, 1995.

Le Bianic, Thomas. "Certified Expertise and Professional Responsibility in Organizations: The Case of Mental Health Practice in Prisons." *Sociological Review* 59, no. 4 (2011): 803–27. https://doi.org/10.1111/j.1467-954X.2011.02029.x.

Leboyer, Marion, and Pierre-Michel Llorca. *Psychiatrie: L'état d'urgence*. Fayard, 2018.

Lefrand, Guy, and Serge Blisko. *Rapport sur la mise en oeuvre de la loi N° 2011–803 du 5 Juillet 2011 relative aux droits et protection des personnes faisant l'objet des soins psychiatriques et aux modalités de leur prise en charge*. N° 4402. Assemblée Nationale, 2012.

Legohérel, Delphine. *Étude sur les soins psychiatriques sans consentement*. Service de Documentation, des études et du Rapport, Cour de cassation, 2014. http://psychiatrie.crpa.asso.fr/IMG/pdf/2014-12-31-etude-sur-les-soins-sans-consentement-cour-de-cassation.pdf.

Legrand, Julia. "L'injonction ou l'injection? Prescriptions de médicaments et reconfigurations contemporaines du pouvoir psychiatrique." *Genèses* 127, no. 2 (2022): 11–32. https://doi.org/10.3917/gen.127.0011.

Le Houérou, Annie. *Dynamiser l'emploi des personnes handicapées en milieu ordinaire*. Assemblée Nationale, 2014.

*Le Monde*. "Le handicap demeure une cause majeure d'exclusion." May 25, 2000.

——. "L'union nationale des amis et parents de personnes handicapées mentales (Unapei) va déposer une pétition." March 20, 2002.

——. "Le Sénat adopte le projet de loi sur l'hospitalisation d'office." May 13, 2011. https://www.lemonde.fr/politique/article/2011/05/13/le-senat-adopte-le-projet-de-loi-sur-l-hospitalisation-d-office_1521848_823448.html.

——. "Editorial: La psychiatrie, un secteur en profonde dépression." August 19, 2018. https://www.lemonde.fr/idees/article/2018/08/18/la-psychiatrie-un-secteur-en-etat-d-urgence_5343765_3232.html.

——. "'Mon soutien psy' ne répond pas à une exigence de qualité des soins, mais à une logique économique." June 5, 2025. https://www.lemonde.fr/idees/article/2025/06/05/mon-soutien-psy-ne-repond-pas-a-une-exigence-de-qualite-des-soins-mais-a-une-logique-economique_6610593_3232.html.

"Les institutions et l'organisation de secteurs psychiatriques." In *Livre blanc de la psychiatrie française*, vol. 2. Éditions Édouard Privat, 1966.

Lewis, Dan, Stephanie Riger, Helen Rosenberg, Hendrik Wagenaar, Arthur Lurigio, and Susan Reed. *Worlds of the Mentally Ill: How Deinstitutionalization Works in the City*. Southern Illinois University Press, 1991.

Light, Donald W., and David Hughes. "Introduction: A Sociological Perspective on Rationing: Power, Rhetoric and Situated Practices." *Sociology of Health & Illness* 23, no. 5 (2001): 551–69. https://doi.org/10.1111/1467-9566.00265.

Lipsky, Michael. *Street-Level Bureaucracy: Dilemmas of the Individual in Public Service*. 30th Anniversary Edition. Russell Sage Foundation, 2010.

Livne, Roi. *Values at the End of Life*. Harvard University Press, 2019.

Lloyd, Stephanie. "Morals, Medicine and Change: Morality Brokers, Social Phobias, and French Psychiatry." *Culture, Medicine, and Psychiatry* 32, no. 2 (2008): 279–97. https://doi.org/10.1007/s11013-008-9092-4.

Lopez, Alain. *La psychiatrie dans la tourmente*. Hygée, 2023.

Lopez, Alain, and Gaëlle Turan-Pelletier. *Organisation et fonctionnement du dispositif de soins psychiatriques, 60 ans après la Circulaire du 15 Mars 1960*. N° 2017-064R. Inspection générale des affaires sociales, 2017.

Lovell, Anne M., Aurélien Troisoeufs, and Marion Mora. "Du handicap psychique aux paradoxes de sa reconnaissance: Éléments d'un savoir ordinaire des personnes vivant avec un trouble psychique grave." *Revue française des affaires sociales* 1–2, no. 1 (2010): 209–27.

Loveman, Mara. *National Colors: Racial Classification and the State in Latin America*. Oxford University Press, 2014.

——. "The U.S. Census and the Contested Rules of Racial Classification in Early Twentieth-Century Puerto Rico." *Caribbean Studies* 35, no. 2 (2007): 79–113.

Loyal, Steven, and Stephen Quilley. "The Particularity of the Universal: Critical Reflections on Bourdieu's Theory of Symbolic Power and the State." *Theory and Society* 46, no. 5 (2017): 429–62. https://doi.org/10.1007/s11186-017-9298-y.

Lucksted, Alicia, and Robert D. Coursey. "Consumer Perceptions of Pressure and Force in Psychiatric Treatments." *Psychiatric Services* 46, no. 2 (1995): 146–52. https://doi.org/10.1176/ps.46.2.146.

Majerus, Benoît. "A Chemical Revolution as Seen from Below: The 'Discovery' of Neuroleptics in 1950s Paris." *Social History of Medicine* 32, no. 2 (2019): 395–413. https://doi.org/10.1093/shm/hkx113.

Makdessi, Yara, and Bénédicte Mordier. *Les établissements et services pour adultes handicapés: Résultats de l'enquête ES 2010*. N° 180. Direction de la recherche, des études, de l'évaluation et des statistiques, 2013.

Mallevoue, Delphine de. "L'hôpital psychiatrique sous contraint." *Le Figaro*, October 17, 2002.

Marques, Ana, Benoît Eyraud, and Livia Velpry. "Les enjeux d'une judiciarisation tardive, inévitable et embarrassante." *L'Information Psychiatrique* 91, no. 6 (2015): 471–77.

Marques, Ana, Sébastien Saetta, and Tonya Tartour. "Des murailles de papier: La contrainte aux soins en ambulatoire." *Revue française des affaires sociales*, no. 6 (2016): 57–74.

Marquis, Nicolas. "Making People Autonomous: A Sociological Analysis of the Uses of Contracts and Projects in the Psychiatric Care Institutions." *Culture, Medicine, and Psychiatry* 46, no. 2 (2022): 248–76. https://doi.org/10.1007/s11013-019-09624-x.

Marquis, Nicolas, and Sophie Pesesse. "De l'incertitude en santé mentale: Analyse de la prise de décision aux urgences psychiatriques." *Sciences sociales et santé* 39, no. 1 (2021): 43–67. https://doi.org/10.1684/sss.2021.0191.

Martin, Jean-Pierre. *Psychiatrie dans la ville: Pratiques et clinique de terrain*. Erès, 2000.

Martinez, Claire. "Systématisation de la judiciarisation des hospitalisations sous contrainte: impact de l'action du Groupe Information Asiles." MD diss., Université de Lille 2, 2016.

Mathieu, Arline. "The Medicalization of Homelessness and the Theater of Repression." *Medical Anthropology Quarterly* 7, no. 2 (1993): 170–84. https://doi.org/10.1525/maq.1993.7.2.02a00030.

Mauchet, Chantal, Simon Babre, Denys Eustace, and Serge Paquy. *Rapport sur les problèmes de securité liés aux régimes d'hospitalisation sans consentement*. N° 04-023-01. Ministère de l'interieur, de la securité interieure et des liberties locales, 2004.

Mauduit, Hélène. "Psychiatrie: Crispations entre le Groupe Hospitalier Paul-Guiraud et le Tribunal de Créteil sur les audiences de patients." *Dépêche APM*, March 16, 2012. h4p://goo.gl/5ch3h.

——. "Soins sans consentement en psychiatrie: Magistrats et avocats favorables à moins de certificats." *Agence Presse Médicale*, February 25, 2013. https://psychiatrie.crpa.asso.fr/2013-02-22-Audition-des-representants-des-professionnels-par-la-mission-la-sante-mentale-et-psychiatrie?lang=fr.

——. "Soins sans consentement en psychiatrie: Plusieurs difficultés constatées sur les décisions de mainlevées." *Agence Presse Médicale*, June 13, 2013. https://psychiatrie.crpa.asso.fr/2013-06-14-APM-Soins-sans-consentement-en-psychiatrie-plusieurs-difficultes-constatees-sur-les-decisions-de-mainlevee?lang=fr.

Mayrl, Damon, and Sarah Quinn. "Defining the State from Within: Boundaries, Schemas, and Associational Policymaking." *Sociological Theory* 34, no. 1 (2016): 1–26. https://doi.org/10.1177/0735275116632557.

McCabe, Brian J. "Ready to Rent: Administrative Decisions and Poverty Governance in the Housing Choice Voucher Program." *American Sociological Review* 88, no. 1 (2023): 86–113. https://doi.org/10.1177/00031224221131798.

McKim, Allison. "'Getting Gut-Level': Punishment, Gender, and Therapeutic Governance." *Gender & Society* 22, no. 3 (2008): 303–23. https://doi.org/10.1177/0891243208317826.

Mechanic, David. "Dilemmas in Rationing Health Care Services: The Case for Implicit Rationing." *BMJ* 310, no. 6995 (1995): 1655–59. https://doi.org/10.1136/bmj.310.6995.1655.

Mechanic, David, and David A. Rochefort. "Deinstitutionalization: An Appraisal of Reform." *Annual Review of Sociology* 16 (1990): 301–27.

Meslé, France, and Jacques Vallin. "La population des établissements psychiatriques: Évolution de la morbidité ou changement de stratégie médicale?" *Population* 36, no. 6 (1981): 1035–68. https://doi.org/10.2307/1532324.

Mignot, H. "Le problème législatif." In *Live blanc de la psychiatrie française*, vol. 1. Éditions Édouard Privat, 1965.

Ministère chargé de la santé et de l'accès aux soins. *Santé mentale et psychiatrie: Mise en œuvre de la feuille de route*. 2025. https://sante.gouv.fr/IMG/pdf/bilan_feuille_de_route.pdf.

Ministère de la santé publique et de la population, *Circulaire du 4 Février 1958 portant organisation du travail des malades mentaux en traitement dans les hôpitaux psychiatriques* (Le ministre de la santé publique, 1958).

——. *Circulaire du 15 Mars 1960 relative au plan directeur des hôpitaux psychiatriques anciens* (Le ministre de la santé publique, 1960).

——. *Circulaire du 15 Mars 1960 relative au programme d'organisation et d'équipement des départements en matière de lutte contre les maladies mentales* (Le ministre de la santé publique, 1960).

Ministère du travail, de la santé, et des solidarités. *Santé mentale et psychiatrie: État d'avancement*. Paris, France, 2024. https://sante.gouv.fr/IMG/pdf/feuille_de_route.sante-mentale-psychiatrie-2024.pdf.

Mission nationale d'expertise et d'audit hospitalier. *L'organisation des centres médico-psychologiques*. Centre medico psychologique, 2008.

Moisy, Muriel. *État de santé et renoncement aux soins des bénéficiaires du RSA*. N° 882. Direction de la recherche, des études, de l'évaluation et des statistiques, 2014.

Mondoloni, A., M. Buard, J. Nargeot, and M.-N. Vacheron. "Le péril imminent dans la loi du 5 Juillet 2011: Quelles implications sur les soins?" *L'encéphale* 40, no. 6 (2014): 468–73.

Mongy, Aymeric. "Les droits, masques de la rationalisation gestionnaire? Processus de traduction des droits des personnes handicapées dans l'action publique départementale." *Droit et société* 113, no. 1 (2023): 91–110. https://doi.org/10.3917/drs1.113.0091.

Monnier, Alain, and Jean-Paul Tachon. "Les commissions départementales de soins psychiatriques: Un pilier de la démocratie sanitaire à consolider." *L'information psychiatrique* 91, no. 6 (2015): 455–58.

Mora, G. Cristina. "Cross-Field Effects and Ethnic Classification." *American Sociological Review* 79, no. 2 (2014): 183–210. https://doi.org/10.1177/0003122413509813.

Moreau, Delphine. "Contraindre pour soigner? Les tensions normatives et institutionnelles de l'intervention psychiatrique après l'asile." PhD diss., Écoles des hautes études en sciences sociales, 2015.

Moreau, Delphine, and Christian Laval. "Care et Recovery: Jusqu'où ne pas décider pour autrui? L'exemple du programme 'Un Chez-Soi d'Abord.'" *Alter* 9, no. 3 (2015): 222–35. https://doi.org/10.1016/j.alter.2014.05.003.

Morgan, Kimberly J., and Ann Shola Orloff eds. *The Many Hands of the State: Theorizing Political Authority and Social Control*. Cambridge University Press, 2017.

Morrissey, Joseph P., and Howard H. Goldman. "Care and Treatment of the Mentally Ill in the United States: Historical Developments and Reforms." *Annals of the American Academy of Political and Social Science* 484 (1986): 12–27.

Mougeot, Frédéric. *Le travail des infirmiers en hôpital psychiatrique*. Érès, 2019.

Mougeot, Frédéric, Elsa Benetos, and Antoine Simon. "Apprendre (de) la violence à l'hôpital: Directives anticipées en psychiatrie et violence des soins." *Rhizome* 8081, no. 2 (2021): 27–28.

Murard, Lion, and François Fourquet. *Histoire de la psychiatrie de secteur ou le secteur impossible?* Recherches, 1975.

Nau, Jean Nves. "La clinique psychiatrique de la borde fait face à de nouvelles difficultés." *Le Monde*, April 3, 1991.

Navon, Daniel. *Mobilizing Mutations: Human Genetics in the Age of Patient Advocacy.* University of Chicago Press, 2019.

Navon, Daniel, and Gil Eyal. "Looping Genomes: Diagnostic Change and the Genetic Makeup of the Autism Population." *American Journal of Sociology* 121, no. 5 (2016): 1416–71. https://doi.org/10.1086/684201.

Nelson, Bryan. "Bellevue Psychiatric: Tales of Despair." *New York Times*, September 20, 1983.

Neuville, Ségolène. "Cap sur la santé mentale," Cérémonie d'ouverture du premier village santé mentale en France, Ministère des affaires sociales et de la santé, Paris, France. May 10, 2016). https://sante.gouv.fr/IMG/pdf/discours_de_segolene_neuville_-_sante_mentale_10052016.pdf.

Nicaise, Pablo, Domenico Giacco, Bettina Soltmann, et al. "Healthcare System Performance in Continuity of Care for Patients with Severe Mental Illness: A Comparison of Five European Countries." *Health Policy* 124, no. 1 (2020): 25–36. https://doi.org/10.1016/j.healthpol.2019.11.004.

Niveau, G., and J. Materi. "Psychiatric Commitment: Over 50 Years of Case Law from the European Court of Human Rights." *European Psychiatry* 22, no. 1 (2007): 59–67. https://doi.org/10.1016/j.eurpsy.2006.05.004.

Noël, David. "Psychiatrie: Sarkozy confond santé et répression." Section d'Hénin-Beaumont du Parti Communiste Français, December 12, 2008.

Norton, Matthew. "Classification and Coercion: The Destruction of Piracy in the English Maritime System." *American Journal of Sociology* 119, no. 6 (2014): 1537–75. https://doi.org/10.1086/676041.

Olafsdottir, Sigrun. "Medicalizing Mental Health: A Comparative View of the Public, Private, and Professional Construction of Mental Illness." PhD diss., Indiana University, 2007.

Oliver, Michael. *The Politics of Disablement: A Sociological Approach.* Palgrave Macmillan, 1990.

Oute, Jeppe, and Susan McPherson. "Conflict and Antagonism Within Global Psychiatry: A Discourse Analysis of Organisational Responses to the UN Reports on Rights-Based Approaches in Mental Health." *Sociology of Health & Illness* 46, no. 3 (2024): 473–94. https://doi.org/10.1111/1467-9566.13717.

Palaric, Ronan, and Valérie Moulin. "Critères intervenant dans le choix de l'expert judiciaire, psychiatre ou psychologue, en France." *Annales Médico-Psychologiques* 172, no. 7 (2014): 489–94. https://doi.org/10.1016/j.amp.2013.07.011.

Palier, Bruno. *Gouverner la sécurité sociale: Les réformes du système français de protection sociale depuis 1945*. Presses Universitaires de France, 2005.

Panfili, Jean-Marc. *L'intervention du juge judiciaire dans les soins psychiatriques sans consentement: Analyse de la jurisprudence depuis la loi 5 Juillet 2011*, 2016. https://psychiatrie.crpa.asso.fr/IMG/pdf/2016-12-31_analyse_de_la_jpdce_loi_du_05-07-2011_mise_a_jour.pdf.

Paris, Valérie, Thomas Renaud, and Catherine Sermet. *Des comptes de la santé par pathologie: Un prototype sur l'année 1998*. Etudes et Résultats. Direction de la recherche, des études, de l'évaluation et des statistiques, 2002.

Payer, Lynn. *Medicine and Culture*. Penguin, 1988.

Pélisse, Jérôme, Caroline Protais, and Keltoume Larchet. *Des chiffres des maux et des lettres: Une sociologie de l'expertise judiciaire en économie, psychiatrie et traduction*. Armand Colin, 2012.

Perera, Isabel M. "Is Psychiatry Different? An Economic Perspective." *Lancet Psychiatry* 6, no. 4 (2019): 282–83. https://doi.org/10.1016/S2215-0366(19)30046-X.

——. "Interest Group Governance and Policy Agendas." *Governance* 35, no. 3 (2022): 869–86. https://doi.org/10.1111/gove.12615.

——. *The Welfare Workforce: Why Mental Health Care Varies Across Affluent Democracies*. Cambridge University Press, 2025.

Perera, Isabel M., and Alex V. Barnard. "Myths of Mental Health: Revelations from the French System for the United States." *Perspectives in Biology and Medicine* 64, no. 1 (2021): 103–18. https://doi.org/10.1353/pbm.2021.0008.

Perlin, Michael L. "On Sanism." *SMU Law Review* 46, no. 2 (1992): 373–408.

Pescosolido, Bernice A., Tait R. Medina, Jack K. Martin, and J. Scott Long. "The 'Backbone' of Stigma: Identifying the Global Core of Public Prejudice Associated with Mental Illness." *American Journal of Public Health* 103, no. 5 (2013): 853–60. https://doi.org/10.2105/AJPH.2012.301147.

Petitnicolas, Catherine. "Les psychiatres appellent au secours." *Le Figaro*, January 19, 2005.

Pettinicchio, David. *Politics of Empowerment: Disability Rights and the Cycle of American Policy Reform*. Stanford University Press, 2019. https://doi.org/10.1515/9781503609778.

Picolet, Élodie, Sarah Jones, Nicolas Chambon, and Marie-Carmen Castillo. "Agir vers son rétablissement avec un handicap psychique: Un parcours de reconnaissance(s)." *Revue française des affaires sociales*, no. 1 (April 2021): 189–210. https://doi.org/10.3917/rfas.211.0189.

Piel, Eric, and Jean-Luc Roelandt. *De la psychiatrie vers la santé mentale*. Rapport de Mission. Ministre de l'Emploi et de la Solidarité, 2001.

Pinel, Phillipe. "A Treatise on Insanity." In *From Madness to Mental Health*, edited by Greg Eghigian. Rutgers University Press, 2010.

Piven, Frances Fox, and Richard Cloward. *Regulating the Poor: The Functions of Public Welfare*. Vintage, 2012.

Piveteau, Denis, Saïd Acef, François-Xavier Debrabant, Didier Jaffre, and Antoine Perrin. *"Zéro sans solution": Le devoir collectif de permettre un parcours de vie sans rupture, pour les personnes en situation de handicap et pour leurs proches*. Ministère des affaires sociales, de la santé, et des droits des femmes, 2014.

Poisson, Marie-Aude, Ayden Tajahmady, Leslie Valon, Benoît Servant, and Élise Proult. *Les parcours des personnes en psychiatrie et santé mentale: Première approche*. L'Agence Nationale d'Appui à la Performance des établissements sanitaires et médico-sociaux, 2015.

Ponge, Rémy. "D'un enjeu politique à un problème personnel: L'individualisation de la réparation des souffrances psychiques liées au travail." *Revue française de sociologie* 61, no. 3 (2020): 435–63. https://doi.org/10.3917/rfs.613.0435.

Porter, Roy. *A Social History of Madness: The World Through the Eyes of the Insane*. Plume, 1989.

Porter, Theodore M. *Trust in Numbers: The Pursuit of Objectivity in Science and Public Life*. Princeton University Press, 1996.

Power, Andrew, Janet E. Lord, and Allison S. DeFranco. "Active Citizenship and Disability in France." In *Active Citizenship and Disability: Implementing the Personalisation of Support*, edited by Andrew Power et al. Cambridge University Press, 2014.
President's New Freedom Commission on Mental Health. *Achieving the Promise: Transforming Mental Health Care in America*. Rockville, MD, 2003.
Prieur, Cécile. "Ministre des Solidarités, de la Santé et de la Famille: 'Je veux donner un nouvel élan au secteur psychiatrique.'" *Le Monde*, February 5, 2005.
Prottas, Jeffrey. *People Processing: The Street-Level Bureaucrat in Public-Service Bureaucracies*. Lexington Books, 1979.
Quah, Stella R. "Rationalization." In *Encyclopedia of Health, Illness, Behavior, and Society*, edited by Stella R. Quah, William Cockerham, and Robert Dingwall. Wiley-Blackwell, 2014. https://doi.org/10.1002/9781118410868.wbehibs019.
Quétel, Claude. *Histoire de la folie*. Tallandier, 2012.
Quidu, Frédérique, and Pascale Roussel. "Liens entre troubles psychiques et recours aux dispositifs du champ du handicap en France." *Santé publique* 31, no. 3 (2019): 417–26.
Reira, Ramiro, Simon Babre, Joëlle Bourquard, Françoise Thomas, Gérard Laurand, and Alain Lopez. *La prise en charge des patients susceptibles d'être dangereux*. N° 020. Inspection générale des affaires sociales, 2006.
Rekenthaler, Nick, and Alex V Barnard. "Chronic, Disruptive, or Resistant? Target Ecologies and the Medicalization of Homelessness in California." *Social Problems* 72, no. 4 (2025): 1339–54. https://doi.org/10.1093/socpro/spae019.
Renault, Marie-Cécile. "Le handicap, une priorité du gouvernement." *Le Figaro*, July 6, 2017, https://www.lefigaro.fr/emploi/2017/07/05/09005-20170705ARTFIG00322-le-handicap-une-priorite-du-gouvernement.php.
République Française, *Loi N° 96-1076 du 11 Décembre 1996 modifiant la loi N° 75-535 du 30 Juin 1975 relative aux institutions sociales et médico-sociales et tendant à assurer une prise en charge adaptée de l'autisme* (1996). https://www.legifrance.gouv.fr/jorf/id/JORFTEXT000000746537.
——. *Loi N° 2005-102 pour l'égalité des droits et des chances, la participation et la citoyenneté des personnes handicapées* (2005). https://www.legifrance.gouv.fr/affichTexte.do?cidTexte=JORFTEXT000000809647&categorieLien=id.
Rhenter, Pauline. "De l'institutionelle au contractuel: Psychiatrie publique et politiques de santé mentale en France (1945–2003)." PhD diss., Université Lumière Lyon 2, 2004.
——. "Usages et mésusages de l'hospitalisation d'office." *Rhizome* 24 (October 2006). http://www.ch-le-vinatier.fr/orspere-samdarra/rhizome/anciens-numeros/rhizome-n24-elus-des-villes-et-sante-mentale/usages-et-mesusages-de-lhospitalisation-doffice-1951.html.
Rhodes, Lorna A. *Emptying Beds: The Work of an Emergency Psychiatric Unit*. University of California Press, 1991.
Rimbault, Eléonore. "Killing Two Birds with One Stone: Mandatory Therapy and the Prevention of Sex Crime in France." *Culture, Medicine, and Psychiatry* 49, no. 1 (2025): 304–27. https://doi.org/10.1007/s11013-024-09882-4.
Robcis, Camille. *Disalienation: Politics, Philosophy, and Radical Psychiatry in Postwar France*. University of Chicago Press, 2021.
Robelet, Magali. "Les transformations des modes de contrôle croisés entre associations et autorités publiques dans le secteur du handicap." *Revue française d'administration publique* 163, no. 3 (2017): 599–612. https://doi.org/10.3917/rfap.163.0599.

Robiliard, Denys. *Sur la proposition de loi relative aux soins sans consentement en psychiatrie*. Rapport d'Information N° 1284. Assemblée Nationale, 2013.

Robiliard, Denys, and Denys Jacquat. *Rapport d'information en conclusion des travaux de la mission d'évaluation de la loi N° 2013–869 du 27 Septembre 2013 modifiant certaines dispositions issues de la loi N° 2011–803 du 5 Juillet 2011 relative aux droits et à la protection des personnes faisant l'objet de soins psychiatriques et aux modalités de leur prise en charge*. N° 4486. Assemblée Nationale, 2017.

Roelandt, Jean-Luc. "Pour en finir avec la confusion entre psychiatrie et justice, hôpital psychiatrique et prison, soins et enfermement." *L'information psychiatrique* 85, no. 6 (2009): 525–35.

Roelandt, Jean-Luc, Paula Bastow, Aude Caria, Nicolas Daumerie, Laurent Defromont, and Jugal Kishore. "Community Mental Health Service: An Experience from East Lille, France." *Journal of Mental Health and Human Behaviour* 19, no. 1 (2014): 10–18. https://doi.org/10.4103/0971-8990.143884.

Roelandt, Jean-Luc, Aude Caria, Laurent Defromont, Anne Vandeborre, and Nicolas Daumerie. "Représentations sociales du 'fou', du 'malade mental' et du 'dépressif' en population générale en France." *L'encéphale* 36, no. 3 (2010): 7–13.

Rolland, Jean-Marie. *Rapport sur la tarification à l'activité dans les établissements de santé*. N° 3265. Assemblée Nationale, 2006.

Romien, Pierre. "À l'origine de la réinsertion professionnelle des personnes handicapées: La prise en charge des invalides de guerre." *Revue française des affaires sociales*, no. 2 (2005): 229–47.

Rose, Nikolas. "Governing Risky Individuals: The Role of Psychiatry in New Regimes of Control." *Psychiatry, Psychology and Law* 5, no. 2 (1998): 177–95.

——. *Powers of Freedom: Reframing Political Thought*. Cambridge University Press, 1999.

——. "Disorders Without Borders? The Expanding Scope of Psychiatric Practice." *BioSocieties* 1, no. 04 (2006): 465–84. https://doi.org/10.1017/S1745855206004078.

Roudinesco, Elisabeth. *Jacques Lacan & Co.: A History of Psychoanalysis in France, 1925–1985*. Translated by Jeffrey Mehlman. University of Chicago Press, 1990.

Sá, Karen de. "Mental Health Spending Creating Haves and Have-Nots in California." *Contra Costa Times*, June 26, 2011, https://www.mercurynews.com/2011/06/25/mental-health-spending-creating-haves-and-have-nots/.

Saeed, Sadia. "Religion, Classification Struggles, and the State's Exercise of Symbolic Power." *Theory and Society* 50, no. 2 (2021): 255–81. https://doi.org/10.1007/s11186-020-09415-z.

Saetta, Sébastien, Emmanuelle Fillion, Ana Marques, and Julie Minoc. "Pas de crise, soyez coopérative!": Les conditions de prise en compte de la parole des patient·e·s dans une unité psychiatrique." *Sciences sociales et santé* 41, no. 2 (2023): 5–29. https://doi.org/10.1684/sss.2023.0245.

Saetta, Sébastien, François Sicot, and Tristan Renard. "Les usages des expertises psy au procès d'assises et les définitions pratiques de la responsabilité." *Déviance et société* 34, no. 4 (2010): 647–69. https://doi.org/10.3917/ds.344.0647.

Saguy, Abigail Cope. *What Is Sexual Harassment? From Capitol Hill to the Sorbonne*. University of California Press, 2003.

Saha, Sukanta, David Chant, Joy Welham, and John McGrath. "A Systematic Review of the Prevalence of Schizophrenia." *PLoS Med* 2, no. 5 (2005): e141. https://doi.org/10.1371/journal.pmed.0020141.

Salize, Hans Joachim, and Harald Dressing. "Epidemiology of Involuntary Placement of Mentally Ill People Across the European Union." *British Journal of Psychiatry* 184, no. 2 (2004): 163–68. https://doi.org/10.1192/bjp.184.2.163.

Samele, Chiara, Stuart Frew, and Norman Urquía. *European Profile of Prevention and Promotion of Mental Health*. European Commission, 2013.

Santé Mentale. "Santé mentale grande cause nationale 2025: Ne pas oublier les soins psychiatriques !" September 25, 2024. https://www.santementale.fr/2024/09/sante-mentale-grande-cause-nationale-2025-ne-pas-oublier-les-soins-psychiatriques/.

Sarkozy, Nicolas. "Déclaration du président de la république sur la réforme de l'hôpital psychiatrique, notamment la prise en charge des patients à risque." Antony, France, December 2, 2008. https://www.vie-publique.fr/discours/173244-declaration-de-m-nicolas-sarkozy-president-de-la-republique-sur-la-re.

Sauleau, Erik A., Hassina Lefèvre, and Pascal Handschumacher. "Approche géographique du recours aux soins en santé mentale." *Journal de gestion et d'économie médicales* 31, no. 7 (2014): 499–516.

Savage, Martha K., Peter Lepping, Giles Newton-Howes, et al. "Comparison of Coercive Practices in Worldwide Mental Healthcare: Overcoming Difficulties Resulting from Variations in Monitoring Strategies." *BJPsych Open* 10, no. 1 (2024): e26. https://doi.org/10.1192/bjo.2023.613.

Scheff, T. J. "The Labelling Theory of Mental Illness." *American Sociological Review* 39, no. 3 (1974): 444–52. https://doi.org/10.2307/2094300.

Scheid, Teresa L. *Tie a Knot and Hang On: Providing Mental Health Care in a Turbulent Environment*. Transaction Publishers, 2004.

——. "Competing Institutional Demands: A Framework for Understanding Mental Health Policy." *Social Theory & Health* 6, no. 4 (2008): 291–308. https://doi.org/10.1057/sth.2008.12.

Scheper-Hughes, Nancy, and Anne M. Lovell. "Breaking the Circuit of Social Control: Lessons in Public Psychiatry from Italy and Franco Basaglia." *Social Science & Medicine* 23, no. 2 (1986): 159–78. https://doi.org/10.1016/0277-9536(86)90364-3.

Scott, James. *Seeing Like a State*. Yale University Press, 1998.

Scull, Andrew. "A New Trade in Lunacy: The Recommodification of the Mental Patient." *American Behavioral Scientist* 24, no. 6 (1981): 741–54. https://doi.org/10.1177/000276428102400602.

——. *Decarceration: Community Treatment and the Deviant*. 2nd ed. Polity Press, 1984.

——. *Social Order/Mental Disorder: Anglo-American Psychiatry in Historical Perspective*. University of California Press, 1989.

——. *The Most Solitary of Afflictions: Madness and Society in Britain, 1700–1900*. Yale University Press, 2005.

——. *Madness in Civilization*. Thames & Hudson, 2015.

Sécretaire d'état en chargé des personnes handicapées. *Feuille de route: MDPH 2022*. Paris, France, 2020.

Secrétariat d'état chargé des personnes handicapées et de la lutte contre l'exclusion. *Stratégie quinquennal de l'évolution de l'offre médico sociale: Volet handicap psychique*. Ministère des affaires sociales et de la santé, 2016.

Seim, Josh. *Bandage, Sort, and Hustle: Ambulance Crews on the Frontlines of Urban Suffering*. University of California Press, 2019.

——. *The Welfare Assembly Line: Public Servants in the Suffering City*. University of California Press, 2026.

Senon, Jean-Louis, and Nemat Jaafari. "La loi du 25 février 2008 relative à la rétention de sûreté: Ne faudrait-il pas clarifier et établir des priorités dans les rapports entre psychiatrie et justice ?" *L'information psychiatrique* 84, no. 6 (2008): 511–18.

Shea, Sheila. "The Mental Hygiene Legal Service at 50: A Retrospective and Prospective Examination of Advocacy for People with Mental Disabilities." *Government, Law, and Policy Journal* 14, no. 2 (2012): 35–41.

Sheridan Rains, Luke, Tatiana Zenina, Marisa Casanova Dias, et al. "Variations in Patterns of Involuntary Hospitalisation and in Legal Frameworks: An International Comparative Study." *Lancet Psychiatry* 6, no. 5 (2019): 403–17. https://doi.org/10.1016/S2215-0366(19)30090-2.

Sirois, Catherine. "Contested by the State: Institutional Offloading in the Case of Crossover Youth." *American Sociological Review* 88, no. 2 (2023): 350–77. https://doi.org/10.1177/00031224231160297.

Société l'évolution psychiatrique. "Conclusions: Résolutions adoptées par la société." In *Livre blanc de la psychiatrie française*, vol. 3. Éditions Édouard Privat, 1967.

Somers, Margaret R., and Fred Block. "From Poverty to Perversity: Ideas, Markets, and Institutions over 200 Years of Welfare Debate." *American Sociological Review* 70, no. 2 (2005): 260–87.

Soss, Joe, Richard C. Fording, and Sanford F. Schram. *Disciplining the Poor: Neoliberal Paternalism and the Persistent Power of Race*. University of Chicago Press, 2011.

Souza Leão, Luciana de. "Optics of the State: The Politics of Making Poverty Visible in Brazil and Mexico." *American Journal of Sociology* 128, no. 1 (2022): 1–46. https://doi.org/10.1086/719936.

Special Committee to Study Commitment Procedures. *Mental Illness and Due Process*. Cornell University Press, 1962.

Starr, Paul. "The Sociology of Official Statistics." In *The Politics of Numbers*, edited by Paul Starr and William Alonso. Russel Sage Foundation, 1987.

Staub, Michael. *Madness Is Civilization*. University of Chicago Press, 2011.

Steensland, Brian. "Cultural Categories and the American Welfare State: The Case of Guaranteed Income Policy." *American Journal of Sociology* 111, no. 5 (2006): 1273–1326. https://doi.org/10.1086/ajs.2006.111.issue-5.

Steering Committee on the Chronically Mentally Ill. *Toward a National Plan for the Chronically Mentally Ill*. US Department of Health and Human Services, 1980.

Strand, Michael. "Where Do Classifications Come From? The DSM-III, the Transformation of American Psychiatry, and the Problem of Origins in the Sociology of Knowledge." *Theory and Society* 40, no. 3 (2011): 273–313. https://doi.org/10.1007/s11186-011-9142-8.

Strohl, Hélène, and Martine Clemente. *Rapport du group nationale d'evaluation de la loi du 27 Juin 1990*. N° 97081. Inspection générale des affaires sociales, 1997.

Subcommittee on Mental Health. *The Dilemma of Mental Commitments in California*. California State Legislature, 1966.

Substance Abuse and Mental Health Services Administration. *Mental Health United States*. DHHS-ADM-85-1378. US Department of Health and Human Services, 1985.

Sweet, Paige L. *The Politics of Surviving: How Women Navigate Domestic Violence and Its Aftermath*. University of California Press, 2021.

Tan, Catherine. *Spaces on the Spectrum: How Autism Movements Resist Experts and Create Knowledge*. Columbia University Press, 2024.

Tartour, Tonya. "L'administration du désordre: Gouverner l'hôpital psychiatrique depuis les années 1980." PhD diss., Sciences Po Paris, 2021.

Tartour, Tonya, and Alex V. Barnard. "Démocratie sanitaire à New York: La participation dans le contrôle judiciaire des soins psychiatriques sans consentement." *Participations* 22, no. 3 (2018): 83–107. https://doi.org/10.3917/parti.022.0083.

"The New York Mental Health Information Service: A New Approach to Hospitalization of the Mentally Ill." *Columbia Law Review*, 67, no. 4 (1967): 672–715. https://doi.org/10.2307/1121084.

The State Commission on Quality of Care for the Mentally Disabled. *Strengthening Patient Advocacy: A Review of the Mental Health Information Service*. 1980.

Thornicroft, Graham, Elaine Brohan, Diana Rose, Norman Sartorius, and Morven Leese. "Global Pattern of Experienced and Anticipated Discrimination Against People with Schizophrenia: A Cross-Sectional Survey." *The Lancet* 373, no. 9661 (2009): 408–15. https://doi.org/10.1016/S0140-6736(08)61817-6.

Tinland, Aurélie, Sandrine Loubière, Frederic Mougeot, et al. "Effect of Psychiatric Advance Directives Facilitated by Peer Workers on Compulsory Admission Among People with Mental Illness: A Randomized Clinical Trial." *JAMA Psychiatry* 79, no. 8 (2022): 752–59. https://doi.org/10.1001/jamapsychiatry.2022.1627.

Touitou-Burckard, Esther, Coralie Gandré, and Magali Coldefy. *Isolement et contention en psychiatrie en 2022: Un panorama inédit de la population concernée et des disparités d'usage entre établissements*. N° 286. Institut de recherche et documentation en économie de la santé, 2024.

Trémine, Thierry. "Y a-t-il une Identité de la Psychiatrie Française?" In *Psychiatrie française/psychiatrie en France*, edited by Frédéric Rouillon. Springer, 2012.

Troisoeufs, Aurélien. "Patients intervenants, médiateurs de santé-pairs: Quelles figures de la pair-aidance en santé ?" *Rhizome* 7576, no. 1 (2020): 27–36. https://doi.org/10.3917/rhiz.075.0027.

Turkle, Sherry. *Psychoanalytic Politics: Jacques Lacan and Freud's French Revolution*. 2nd ed. Guilford Press, 1992.

Union nationale de familles et amis de personnes malades. *Le livre blanc des partenaires de santé mentale France, associations d'usagers de la psychiatrie, de soignants et de responsables du social dans la cité*, 2001.

United States Department of Justice. *Breaking Down Barriers to Employment of People with Disabilities*. October 14, 2015. https://www.justice.gov/archives/opa/blog/breaking-down-barriers-employment-individuals-disabilities.

United States Department of Health and Human Services. *Health, United States*. Nos. 78–1232. Rockville, MD. 1978.

Vaillant, Corine. *Conclusions par avocat de la Groupe Information Asilés*. N° QPC 2010–71. Conseil constitutionnel, 2010.

Vallade, Florence. "Le problème public de l'autisme dans la presse française." *Alter* 10 (2016): 263–76. https://doi.org/10.1016/j.alter.2016.05.001.

Vallée, Manuel. "The Countervailing Forces Behind France's Low Ritalin Consumption." *Social Science & Medicine* 238 (2019): 112492. https://doi.org/10.1016/j.socscimed.2019.112492.

Vassy, Carine. "Categorisation and Micro-Rationing: Access to Care in a French Emergency Department." *Sociology of Health & Illness* 23, no. 5 (2001): 615–32. https://doi.org/10.1111/1467-9566.00268.

Velpry, Livia. *Le quotidien de la psychiatrie: Sociologie de la maladie mentale*. Armand Colin, 2008.

Velpry, Livia, and Benoît Eyraud. "Confinement and Psychiatric Care: A Comparison Between High-Security Units for Prisoners and for Difficult Patients in France." *Culture, Medicine, and Psychiatry* 38, no. 4 (2014): 550–77. https://doi.org/10.1007/s11013-014-9400-0.

Verdes-Leroux, Jeannine. *Le travail social*. Les Editions de Minuit, 1978.

Vincent, Catherine. "La très grande souffrance de la psychiatrie française." *Le Monde*, July 18, 2020, https://www.lemonde.fr/sante/article/2020/07/17/la-tres-grande-souffrance-de-la-psychiatrie-francaise_6046447_1651302.html.

Vogler, Stefan. *Sorting Sexualities: Expertise and the Politics of Legal Classification*. University of Chicago Press, 2021.

Vine, Phyllis. *Fighting for Recovery: An Activists' History of Mental Health Reform*. Beacon Press, 2022.

Wacquant, Loïc. *Punishing the Poor: The Neoliberal Government of Social Insecurity*. Duke University Press, 2009.

Waldschmidt, Anne. "Disability Policy of the European Union: The Supranational Level." *Alter* 3, no. 1 (2009): 8–23. https://doi.org/10.1016/j.alter.2008.12.002.

Warren, Carol. *The Court of Last Resort*. University of Chicago Press, 1982.

Warren, Sasha. *Storming Bedlam: Madness, Utopia, and Revolt*. Common Notions Press, 2024.

Watkins-Hayes, Celeste. *The New Welfare Bureaucrats: Entanglements of Race, Class, and Policy Reform*. University of Chicago Press, 2009.

Watters, Ethan. *Crazy Like Us: The Globalization of the American Psyche*. Free Press, 2011.

Weber, Eugen. *Peasants into Frenchmen: The Modernization of Rural France, 1870–1914*. Stanford University Press, 1976.

Weber, Florence. *Handicap et dépendance: Drames humains, enjeux politiques*. Éditions Rue d'Ulm, 2011.

Weiner, Dora B. "Philippe Pinel in the Twenty-First Century." In *History of Psychiatry and Medical Psychology*, edited by Edwin R. Wallace and John Gach. Springer, 2008. https://doi.org/10.1007/978-0-387-34708-0_8.

Whiting, Daniel, Paul Lichtenstein, and Seena Fazel. "Violence and Mental Disorders: A Structured Review of Associations by Individual Diagnoses, Risk Factors, and Risk Assessment." *Lancet Psychiatry* 8, no. 2 (2021): 150–61. https://doi.org/10.1016/S2215-0366(20)30262-5.

Whooley, Owen. *A Mad Mess: Community Mental Health in Crisis*. University of Chicago Press, 2026.

Wilsford, David. *Doctors and the State: The Politics of Health Care in France and the United States*. Duke University Press, 1991.

Wipond, Rob. *Your Consent Is Not Required: The Rise in Psychiatric Detentions, Forced Treatment, and Abusive Guardianships*. Ben Bella Press, 2023.

Wolfe, Matthew. "Policing the Lost: The Emergence of Missing Persons and the Classification of Deviant Absence." *Theory and Society* 51, no. 3 (2022): 511–41. https://doi.org/10.1007/s11186-021-09466-w.

Zagury, Daniel. "'La psychiatrie publique est devenue un enfer.'" *Le Monde*, June 12, 2018. https://www.lemonde.fr/idees/article/2018/06/12/la-psychiatrie-publique-est-devenue-un-enfer_5313233_3232.html.

Zambrowski, François. *Moderniser et diversifier les modes de prise en charge de la psychiatrie française*. Ministre de la Solidarité, de la Santé, et de la Protection Sociale, 1986.

Zerubavel, Eviatar. "Lumping and Splitting: Notes on Social Classification." *Sociological Forum* 11, no. 3 (1996): 421–33.

# INDEX

Printed and bound by CPI Group (UK) Ltd, Croydon, CR0 4YY

16/09/2026

14963453-0002